Feminism
and Community

Feminism
and Community

Edited by Penny A. Weiss and Marilyn Friedman

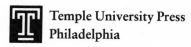
Temple University Press
Philadelphia

Temple University Press, Philadelphia 19122
Copyright © 1995 by Temple University. All rights reserved
Published 1995
Printed in the United States of America

Text design by Alexa Dilworth

Library of Congress Cataloging-in-Publication Data

Feminism and community / edited by Penny A. Weiss and Marilyn
Friedman.
      p.   cm.
    Includes bibliographical references.
    ISBN 1-56639-276-4. — ISBN 1-56639-277-2 (pbk.)
    1. Feminism.   2. Community.   3. Women in community
organization.   I. Weiss, Penny A.   II. Friedman, Marilyn,
1945-
HQ1190.F419   1995
305.42 — dc20   94-48374

To our children,

Elizabeth May, Linden Weiswerda,
Brennin Weiswerda, and Avian Weiswerda,

**and to all the communities, both real and ideal,
in which they can flourish.**

Contents

II Women in Feminist Communities

III Feminist Communitarianism

Preface

Does feminism reject family and community? Have feminists embraced a radically individualist philosophy that is antithetical to those social forms? Contemporary popular culture and academic theorizing sometimes incorrectly answer yes to these questions. Such answers misrepresent both the wide variety of feminist viewpoints and their most characteristic concerns. We have chosen to focus on community and have assembled a collection of empirical and theoretical papers that show the strong feminist interest in this form of social life, particularly those communities that provide women with wide-ranging prospects for human fulfillment. The authors in our collection include independent writers and activists as well as academicians from political science, philosophy, women's studies, English, history, sociology, and anthropology.

To avoid rigidity, we have deployed the notion of community in a flexible manner. We count among our samples of community, for example, what some traditionalists might regard as mere collectives or special-interest associations. Even collectives, however, foster complex and integrated patterns of affiliation among their members. More important, collective association offers structures and modes of interrelationship that are more flexible and adaptable than those of the traditional patriarchal communities of family, neighborhood, church, or nation. This flexibility enables collective associations whose members desire to do so to experiment with gender-innovative practices. The feminist potential of such options is obvious.

Despite space limitations, this collection of essays reveals a great deal of the diversity in women's lives worldwide. Here, readers will encounter women of different nations, races, religious affiliations, sexual identities, and political commitments. Writings by or about Bedouin, Chinese, African American, Latina, European Jewish, and American white women, among others, are represented in these pages.

Our investigation begins with essays that illuminate some aspects of women's experiences in traditional communities. These writings suggest the complexity of life for women in traditional communities. Even though women are everywhere largely subordinate to men, they often have access to resources sufficient to enable their survival and sometimes have substantial freedom and control in what is regarded as their proper domain. The essays on traditional communities also survey some of the restrictions, deprivations, and abuses facing women in those contexts. Occasionally women are able to surmount the gender-based restrictions on their lives, but traditional communities usually limit and penalize women's resistance to their own subordination.

The essays on traditional community, together with those that follow, reveal the crucial significance of female communal networks. Women who derive value from their lives in traditional communities often do so only by virtue of the support and care provided by female kin, female friends, and wider female enclaves. Women who suffer the harshest and most oppressive of traditional communal practices depend all the more on female support networks to enable them to cope with those conditions. The critical importance of women's social networks cannot be overemphasized. This theme pervades the literature on women in communities and, as this volume reveals, it undergirds most of the theoretical developments in feminist communitarianism.

From our very brief survey of the experiences of (some) women in traditional communities, we move on to feminist communities. We label a community as feminist when women rather than men establish the community or the roles and projects of women within it, and when it is dedicated to overcoming specifically gender-based obstacles to women's survival and flourishing — as understood first and foremost by the women in the community. Traditional communities and feminist communities, however, are neither totally dissimilar nor radically disconnected. Both can be the sites of genuine friendship, social support, and collaborative political activism among women. Women working within a traditional community can evolve together toward activities that unselfconsciously refashion the gender practices of those communities in substantially feminist directions. Women's subgroups within traditional communities can also become self-consciously and explicitly feminist.

The feminist communities surveyed here show their own sorts of diversity. They span a historical period of more than one hundred years. They include among them middle-class, working-class, black, white, lesbian, and heterosexual members. For some of those feminist groups, these categories constitute additional and explicit dimensions of their self-identification.

Feminist communities of recent decades were sometimes short-lived, and it is crucial to know why this was so. In some cases, such as that of the underground abortion collective called "Jane," they accomplished what they set out to do and changing external circumstances made their continued existence unnecessary. In other cases, however, feminist communities struggled with internal obstacles to communal flourishing. Some of those obstacles arose from the internalization of societal patterns of domination such as racism or class antagonism.

Racism and other oppressive hostilities are not unique to feminist groups; they are pervasive throughout white society. If feminist communities struggle over these problems more than other social groups, this probably reflects the high ideals that feminists set for communal life. Any signs of hierarchy or domination within feminist communities are occasions for communal self-reflection and readjustment. For most feminists, in theory at least, it is not enough to form homogeneous communal enclaves that merely protect "our own" members at the expense of outsiders and that disregard the wider world of political oppression. Considering the opposition by traditional institutions and practices to feminist ideals, the survival of any feminist community for any length of time is a successful experiment and a welcome opportunity to learn how better to forge ideal communities of feminist aspiration.

The glimpses provided here of women's experiences in both traditional and feminist communities compose the empirical background for the theoretical essays that form the second half of the book. Some of these essays present feminist critiques of nonfeminist communitarian thought as well as of nonfeminist social theorizing in general. More important, however, are the impressively varied feminist contributions to communitarian theory. Here we find an endorsement of traditional communities as well as a defense of voluntary associations, a maternal paradigm for feminist community along with an urban model of communal diversification. We encounter a challenge to the unqualified celebration of women's traditional nurturant values and a realistic call for the difficult but all-important work of female coalition-building. Still other theorists defend separatism in light of lesbian communal experiences, explore the female-coded communal underpinnings of democratic government, and envisage the requirements for global feminist community.

The accounts throughout our book take us from the realm of small-scale female friendships to ambitious dreams for worldwide feminist affiliation. These provocative explorations of women and community chart a vigorous and burgeoning domain of contemporary feminist theory.

We owe an immense debt of gratitude to Jane Cullen, our former philosophy acquisitions editor at Temple University Press, for her abundant support and encouragement of our project despite its lengthy delays and other birthing agonies. Her astute suggestions did much to improve the quality of this volume. She never lost faith in us — nor we in her.

We are also grateful to the authors of the essays in this collection and their publishers for permission to reprint their materials.

Introduction

Feminist Reflections on Community

Penny A. Weiss

Feminist attraction to communitarianism is easily understandable. Having rejected the self-interested, autonomous individual of liberalism as both mythical and undesirable, feminists find that a more social view of the self and a more collective, interdependent, and cooperative model of social relations has an obvious and reasonable appeal. Further, given women's history and continued practice of attachment to others through traditional female roles and networks, feminist visions might even be expected to be communitarian.

But feminist rejection of communitarianism would also be understandable. The misogynist history of communitarian theorizing about what the principles and who the members of communities should be dates from at least Plato and continues today. That history has called for women, much more than men, to sacrifice themselves in the supposed interest of familial and civic communities. Communities can have troubling origins and devastating consequences. The very division of people into distinct communities (the gay community, the Black community, etc.) can be caused by a dominant group's enforcement of particular identities and can impose great costs. Further, political and social gains in recent history have often involved calling for treatment of women and men as *individuals,* rather than as members of a gender group whose traits all supposedly do or should share. A feminist reliance, then, on a more individualistic ideal would not be entirely unwarranted.

It seems clear, however, that communities are essential to sexual equality and that those capable of contributing to liberation must differ from those few still widely lauded in popular and academic thinking:

communities based on common household, church, or bloodline. Many of the institutions and practices central to patriarchy cannot be reconceived and replaced without the formation of new communities that alter how we meet our material, political, intellectual, and emotional needs. Audre Lorde's comment is precise and provocative: "Without community there is no liberation, only the most vulnerable and temporary armistice between an individual and her oppression."[1]

In designing and implementing communities that empower and liberate, feminists are doing what seems never to have occurred to other communitarians: taking advantage of the opportunity to learn about the dynamics, costs, and benefits of traditional and alternative communities by listening to the voices of women who have lived in them. This is a task essential to feminist theory and practice and one we need to engage in critically — consciously aware of two tantalizing paths that turn abruptly into dead ends. The first of these opposing tendencies is simply to applaud and then attempt to extend into more areas women's experiences in traditional communities. This tendency is born, perhaps, out of the excitement of recovering a history of female communities, out of admiration for how women in all conditions and circumstances tried to survive with and through each other, and out of a real need to counter the patriarchal lies that women cannot get along together, that women have always been passive and accepting of their oppression, and that the relations of men in friendship, business, and politics constitute the human norm and ideal. A second tendency is to disregard or condemn those same experiences because of the oppressive environments in which they occurred, environments to which they adapted. At its worst this tendency is fed by acceptance of the patriarchal evaluations of women and all we do; at its best, it is fed by loathing to celebrate anything that has had a part in maintaining patriarchy, lest that contribute to patriarchy's perpetuation. But a willingness to listen to and learn from women as members of communities is crucial, whether those women have been joined in a harem or on lesbian separatist land, have been members of a feminist collective or of the Women's Christian Temperance Union. By listening we live out the feminist belief that women have something important and distinctive to say; by listening critically we practice the honesty and intellectual searching essential to establishing and maintaining relations of freedom and equality. We need very much to know what it is in communities — what practices, structures, and values — have made them or allowed them to be exclusionary, devouring, and violent, and what has made or allowed them to be sustaining, empowering, and respectful of individuality.

In this introductory chapter I look at the wide range of traditional and feminist women's communities represented in this volume and elsewhere, as reported by scholars across the disciplines and by women who have lived or worked in them. In the first section I lay out some of the major issues concerning community that continue to draw attention and provoke debate within feminist discourse. In the next two sections I turn to the studies and stories first of traditional women's communities and then of feminist communities, focusing on what theoretical and practical lessons we can draw from them. In the conclusion I reflect on what this literature reveals about feminism and community.

Contested Issues

This volume makes abundantly clear that feminists do not speak about community with one voice. There are, for example, essays that stress the destructiveness of traditional families and that stress their worthiness; pieces that challenge community as a goal and that argue for community's central role in liberation; entries that applaud separatist communities and that focus on building communities across differences. A published debate between Jean Elshtain and Barbara Ehrenreich is another instance of self-identified feminists challenging each other's understanding of the nature and value of various communities, and one that is useful in distilling some of the contested issues.[2]

Elshtain's central argument is that feminism treats family and traditional community as reactionary and repressive and that such treatment is a substantive misrepresentation and a political error that feeds the continuing conservative backlash. According to Elshtain, feminism has embraced individualism too completely and reduced community to an "abstract ideology" and an "empty term." She praises the potential of family and traditional community to "challenge corporate power and antidemocratic, managerial elites," to answer "legitimate human needs for intimacy and security," to help our "lives make sense," and to turn "disparate elements" into parts of a community with shared values, a community that cares for its members throughout their lives and is based on "solemn commitment." Like the communitarians many feminists critique today, Elshtain celebrates "historic identity," "traditional values," "social responsibility," and "particular ties" while disparaging "untempered liberalism," "self-actualization," "contract," "nonbinding commitment," and "possessive individualism." Elshtain believes that "rather than denying women the meaning their traditional world provided, even under conditions of male domination, feminists should move to challenge a society that downgrades female-created and -sustained values."

In her response, Ehrenreich criticizes Elshtain for failing to deal adequately with the ways traditional families and communities have perpetuated capitalism and patriarchy and for urging that we "roll back most of liberalism" (Ehrenreich 103) as liberalism is embodied in our practices of divorce, day care, and public social services. As Ehrenreich sees things, Elshtain "totally neglects sisterhood" and other nontraditional communities such as support groups, "imagines that the 'feminine values' are uniquely engendered by the traditional family" (Ehrenreich 104), and does not connect the " 'female-sustained,' non-market values of nurturance and compassion" (Ehrenreich 105) with programs such as child care or AFDC.

This debate within feminism over community raises difficult and important questions, questions I think can usefully be broken down into three areas of dispute and uncertainty. One set of questions concerns approaches to traditional families and communities. Are feminist critiques of the family unwise and unnecessary dismissals of a satisfying form of community? How much can and should feminist communities adopt from traditional ones? To what extent has communitarianism been compromised by using as desirable examples traditional communities (including the family) that oppress women? And, given their focus on families, cities, guilds, professions, tribes, and nations,[3] with what consequences has communitarian theory omitted or dismissed a wide range of "alternative" communities?

The relationship between autonomy and community is a second contested issue, giving rise to questions such as: To what extent does the feminist endorsement of power and freedom for women undermine the possibility of community? Does feminist disenchantment with autonomy as an overriding value leave feminism defenseless against the totalizing potential of community? And what assumptions lie behind the belief that respect for the individual and attachment to the community correlate negatively?

A last set of issues concerns the locations of and opportunities for community. What practices, values, and structures have made traditional and feminist groups more or less able to realize community? What range of opportunities and sources exist for fostering community? Is, for example, the existence of community and tradition compatible with voluntarily chosen associations? Is there something unique about the female or the realm of the private that makes them alone capable of nurturing community, or can this ability be extended? And what communities present the greatest opportunities for liberty and equality?

Women in Traditional Communities

Some of the debate between feminists on the worth, values, sources, and forms of traditional communities hinges on a fair hearing and evaluation of women's experiences in them. In addition to essays in this volume I draw on work about the status of Hopi women in a sexually differentiated but often egalitarian culture,[4] about women's relationships as portrayed in some popular and often-revealing fairy tales,[5] about female activism based on women's traditional roles, institutions and networks,[6] about women's traditions in the Sanctified Church,[7] about race and gender in neighborhoods,[8] and about the women's community in Hull House.[9] Based on these readings, I see the outcome of feminist reappraisal thus far as both a reclaiming and rejection of different aspects of women's traditional communities, which I summarize in five themes running through the literature.

First, and I hope most obviously, traditional families and communities can be destructive communities, damaging both to those within and those outside of them. Thus there can be no simple, unqualified endorsement of them. Traditional families and communities often are not the guaranteed preserves against the forces of oppression and totalitarianism that Elshtain, Albert,[10] and Fox-Genovese[11] can sometimes make them out to be; instead, those very forces can live within and be propagated by them. As Andrea Dworkin suggests, the sex roles of traditional families and communities are themselves "annihilating [and] totalitarian" (Dworkin 34).

In her interpretive study of fairy tales — stories in which "we find what the culture would have us know about who we are" (Dworkin 32) — Dworkin helps us see that traditional roles and families do not lead to or constitute community. The patriarchal imperative to be the most beautiful and thus the most cherished woman leads the queen to order Snow White killed. The patriarchal need to find good marriages for her daughters drives Cinderella's stepmother to abuse Cinderella and mutilate her own daughters. Fairy-tale fathers are unattached and indifferent to their children. If there is something worth celebrating in these relationships, taken in context, Dworkin implies, the dangers of romanticizing traditional families are nevertheless crystal clear. The real lessons of fairy tales and the lives they reflect are that families are not necessarily real communities, that their failure to be real communities is tied to their inegalitarianism — an inequality they also perpetuate — and that those who suffer from inequality in families may or may not become more caring themselves. Dworkin's conclusions are largely supported by Del Martin's "Letter from a Battered Woman," written by a woman who has "learned that no one believes me and that I cannot depend upon any outside help. All I have left is the hope that I can get away before it is too late." They are also supported by Williams's multiple encounters with hostility to her very presence and resistance to the expression of her own voice.

Diane LeBow's study of the Hopi indicates that a traditional and fundamental sexual division of labor, even in a culture with what she calls "balanced status" (LeBow 18), will give rise to various hierarchies and barriers between and among the sexes (LeBow 12). Further, as bell hooks demonstrates, sexism and racism divide people in a number of ways. Racism creates "a barrier to solidarity between women," while "sexism teaches women woman-hating, and both consciously and unconsciously we act out this hatred in our daily contact with one another." Paulette Childress White does indeed feel "separated" from certain other women, each in her own bird cage in the same neighborhood. And this mother of four finds no room in the traditional family for who she is becoming: "this discontent, this willful woman . . . who is not mindful; who talks of independence and personhood and freedom" (White 52–53). Kate Rushin's essay vividly reminds us of the endless assaults to women's integrity occurring in "traditional" neighborhoods and workplaces.

Second, Joan Ringelheim's studies of Jewish women in the Holocaust, Lila Abu-Lughod's observations of Bedouin women in Egypt, and Cheryl Gilkes's work on Black women in the Sanctified Church make clear that even in the restrictive and violent conditions of patriarchy, women's relationships with each other often sustain them. Thus it is that the secluded women in a community in Egypt — women who are economically dependent and politically unrepresented, who find themselves in arranged and polygamous marriages and who must avoid and defer to many men — create a separate world that is "a genuine community."

That world, according to Abu-Lughod, is characterized by "easy familiarity," "relaxed closeness," "companionable warmth and even raucous good spirits." Similarly, Jewish women in ghettos and concentration camps, drawing on deep friendships and recreated families, often "got each other through," covering each other's illnesses from the Nazis, sharing sparse food, and exchanging a humane touch, as Ringelheim details. Honig shows how female co-workers in early to mid-twentieth-century Shanghai formed sisterhoods whose members "walked together to work in order to protect each other from hoodlums on the street." Kathryn Sklar emphasizes the "loving friendship" (Sklar 661) among women at Hull House. Patriarchy, then, neither turns all women against each other nor creates women who find their primary identity and support only through men. In even the most traditional and the most destructive circumstances, women have resisted making patriarchal values their own and have valued members of their own sex.

It seems that the traditional communities in which women fared best were those in which sexual segregation so removed men from significant aspects of the women's world that within it they regulated their own affairs, relatively free from male control, an argument made persuasively by Estelle Freedman. This women's space could involve almost total sexual segregation, as among the Bedouin women, or a "women's department," as in the Sanctified Church's denominations. What is important is that there be "an institutional basis for women's self-consciousness" (Gilkes 680).

A third conclusion about women in traditional communities is that their relationships with each other have often served not only to maintain them, but, under certain conditions, to provide them with the material, emotional, and intellectual resources to challenge their conditions. For example, the Women's Christian Temperance Union "was an open and democratic female environment within which women experimented and pushed their traditional self-definitions past the boundaries of domesticity and into the broadest demand for full political participation" (Evans and Boyte 88). Similarly, Freedman argues that "a major strength of American feminism prior to 1920 was the separate female community that helped sustain women's participation in both social reform and political activism." In no small part, the potential of women's communities to give rise to movements for our liberation is linked to the unwillingness of men in mixed-sex groups to work for women. It is also testimony to the relevance of "networks of love and support . . . [to] our ability as women to work in a hostile world."[12] It is a guide for under-standing important facets of the relationship between lesbianism and feminism and an argument for making (at least aspects of) feminist organizations communal, intimate, and noncompetitive.

A fourth conclusion drawn from the literature on women in tradi-tional communities is that aspects of culture and society that contribute to community can curb at least some of the worst excesses of male domination, and vice versa. As Dworkin finds in patriarchy relations that preclude community, LeBow offers useful evidence that sexual equality and community are sustained by many of the same practices and values and that each can contribute to the other. For example, the Hopi emphasis on social responsibility and tribal welfare limits the drive for individual privilege, prestige, and power and embodies an "ethic of humility and non-competitiveness" (LeBow 13) that eliminates certain motives for and manifestations of both self-absorption and of male dominance. Similarly, the extension of family bonds to a larger kinship unit helps establish a common good outside both the self and the privat-ized family, does away with female economic dependence on a male and on marriage, and lightens what Virginia Woolf calls "the claims and tyrannies of . . . families."[13] There is, as part of this conclusion, an argument that we suffer from no shortage of practices and principles valuable to both community and sexual equality: participation of both sexes in mundane and daily toil as well as in ceremonial rites, generally identical treatment of prepubescent children, "respect for individual autonomy," and social values that are "peace-loving, egalitarian, and [reverence] life" (LeBow 9–13).

The final conclusion from the literature on women in traditional communities is that women's ability to sustain each other and to chal-lenge patriarchy from positions of dependence and subjugation is often sporadic, of limited scope, and less than universal. As Ringelheim's study makes so clear, one woman's ability to hold up a falling friend during Nazi inspection did not mean the Nazi torture or killing stopped. Only a few could be saved, sometimes only for a while. Similarly, the positive traditions of Black evangelical church women only limit certain aspects of the church's patriarchy and do not do even that completely. Women's traditional financial support is so utterly crucial to the survival of the Sanctified Church that women can oppose efforts "to achieve the pure patriarchy" many male members want (Gilkes 697) and can force "the most sexist and domineering pastor to advocate financial support for the local, district, and national women's work" (Gilkes 691), but the Church is still characterized as "the most authoritarian and least democratic of formal organizations" (Gilkes 680). Similarly, the community of Bedouin women, for all its mirth and closeness, cannot change the restrictive codes of sexual propriety, cannot challenge the hierarchies that create and structure it, and cannot do away with the "frustration," "sadness, bitterness, and pain" the women express about their relations with men. And while we may be glad to know that among the Bedouin women "hierarchy is not pronounced," it is sobering to think this may be "because all women lack access to resources." As Honig further warns, "the communities formed by women workers in Shanghai — communities in which women drew on traditional social relationships to survive . . . suggest that organizations formed by women workers are not necessarily expressions of working-class or feminist consciousness. And once formed, the sisterhoods did not inevitably lead their members to see that by acting collectively they could change their circumstances."

When we rediscover and reassess traditional women's communities these limitations have to be central. That we have sometimes fed each other in rough times does not mean that no one starved, or that we do not need to change the conditions that gave rise to the shortage. That we have sometimes enabled each other to resist does not mean we could not resist more completely and less self-destructively under other circumstances, and does not lessen the evil of what we are resisting. There are cracks in patriarchy, and women's communities have lived in those spaces, have pushed back the borders, and have even done the hammering and chiseling to create and widen them. Women's experiences give us cause to be proud of a long-standing commitment to something far richer than patriarchy, and of our ability to use, with some successes, even our traditional roles and practices for the sake of our liberation. As Ringelheim makes clear, however, this does not mean that we ought to turn "the very 'femininity' that seemed oppressive earlier in the women's movement [into something] . . . sacred." We also still need to ask whether the "values, ways of life, and skills . . . [that] have arisen with an oppressive situation . . . [can] become free of oppression or of its effects." Further, Annie Popkin reminds us, "The progression from sisterhood as shared suffering to sisterhood as shared strength was necessary to make Bread and Roses and the women's liberation movement instruments of change rather than of support for existing conditions."[14]

Women in Feminist Communities

Feminist communities have been experiments in feminist living carried out in a range of environments, for a variety of purposes, and with varying degrees of "bumpiness" and success. The range of communities considered in this volume and elsewhere gives a clear sense of the possibilities before us and encourages us to learn from sources previously silenced or ignored. Again I will focus on major themes running through tales and studies of these communities.

The first theme in the literature on feminist communities is that they generally ignore the boundaries between friendships, families, the social, and the political, integrating them in a variety of ways. Rita Mae Brown documents that women in the Furies Collective shared almost everything, from clothes and chores to political actions and study groups. Leila Rupp claims that women in the National Woman's Party offered each other support, meaningful work, and quasifamilial relations; it served as both a living social community and a political organization.[15] Pauline Bart documents the commitment to each other, to the issue of reproductive freedom, and to clients found in Jane, the illegal feminist abortion collective. In Dorothy Allison's words, "organizing is as much a process of developing mutual intimacy and group and individual skills, as it is of achieving specific goals."[16]

Community is essential to feminist survival. Female support networks support activism by making "it possible for feminists to maintain their commitment in the hostile environment" (Rupp 739). External forces take their toll, whether they be the lack of support from men in the left, the homophobia of straight women or racism of white women in the women's movement, or the antifeminism of the right. Feminist groups have not discarded the supportive female relationships seen in some traditional female communities; in fact, feminist communities have often relied heavily upon them. But feminist groups have reinforced those ties via political action and have also thereby redirected them more constructively toward liberation and practices compatible with it.

Because feminist communities combine the forms and functions often separated by patriarchy, they are often confronted with distinctive problems that they must meet with resources tailored to them. The satisfaction one derives from successful political activity can translate into a commitment to work through personal problems, and vice versa. For example, the strain of confronting homophobia politically may be more tolerable among a group that also shares the success of publishing a feminist newspaper. More destructively, in the National Woman's Party, friendship and devotion to Alice Paul could "so infuse political conflicts with personal loyalties or hatreds that the community itself was endangered" (Rupp 739). The distinctive characteristics of feminist communities call for closer attention to their dynamics.

A second conclusion drawn from a survey of the literature on feminist communities is that feminist communities all struggle. "An effective collective is capable of confrontation" (Allison 82). The most successful communities may be those that adopt ways to raise and address issues on an ongoing basis, such as through regular meetings or rituals for confrontation and dispute resolution. In some respects this is a tough issue, for many of us are still recovering from the notions that all women or all feminists or all friends or all lovers should get along "naturally," that disagreement means disaster and that unilateral accommodation is preferable to confrontation. Yet there is potentially great gain to be had from learning to live and work with differences. The patriarchal model copes with differences and solves problems according to hierarchical, sexist, and racist dictates. True, under patriarchy, there may be fewer fights over whose turn it is to do the dishes or cook dinner, mow the yard, or relocate for a job. But of course there is still conflict. Patriarchy just drives it underground and leaves it up to women to accommodate for the supposed sake of the relationship. What feminist experiments with community show us is that there is more from which to choose than sacrificing oneself for the supposed sake of the group or committing sacrilege by bringing conflict into the open. Struggle "serves so well to clarify politics and goals" (Allison 84). Creating other options means reconceiving personal and political relationships as things requiring and deserving hard and messy work, and demanding the explicit cultivation of skills for nonviolent conflict resolution. In fact, bell hooks makes clear that some of our most serious problems occur when "Sisterhood [is] *not* viewed as a revolutionary accomplishment women would work and struggle to obtain" (emphasis added). Marilyn Frye's essay is most important for shattering the myth of "unitary" community: "Probably the most obvious thing about what makes this community a community is that it is *not* that we agree on everything."

Third, it seems clear from the literature on feminist communities that among the most successful are those that are based on and address women's self-defined needs and that build in ways to keep women's voices at the center. "All Jane members counseled, whatever their other tasks, so that their work would be grounded in the woman's experiences." Michele Russell describes how, in her teaching, she "start[s] where [her students] are," learns from them about "daily survival wisdom," and uses their experiences as the basis for building knowledge.[17] Byllye Avery writes that "hearing these women's stories . . . led me to start conceptualizing the National Black Women's Health Project." The Project continues to employ a creative variety of conferences, retreats, support groups, and workshops that bring women together not only to define their own needs but also to design their own individualized remedies. "A movement which began with the individual process of self-discovery cannot assume only one solution to . . . [any] problem. We are a movement of many different women, each existing in a network of different circles, and we need not just one, but a range of models" (Allison 76).

Fourth, and related to the preceding themes, feminist communities have not seen community and autonomy as necessarily negatively correlated. Instead, the two can feed each other and can exist in different proportion according to the relationship and the personal, social, and economic situation. This positive correlation can be found, for example, in practices that encourage multiple solutions to collective concerns, that establish both private and communal space or money, and that embody group support of individual differences. If feminist communities tend to err more in one direction than another (thinking linearly, for the moment), it would seem to be toward suspicion of the private. As Rita Mae Brown recalls from the Furies Collective, the two members who were writers "were forever suspect because we spent so much time at our desks." Thus Allison suggests that feminist communities should "put a strong emphasis on allowing and encouraging individual differences" (Allison 85–86). She says of her collective: "We try to emphasize individual creativity by consciously nurturing each other as artists, activists, and individuals" (Allison 87).

A negative lesson to be learned from experiments with feminist communities is that racism, classism, and homophobia limit what a group can accomplish externally and threaten the group internally. In fact, this conclusion can also be drawn from studies of women in traditional communities, leading to the conclusion that current work in the women's movement on issues of diversity is absolutely crucial to the success of feminist politics. Similarity of family backgrounds, race, political commitment, educational experiences, and sexuality *can* give rise to the solidarity that contributes to a community's political successes, as it may have done for women at Hull House and in the Furies. But it also means exclusion, "elitism and isolation," as is obvious in the case of the National Woman's Party (Rupp 739). The Women's Christian Temperance Union, similarly, "could not transcend the biases of its base, with its increasing hostility to the lower classes, to immigrants, and to blacks" (Evans and Boyte 90). Of the Furies Rita Mae Brown says "we ignored the psychology of class differences. In the end, it was this issue and the issue of identity which destroyed our collective." The "walls" that arose from different class-based perspectives "prevent[ed] effective political commitments." This exclusion has consequences that go well beyond the dynamics and longevity of any particular community. Popkin writes of Bread and Roses that the "loss of an inclusiveness that could have helped diversify the group" directly limited the ability of its consciousness-raising groups to develop effective strategies for change based on experience: "a more diverse membership would be necessary before valid speculations about 'all women' could be made" (Popkin 184).

Conclusions

One reason I am attracted to feminist reflections on community is that they are a way of countering nonfeminist communitarians, for while the latter are so dreary, their verdicts continue to carry great weight. Nonfeminist communitarians have assumed that community can exist in the face of sexual inequality (as well as other forms of inequality), have held up as desirable examples communities in which it is not clear that women experienced a high quality of life, have failed to "anticipate questions feminists might ask . . . about the implications of their analysis" (Albert 84), and have neglected political practices, values, and structures needed for liberatory communities. Nonfeminist communitarians often criticize individualistic society for its absence of bonds, affiliation, socialization, and rituals because they ignore or discount those affiliations and rituals that "do not conform to patriarchal nuclear family norms."[18] Thus, their communitarianism becomes a thinly veiled means for disparaging "the bonds and rituals of members of this pluralistic society who do not share . . . [their] religious connections or views on sexual politics" (Card 371).

The failure of nonfeminist communitarians to wrestle honestly and deeply with feminism has real consequences. To the extent they do address feminism they converse with a distorted, mythical version of it — feminists as man-haters, as selfish individuals out for power — that is unlikely to be very enlightening for anyone. The failure to engage feminism in discussions of community increases the likelihood of repeating past mistakes: either resurrecting naively idealized traditional communities that have been built upon women's oppression, or ignoring the strengths of communities sustained by women. Nonfeminist communitarians fail to take advantage of the opportunity to learn about the costs and benefits of various forms of community by listening to the voices of women.

Feminist work on community challenges many traditional political assumptions. It makes clear that we cannot accurately characterize people as self-interested individuals attempting to maximize their narrow interests. Instead, women are shown to have been and to be active members of various communities who participate not only for themselves but also out of concern for and connection with others. Further, women's communities show women as positively drawn to each other, as active, and as resisters of oppression.

Both feminist communities and activism rooted in women's traditional roles, relations, and networks blur the distinction between public and private and, related to that, upset the easy association of the private with the female and the public with the male. And once the dichotomy between public and private is smudged, so too do other dualisms become suspect: the division between liberal and communitarian, between individualism and commitment, between self-interest and the common good, between concern for rights and for relationships.

The relatedness of many women's lives forces us to redefine the political in a way that reflects and encourages a broader range of participation and to understand networks of relationships as motivating political activism. Such "a model of social struggle, rooted in and nourished by ongoing social relationships, [should] replace the pluralist model of interest-group bargaining, a model that masks both the intensity of the feelings and commitments people bring to political life and the power relationships that structure their interactions."[19] This redefinition allows us to build on the radical potential of daily life. It respects the fact that women have had primary responsibility for sustaining communities and looks to that fact for understandings of connectedness and community not tied to women's biology or domestic roles per se.

Feminist critiques of traditional families and communities do not necessarily devalue female-created and -sustained values. Nor do they generally argue, however, that such values alone can end women's oppression, or can, unaltered or unsupplemented, constitute the entirety of a feminist moral framework. Endorsement of power for women does not undermine the possibility of community when we reconceive the nature of both power and solidarity, and devices that encourage individuality can creatively limit the totalizing potential of community without leading to atomized individualism.

We need not accept individualism and commitment as an either/or proposition, any more than we need to see good motherhood and paid employment as mutually exclusive, or affirmative action and fairness. The very way the alternatives are established is oppressive, distorted, and unimaginative. That, I think, is one of the fundamental insights of feminist theorizing, both in general and on community in particular. It probably cannot be uttered often enough.

> Women do not need to eradicate difference to feel solidarity. We do not need to share common oppression to fight equally to end oppression. We do not need anti-male sentiments to bond us together, so great is the wealth of experience, culture, and ideas we have to share with one another. We can be sisters united by shared interests and beliefs, united in our appreciation for diversity, united in our struggle to end sexist oppression, united in political solidarity. (hooks)

Notes

1. Audre Lorde, "The Master's Tools Will Never Dismantle to the Master's House," *Sister Outsider: Essays and Speeches* (Freedom, Calif.: The Crossing Press, 1984), 112.

2. Elshtain's article is reprinted in this volume (Chapter 16). Ehrenreich's response to it, "On Feminism, Family, and Community," was published in *Dissent* (Winter 1983): 103–6. Page numbers are given in the text for articles not included in this anthology.

3. See, for example, Alasdair MacIntyre, *After Virtue: A Study in Moral Theory* (Notre Dame, Ind.: University of Notre Dame Press, 1981), esp. 204–5.

4. Diane LeBow, "Rethinking Matriliny among the Hopi," in *Women in Search of Utopia*, ed. Ruby Rohrlich and Elaine Hoffman Baruch (New York: Schocken Books, 1984), 8–20.

5. Andrea Dworkin, *Woman Hating* (New York: E. P. Dutton, 1974).

6. Sara Evans and Harry Boyte, "Beyond the Dictates of Prudence," *Free*

Spaces: The Sources of Democratic Change in America (Harper & Row, 1986), 69–108.

7. Cheryl Townsend Gilkes, " 'Together and in Harness': Women's Traditions in the Sanctified Church," *Signs: Journal of Women in Culture and Society* 10 (Summer 1985): 678–99.

8. Paulette Childress White, "The Bird Cage," in Mary Helen Washington, ed., *Black-Eyed Susans/Midnight Birds: Stories By and About Black Women* (New York: Anchor Books, 1990): 45–53.

9. Kathryn Kish Sklar, "Hull House in the 1890's: A Community of Women Reformers," *Signs: A Journal of Women in Culture and Society* 10 (Summer 1985): 658–77.

10. M. Elizabeth Albert, "In the Interest of the Public Good? New Questions for Feminism," in *Community in America: The Challenge of Habits of the Heart*, ed. Charles Reynolds and Ralph Norman (Berkeley: University of California Press, 1988), 297–313.

11. Elizabeth Fox-Genovese, "Women and Community," *Feminism without Illusions: A Critique of Individualism* (Chapel Hill: University of North Carolina Press, 1991), 33–54.

12. Blanche Wiesen Cook, "Female Support Networks and Political Activism: Lillian Wald, Crystal Eastman, Emma Goldman," *Chrysalis* 3 (1977): 43–61, 44.

13. Virginia Woolf, *A Room of One's Own* (New York: Harcourt Brace Jovanovich, 1929), 54.

14. Annie Popkin, "The Social Experience of Bread and Roses: Building a Community and Creating a Culture," in *Women, Class, and the Feminist Imagination: A Socialist-Feminist Reader*, ed. Karen V. Hansen and Ilene J. Philipson (Temple University Press, 1990), 182–212, 188.

15. Leila J. Rupp, "The Women's Community in the National Woman's Party, 1945 to the 1960's," *Signs: Journal of Women in Culture and Society* 10 (Summer 1985): 715–40.

16. Dorothy Allison, "Weaving the Web of Community," *Quest: A Feminist Quarterly* 4 (Fall 1978): 75–92, 75.

17. Michele Russell, "Black-Eyed Blues Connections: Teaching Black Women," in *All the Women Are White, All the Blacks are Men, but Some of Us Are Brave*, ed. Gloria D. Hull, Patricia Bell Scott, and Barbara Smith (New York: Feminist Press, 1982), 197.

18. Claudia Card, review of Andrew Oldenquist, *The Non-Suicidal Society*, *Teaching Philosophy* 10 (December 1987): 371.

19. Martha A. Ackelsberg, "Communities, Resistance, and Women's Activism: Some Implications for a Democratic Polity," *Women and the Politics of Empowerment*, ed. Ann Bookman and Sandra Morgen (Temple University Press, 1988), 297–313.

I

Women in Traditional Communities

1

A Community of Secrets
The Separate World of Bedouin Women

Lila Abu-Lughod

The terms "harem" and "seclusion," so intertwined with popular and scholarly conceptions of Arab women, are in most respects grossly misleading. Conjuring up provocative images of groups of idle women imprisoned in sumptuous quarters awaiting the attentions of their master, or submissive veiled shadows scurrying down alleys, confined behind high walls, and excluded from the bustle of the public male world, these terms suggest the nadir of women's status and autonomy. They also suggest male initiative in the creation of separate worlds and direct male control over groups of women. Although these interpretations misrepresent reality, the images evoked by the terms, which indicate that women spend much of their time apart from men living in a separate world and form some sort of community within the larger society, capture an essential truth of social life in the Arab world, if not in other Muslim societies as well. By shifting our gaze and assuming the perspective of those for whom this community of women is the primary arena of social life, we get a more accurate and nuanced view not only of its connection to the men's world, but of the nature of women's experiences and relationships within the community.

Although the generalized principle of mutual avoidance applies in many traditional Middle Eastern societies,[1] the degree to which sexual segregation structures people's lives and the actual patterns it creates vary considerably depending on how it articulates with social and economic organization and historical circumstances. Lumping rural and urban groups; pastoral, peasant, and mercantile economies; or different geographic and cultural areas only confuses the issue. Thus I confine my description to one society in the Middle East, that of the Awlad 'Ali Bedouins of the Egyptian Western Desert.[2] I know this case intimately because I lived in an Awlad 'Ali camp made up of the households of my host, his brothers and cousins, some distant relatives, and some clients. The role of adoptive daughter within the household was open to me because of my Arab and Muslim background and the circumstances of my introduction to the families,[3] and I embraced it for the acceptance it provided in a society in which, first, kinship defines relationships and, second, young women never live alone. Thus I traded access to a wide network for the advantages of close relationships within the smaller community in which most people lived their lives. Although in the first phase of my fieldwork I moved back and forth from the men's world to the women's, I soon realized that my contact with men — boring and frustrating because of barriers to conversation about personal matters created by the rules of propriety and the formality of men's gatherings — also foreclosed the possibility that the women would trust me. Since I wished to study interpersonal relations (those between men and women in particular) and the ideology of social life, topics that could not be studied without people's willingness to talk openly about their personal lives and feelings, I chose to declare my loyalty to the women.

In this article I explore in detail the sense in which the Bedouin women with whom I spent nearly two years live in a separate community — a community that could also be considered a subsociety: separate from and parallel to the men's, yet cross-cut by ties to men and encompassed in the larger world defined by kinship in a tribal structure; characterized by complex and intense interpersonal relations; and maintained by shared secrets, conveyed most poignantly through poetry. More importantly, I consider the women's attitudes about this community and about their separation from men, and the apparent consequences of such arrangements with regard to women's autonomy, personal development, and interpersonal relations. This study will also contribute to our general understanding of the forces that create and shape communities of women and the advantages and dilemmas that face women who live in separate communities.

Sexual Segregation among Awlad 'Ali

Living in camps and towns scattered throughout the coastal region of the Egyptian Western Desert, the Bedouins known collectively as Awlad 'Ali are seminomadic pastoralists in the process of sedentarization. Their traditional economy was based on sheep and camel herding, supplemented by rain-fed barley cultivation and trade (recently replaced by smuggling and legal commercial ventures). Arabic speakers and Muslims who migrated from Cyrenaica (Eastern Libya) at least two hundred years ago, they proudly differentiate themselves from the peasants and urbanites of the Nile Valley by the tribal ideology that shapes their social and political organization, not to mention their interpersonal relations, and by their stricter adherence to a moral code of honor and modesty. A key entailment of this code is sexual propriety facilitated by sexual segregation.[4]

The Bedouins' everyday social world is divided in two. In one half are adult men, in the other are women and children. The division does not take the form of a rigidly demarcated ecological separation between home, or the private sphere, and public space, as it does in other parts of the Middle East, particularly in urban areas. The locus of most activities for both men and women was, until recently, the camp and its environs. The division of space is relatively informal and flexible, segregation depending on mutual avoidance and the separation of activities that results from the sexual division of labor.[5] Yet even when they are not working, men and women rarely socialize together. Indeed, my host's senior wife confessed to me that before I had come to live with them and to spend time chatting with my host in her room, she had never spent an entire evening in his company.

The two worlds coexist side by side, a function not of the wishes and power of particular men, but of the sexual division of labor and a social system structured by the primacy of agnatic bonds (those between male and female paternal kin) and the authority of senior kinsmen, and maintained by individuals whose attitudes and actions are guided by a shared moral ideology. This code of honor and modesty discourages expression of sexuality because it constructs a set of personal ideals revolving around notions of independence and autonomy in which a person's status depends on his or her distance from social and natural sources of weakness and lack of control.[6] The denial of sexuality is best expressed by avoiding members of the opposite sex with whom one might have a sexual relationship, and deferring, through modest avoidance, to those senior kinsmen who embody and represent the social ideals of independence and the triumph of agnation.[7] Hence develops the system of sexual segregation, upheld equally by men and women who wish to be respectable members of their communities and who derive their social positions and support through family and tribe.

The degree to which contact between men and women is determined by their social categories is evidence that this separation of the sexes has to do with the avoidance of sexuality and deference to senior kinsmen. The boundaries between the men's and women's worlds are no more impermeable than the woven blanket that in the past used to divide the Bedouin tent into women's and men's sections. Men may more easily enter the women's world than vice versa, but the men who do so are those considered neither sexual threats nor authority figures. They are young kinsmen or household members and low-status men of the community. In fact, interactions between individual men and women range from relaxed familiarity to extremely formal avoidance, marked by women's veiling and men's aversion of gaze. Kinship relation, relative age, and social status determine the types of interaction. Sons, nephews, and younger kinsmen are greeted warmly and engaged in lively conversation. Fathers, paternal uncles, or fathers-in-law radically transform the atmosphere of the women's world; their intrusions bring a sudden hush to a roomful of garrulous women and boisterous children. Men who are not kin, especially those of high status, would not even come close to an area where a group of women was gathered.

Structural Dependence and Cross-Cutting Ties

The character of the community of women is shaped by the same social system whose by-product it is. Kinship is the primary idiom of social, political, and economic relationships in this tribal society, and the women's community is embedded in that society and cross-cut by numerous ties. Structurally, the community is by no means autonomous; it is neither self-contained nor economically self-sufficient. It controls no particular property or space, has no formal political presence or representation within the larger system, nor even an informal means of acting as an interest group. It is fragmented because its members define their primary ties and allegiances not to one another but to their kin groups.

The community is composed of individual women, all of whom are economically dependent and each of whom derives her right to support through links to kinsmen or husbands or both. In this, women are not much different from other dependent persons, including poor and young men. Among Awlad 'Ali, senior men of each lineage control the resources and are responsible for supporting kin, male and female. Dependents face serious restrictions on their autonomy in decision making. Senior kinsmen arrange marriages for daughters (and sons) and can order a young kinswoman to abandon a marriage, for example, if her own lineage and that of her husband have a serious fight. A woman who wants a divorce depends on the cooperation of senior male kin or senior males forced to take on the role of kin.[8] Given these facts, it should not be surprising that kinship bonds are affectively charged. In a very real sense, a woman's interests are one with those of her kin group, as her reputation and status are linked to theirs.

Thus kinship creates structural pulls that divide the women's community. Solidarity and identification with agnatic kin override bonds based on gender, common experience, or a shared daily life. One of the first questions asked of any stranger is "Where are you from?" The answer is not, as one would expect, a geographic area, but rather a tribal or lineage affiliation. Women retain their tribal identity even after marriage, although their children belong to the husband's tribe. More importantly, the ideology of the unbreakable and special bond among patrikin pervades the Awlad 'Ali's vision of their social relations. This is as true for women as for men, which means that women conceive of their primary bonds as those to kin, not to one another. In short, the women's community is encompassed and penetrated; it has no structural independence, and its members have their primary structural ties to those outside the community.

A Women's Society

In day-to-day life, however, sexual segregation effectively separates the social worlds of men and women. Women constitute a separate society, which has an internal structure that ranks women and defines their relations, both within the residential unit and outside the camp, in an often wide network maintained by reciprocal visiting and gift exchange. Yet women's social links are not defined independently. The same system that structures the social relations between men determines those between women. Personal networks depend on the principles of kinship, coresidence, and affinity. Rank and residence depend on a woman's relations to men, either kin or spouses. Thus while the women's society functions separately, its structure is derivative. In the women's own experience, it is not subordinate, however, but parallel.

Members of a residential community do not choose to live with one another but are thrown together by their ties to men who live together. Camps or settled hamlets are usually formed around a core of agnates and their dependents. Unmarried or divorced sisters and daughters of the core men, and often their mothers (who if widowed usually provide the social and emotional focus of the whole camp), are the core of the women's community. The prevalence of endogamous marriages ensures that many of the wives of men in the community are also related to the core women. Unrelated wives fill out the ranks.[9] Most camps also include permanent or temporary client households. The men of these households have contractual ties to individual core men or nonspecific ties of clientship, often for generations, to the core lineage; their female dependents join the women's community.

Within the community of women hierarchy is not pronounced, perhaps because all women lack access to resources. The patterns of formality and ritualized avoidance that mark deferential behavior toward men occur in only the most attenuated form among women, who never veil for each other.[10] Hierarchy is expressed in who performs services for whom, who greets versus who serves guests, and who has more freedom to move around and outside the camp. Kinswomen of the core agnates are in positions of strength. A kinswoman has rights, through her father, to all lineage property, while a wife is not entitled to much. The camp is the kinswoman's home; a wife can be divorced and sent home to her family. Senior women, even if of a different tribe, gain status in the camp not only because of old age but because of their relationship to adult sons. A woman's status is also tied to that of her husband. Younger wives of core senior agnates, for example, have higher status than do older wives of less important men.

In relations with the larger community of women outside the camp, a woman's status rests more on seniority and the reputation of her lineage or tribe, or on her husband and his. Within these constraints, personal qualities such as character, intelligence, wit, humor, and talent, and moral qualities such as generosity can make a big difference, if not for status then for centrality and influence. They certainly affect popularity.

Women's social positions may be enhanced, but never transformed, by the adoption of specialized roles.[11]

The women's community is not only internally structured by the same principles — primarily kinship and seniority — that structure society as a whole, but in many ways replicates and parallels the men's community. Since identity is defined by kinship, men and women represent their kin groups in the separate spheres. This can be seen most clearly in the way high-status guests are received in the camp. Men go directly to the men's section, are greeted and entertained by the senior agnates, while younger men and clients serve them and remain quiet on the fringes. High-status women visitors, coming alone or with the men, go directly to the women's quarters, where they are entertained by the senior core women; younger women prepare the food and tea, sometimes participating in the conversation, sometimes not.

Women have their own social networks and obligations, established on the same principles that organize the society as a whole. Persons in a network offer condolences at funerals and attend celebrations of weddings, boys' circumcisions, and feasts that mark the return from the holy pilgrimage to Mecca, the building of a new house, or the release from prison or hospital. A smaller network of closely related persons pays sick calls, and only women, mostly those living nearby, go to see one another after childbirth. Visits on most of these occasions generally include the exchange of gifts and services. Since socializing, particularly at formal gatherings where nonkin are present, is a single-sex activity, men and women visit and exchange gifts with different individuals. However, most of these occasions are considered family affairs, and so related men and women usually attend the same functions. In general, while the dominant links for both men and women are those of kinship and affinity, the structure of women's networks differs because in them co-residence and neighborhood are also highly valued.

Autonomy and the Women's World

When one turns one's attention from structural concerns to women's day-to-day activities and their experiences of living together within Awlad 'Ali female society, the women's community takes on a more independent appearance. The community regulates its internal affairs free from the interference and often the knowledge of men. Sexual segregation is also a source of personal autonomy for women. Rather than feeling deprived or excluded from the men's world, women are oriented toward each other and concerned to guard the boundaries of their exclusive world.[12] Adult men's intrusions are infrequent and for the most part unwelcome; women are always anxious to shake off husbands and their male guests. When men are about, an often-heard question among the women is, "Have they gone?" The relief at their departure is palpable. One of the complaints I most frequently heard from a particular group of women concerned the layout of their new house. They thought the men's and women's sections were not sufficiently far apart, and they resented the way this interfered with their privacy.

Bedouin women collude to erect a barrier of silence about their world. Information flows unidirectionally from the men's arena into the women's and not vice versa. Since women become deferentially silent in the presence of most adult men, men generally do not overhear the natural conversations of women.[13] Young and low-status men have easy access to the women's community, and they bring information to the women about what goes on in the male world. But such men, because they are circumspect in their own community and must be deferential to senior males, do not report back about what goes on among women. The extent to which women collude to keep men out of their world is apparent from the reaction of one Bedouin woman who discovered that her brother-in-law had gotten wind of something she had said about him. She guessed that the comment must have been passed on to him by his new bride. She fumed: "We [the women in the core community] have lived together for seventeen years and never has any woman brought women's talk to the men! In our community we have one way. Women don't tell the men what goes on between women. Even the old women — why, they talk to the men, but they don't expose the secrets."

In her analysis of urban Moroccan women, Daisy Dwyer notes that women support men's avoidance of them in part because it offers the women opportunity for independence and defiance.[14] Bedouin women appreciate this aspect of sexual segregation as well. When men are absent, women can engage in activities that are forbidden in men's presence. Smoking, for example, is considered improper for women, but most Bedouin women like to smoke cigarettes and do so whenever they can. When a child or someone's loud throat clearing warns them of a man's approach, they hide the cigarettes. Similarly, when men are not around, women go places without permission. Often they visit local healers to get treatments or holy men to get amulets and charms. Other women cover for them if spouses or male kinsmen return unexpectedly.

Social Responsibility

The separation of male and female worlds grants women more than freedom to indulge in minor defiances of the system and the men in control. It allows for the development of social responsibility. Within their community, women run their own daily affairs. They manage their households with little interference from men, dividing up the tasks and seeing to it that the necessary work that is women's province gets done each day. During slack periods, women occupy themselves as they wish, weaving, paying visits to neighbors, or just sitting around. Since men are gone for much of the day, seeing to the sheep and to business concerns, they impose themselves on women only rarely, usually at mealtimes.

More importantly, women are the arbiters of women's morality. Social control over women is in the hands of other women and is guided by a set of moral ideals that girls learn as they grow up in the women's community. Women correct one another well into adulthood through gossip, teasing, and other forms of indirect criticism, even poetry. Men interfere only when serious infractions of basic norms occur — particularly those of sexual propriety. They have no direct authority over the community as a whole, and their legitimate control over individual women derives from their kinship ties. Husbands have limited authority because wives have recourse to kin for protection. And because the worlds are so separate, men are generally ignorant of what women do, which also effectively restricts male control.

Children are socialized into Bedouin society by women. Women teach children to be modest or deferential in the proper situations. Girls are more harshly criticized for immodesty and insubordination, and heavy pressure begins to fall on them as they reach puberty. Girls watch and listen, learning a great deal about moral standards from women's conversations. Neither punishment nor force is used, although threats abound. Often, older women show their disapproval in a humorous way. The following incident illustrates such indirect social control. Female peddlers in the desert areas had just begun to carry western-style negligées. The adolescent girls were enthralled and, in one camp, two of them had bought negligées for their trousseaus. Their grandmothers were outraged. As she sat with a group of women, one grandmother demanded that the negligée be brought to her. She showed it to the other women, asking if indeed this wasn't the most shameless thing they had ever seen. She then pulled the sheer lime-green nightgown over her bulky dresses and danced provocatively around the room, threatening to go outside and show it to the men. The women wailed with laughter and dragged her away from the doorway. The other grandmother then threatened to take a match to the negligées and suggested that the girls return them to the peddler.

Adult women are more tactful in criticizing one another. Much of the frequent teasing among women serves to highlight societal standards, since it involves joking accusations of behaviors and desires that are contrary to the ideals. For example, women often tease each other about sexuality, which above all else violates concepts of propriety. A woman will respond instantly with vehement denials to the accusation that she enjoys sleeping with her husband, or even the insinuation that she does. One woman, teased about her closeness to her husband, protested that she much preferred it when he slept with her co-wife because then she could surround herself with her children who kept her warm. When a second woman agreed with the first, the others interrogated her about what in the world could account for her obviously pregnant belly.

When someone has actually done something wrong, the women of the community let her know that they disapprove, often through oblique references. On one occasion a new bride ran away from her husband without complaining first to her husband's kin or returning directly to her family; instead she took refuge among some neighbors of a different tribe. Everyone disapproved. After she was persuaded to return to her husband, each of the women in the community came to see her. They recounted stories about their own and others' experiences of running away in the proper manner. With a kind smile and a twinkle in her eyes, an older woman in the bride's household told the young woman she deserved a good beating. The women joked about "evil spirits" a good deal, because the bride had claimed that her husband suddenly looked like an evil spirit and frightened her.

The assumption of social control by women, particularly senior women, could be viewed as an expression of false consciousness. One could argue that when women enforce societal standards that support the male-dominant status quo, they help to maintain the system that keeps them subordinate. On the other hand, by regulating their own affairs rather than letting men do so, they avoid direct experiences of their own subordination and dependency. By participating equally in the maintenance of cultural ideals and social standards, women can come to see themselves as responsible moral beings, not powerless pawns whose only hope for gain lies in manipulation and subversion. They can have honor and command respect just as men do. And within their own unsupervised and autonomous arena, managing their own affairs allows women to develop both competence and dignity.

Personal Development

These observations regarding the effects of women's social responsibility raise other questions about the relationship between sexual segregation and female "personality" or the cultural construction of the ideal woman. Perhaps most critical to Bedouin women's personal development are their minimal interaction with those to whom they are subordinate and the de-emphasis of sexuality as an orientation in social life. These two circumstances encourage women to develop in terms of the cultural ideals of pride and independence.

The ideals of feminine personality are context dependent in Bedouin culture. Both men and women agree that women should be "modest," but this only applies in certain social situations. Modesty is a complex cultural concept that refers to both an internal state of embarrassment and shyness, and a repertoire of behaviors indicative of this state, including downcast eyes, silence, and a general self-effacement, made literal among married women by use of the veil. It relates in a sense to sexual propriety in that it indicates respect for a social system threatened by sexual bonds and for those who are most responsible for upholding such a system (kinsmen and elders). Modesty is thus the spontaneous and appropriate response to encounters with status superiors and is the path to honor for the socially weak.

In interactions among women, modesty is not an issue since neither sexuality nor hierarchy (except in the most understated form) are relevant. There is another set of standards at work in the separate women's world. The attributes Bedouin women value in one another are not those of passivity or delicacy often associated with the feminine ideal in the West, but rather those of energy, industry, enterprise, and emotional and physical toughness. Wisdom, intelligence, and verbal skill, exemplified in storytelling and singing, are also much admired. The active capabilities of women are even celebrated in the ideals of feminine beauty. For the Bedouins a beautiful woman has a robust build and shines with the rosy glow of good health. They abhor slenderness, weakness, or sickliness as much in women as in men.

Like Bedouin men, women are expected to be proud, bold, and assertive, responding angrily to insults or affronts to their dignity. Within the limits set by their actual dependence on men, women are also expected to be independent. They express this quality mostly through vehement denials of attachment or vulnerability to others, particularly the spouse. They respond to major and minor personal losses with defensive stances, anger at others, or stoic denial of concern.

Pride is antithetical to subordination. To realize the culturally shared ideals of the code of honor, including pride, women must avoid situations in which their capacity to act in accordance with the ideal is compromised. This means avoiding confrontations with status superiors or persons on whom they are dependent, since either could undermine their sense of independence by coercing them or directly asserting authority over them. Living in their sex-segregated world, women can, for most of their lives, manage to keep such encounters to a minimum. The separate community of women provides a social environment in which women can develop personal qualities which would be stifled were they always in situations that called for subordination and deference.[15]

Modesty, or the denial of sexuality, is the way that women demonstrate their morality in order to gain status within the system (sexuality representing the potential for both vulnerability to others and defiance of senior kinsmen). In concert with the ideal of pride, the emphasis on modesty profoundly shapes women's personal development and social style. Flirtation, display of sexual charms, pandering to men, or any sign of orientation toward men achieve little for women besides a bad reputation. Rather than using sexuality as a tool for personal gain, women in Bedouin society must deny it. The basis for a woman's good reputation and her sense of self-worth is a respectability that centers on her modest behavior. A girl's chances of marrying well have more to do with her kin group's reputation and their connections than with her attractiveness to men, especially since the best thing that can be said of her is that she has not been seen by men.

The consequences of this orientation away from men and sexuality are sometimes ruefully noted by Bedouin men. One husband who was acquainted with non-Bedouins complained that his wives were coarse and "unfeminine" and that going to bed with one of them was like going to bed with a man. A bold and outspoken old aunt teased her nephew, a distinguished middle-aged man with three wives, for living a dog's life. She observed that his wives ignored him, that they were too busy to take good care of him. Her own son had recently married a city girl and she described with amusement how the young woman prepared his clothes for him, dressed him, and pampered him in many ways. She joked that the nephew should get himself a nice city girl who would spoil him. Given that the Bedouins consider non-Bedouins morally inferior, this was not a serious recommendation. But the story does highlight Bedouin women's independence from men, which can be characterized by contempt or hostility or merely respectful distance depending on the woman and the relationship in question.

Social Intimacy

Having examined the individual woman's development, we now turn to interactions within the women's world. Here we can see most clearly how the separate sphere of Bedouin women forms a genuine community. My field journals are punctuated with notes to myself about the importance of remembering the texture and tone of interpersonal relations among women. In every description of a women's gathering, I note the relaxed informality, the physical intimacy, the warmth and animated conversation. Lounging against each other in close, disorganized circles, veils in disarray, bodies touching — a head in another's lap, an arm draped around a shoulder, a child clambering on a back or tugging on an earring, an infant being nursed casually — a group of women with expressive voices interrupt each other, break into laughter, and absent-mindedly respond to demands of children in the midst of intense discussions. Even in encounters with strangers, women bridge the distance by talking about common acquaintances, exchanging life stories, or offering small services like braiding or grooming hair.

The easy familiarity in interactions between women of various ages and social statuses in all-female gatherings contrasts sharply with the formality that characterizes their interactions with men. In mixed-sex groups women are usually restrained and unexpressive. The only exceptions are settings that involve young unmarried kinsmen, whom aunts and mothers adore and treat with affectionate ease. Young and low-status men often find relief in the women's world where deferential behavior is unnecessary. Yet even their entrance into a group of women changes its tone and reorients conversation. The interlopers rarely stay long, moreover. Men appear in the women's world as periodic disruptions of the ongoing flow of daily life. Men spend their time with other men, in a social world that is more hierarchical and less intimate than that of the women.

The relaxed closeness of female community is epitomized in the gathering that follows the birth of a child. Pregnancy, delivery, and postpartum recovery are women's affairs in which men play no part. Midwives or other women in the community assist with delivery, and men stay as far away as possible. Following Muslim custom, the Bedouins observe, at least in theory, a forty-day postpartum sex taboo. During this period, the husband should not even share a room with his wife. In practice, husbands rarely stay away for the full forty days, but they do always sleep elsewhere for the first week of the wife's confinement. During that week she does not leave her room but rests, recovers, and receives her visitors. All the women in her social network visit her, bringing obligatory money gifts and also chickens, eggs, soaps, incense, and sometimes handsewn clothes for the newborn. Each guest receives a special meal, *kohl* (eyeliner) for her eyes, and aromatic olive oil for her hair. Close friends and relatives who can be spared from their own households assist with the delivery and stay for several days, bringing their youngest children with them. They take over the new mother's household chores, make her special drinks for cramps, care for her children, and keep her company.

In the evening, when all the work is done, the women and their children squeeze into her room to sleep contentedly on the straw mats that line the floor. Throughout the day and late into the night, the women gossip, exchange news, joke and tell stories, sing and smoke cigarettes. They show their concern for the new mother, who is often too weak to participate much, through the favors they do for her, the stories they tell of their own birthing experiences, and the advice they offer. In this female community, women are free to do as they wish with no fear of sudden intrusions or interruptions. Bedouin women enjoy these periods, cherishing the atmosphere of companionable warmth and even raucous good spirits.

Women are most at ease in the company of other women, but individual relationships among women are not always harmonious. Because the female community is not merely a residual arena where women pass the time while waiting for spouses, but rather the social and emotional world in which women live out most of their lives, the relationships within it are emotionally charged and invested with meaning. Interactions between women are intense — if not quick-paced teasing and banter, then urgent confidences or heated arguments complete with insults, tears, and stony silences. From intimate sharing to hostile avoidance, the relationships span the range of emotions and can change from day to day.

The closest relationships in the women's world are those between kinswomen — sisters and cousins who grew up together, aunts and nieces, and mothers and daughters. Particularly when they marry kinsmen or neighbors and thus remain in the same camp or nearby, kinswomen stay in close, if not daily, contact all their lives. They have much shared experience, not to mention the shared interests and concerns created by membership in the same kin group or tribe. They attend all the same functions, since any time there is a wedding, funeral, or even an illness in the lineage, they must all be there, no matter where they live.

Mothers and daughters are particularly close and interdependent. Of all women, they spend the most time together, especially as daughters are growing up. Daughters remain emotionally dependent on their mothers all their lives. As adults they treasure their mothers' visits to them, at childbirth or other special occasions. They confide in their mothers and appeal to them for advice. Whenever I looked sad, the women asked me if I missed my mother, and they assumed that my greatest hardship during fieldwork was my distance from her. Mothers rely heavily on their daughters for help with work, for companionship, and, later in life, for care. They speak openly in front of their daughters, if not directly to them, so there are few secrets between them. Daughters rush to their mothers' sides in any crisis, leaving husbands and children behind. Even if they want sons for social security, mothers have a special place in their hearts for their daughters. This was brought home to me one day when, in a discussion of the relative value of sons and daughters, an old woman told me the following folktale:

> There once was a woman who had nine daughters. When she became pregnant again she prayed for a boy and made an oath to give up one of her daughters as an offering if she were granted a son. She did give birth to a boy. When they moved camp, riding off on their camels, she left behind one daughter.
> Soon a man came by on a horse and found the girl tied up. He asked her story, untied her, took her with him, and cared for her.
> Meanwhile, the boy grew up and took a wife. His wife demanded that he make his mother a servant. He did this and the old mother was forced to do all the household work for her daughter-in-law. One day they decided to move camp. They loaded up the camels and traveled and traveled. The old mother had to walk and drive the sheep. She got tired and eventually was left

behind. Lost, she wandered and wandered until she came upon a camp.

The people in the camp called to her and invited her in. They asked her story. She told them she had not always been a servant and recounted her tale. When the people in the camp heard this story they went running to tell one of the women. It turned out that she was the old woman's daughter who had been abandoned as a child. She came, questioned the old woman, and was convinced that she was really her mother. She embraced and kissed her, took her to her tent, washed her clothes for her, fed her, and cared well for her.

By and by, the son came looking for his mother. He rode up to the camp and asked people, "Haven't you seen an old servant wandering around?" The woman who (unknown to him) was his sister invited him into her tent. She demanded that a ram be brought and slaughtered in his honor. She then asked him, "Where is the *rihm* [womb] of the ram? I want it." The brother looked at her in surprise, answering, "A ram has no *rihm* [womb], didn't you know?"

She then revealed her identity and told him her story. She refused to let him take his mother back and scolded him for having mistreated her.

The moral of the story turns on the double meaning of the triliteral root *rahama* from which the word "womb" is derived. Another word from the same root means "pity, compassion, or mercy." Thus the story links the womb (femaleness) with compassion and caring. The old woman who told me the story added the following commentary: "You see, the male has no womb. He has nothing but a little penis, just like this finger of mine [laughing and wiggling her finger in a contemptuous gesture]. The male has no compassion. But the female is tender and compassionate. It is the daughter who will care for her mother, not the son."

Close relationships also develop between coresident women, whatever their kinship ties. In the community in which I lived, there were at least two adult women in each household and usually several adolescent girls as well. They worked together most of the day. Once they finished their share of the household work, most visited with women in other households, using an excuse like the need to borrow or return something, or the appearance of a guest in the camp. Close neighbors usually spent the evening hours chatting companionably around a lantern as the children dropped off to sleep on their laps.

Many women in a community have known one another all their lives. They have seen each other through all the major and minor events that have touched them; they have celebrated joyous occasions together and known each other's grief. Those who share circumstances such as divorce or widowhood often develop special friendships. The women of a community tend to know every detail of one another's lives, down to when they are menstruating. In general, their most frequent and preferred topic of conversation is other women. They recount life histories for the benefit of those who do not know them, and they discuss recent news of other women brought by visitors or garnered during trips to distant camps. Women talk about themselves, explaining their actions, detailing their responses to things, and sharing their experiences and knowledge.

Shared Experience

The greatest sense of community is created through the shared experience of being women in Bedouin society. Most women's lives follow much the same pattern: they grow up with kin, marry (sometimes moving to another community, sometimes not), have many children, and grow old. With luck, they are given to a good husband who does not mistreat them, their husband's kinswomen are kind, their kin support them, and their children are healthy. Most likely, however, they will face a number of difficult experiences in the course of their lives. Women agree that their lives are not easy. They work hard, often handicapped by poor health due to inadequate nutrition and constant childbearing. Even more trying are the hardships in the interpersonal sphere. Separations from loved ones are a fact of life, especially in a society that was until recently nomadic. Children and loved ones fall ill. More than anything, though, women seem troubled in their relations to men. However much women try to minimize their importance, love and marriage are matters of deep concern and often sources of unhappiness.

One of the ways women share their sentiments is through a particular genre of traditional oral lyric poetry.[16] They often punctuate their conversations with spontaneous recitations of short poems or break into song when alone or with a few close companions. Through these poignant poems, women communicate their responses to situations that arise in their personal lives. Although it was my impression that women experiencing crises tended to sing or recite more often than others, Bedouins do respond with poetry to all sorts of meaningful events.

Those who hear the poems appreciate them for what they reveal about the experiences of those reciting. Despite the intrinsic ambiguity of such condensed and formulaic poetic statements, for those in the community they are easily interpretable because women have such intimate knowledge of the particular circumstances of one another's lives. The poems are moving because the contours of women's experiences are so similar; women empathize with other women and are moved by their sufferings. They try to offer comfort, either through understanding, advice, or words of wisdom about the virtues of patience and trust in God. A woman who feels wronged or mistreated by her husband often appeals to her mother-in-law or her husband's kinswomen, whose loyalties are with the husband, confident that the bond of common womanhood will prevail and that these others will sympathize, if not intervene on her behalf.

Poems are considered both revealing and confidential, and women are especially concerned that men not hear them. Men too recite this poetry among themselves, but there are social taboos against mentioning the very word for this type of poem (*ghinnaawa*) in mixed-sex company. Thus the poems can be viewed as secrets, which, as Georg Simmel observes, function to exclude those who do not share them (in this case, members of the opposite sex), to bind closely those who do, and to give special value to that which is hidden.[17] Thus, like the conspiratorial silences about what goes on in the women's world, the sharing of poems enhances the cohesion and sense of community among Bedouin women.

More often than not, the poems voice sentiments of sadness, unfulfilled longing, or suffering caused by painful losses or sense of abandonment. What is striking is that most often, the poems seem to concern love relationships with men — the very relationships whose importance is continually minimized in ordinary social interaction. Women — who otherwise vehemently denied attachment to their spouses, seemed unconcerned with their marriages, and admitted no interest in sexual matters or in members of the opposite sex — recited poems that expressed their vulnerability to and emotional dependence on men.

The poems betray the fact that many of the most significant crises in the lives of Bedouin women revolve around marriage. Marriage itself can be traumatic, the more so if the husband is a stranger and the new bride must move to a distant area far from her kin. Women are sometimes forced to remain with a husband they do not want in order to refrain from defying and hence losing the support of their kin. Many men are difficult and temperamental, causing their wives (and others) endless agony. But the most poignant poems come from women who have lost their husbands' affections. These expressions have little to do with women's dependence on the marital relationship for social status. The sadness, bitterness, and pain conveyed through their poems attest to the importance of heterosexual love and the depth of the affective bonds that can develop over time between husbands and wives.

Although space constraints prevent me from elaborating on the nature and use of this poetry in social life, a few brief examples will suffice to convey its flavor. One unhappy bride whose kinsmen insisted that she accept the marriage they had arranged for her could not express her objections without alienating her kinsmen or insulting the women in her new community, kinswomen of her husband. She rarely said much but recited numerous poems and often sang to herself while she worked. One of the poems she recited was the following:

> Without being dead I placed
> a tombstone on my breast, dear one . . .

A young widow whose husband had been killed in a fight did not speak of him. She was cheerful and her sense of humor endeared her to the community. She seemed content to forgo remarriage, preferring to remain with her children and the women among whom she had grown up. One night she recited a number of poems, including the following, that saddened and moved the women who heard them:

> Drowning in despair
> the eye says, Oh my fate in love . . .

A married woman whose husband of fifteen years wished to take a second wife admitted no concern, expressing only anger at his failure to buy her the proper gifts and his unconventional decision to hold the wedding in his brother's house rather than her own. Yet she indicated her sense of hurt by myriad poems including:

> Long shriveled from despair
> are the roots that fed my soul . . .

> Patience is my mourning for the loved one
> and your job, oh eyes, is to cry . . .

Other women in the community tried to console her by comparing her fate to that of other women ("Do you think you are the first woman whose husband ever took a second wife?"), cynically commenting that men are all "like that" (as soon as they can afford it, they seek another wife and more children), or telling her to be grateful for her six wonderful children. They indicated empathetic concern by reciting in her presence poems that voiced what they assumed she was feeling:

> Despair of them, dear one, left you
> abjectly turning a water wheel . . .

> At midday in the eye of the murdered
> they were but a trace, a caravan moving off . . .

In the second poem "midday" refers to a wedding and "the murdered" to a person betrayed (the first wife who watches her husband go off with another woman). By expressing sentiments from her point of view, rather than offering advice, her companions emphasized the sense of community and commonality of experience among women.

Another woman had recurring problems with her moody and poverty-stricken brother, who lived with her. Her marital history was sad. Her husband had taken a dislike to her shortly after their marriage and become abusive, later divorcing her. To make matters worse, she had a painful skin disease that had first manifested itself during the difficult period before the divorce and had broken out periodically since. She also recited many poems, one of which perhaps many women could understand all too well:

> I wonder, is despair
> a passing shadow or a companion for life . . .

Conclusion

Awlad 'Ali women live neither in harems nor in seclusion. But like their sisters in societies or classes that can afford to keep women indoors, they live in a world where the general principle of sexual segregation structures social life. Rather than assuming the male perspective and viewing one-half of the bifurcated world as residual or even excluded, we saw, by looking closely at actual lives, that two coexisting communities are created when persons associate primarily with members of their own sex. Even if cross-cut by various ties, each has its integrity and must be examined in its own right. Among Bedouins, the ideological predominance of patrilateral, patrilineal kinship in economic and social relationships and its impact on identity and identification necessarily preclude the structural independence of the women's community. Further, a woman's economic and social dependency severely curtails her autonomy, particularly in making major life decisions.

Yet sexual segregation is not inherently bad for women. In this case, it seems clear that the separation of the worlds mitigates the negative effects of sexual inequality and women's dependence. By taking responsibility for regulating their own conformity to social norms and by avoiding encounters with men who have authority over them, women escape the direct experience of their subordination and gain the respect accorded those who do their share to uphold the social order. Women enthusiastically support the segregation that allows them to carve out significant fields for autonomous action in their relatively unsupervised and egalitarian world. In the women's community, they have an arena for self-assertion. Individual development among women does not occur in opposition to male development; indeed cultural ideals of the feminine "personality" resemble the masculine and include enterprise, boldness, pride, and independence. Because of the denial of sexuality among Awlad 'Ali, women do not orient themselves toward men or try to please them. Instead they value competence, self-sufficiency, and respectful distance. They orient themselves toward other women.

The community of Bedouin women is, above all, a rich world of close ties, intimacy, and shared experience. Because power and authority are hardly at issue in the relations among women, their world is one of relaxed informality, familiarity, and a certain honesty. Although not the result of a self-conscious feminist separatism or a deliberate fostering of bonds of sisterhood, the tone, intensity, and closeness of relations within the Bedouin women's community approach those idealized by feminists. Yet the poems through which women share many of their most intimate sentiments reveal another dimension of experience. Not all women's poems describe love and attachment or concern relationships with men. Nor are all as tragic as the ones presented above. But enough of them revolve around such themes to suggest that women develop deep affective bonds with men — lovers and husbands as well as kin. For the Awlad 'Ali Bedouins, the bonds of womanhood that integrate the world of women have much to do with shared suffering and longing for those outside their community.

Notes

Acknowledgments: The research on which this essay is based was conducted in Egypt between October 1978 and May 1980. I am grateful to many who facilitated my research there but most of all to the community of Awlad ʿAli Bedouins with whom I lived. For financial support for my research in Egypt and writing at Harvard, I am grateful to the National Institute of Mental Health and the American Association of University Women. For encouragement, comments, and help in preparing this essay for presentation at the conference "Communities of Women" I want to thank Barb Smuts and John Watanabe. For inspiration and critical response I must thank the organizers of and participants in that conference sponsored by *Signs* and the Center for Research on Women at Stanford University, and for thought-provoking comments, the anonymous readers of the manuscript for *Signs*.

1. On sexual segregation outside the Middle East, see Janet Bujra, "Introductory: Female Solidarity and the Sexual Division of Labour," in *Women United, Women Divided,* ed. Patricia Caplan and Janet Bujra (Bloomington: Indiana University Press, 1979), pp. 13–45, esp. p. 31; Ursula Sharma, "Segregation and Its Consequences in India: Rural Women in Himachal Pradesh," in the same volume, pp. 259–82.

2. This is an anglicized version of the name by which these tribes are collectively known. The correct Arabic transcription is *Awlaad ʿAlii.* For ethnographic material, see Ahmed H. Abou-Zeid, "Honour and Shame among the Bedouins of Egypt," in *Honour and Shame: The Values of Mediterranean Society,* ed. Jean Peristiany (Chicago: University of Chicago Press, 1966), pp. 243–59; Abdalla Bujra, "The Social Implications of Development Policies: A Case Study from Egypt," in *The Desert and the Sown: Nomads in the Wider Society,* ed. Cynthia Nelson (Berkeley: University of California, Institute of International Studies, 1973), pp. 143–57; Safia Mohsen, "Legal Status of Women among the Awlad ʿAli," *Anthropological Quarterly* 40, no. 3 (July 1967): 153–66.

3. These circumstances and the consequences of having been accompanied initially by my father are detailed in the first chapter of Lila Abu-Lughod, *Veiled Sentiments: Honor and Poetry in a Bedouin Society* (Berkeley: University of California Press, 1986).

4. The analysis of the code of honor and modesty on which the arguments of this article hinge is far too complex to present here. For elaboration, see ibid.

5. In the traditional economy, subsistence depended on the joint labor of all members of one or more households. Men now travel a great deal and much of their work takes them outside the camp. What may have been a more informal separation of men and women on the basis of separate tasks has become rigid and extreme. For a similar case, see Lois Beck, "Women among Qashqaʾi

Nomadic Pastoralists in Iran," in *Women in the Muslim World,* ed. Lois Beck and Nikki Keddie (Cambridge, Mass.: Harvard University Press, 1978), pp. 351–73.

6. In this article references to sexuality are to heterosexuality, which is in keeping with Awlad ʿAli ways of thinking about sexuality.

7. See Abu-Lughod, *Veiled Sentiments.*

8. The customary procedure for obtaining a divorce is either to return to one's natal home and have one's father or older male kin negotiate the divorce, or to "throw oneself" at the mercy of a tribal leader or religious figure. See Mohsen (n. 2 above), esp. pp. 163–65.

9. Polygyny, usually initiated by men, swells the women's community both by increasing the actual number of women in a household and by enabling individual women to participate more in the women's world. Co-wives spend more time with each other than either does with the husband, and they are also free to mingle with other women more often since they split the work and the time involved in meeting the husband's demands.

10. Ursula Sharma, in "Women and Their Affines: The Veil as a Symbol of Separation," *Man* 13, no. 2 (June 1978): 727–56, esp. 226, cites Doranne Jacobson, "Hidden Faces: Hindu and Muslim Purdah in a Central Indian Village" (Ph.D. diss., Columbia University, 1970), who shows that women veil for certain female affines. Like the North Indian villagers studied by Sharma, Awlad ʿAli women veil only for men, although, in contrast, they veil not only for affines but also for kinsmen of certain categories.

11. Nancy Tapper, "The Women's Subsociety among the Shahsevan Nomads of Iran," in Beck and Keddie, eds. (n. 5 above), directed my attention to issues of rank and network in the women's community.

12. For a similar observation regarding urban Yemen, see Carla Makhlouf, *Changing Veils: Women and Modernisation in North Yemen* (London: Croom Helm, 1979), p. 28.

13. For a similar situation among peasants in southern France, see Susan Carol Rogers, "Female Forms of Power and the Myth of Male Dominance: A Model of Female/Male Interaction in a Peasant Society," *American Ethnologist* 2, no. 4 (November 1975): 727–56, esp. 741.

14. Daisy Hilse Dwyer, *Images and Self-Images: Male and Female in Morocco* (New York: Columbia University Press, 1978), p. 163.

15. Lloyd Fallers and Margaret Fallers, "Sex Roles in Edremit," in *Mediterranean Family Structures,* ed. Jean Peristiany (Cambridge: Cambridge University Press, 1976), pp. 243–60, esp. pp. 254, 260, and Sharma, "Segregation and Its Consequences in India" (n. 1 above), make similar observations about the relationship between sexual segregation and women's development in Turkey and India, respectively.

16. Called the *ghinnaawa,* this type of poem or song is marked by its length

(only one line) and its lack of rhyme. Longer rhyming poems are recited mostly by men. The structure of the genre and the role of poetry in Bedouin social life are the subjects of my book *Veiled Sentiments* (n. 3 above).

17. Georg Simmel, "The Secret and the Secret Society," in *The Sociology of Georg Simmel,* ed. Kurt Wolff (Glencoe, Ill.: Free Press, 1950), pp. 307–76.

2

A Letter from a Battered Wife

Del Martin

A friend of mine received the following letter after discussing wife-
beating at a public meeting.

> I am in my thirties and so is my husband. I have a high school
> diploma and am presently attending a local college, trying to obtain
> the additional education I need. My husband is a college graduate
> and a professional in his field. We are both attractive and, for the
> most part, respected and well-liked. We have four children and live
> in a middle-class home with all the comforts we could possibly
> want.
>
> I have everything, except life without fear.
>
> For most of my married life I have been periodically beaten by
> my husband. What do I mean by "beaten"? I mean that parts of my
> body have been hit violently and repeatedly, and that painful
> bruises, swelling, bleeding wounds, unconsciousness, and
> combinations of these things have resulted.
>
> Beating should be distinguished from all other kinds of physical
> abuse—including being hit and shoved around. When I say my
> husband threatens me with abuse I do not mean he warns me that
> he may lose control. I mean that he shakes a fist against my face or
> nose, makes punching-bag jabs at my shoulder, or makes similar
> gestures which may quickly turn into a full-fledged beating.

I have had glasses thrown at me. I have been kicked in the abdomen when I was visibly pregnant. I have been kicked off the bed and hit while lying on the floor — again, while I was pregnant. I have been whipped, kicked and thrown, picked up again and thrown down again. I have been punched and kicked in the head, chest, face, and abdomen more times than I can count.

I have been slapped for saying something about politics, for having a different view about religion, for swearing, for crying, for wanting to have intercourse.

I have been threatened when I wouldn't do something he told me to do. I have been threatened when he's had a bad day and when he's had a good day.

I have been threatened, slapped, and beaten after stating bitterly that I didn't like what he was doing with another woman.

After each beating my husband has left the house and remained away for days.

Few people have ever seen my black and blue face or swollen lips because I have always stayed indoors afterwards, feeling ashamed. I was never able to drive following one of these beatings, so I could not get myself to a hospital for care. I could never have left my young children alone, even if I could have driven a car.

Hysteria inevitably sets in after a beating. This hysteria — the shaking and crying and mumbling — is not accepted by anyone, so there has never been anyone to call.

My husband on a few occasions did phone a day or so later so we could agree on the excuse I would use for returning to work, the grocery store, the dentist appointment, and so on. I used the excuses — a car accident, oral surgery, things like that.

Now, the first response to this story, which I myself think of, will be "Why didn't you seek help?"

I did. Early in our marriage I went to a clergyman who, after a few visits, told me that my husband meant no real harm, that he was just confused and felt insecure. I was encouraged to be more tolerant and understanding. Most important, I was told to forgive him the beatings just as Christ had forgiven me from the cross. I did that, too.

Things continued. Next time I turned to a doctor. I was given little pills to relax me and told to take things a little easier. I was just too nervous.

I turned to a friend, and when her husband found out, he accused me of either making things up or exaggerating the situation. She was told to stay away from me. She didn't, but she could no longer really help me. Just by believing me she was made to feel disloyal.

I turned to a professional family guidance agency. I was told there that my husband needed help and that I should find a way to control the incidents. I couldn't control the beatings — that was the whole point of my seeking help. At the agency I found I had to defend myself against the suspicion that I wanted to be hit, that I invited the beatings. Good God! Did the Jews invite themselves to be slaughtered in Germany?

I did go to two more doctors. One asked me what I had done to provoke my husband. The other asked if we had made up yet.

I called the police one time. They not only did not respond to the call, they called several hours later to ask if things had "settled down." I could have been dead by then!

I have nowhere to go if it happens again. No one wants to take in a woman with four children. Even if there were someone kind enough to care, no one wants to become involved in what is commonly referred to as a "domestic situation."

Everyone I have gone to for help has somehow wanted to blame me and vindicate my husband. I can see it lying there between their words and at the end of their sentences. The clergyman, the doctor, the counselor, my friend's husband, the police — all of them have found a way to vindicate my husband.

No one has to "provoke" a wife-beater. He will strike out when he's ready and for whatever reason he has at the moment.

I may be his excuse, but I have never been the reason.

I know that I do not want to be hit. I know, too, that I will be beaten again unless I can find a way out for myself and my children. I am terrified for them also.

As a married woman I have no recourse but to remain in the situation which is causing me to be painfully abused. I have suffered physical and emotional battering and spiritual rape because the social structure of my world says I cannot do anything about a man who wants to beat me. . . . But staying with my husband means that my children must be subjected to the emotional battering caused when they see their mother's beaten face or hear her screams in the middle of the night.

I know that I have to get out. But when you have nowhere to go, you know that you must go on your own and expect no support. I have to be ready for that. I have to be ready to support myself and the children completely, and still provide a decent environment for them. I pray that I can do that before I am murdered in my own home.

I have learned that no one believes me and that I cannot depend upon any outside help. All I have left is the hope that I can get away before it is too late.

I have learned also that the doctors, the police, the clergy, and my friends will excuse my husband for distorting my face, but won't forgive me for looking bruised and broken. The greatest tragedy is that I am still praying, and there is not a human person to listen.

Being beaten is a terrible thing; it is most terrible of all if you are not equipped to fight back. I recall an occasion when I tried to defend myself and actually tore my husband's shirt. Later, he showed it to a relative as proof that I had done something terribly wrong. The fact that at that moment I had several raised spots on my head hidden by my hair, a swollen lip that was bleeding, and a severely damaged cheek with a blood clot that caused a permanent dimple didn't matter to him. What mattered was that I tore his shirt! That I tore it in self-defense didn't mean anything to him.

My situation is so untenable I would guess that anyone who has not experienced one like it would find it incomprehensible. I find it difficult to believe myself.

It must be pointed out that while a husband can beat, slap, or threaten his wife, there are "good days." These days tend to wear away the effects of the beating. They tend to cause the wife to put aside the traumas and look to the good — first, because there is nothing else to do; second, because there is nowhere and no one to turn to; and third, because the defeat is the beating and the hope is that it will not happen again. A loving woman like myself always hopes that it will not happen again. When it does, she simply hopes again, until it becomes obvious after a third beating that there is no hope. That is when she turns outward for help to find an answer. When that help is denied, she either resigns herself to the situation she is in or pulls herself together and starts making plans for a future life that includes only herself and her children.

For many the third beating may be too late. Several of the times I have been abused I have been amazed that I have remained alive. Imagine that I have been thrown to a very hard slate floor several times, kicked in the abdomen, the head, and the chest, and still remained alive!

What determines who is lucky and who isn't? I could have been dead a long time ago had I been hit the wrong way. My baby could have been killed or deformed had I been kicked the wrong way. What saved me?

I don't know. I only know that it has happened and that each night I dread the final blow that will kill me and leave my children motherless. I hope I can hang on until I complete my education, get a good job, and become self-sufficient enough to care for my children on my own.

3

The Death of the Profane

(a commentary on the genre of legal writing)

Patricia J. Williams

Buzzers are big in New York City. Favored particularly by smaller stores and boutiques, merchants throughout the city have installed them as screening devices to reduce the incidence of robbery: if the face at the door looks desirable, the buzzer is pressed and the door is unlocked. If the face is that of an undesirable, the door stays locked. Predictably, the issue of undesirability has revealed itself to be a racial determination. While controversial enough at first, even civil-rights organizations backed down eventually in the face of arguments that the buzzer system is a "necessary evil," that it is a "mere inconvenience" in comparison to the risks of being murdered, that suffering discrimination is not as bad as being assaulted, and that in any event it is not all blacks who are barred, just "17-year-old black males wearing running shoes and hooded sweatshirts."[1]

The installation of these buzzers happened swiftly in New York; stores that had always had their doors wide open suddenly became exclusive or received people by appointment only. I discovered them and their meaning one Saturday in 1986. I was shopping in Soho and saw in a store window a sweater that I wanted to buy for my mother. I pressed my round brown face to the window and my finger to the buzzer, seeking admittance. A narrow-eyed, white teenager wearing running shoes and feasting on bubble gum glared out, evaluating me for signs that would pit me against the limits of his social understanding. After about five seconds, he mouthed "We're closed," and blew pink rubber at me. It was two Saturdays before Christmas, at one o'clock in the afternoon; there were several white people in the store who appeared to be shopping for things for *their* mothers.

I was enraged. At that moment I literally wanted to break all the windows of the store and *take* lots of sweaters for my mother. In the flicker of his judgmental gray eyes, that saleschild had transformed my brightly sentimental, joy-to-the-world, pre-Christmas spree to a shambles. He snuffed my sense of humanitarian catholicity, and there was nothing I could do to snuff his, without making a spectacle of myself.

I am still struck by the structure of power that drove me into such a blizzard of rage. There was almost nothing I could do, short of physically intruding upon him, that would humiliate him the way he humiliated me. No words, no gestures, no prejudices of my own would make a bit of difference to him; his refusal to let me into the store — it was Benetton's, whose colorfully punnish ad campaign is premised on wrapping every one of the world's peoples in its cottons and woolens — was an outward manifestation of his never having let someone like me into the realm of his reality. He had no compassion, no remorse, no reference to me; and no desire to acknowledge me even at the estranged level of arm's-length transactor. He saw me only as one who would take his money and therefore could not conceive that I was there to give him money.

In this weird ontological imbalance, I realized that buying something in that store was like bestowing a gift, the gift of my commerce, the lucre of my patronage. In the wake of my outrage, I wanted to take back the gift of appreciation that my peering in the window must have appeared to be. I wanted to take it back in the form of unappreciation, disrespect, defilement. I wanted to work so hard at wishing he could feel what I felt that he would never again mistake my hatred for some sort of plaintive wish to be included. I was quite willing to disenfranchise myself, in the heat of my need to revoke the flattery of my purchasing power. I was willing to boycott Benetton's, random white-owned businesses, and anyone who ever blew bubble gum in my face again.

My rage was admittedly diffuse, even self-destructive, but it was symmetrical. The perhaps loose-ended but utter propriety of that rage is no doubt lost, not just to the young man who actually barred me, but to those who would appreciate my being barred only as an abstract precaution, who approve of those who would bar even as they deny that they would bar *me*.

The violence of my desire to burst into Benetton's is probably quite apparent. I often wonder if the violence, the exclusionary hatred, is equally apparent in the repeated public urgings that blacks understand the buzzer system by putting themselves in the shoes of white store-owners — that, in effect, blacks look into the mirror of frightened white faces for the reality of their undesirability; and that then blacks would "just as surely conclude that [they] would not let [themselves] in under similar circumstances."[2] (That some blacks might agree merely shows that some of us have learned too well the lessons of privatized intimacies of self-hatred and rationalized away the fullness of our public, participatory selves.)

On the same day I was barred from Benetton's, I went home and wrote the above impassioned account in my journal. On the day after that, I found I was still brooding, so I turned to a form of catharsis I have always found healing. I typed up as much of the story as I have just told, made a big poster of it, put a nice colorful border around it, and, after Benetton's was truly closed, stuck it to their big sweater-filled window. I exercised my first-amendment right to place my business with them right out in the street.

So that was the first telling of this story. The second telling came a few months later, for a symposium on Excluded Voices sponsored by a law review. I wrote an essay summing up my feelings about being excluded from Benetton's and analyzing "how the rhetoric of increased privatization, in response to racial issues, functions as the rationalizing agent of public unaccountability and, ultimately, irresponsibility." Weeks later, I received the first edit. From the first page to the last, my fury had been carefully cut out. My rushing, run-on-rage had been reduced to simple declarative sentences. The active personal had been inverted in favor of the passive impersonal. My words were different; they spoke to me upsidedown. I was afraid to read too much of it at a time — meanings rose up at me oddly, stolen and strange.

A week and a half later, I received the second edit. All reference to Benetton's had been deleted because, according to the editors and the faculty adviser, it was defamatory; they feared harassment and liability; they said printing it would be irresponsible. I called them and offered to supply a footnote attesting to this as my personal experience at one particular location and of a buzzer system not limited to Benetton's; the editors told me that they were not in the habit of publishing things that were unverifiable. I could not but wonder, in this refusal even to let me file an affadavit, what it would take to make my experience verifiable. The testimony of an independent white bystander? (a requirement in fact imposed in U.S. Supreme Court holdings through the first part of the century[3]).

Two days *after* the piece was sent to press, I received copies of the final page proofs. All reference to my race had been eliminated because it was against "editorial policy" to permit descriptions of physiognomy. "I realize," wrote one editor, "that this was a very personal experience, but any reader will know what you must have looked like when standing at that window." In a telephone conversation to them, I ranted wildly about the significance of such an omission. "It's irrelevant," another editor explained in a voice gummy with soothing and patience; "It's nice and poetic," but it doesn't "advance the discussion of any principle. . . . This is a law review, after all." Frustrated, I accused him of censorship; calmly he assured me it was not. "This is just a matter of style," he said with firmness and finality.

Ultimately I did convince the editors that mention of my race was central to the whole sense of the subsequent text; that my story became one of extreme paranoia without the information that I am black; or that it became one in which the reader had to fill in the gap by assumption, presumption, prejudgment, or prejudice. What was most interesting to me in this experience was how the blind application of principles of neutrality, through the device of omission, acted either to make me look crazy or to make the reader participate in old habits of cultural bias.

That was the second telling of my story. The third telling came last April, when I was invited to participate in a law-school conference on Equality and Difference. I retold my sad tale of exclusion from Soho's most glitzy boutique, focusing in this version on the law-review editing process as a consequence of an ideology of style rooted in a social text of neutrality. I opined:

> Law and legal writing aspire to formalized, color-blind, liberal
> ideals. Neutrality is the standard for assuring these ideals; yet the
> adherence to it is often determined by reference to an aesthetic of
> uniformity, in which difference is simply omitted. For example,
> when segregation was eradicated from the American lexicon, its
> omission led many to actually believe that racism therefore no

longer existed. Race-neutrality in law has become the presumed antidote for race bias in real life. With the entrenchment of the notion of race-neutrality came attacks on the concept of affirmative action and the rise of reverse discrimination suits. Blacks, for so many generations deprived of jobs based on the color of our skin, are now told that we ought to find it demeaning to be hired, based on the color of our skin. Such is the silliness of simplistic either-or inversions as remedies to complex problems.

What is truly demeaning in this era of double-speak-no-evil is going on interviews and not getting hired because someone doesn't think we'll be comfortable. It is demeaning not to get promoted because we're judged "too weak," then putting in a lot of energy the next time and getting fired because we're "too strong." It is demeaning to be told what we find demeaning. It is very demeaning to stand on street corners unemployed and begging. It is downright demeaning to have to explain why we haven't been employed for months and then watch the job go to someone who is "more experienced." It is outrageously demeaning that none of this can be called racism, even if it happens only to, or to large numbers of, black people; as long as it's done with a smile, a handshake and a shrug; as long as the phantom-word "race" is never used.

The image of race as a phantom-word came to me after I moved into my late godmother's home. In an attempt to make it my own, I cleared the bedroom for painting. The following morning the room asserted itself, came rushing and raging at me through the emptiness, exactly as it had been for twenty-five years. One day filled with profuse and overwhelming complexity, the next day filled with persistently recurring memories. The shape of the past came to haunt me, the shape of the emptiness confronted me each time I was about to enter the room. The force of its spirit still drifts like an odor throughout the house.

The power of that room, I have thought since, is very like the power of racism as status quo: it is deep, angry, eradicated from view, but strong enough to make everyone who enters the room walk around the bed that isn't there, avoiding the phantom as they did the substance, for fear of bodily harm. They do not even know they are avoiding; they defer to the unseen shapes of things with subtle responsiveness, guided by an impulsive awareness of nothingness, and the deep knowledge and denial of witchcraft at work.

The phantom room is to me symbolic of the emptiness of formal equal opportunity, particularly as propounded by President Reagan, the Reagan Civil Rights Commission and the Reagan Supreme Court. Blindly formalized constructions of equal opportunity are the creation of a space that is filled in by a meandering stream of unguided hopes, dreams, fantasies, fears, recollections. They are the presence of the past in imaginary, imagistic form — the phantom-roomed exile of our longing.

It is thus that I strongly believe in the efficacy of programs and paradigms like affirmative action. Blacks are the objects of a constitutional omission which has been incorporated into a theory of neutrality. It is thus that omission is really a form of expression, as oxymoronic as that sounds: racial omission is a literal part of original intent; it is the fixed, reiterated prophecy of the Founding Fathers. It is thus that affirmative action is an affirmation; the affirmative act of hiring — or hearing — blacks is a recognition of individuality that re-places blacks as a social statistic, that is profoundly interconnective to the fate of blacks and whites either as sub-groups or as one group. In this sense, affirmative action is as mystical and beyond-the-self as an initiation ceremony. It is an act of verification and of vision. It is an act of social as well as professional responsibility.

The following morning I opened the local newspaper, to find that the event of my speech had commanded two columns on the front page of the Metro section. I quote only the opening lines: "Affirmative action promotes prejudice by denying the status of women and blacks, instead of affirming them as its name suggests. So said New York City attorney Patricia Williams to an audience Wednesday."[4]

I clipped out the article and put it in my journal. In the margin there is a note to myself: eventually, it says, I should try to pull all these threads together into yet another law-review article. The problem, of course, will be that in the hierarchy of law-review citation, the article in the newspaper will have more authoritative weight about me, as a so-called primary resource, than I will have; it will take precedence over my own citation of the unverifiable testimony of my speech.

I have used the Benetton's story a lot, in speaking engagements at various schools. I tell it whenever I am too tired to whip up an original speech from scratch. Here are some of the questions I have been asked in the wake of its telling:

Am I not privileging a racial perspective, by considering only the black point of view? Don't I have an obligation to include the "salesman's side" of the story?

Am I not putting the salesman on trial and finding him guilty of racism without giving him a chance to respond to or cross-examine me?

Am I not using the store window as a "metaphorical fence" against the potential of his explanation in order to represent my side as "authentic"?

How can I be sure I'm right?

What makes my experience the real black one anyway?

Isn't it possible that another black person would disagree with my experience? If so, doesn't that render my story too unempirical and subjective to pay any attention to?

Always a major objection is to my having put the poster on Benetton's window. As one law professor put it: "It's one thing to publish this in a law review, where no one can take it personally, but it's another thing altogether to put your own interpretation right out there, just like that, uncontested, I mean, with nothing to counter it."[5]

Notes

1. "When 'By Appointment' Means Keep Out," *New York Times*, December 17, 1986, p. B1. Letter to the Editor from Michael Levin and Marguerita Levin, *New York Times*, January 11, 1987, p. E32.

2. *New York Times*, January 11, 1987, p. E32.

3. See generally *Blyew v. U.S.*, 80 U.S. 581 (1871), upholding a state's right to forbid blacks to testify against whites.

4. "Attorney Says Affirmative Action Denies Racism, Sexism," *Dominion Post* (Morgantown, West Virginia), April 8, 1988, p. B1.

5. These questions put me on trial — an imaginary trial where it is I who have the burden of proof — and proof being nothing less than the testimony of the salesman actually confessing yes yes I am a racist. These questions question my own ability to know, to assess, to be objective. And of course, since anything that happens to me is inherently subjective, they take away my power to know what happens to me in the world. Others, by this standard, will always know better than I. And my insistence on recounting stories from my own perspective will be treated as presumption, slander, paranoid hallucination, or just plain lies.

Recently I got an urgent call from Thomas Grey of Stanford Law School. He had used this piece in his jurisprudence class, and a rumor got started that the Benetton's story wasn't true, that I had made it up, that it was a fantasy, a lie that was probably the product of a diseased mind trying to make all white people feel guilty. At this point I realized it almost didn't make any difference whether I was telling the truth or not — that the greater issue I had to face was the overwhelming weight of a disbelief that goes beyond mere disinclination to believe and becomes active suppression of anything I might have to say. The greater problem is a powerfully oppressive mechanism for denial of black self-knowledge and expression. And this denial cannot be separated from the simultaneously pathological willingness to believe certain things about blacks — not to believe them, but things about them.

When students in Grey's class believed and then claimed that I had made it all up, they put me in a position like that of Tawana Brawley. I mean that specifically: the social consequence of concluding that we are liars operates as a kind of public absolution of racism — the conclusion is not merely that we are troubled or that I am eccentric, but that we, as liars, are the norm. Therefore, the nonbelievers can believe, things of this sort really don't happen (even in the face of statistics to the contrary). Racism or rape is all a big fantasy concocted by troublesome minorities and women. It is interesting to recall the outcry in every national medium, from the *New York Post* to the *Times* to the major networks, in the wake of the Brawley case: who will ever again believe a black woman who cries rape by a white man? Now shift the frame a bit, and imagine a white male facing a consensus that he lied. Would there be a difference? Consider Charles Stuart, for example, the white Bostonian who accused a black man of murdering his pregnant wife and whose brother later alleged that in fact the brothers had conspired to murder her. Most people and the media not only did not claim but actively resisted believing that Stuart represented any kind of "white male" norm. Instead he was written off as a troubled weirdo, a deviant — again even in the face of spousal-abuse statistics to the contrary. There was not a story I could find that carried on about "who will ever believe" the next white man who cries murder.

4

Burning Incense, Pledging Sisterhood

Communities of Women Workers in the Shanghai Cotton Mills, 1919–1949

Emily Honig

When we swore sisterhood we would go to a temple and burn incense. Everyone would have to make a pledge. We pledged to be loyal through life and death. And if someone was halfhearted in their loyalty, then we prayed that when they got on a boat, that boat would turn over.
— *A woman who worked in the Shanghai cotton mills in the 1920s*

During the thirty years between the end of World War I and Liberation in 1949, it was common for women who worked in the cotton mills of Shanghai to form sisterhood societies (*jiemei hui*). After working together for several years, six to ten women would formalize their relationship with one another by pledging sisterhood. Sometimes this simply involved going to a restaurant, eating a meal together, drinking a cup of "one-heart wine," and toasting their loyalty to one another. Because large numbers of women workers were Buddhists, it was more common for those forming sisterhoods to go to a Buddhist temple, burn incense before the statue of a deity, and pledge to be loyal to one another "through life and death."

Reprinted from *Signs* 10 (Summer 1985): 700–714, by permission of the author and the publisher. © 1985 by The University of Chicago. All rights reserved.

Once they had formed a sisterhood, the members would call each other by kinship terms based on their age: the oldest was "Big Sister," the next oldest "Second Sister," and so forth. Often members of the sisterhoods contributed money to buy a cloth in order to make each member an identical Chinese-style, long blue cotton gown. They wore the gowns when they went out together to express their unity.[1]

Women displayed their loyalty to one another both inside and outside the mills. Members of sisterhoods walked together to work in order to protect each other from hoodlums on the street. During the twelve-hour shifts they worked in the factory, one woman would do the work of two while the other ate lunch, went to the bathroom, or hid in a yard bin to take a nap. They defended each other if a male worker or overseer threatened one of them. Often the sisterhoods functioned as an economic mutual aid society: in order to avoid borrowing from "stamp-money lenders" who charged over 100 percent in interest, women paid a monthly "sisterhood fee." Then if one of the members faced an extraordinary expense such as a wedding, a funeral, or an illness, she could draw on this fund.[2] Members of sisterhoods socialized together: they would get together at one member's house to chat on Sundays, to go window-shopping, or to hear performances of local opera, a favorite form of entertainment among women workers in Shanghai.

These sisterhoods are scarcely mentioned in contemporary surveys of working-class life in Shanghai. This is not because those conducting the surveys failed to observe and record the conditions of women cotton-mill workers, whose number represented over one-third of the ranks of the famed Shanghai proletariat.[3] Historians have used these contemporary records to describe the transformation of women workers from passive, ever-suffering victims of industrial poverty to heroines of the organized labor movement and, in some cases, to class-conscious revolutionaries.

The interviews I conducted with women who had worked in Shanghai cotton mills during the three decades before 1949 suggest that the majority of women working in Shanghai were not lonely, isolated individuals; but neither were they members of trade unions, political organizations, or the Chinese Communist Party (CCP).[4] They survived by forming ties with other women workers who helped and protected them. These informal groups in time formalized as sisterhoods.

Although all women can recall in great detail the ways in which they depended on each other, questions about the sisterhoods provoked a number of seemingly contradictory answers. Some said that only women who had worked for many years pledged sisterhood, while others disdainfully described the sisterhoods as a phenomenon most prevalent among young women workers who liked to go out shopping, dress up, and hear local opera. Some said they were hoodlum organizations, while others insisted they were formed by women who wanted to protect themselves against hoodlums. Some remembered that only the most ideologically "backward" women pledged sisterhood, while others said the sisterhoods had been organized by the CCP. And finally, there were women who, when asked about the sisterhoods, exclaimed, "We women mill workers — we *all* used to pledge sisterhood!"

This variety of explanations suggests that there was no single type of sisterhood, that sisterhoods were formed for a host of reasons, and that they engaged in many different kinds of activities. There were some sisterhoods, however, that encompassed all these contradictory aspects, and one purpose of this article is to explain this phenomenon.

The major focus of this article, though, is to evaluate the significance of the sisterhoods. It would be tempting when studying these organizations formed by women workers, largely to serve the needs of women workers, to assume that they represent members' development of a consciousness as women and as workers. By looking more closely at these sisterhoods — at the women who formed them and at their activities — this article will suggest that associations constituted solely of workers are not necessarily an expression of working-class consciousness and that neither are autonomous women's groups inherently an expression of female consciousness. When examined in their cultural and historical context, working women's organizations, such as the Chinese sisterhoods, may as easily confirm and perpetuate traditional social relationships as challenge them.

Who Are Our Sisters?

In order to understand the development of sisterhoods, we must first look at the conditions inside the cotton mills and working-class districts that made it necessary for women workers to depend on one another. It was this need for mutual aid that led to the development of a sense of community among women workers and, ultimately, to the sisterhoods.

The daily work routine in the mills — if women had adhered to the rules — would have been grueling. They were required to work twelve-hour shifts with only a ten-minute break for lunch. Even while they ate, the machines continued to run. But women did not passively accept these rules. They often made work-sharing arrangements with those who labored beside them. "Those who got along well," a worker named Gu Lianying recalled, "one would help the other work, so that the other could eat." If a woman was exhausted and wanted to sleep for a few hours, another worker watched her machine and woke her up when the overseer made his rounds through the workshop. Sometimes women had to leave the mill for several hours to take care of a child. Since requesting formal permission would have jeopardized their jobs, they instead asked a friend to guard their machine while they were gone.

The world outside the mills was equally threatening, and women were compelled to help each other if they were to survive. Local toughs — many of whom belonged to Shanghai's powerful gang organizations — gathered at the mill gates, then flirted with and even pursued women walking home from work. On payday they seized women's wages, and on ordinary days they collected some cash by engaging in an activity called "stripping a sheep" — robbing a woman of her clothes, which they then sold.[5] While sexual abuse by male hoodlums was the most common problem, women mill workers had reason to be equally fearful of female gangsters, who specialized in the lucrative business of kidnapping young girls for sale to brothels or as future daughters-in-law.[6] All women workers had family members or friends who had been raped, beaten, or kidnapped by neighborhood hoodlums. For protection they almost always walked to and from the mills in groups — accompanied by parents when they were young and by siblings and neighbors as they grew older.

Part of the experience of growing up in the mills, for girls who had begun working when they were ten or eleven, was developing a network of "sisters" on whom they could depend for both help and protection. "We younger workers would not help each other in the workshop," one woman recalled, "but when I was older, I also had 'little sisters.' Then when I would eat, one of them would tend my machine. It was the girls in the lane next to me — we would help each other. This started when I was about fifteen." As women developed such relationships in the mills, they began to socialize with these other women workers as well. "After working a long time, then you'd start to have friends," the same woman continued. "And on Sundays, if you had time, you could go visit their house. Maybe that started when I was seventeen or eighteen. All of my friends then were cotton-mill workers." These relationships often continued after women were married. "We used to love to go see Subei operas," Chen Zhaodi recalled. "We would go in the evening, from seven to eleven. We almost never went with our husbands or children. It was usually some of us women who worked together who would go. But I would not tell my family where I was going. My mother-in-law would never have let me go. I just went secretly, with my 'sisters.'"

These relationships often remained casual, but frequently they were formalized as sisterhoods. One woman described this process: "Originally we would go to work together, and leave work together, because then it was not good to walk alone. After a while we would get to know each other. Then, if I thought that person was very decent, I would say to her, 'Why don't we pledge loyalty? Then if you have some problems I'll help you, and if I have some problems you can help me.'" It was at this point that they would go to a Buddhist temple and burn incense to establish their sisterhood. Women who pledged sisterhood were thus formalizing relationships with people outside their families as they began to perceive the women with whom they worked in the factory as their sisters.

This does not mean, however, that individual women perceived all other women mill workers, or even all other women who worked in the same mill, as potential sisters. In fact, most of the relationships of work sharing and mutual assistance that I have described were based on traditional connections between those from the same native place. In order to understand the nature of communities formed by women workers — and ultimately the nature of the sisterhoods — we must look briefly at the workers' origins and the extent to which their native place determined their experience in Shanghai, both inside and outside the mills.

Although some women who worked in the cotton mills were natives of Shanghai, throughout this thirty-year period the overwhelming majority of women came from rural villages in the provinces of Jiangsu and Zhejiang. (Shanghai is located at the southeastern corner of Jiangsu, on the border of Zhejiang.) They came from villages with almost every kind of economy imaginable — from places that relied on salt production to ones that depended on rice cultivation to ones where cotton was the major crop, from areas where handicraft industries such as silk or cotton spinning and weaving were a vital part of the peasant household economy to ones where handicrafts were almost nonexistent. They came from locales where foot-binding was still common in the 1930s as well as from places where the practice had long since ceased.

The villages from which women came can be roughly divided into two groups: those located in Subei, the part of Jiangsu Province north of the Yangzi River, and those located in the Jiangnan, the area south of the river. (The Yangzi River flows just north of Shanghai.) The Jiangnan has historically been one of the richest agricultural areas in China. Although no systematic research has considered the role of women in the rural economy, it appears that most peasant women in this area engaged in handicraft work. The places in the Jiangnan from which the mill workers came, such as Wuxi and Changzhou, had also exported many mill owners and technicians to Shanghai.

Subei was a much poorer area. Handicraft industries were less developed than in the south, and most peasant women played an active role in agricultural work. Throughout the early twentieth century vast numbers of families fled villages in the north that had been devastated by floods. Ever since that time, refugees from northern Jiangsu had performed the coolie jobs — such as collecting night soil and pulling rickshaws — that locals considered too demeaning to do themselves.[7]

These basic differences in the rural economies north and south of the river were replicated and perpetuated in the mills of Shanghai. In general, women from Subei, considered strong, robust, and accustomed to dirt, were channeled into the mill workshops, where the labor was most arduous and dirty. Often they did the jobs that in earlier stages of industrialization had been performed by male workers and that women from Shanghai proper or from villages of Jiangnan were not willing to do. Women from Jiangnan concentrated in the workshops where the labor was lighter and better paying. They also had the possibility of being promoted to supervisory positions.

Individual departments in the cotton mills were usually staffed by workers from a particular village.[8] This does not appear to have been the result of a management strategy to create divisions in the labor force, even though it had that effect. Hiring in the Shanghai mills was not controlled by a central personnel office but rather was the prerogative of the "Number Ones" (forewomen) in the workshops, and women secured jobs by dint of their "connections" with a Number One. When women who had migrated from the countryside arrived in Shanghai in search of work, they sought out people from their hometown who could introduce them to a Number One, usually someone from the same town. People from the same native place considered it their duty to help others from their district.[9]

The cotton mills were the only enterprise in Shanghai that brought several thousand women of disparate origins together under one roof. But they did not necessarily provide a setting where traditional patterns of localism were dissolved. Women from the same village were likely to be employed in the same workshop, surrounded by relatives and neighbors who came from their town, shared their customs, and spoke their particular dialect of Chinese. Furthermore, in the course of a working day, women had little reason to leave their workshop and have contact with women from others.

This localism pervaded the lives of women outside the mills as well. They usually lived in neighborhoods where people from their hometown had gathered.[10] Their hairstyles and eating habits often reflected the traditions of their native villages, and, as Chen Zhaodi observed:

> People from each place had different styles of dress. People from Subei liked to wear red, brightly colored clothes. People from Wuxi, Changzhou, and Tongzhou had their own looms, so they wore clothing they had woven themselves. They had little square scarves they would wrap on their heads. They also had long aprons. People from Nantong liked to wear long aprons. People from Yangzhou liked to dress up their hair. They would wear a bun. People from Changzhou and Wuxi liked to wear hairpins.

When they socialized on Sundays or holidays, they almost always did so with friends from their native place. Women from Zhejiang socialized with relatives and other people from Zhejiang and "did not bother too much with other people." When attending performances of local opera, Subei women went to theaters where they could hear Yangzhou opera, women from Wuxi went to hear Wuxi opera, and those from Zhejiang attended performances of Shaoxing (a city in Zhejiang) opera. When they married, their spouses were inevitably from the same district.

Place of origin was the major way in which women perceived themselves as similar to or different from others. Their attitude toward women from other villages was indifferent, at best, and sometimes overtly hostile. Women from Shanghai and from villages in the Jiangnan were contemptuous of women from Subei and often swore at them, "You Jiangbei swine!" It was not unheard of for a Subei woman to dump a bucket of night soil on the head of a fellow worker from Jiangnan or to shove a woman from Jiangnan into one of the rivers or canals that crisscrossed Shanghai.[11] Regional animosity — often the cause of bloody battles between male laborers — was also expressed by women who worked in the mills.[12]

When women pledged sisterhood, they were perpetuating both intra-regional bonds and interregional divisions. No systematic information about the membership of sisterhoods is available. Yet based on what we know about patterns of migration to and settlement in Shanghai and about hiring practices, which usually resulted in concentrations of people from the same village in particular workshops, it seems safe to assume that, when women pledged sisterhood, it was with women from the same village. This is confirmed by the comment of a woman from Wuxi who, when asked whether she had ever joined a sisterhood, replied, "There was no one else in my workshop from Wuxi, so with whom could I pledge sisterhood?"

Thus the sisterhoods were not organizations that drew and bonded all women workers together. The women who joined them by no means perceived themselves as sisters to all women who shared their predicament. The important commonality was a shared native place. Yet the sisterhoods involved something more than traditional relationships. It is important to remember that new workers did not have a group of sisters on whom they could depend. To some degree the relationships embodied in the sisterhoods were ones that developed during the time women worked in the mills, and in that sense they were indeed a product of factory life.

Sisters, Not Brothers

Even if women in the Shanghai cotton mills did not perceive themselves as sisters to all women workers, they did indeed enter into formal organizations with some of their fellow laborers. They could have simply continued to help each other at work, walk with one another to and from the mill, and socialize together without bothering to go to Buddhist temples, burn incense, and pledge sisterhood. Thus we must return to the question, What does it mean that women mill workers formed autonomous female organizations?

Before confronting this question, I must point out that there is some evidence that the sisterhoods were not exclusively female. In describing the sisterhoods, one woman explained, "When ten of us women workers pledged sisterhood, we usually included one male worker and two or three tough women workers. Otherwise our group would not have power for defense." That this was not an atypical situation is suggested by a similar phenomenon among prostitutes in Shanghai. "Wild chickens," the lowest class of prostitutes in Shanghai, and the only ones who went out onto the streets to attract customers, also formed sisterhood societies. Their sisterhoods are described as consisting of nine prostitutes plus one male, usually a petty gangster who had connections with the local police, who was supposed to help protect the women if anyone tried to abuse them while they were out at night.[13]

Unfortunately, we do not know if the practice of including men in the sisterhoods of women mill workers was widespread. Nor do we know what role the men played. It is possible, for example, that they were part of the sisterhood simply to give physical protection when necessary but did not participate in the other functions of the sisterhood such as work sharing, providing economic mutual aid, and socializing.

While the evidence of men's inclusion in the sisterhoods is perplexing, what we know about male membership at this point is not enough to negate our consideration of the sisterhoods as organizations formed primarily for and by women. This is confirmed by the simultaneous existence of "brotherhoods" among male workers in the mills. Groups of eight to ten male workers pledged loyalty to each other by burning incense, and members of brotherhoods referred to each other as "Oldest Brother," "Second Brother," and so forth. If women did not intend to form separate, autonomous organizations, then why did they not form "brother-sister societies" or simply "workerhoods"? The answer to this question, I would argue, is found in the historical and cultural context in which sisterhoods developed.

During the three decades before Liberation, it was socially acceptable for women to participate in activities or associations with other women but not with men. This was a reality that even radical organizers in the CCP—who would have preferred to develop organizations that included both men and women—had to accept in order to mobilize women. "Although I am an extreme supporter of the belief that men and women should study together," Xiang Jingyu, head of the Women's Bureau of the CCP, wrote in 1924, "when it comes to establishing workers' schools, I am an absolute advocate of male and female separatism. . . . It is only by setting up schools especially for women that women will be willing to come, and that their fathers and husbands will be willing to let them come and study."[14] That year, the first Party-sponsored workers' schools were established in one of Shanghai's cotton-mill districts: one for men and one for women.[15] A year later Xiang Jingyu extended this principle to unions, suggesting that, in order to attract female members, there would have to be separate unions for women.[16] As late as 1941, when the Party was trying to organize underground during the Japanese occupation, the person responsible for organizing in the cotton mills lamented that it was still necessary to establish separate Party branches for women workers.[17]

In this context, forming a mixed-gender group may have presented a more profound challenge to traditional social relationships than forming a women's organization. Or, more modestly put, establishing a women's association and calling it a sisterhood did not necessarily indicate that women desired autonomy from men. In Shanghai (and in most of China) separate female organizations were traditional, not radical.

This does not mean, however, that the formation of autonomous women's groups was inherently conservative. It would have been equally possible for women to have established organizations that expressed their determination to challenge the existing social order. This is in fact what happened in the Canton delta during the late nineteenth and early twentieth centuries, according to Marjorie Topley. Many peasant women in this area, who played a critical role in sericulture, formed sisterhoods to resist marriage. Groups of women pledged loyalty to one another before a deity in a Buddhist temple and made vows never to marry. This was possible because they could support themselves through the wages they earned as silk workers.[18]

Although women in the Shanghai mills, like peasant women in Canton, enjoyed independent incomes, there is little similarity between the two types of sisterhoods besides the name and ceremony of pledging loyalty. The women in Shanghai were not coming together to demand change in their status either as women or as workers. The majority of women who joined sisterhoods in Shanghai accepted what they probably considered to be their fate: they would work twelve hours a day in a mill only to return home to face the task of maintaining a household; they were vulnerable to sexual abuse by overseers inside the mills and thugs on the streets; they would marry the person who had been chosen for them by their parents, often when they were only children. The purpose of the sisterhoods was not to advocate change or express resistance but simply to help each other survive within the context of traditional social relationships.

Sisterhoods were not the only associations women workers formed to ensure their survival in Shanghai. To protect themselves from the wrath of the Number Ones in the mills and from attacks by hoodlums outside, many women workers also "pledged godmothers" (*bai ganniang*). "For protection from the gangs, you could make arrangements with one gang member," Zhu Fanu recalled. "Male workers would find a male gang leader, and women workers would find a woman. This was called pledging a godmother. When you found the person who would protect you, you would send her presents. Then if another gangster ever bothered you, you could go tell your godmother, and she would take care of you, because she had power." Often women mill workers pledged loyalty to the Number One in their workshop as their godmother. Most of the Number Ones not only had the power commensurate with their position in the mills but also were members of the gangs (or were married to gang members) and therefore were influential in the neighborhood as well. With such godmothers, women workers had protection both on and off the job.

Like pledging sisterhood, pledging loyalty to a godmother also involved a ceremony: burning incense, kneeling, and reciting a vow in front of an altar. Once a woman had a godmother, she was expected to demonstrate her appreciation by periodically sending gifts, preferably cash. Whenever the godmother had a pretext—such as a birthday or holiday—she would send invitations to all her "godchildren" to partake in a celebration (*chi jiu*). "You had to go, and when you went, you had to send them money. That was the main purpose," one worker commented.

Sometimes the distinction between pledging sisterhoods and pledging a godmother blurred. While individual women may have chosen either to pledge sisterhood or to pledge a godmother, some may have pledged both. More important, there is some evidence that the two practices sometimes merged—that some sisterhoods included a godmother. One woman, for example, described the sisterhoods as including "one male and two or three tough women." More compelling evidence comes from a description of organizing strategies developed by the CCP during the Anti-Japanese War (1937–45). According to this account, the Party, in an attempt to adapt organizational forms familiar to women workers, established sisterhoods that included several ordinary mill workers, a woman who was a Number One, and an older woman who was married to a gang leader.[19] In these cases women of different ages and of different status in the mill were bonded together in the sisterhoods.

This information affects how we ultimately assess the relationships among the members of sisterhoods. The term "sisterhood" usually evokes the notion of equality, and it is appealing to think of the associations as ones composed of women who saw themselves as sisters, hence equals. Even if these "hybrid" sisterhoods were the exception, not the rule, they caution us not to assume uncritically that sisterhoods are egalitarian organizations.

Sisters in Revolution

Although the sisterhoods were not self-consciously political, they often took actions that had political implications. This was particularly evident when groups of sisters, banding together to protect one member, opposed — or even physically attacked — their employers. "One time a girl worker was being harassed by an overseer," one woman remembered. "She told us sisters, and we all attacked that overseer and beat him up." Sometimes their commitment to mutual protection put them in strikelike situations. If a Number One threatened to fire a woman who belonged to a sisterhood, her sisters would refuse to work until the Number One revoked her threat. These were common, spontaneous incidents, but it does not require much stretch of the imagination to recognize how these loyalties might be appropriated in an organized labor movement. If one member of a sisterhood shut off the motor of her spinning frame or loom as part of a strike, her sisters could be expected to shut off their machines too, even if for no reason other than personal loyalty.

The most vivid example of how the sisterhoods were used to advocate principles very different from those that characterized their original purpose comes from CCP actions during the Anti-Japanese War and during the Civil War from 1946 to 1949. The political situation during both conflicts made only the most covert means of organizing possible, and Party members began to pay closer attention to preexisting social networks among workers, such as sisterhoods, viewing them as potentially revolutionary organizations. In one of the only available reports on this phenomenon, the Party in 1941 instructed local organizers:

> Because of the subjective and objective circumstances of women's lives, they must often help each other. In order to prevent strangers from flirting with them, or thieves from trying to take away their wages, they often walk together. On their time off, when they go buy things, they also usually go in groups of seven or eight. In all of

these groups there is always one or two people who are at the center. If we can attract them, then it is easy to attract the others in their group. More and more of these groups are developing in the areas occupied by the Japanese, where women want to protect themselves. So, it is not just important to unite with these elements in struggle, but also important to do this in their everyday organizations.[20]

Thus, instead of encouraging the members of sisterhoods to read progressive literature, to participate in discussions of the workers' movement, or to go to secret screenings of Russian movies, organizers initially went shopping with their "sisters" or played in parks with them. "First we just tried to develop friendships," a woman who was active in the Party underground in the late 1930s and 1940s recalled, "and then later we could talk about the conditions of women workers."

In some cases Party activists did not simply join sisterhoods that already existed but actually began forming sisterhoods themselves. In order to do so, however, they had to adhere to the practices that made pledging sisterhood meaningful to ordinary women workers, no matter how far they may have diverged from the principles upheld by the Party. Thus, when the CCP formed sisterhoods, the Party activists had to go along with the other members to a Buddhist temple, where they all burned incense, knelt in front of a statue of a deity, and took oaths to "be loyal to each other through life and death."[21]

If these new sisterhoods differed from the traditional ones, the differences were small, almost imperceptible. At the Da Kang mill, for instance, after a group of women pledged such a Party-supported sisterhood, they each contributed a small sum of money to buy a piece of white cloth. They cut the cloth into squares, sewed handkerchiefs, and on each one embroidered the words "working together with one heart." Each member of the sisterhood kept a handkerchief as a souvenir.[22] While members of traditional sisterhoods occasionally made identical gowns — or may even have made identical handkerchiefs — to symbolize their relationship, they were not likely to have expressed their common interests as workers as did the new sisters with their embroidered emblem.

Similarly, it had always been common for members of sisterhoods to get together on Sundays, to go out window-shopping, or to go to a park. Party members encouraged and participated in these activities and gradually introduced new dimensions. When they went to parks, for example, Party members spent part of the time telling their sisters about the progress women had made through the Russian Revolution and about the work of the CCP in Yanan.[23] Women who were sympathetic to these ideas were enlisted by the Party organizers to attend schools for women workers run by the YWCA.[24] Some eventually joined the CCP themselves.[25]

This strategy was apparently successful, for during the Civil War, unprecedented numbers of women workers continuously participated in strikes, for the first time demanding and winning benefits specifically for women, such as maternity leave and nurseries. For some women, the potential for the development of worker and female solidarity that had been inherent in the sisterhoods was finally realized.

Conclusion

The significance of the sisterhoods, then, is that they indicate the ways in which women were not passive victims of industrial poverty. They demonstrate women's resistance to unbearably long work hours, beatings by overseers, and physical abuse by neighborhood gangsters. They also characterize the communities formed by women workers in Shanghai—communities in which women drew on traditional social relationships to survive in a new, unfamiliar, and threatening environment. The Shanghai sisterhoods suggest that organizations formed by women workers are not necessarily expressions of working-class or feminist consciousness. And once formed, the sisterhoods did not inevitably lead their members to see that by acting collectively they could change their circumstances. Nevertheless, the sisterhoods do provide a critical link in the story of how some women became revolutionaries. It was only when Communist Party organizers burned incense and pledged sisterhood that women workers, as sisters, became active participants in the Chinese revolution.

Notes

Acknowledgments: I would like to thank Margery Wolf, Lisa Rofel, and Marilyn Young for discussions of the ideas developed in this essay as well as for comments on earlier drafts.

1. Materials provided by the Institute for Historical Research, Shanghai Academy of Social Sciences. These materials include unpublished factory histories, transcripts of interviews, and accounts of strikes collected as part of an

effort undertaken in the 1950s to chronicle the history of the pre-Liberation labor movement in Shanghai. The documents are not labeled or cataloged. Further information about these materials can be obtained by contacting me.

2. Cora Deng, "The Economic Status of Women in Industry in China, with Special Reference to a Group in Shanghai" (M.A. thesis, New York University, 1941), p. 73.

3. In 1929, when the industry was close to its peak of development, there were sixty-one cotton mills in Shanghai, employing 110,882 workers. Of these, 84,270 (76 percent) were women (Shanghai Bureau of Social Affairs, *Wages and Hours of Labor, Greater Shanghai, 1929* [Shanghai, 1929]). Throughout the period from World War I through Liberation in 1949, Shanghai was the largest industrial center in China, and the cotton industry was Shanghai's major industry.

4. I conducted these interviews during two research trips to Shanghai. Under the auspices of the Committee on Scholarly Communication with the People's Republic of China and the Social Science Research Council, I was an exchange scholar at Fudan University in Shanghai from 1979 to 1981. I returned to conduct follow-up research in September and October of 1982. The interviews with women workers were almost all arranged by Fudan University and usually took place at the cotton mills. I interviewed approximately fifty women. Often these interviews were set up as "round-table discussions," in which I questioned four or five women during a single three-hour session. There was almost no opportunity to conduct follow-up interviews with individual women. Unless otherwise cited, all quotations in the text are from these interviews.

5. For a discussion of these problems, see Liu Ta-chun, *The Growth and Industrialization of Shanghai* (Shanghai: China Institute of Pacific Relations, 1936), p. 169; and Shanghai shehui kexueyuan, jingji yanjiusuo (Institute for Economic Research, Shanghai Academy of Social Sciences), ed., *Shanghai penghuqude bianyi* (Changes in the squatter settlements of Shanghai) (Shanghai: Shanghai renmin chubanshe, 1965), p. 24.

6. Mary Ninde Gamewell, *Gateway to China: Pictures of Shanghai* (New York: Fleming H. Revell Co., 1916), p. 210. See also *Shanghai heimo yiqian zhong* (A thousand kinds of shady plots in Shanghai) (Shanghai: Shanghai chunming shudian yinxing, 1939), pp. 1–31.

7. For a more detailed discussion of the workers' origins, see Emily Honig, "Women Cotton Mill Workers in Shanghai, 1919–1949" (Ph.D. diss., Stanford University, 1982).

8. See, e.g., Zhongguo fangzhi jianshe gongsi (China Textile Reconstruction Corp.), *Shanghai dishisi fangzhichang sanshiwuniande gongzuo nianbao* (Yearly report on the work at the Shanghai Number Fourteen Textile Mill, 1946) (Shanghai, 1946), pp. 63–65. See also *Xin qingnian* (New youth) (Bei-

jing), vol. 7, no. 6 (May 1920). This segregation of workers by place of origin is also documented by the retirement cards from one of the largest cotton mills in Shanghai. These cards — filled out when a worker retires — are part of the personnel records at each mill. They indicate the worker's name, place and date of birth, and work history.

9. For a more extensive discussion of hiring practices in the cotton mills, see Honig, "Women Cotton Mill Workers," pp. 95–104. See also Jean Chesneaux, *The Chinese Labor Movement, 1919–1927* (Stanford, Calif.: Stanford University Press, 1968). These patterns of people from the same hometown helping each other are not unique to workers. See, e.g., Susan Mann Jones, "The Ningpo Pang and Financial Power at Shanghai," in *The Chinese City between Two Worlds,* ed. Mark Elvin and G. W. Skinner (Stanford, Calif.: Stanford University Press, 1974), pp. 73–96.

10. This observation is based on interviews as well as on Herbert Lamson, "The Problem of Housing for Workers in China," *Chinese Economic Journal* 11, no. 2 (August 1932): 139–62.

11. *Shen Bao* (The Huangpu Daily) (Shanghai) (May 6, 1924).

12. For a discussion of regional rivalries in Shanghai, see Chesneaux, *The Chinese Labor Movement,* p. 123; and Leung Yuen Sang, "Regional Rivalry in Mid-Nineteenth Century Shanghai: Cantonese vs. Ningpo Men," *Ch'ing shih wen-t'i* 4, no. 8 (December 1982): 29–50.

13. Materials provided by the Institute for Historical Research, Shanghai Academy of Social Sciences. The source does not explain the relationship of the men to the sisterhoods of prostitutes. Since the men who acted as pimps are discussed in a separate section of the article, it seems safe to assume that these men were not pimps.

14. *Xiang Jingyu wenji* (The collected works of Xiang Jingyu) (Changsha: Hunan renmin chubanshe, 1980), pp. 146–47.

15. Shanghai shehui kexueyuan lishi yanjiusuo (Institute for Historical Research, Shanghai Academy of Social Sciences), ed., *Wusa yundong shiliao* (Historical materials on the May Thirtieth Movement) (Shanghai: Shanghai renmin chubanshe, 1981), 1:270.

16. *Xiang Jingyu wenji,* p. 216.

17. Materials provided by the Institute for Historical Research, Shanghai Academy of Social Sciences.

18. Marjorie Topley, "Marriage Resistance in Rural Kwangtung," in *Women in Chinese Society,* ed. Margery Wolf and Roxane Witke (Stanford, Calif.: Stanford University Press, 1975), pp. 67–68.

19. Materials provided by the Institute for Historical Research, Shanghai Academy of Social Sciences.

20. Ma Chunji, "Shanghai nugong gongzuo baogao" (Report on work among women workers in Shanghai) (Yanan, 1941), reprinted by Zhonghua

quanguo zonggonghui ziliaoshi (Materials Department of the All-China Federation of Labor) (1954).

21. Materials provided by the Institute for Historical Research, Shanghai Academy of Social Sciences.

22. Ibid.

23. Ibid.

24. Tang Guifen, "Huxi shachang gongren douzhengde gaikuang" (General conditions of the cotton workers' struggle in western Shanghai), in *Shanghai gongren yundong lishi ziliao* (Materials on the history of the Shanghai workers' movement) (Shanghai, 1956, mimeographed). Starting in the 1920s, the YWCA operated a number of night schools for women industrial workers. Ostensibly the schools taught literacy, but they were known for teaching women workers to understand their position in the social and economic system. They also taught women skills, such as public speaking, that were useful in labor organizing. By the 1940s, the CCP began using the schools to organize women workers, and many teachers in them were Party members (interview with Cora Deng, Shanghai, 1980; Robin Porter, "The Christian Conscience and Industrial Welfare in China, 1919–1941" [Ph.D. diss., University of Montreal, 1977]; Wang Zhijin et al., "Huiyi Shanghai nuqingnianhuide nugong yexiao" [Recalling the YWCA night schools for women workers in Shanghai], *Shanghai wenshi ziliao xuanji* [Selected materials on Shanghai culture and history], no. 5 [Shanghai, 1979], pp. 83–93).

25. Shanghai gongren yundong shiliao weiyuanhui (Shanghai Labor History Committee), ed., *Shanghai guomian shichang gongren douzheng lishi ziliao* (Materials on the history of the workers' struggles at the Number Ten Textile Mill in Shanghai) (Shanghai, 1954, mimeographed).

5

The Tired Poem

Last Letter from a Typical Unemployed Black Professional Woman

Kate Rushin

So it's a gorgeous afternoon in the park
It's so nice you forget your Attitude
The one your mama taught you
The one that says Don't-Mess-With-Me
You forget until you hear all this
Whistling and lip smacking
You whip around and say
I ain't no damn dog
It's a young guy
His mouth drops open
Excuse me Sister
How you doing
You lie and smile and say
I'm doing good
Everything's cool Brother

Then five minutes later
Hey you Sweet Devil

Hey Girl come here
You tense   sigh   calculate
You know the lean boys and bearded men
Are only cousins and lovers and friends
Sometimes when you say Hey
You get a beautiful surprised smile
Or a good talk

And you've listened to your uncle when he was drunk
Talking about how he has to scuffle to get by and
How he'd wanted to be an engineer
And you talk to Joko who wants to be a singer and
Buy some clothes and get a house for his mother
The Soc. and Psych. books say you're domineering
And you've been to enough
Sisters-Are-Not-Taking-Care-Of-Business discussions
To know where you went wrong
It's decided it had to be the day you decided to go to school
Still you remember the last time you said hey
So you keep on walking
What   you too good to speak
Don't nobody want you no way

You go home   sit on the front steps   listen to
The neighbor boy brag about
How many girls he has pregnant
You ask him if he's going to take care of the babies
And what if he gets taken to court
And what are the girls going to do
He has pictures of them all
This real cute one was supposed to go to college
Dumb broad knew she could get pregnant
I'll just say it's not mine
On the back of this picture of a girl in a cap and gown
It says something like
I love you in my own strange way
Thank you

Then you go in the house
Flip through a magazine and there is

An-Ode-To-My-Black-Queen poem
The kind where the Brother
Thanks all of the Sisters Who Endured
Way back when he didn't have his Shit Together
And you have to wonder where they are now
And you know what happens when you try to resist
All of this Enduring
And you think how this
Thank-you poem is really
No consolation at all
Unless you believe
What the man you met on the train told you
The Black man who worked for the State Department
And had lived in five countries
He said Dear
You were born to suffer
Why don't you give me your address
And I'll come visit

So you try to talk to your friend
About the train and the park and everything
And how it all seems somehow connected
And he says
You're just a Typical Black Professional Woman
Some sisters know how to deal
Right about here
Your end of the conversation phases out
He goes on to say how
Black Professional Women have always had the advantage
You have to stop and think about that one
Maybe you are supposed to be grateful for those sweaty
Beefy-faced white businessmen who try to
Pick you up at lunchtime
And you wonder how many times your friend had
Pennies thrown at him
How many times he's been felt up in the subway
How many times he's been cussed out on the street
You wonder how many times he's been offered
$10 for a piece of himself

$10 for a piece
So you're waiting for the bus
And you look at this young Black man
Asking if you want to make some money
You look at him for a long time
You imagine the little dingy room
It would take twenty minutes or less
You only get $15 for spending all day with thirty kids
Nobody is offering you
Any cash for your poems
You remember again how you have the advantage
How you're not taking care of business
How this man is somebody's kid brother or cousin
And could be your own
So you try to explain how $10 wouldn't pay for
What you'd have to give up
He pushes a handful of sticky crumpled dollars
Into your face and says

Why not
You think I can't pay
Look at that roll
Don't tell me you don't need the money
Cause I know you do
I'll give you fifteen

You maintain your sense of humor
You remember a joke you heard
Well no matter what
A Black Woman never has to starve
Just as long as there are
Dirty toilets and . . .
It isn't funny
Then you wonder if he would at least
Give you the money
And not beat you up
But you're very cool and say
No thanks
You tell him he should spend his time

Looking for someone he cares about
Who cares about him
He waves you off
Get outta my face
I don't have time for that bullshit
You blew it Bitch

Then
(Is it suddenly)
Your voice gets loud
And fills the night street
Your voice gets louder and louder
Your bus comes
The second-shift people file on
The security guards and nurse's aides
Look at you like you're crazy
Get on the damn bus
And remember
You blew it
He turns away
Your bus pulls off
There is no one on the street but you

And then
It is
Very
Quiet

II

Women in Feminist Communities

6

Separatism as Strategy
Female Institution Building and American Feminism, 1870–1930

Estelle Freedman

Scholarship and Strategies

The feminist scholarship of the past decade has often been concerned, either explicitly or implicitly, with two central political questions: the search for the origins of women's oppression and the formulation of effective strategies for combating patriarchy. Analysis of the former question helps us to answer the latter; or as anthropologist Gayle Rubin has wryly explained:

> If innate male aggression and dominance are at the root of female oppression, then the feminist program would logically require either the extermination of the offending sex, or else a eugenics project to modify its character. If sexism is a by-product of capitalism's relentless appetite for profit, then sexism would wither away in the advent of a successful socialist revolution. If the world historical defeat of women occurred at the hands of an armed patriarchal revolt, then it is time for Amazon guerrillas to start training in the Adirondacks.[1]

This article is reprinted from *Feminist Studies*, vol. 5, no. 3 (Fall 1979): 512–29, by permission of the author and the publisher, Feminist Studies, Inc., c/o Women's Studies Program, University of Maryland, College Park, MD 20742.

Another anthropologist, Michelle Zimbalist Rosaldo, provided an influential exploration of the origins-strategy questions in her 1974 theoretical overview of women's status.[2] Rosaldo argued that "universal sexual asymmetry" (the lower value placed on women's tasks and roles in all cultures) has been determined largely by the sexually defined split between domestic and public spheres. To oversimplify her thesis: the greater the social distance between women in the home and men in the public sphere, the greater the devaluation of women. The implications for feminist strategy become clear at the end of Rosaldo's essay in which she says that greater overlap between domestic and public spheres means higher status for women. Thus to achieve an egalitarian future, with less separation of female and male, we should strive not only for the entrance of women into the male-dominated public sphere, but also for men's entry into the female-dominated domestic world.

Rosaldo also discusses an alternative strategy for overcoming sexual asymmetry, namely, the creation of a separate women's public sphere; but she dismisses this model in favor of integrating domestic and public spheres. Nonetheless, the alternative strategy of "women's societies and African queens" deserves further attention.[3] Where female political leaders have power over their own jurisdiction (women), they also gain leverage in tribal policy. Such a separate sexual political hierarchy would presumably offer women more status and power than the extreme male-public/female-domestic split, but it would not require the entrance of each sex into the sphere dominated by the other sex. At certain historical periods, the creation of a public female sphere might be the only viable political strategy for women.

I would like to argue through historical analysis for the alternative strategy of creating a strong, public female sphere. A number of feminist historians have recently explored the value of the separate, though not necessarily public, female sphere for enriching women's historical experience. Carroll Smith-Rosenberg's research[4] has shown how close personal relationships enhanced the private lives of women in the nineteenth century. At the same time, private "sisterhoods," Nancy Cott has suggested, may have been a precondition for the emergence of feminist consciousness.[5] In the late nineteenth and early twentieth centuries, intimate friendships provided support systems for politically active women, as demonstrated by the work of both Blanche Cook and Nancy Sahli. However, the women's culture of the past — personal networks, rituals, and relationships — did not automatically constitute a political strategy.

As loving and supportive as women's networks may have been they could keep women content with a status which was inferior to that of men.[6]

I do not accept the argument that female networks and feminist politics were incompatible. Rather, in the following synthesis of recent scholarship in American women's history, I want to show how the women's movement in the late nineteenth and early twentieth centuries provides an example of the "women's societies and African queens" strategy that Rosaldo mentioned. The creation of a separate, public female sphere helped mobilize women and gained political leverage in the larger society. A separatist political strategy, which I refer to as "female institution building," emerged from the middle-class women's culture of the nineteenth century. Its history suggests that in our own time, as well, women's culture can be integral to feminist politics.[7]

What Happened to Feminism?

My desire to restore historical consciousness about female separatism has both a personal and an intellectual motivation. As a feminist working within male-dominated academic institutions, I have realized that I could not survive without access to the feminist culture and politics that flourish outside of mixed institutions. How, I have wondered, could women in the past work for change within a men's world without having this alternative culture? This thought led me to the more academic questions. Perhaps they could not survive when those supports were not available; and perhaps this insight can help explain one of the most intriguing questions in American women's history: What happened to feminism after the suffrage victory in 1920?

Most explanations of the decline of women's political strength focus on either inherent weaknesses in suffragist ideology or on external pressures from a pervasively sexist society.[8] But when I survey the women's movement before suffrage passed, I am struck by the hypothesis that a major strength of American feminism prior to 1920 was the separate female community that helped sustain women's participation in both social reform and political activism. Although the women's movement of the late nineteenth century contributed to the transformation of women's social roles, it did not reject a separate, unique female identity. Most feminists did not adopt the radical demands for equal status with men that originated at the Seneca Falls Convention of 1848. Rather, they preferred to retain membership in a separate female sphere, one which they did not believe to be inferior to men's sphere and one in which women could be free to create their own forms of personal, social, and political relationships. The achievements of feminism at the turn of the century came less through gaining access to the male domains of politics and the professions than in the tangible form of building separate female institutions.

The self-consciously female community began to disintegrate in the 1920s just as "new women" were attempting to assimilate into male-dominated institutions. At work, in social life, and in politics, I will argue, middle-class women hoped to become equals by adopting men's values and integrating into their institutions. A younger generation of women learned to smoke, drink, and value heterosexual relationships over female friendships in their personal lives. At the same time, women's political activity epitomized the process of rejecting women's culture in favor of men's promises of equality. The gradual decline of female separatism in social and political life precluded the emergence of a strong women's political block which might have protected and expanded the gains made by the earlier women's movement. Thus the erosion of women's culture may help account for the decline of public feminism in the decades after 1920. Without a constituency a movement cannot survive. The old feminist leaders lost their following when a new generation opted for assimilation in the naive hope of becoming men's equals overnight.

To explore this hypothesis, I shall illustrate episodes of cultural and political separatism within American feminism in three periods: its historical roots prior to 1870; the institution building of the late nineteenth century; and the aftermath of suffrage in the 1920s.

Historical Roots of Separatism

In nineteenth-century America, commercial and industrial growth intensified the sexual division of labor, encouraging the separation of men's and women's spheres. While white males entered the public world of wage labor, business, the professions and politics, most white middle-class women remained at home where they provided the domestic, maternal, and spiritual care for their families and the nation. These women underwent intensive socialization into their roles as "true women." Combined with the restrictions on women which denied them access to the public sphere, this training gave American women an identity quite separate from men's. Women shared unique life experiences as daughters, wives, childbearers, childrearers, and moral guardians. They passed on their values and traditions to their female kin. They created what Smith-Rosenberg has called "The Female World of Love and Ritual," a world of homosocial networks that helped these women transcend the alienation of domestic life.[9]

The ideology of "true womanhood" was so deeply ingrained and so useful for preserving social stability in a time of flux that those few women who explicitly rejected its inequalities could find little support for their views. The feminists of the early women's rights movement were certainly justified in their grievances and demands for equal opportunity with men. The Seneca Falls Declaration of Sentiments of 1848, which called for access to education, property ownership, and political rights, has inspired many feminists since then, while the ridicule and denial of these demands have inspired our rage. But the equal rights arguments of the 1850s were apparently too radical for their own times.[10] Men would not accept women's entry into the public sphere, but more importantly, most women were not interested in rejecting their deeply rooted female identities. Both men and women feared the demise of the female sphere and the valuable functions it performed. The feminists, however, still hoped to reduce the limitations on women within their own sphere, as well as to gain the right of choice — of autonomy — for those women who opted for public rather than private roles.

Radical feminists such as Elizabeth Cady Stanton and Susan B. Anthony recognized the importance of maintaining the virtues of the female world while eliminating discrimination against women in public. As their political analysis developed at mid-century, they drew upon the concepts of female moral superiority and sisterhood, and they affirmed the separate nature of woman. At the same time, their disillusionment with even the more enlightened men of the times reinforced the belief that women had to create their own movement to achieve independence. The bitterness that resulted when most male abolitionists refused to support women's rights in the 1860s, and when they failed to include Woman Suffrage in the Fifteenth Amendment (as well as the inclusion of the term "male citizen" in the Fourteenth Amendment) alienated many women reformers. When Frederick Douglass proclaimed in defense that "This is the Negro's Hour," the more radical women's rights advocates followed Stanton and Anthony in withdrawing from the reform coalition and creating a separatist organization. Their National Woman Suffrage Association had women members and officers; supported a broad range of reforms, including changes in marriage and divorce laws; and published the short-lived journal, *The Revolution*. The radical path proved difficult, however, and the National Woman Suffrage Association merged in 1890 with the more moderate American Woman Suffrage Association. Looking back on their disappointment after the Civil War, Stanton and Anthony wrote prophetically in 1881:

> Our liberal men counselled us to silence during the war, and we were silent on our own wrongs; they counselled us to silence in Kansas and New York (in the suffrage referenda), lest we should defeat "Negro Suffrage," and threatened if we were not, we might fight the battle alone. We chose the latter, and were defeated. But standing alone we learned our power: we repudiated man's counsels forevermore; and solemnly vowed that there should never be another season of silence until woman had the same rights everywhere on this green earth, as man. . . .
>
> We would warn the young women of the coming generation against man's advice as to their best interests. . . . Woman must lead the way to her own enfranchisement. . . . She must not put her trust in man in this transition period, since while regarded as his subject, his inferior, his slave, their interests must be antagonistic.[11]

Female Institution Building

The "transition period" that Stanton and Anthony invoked lasted from the 1870s to the 1920s. It was an era of separate female organization and institution building, the result on the one hand, of the negative push of discrimination in the public, male sphere, and on the other hand, of the positive attraction of the female world of close, personal relationships and domestic institutional structures. These dual origins characterized, for instance, one of the largest manifestations of "social feminism" in the late nineteenth century — the women's club movement.

The club movement illustrated the politicization of women's institutions as well as the limitations of their politics. The exclusion of women reporters from the New York Press Club in 1868 inspired the founding of the first women's club, Sorosis. The movement then blossomed in dozens and later hundreds of localities, until a General Federation of

Women's Clubs formed in 1890. By 1910, it claimed over one million members. Although club social and literary activities at first appealed to traditional women who simply wanted to gather with friends and neighbors, by the turn of the century women's clubs had launched civic reform programs. Their activities served to politicize traditional women by forcing them to define themselves as citizens, not simply as wives and mothers. The clubs reflected the societal racism of the time, however, and the black women who founded the National Association of Colored Women in 1896 turned their attention to the social and legal problems that confronted both black women and men.[12]

The Women's Christian Temperance Union had roots in the social feminist tradition of separate institution building. As Ellen DuBois has argued, the WCTU appealed to late nineteenth-century women because it was grounded in the private sphere — the home — and attempted to correct the private abuses against women, namely, intemperance and the sexual double standard.[13] Significantly, though, the WCTU, under Frances Willard's leadership, became a strong prosuffrage organization, committed to righting all wrongs against women, through any means, including the vote.

The women's colleges that opened in these same decades further attest to the importance of separate female institutions during this "transition period." Originally conceived as training grounds of piety, purity, and domesticity, the antebellum women's seminaries, such as Mary Lyon's Mt. Holyoke and Emma Willard's Troy Female Academy, laid the groundwork for the new collegiate institutions of the postwar era. When elite male institutions refused to educate women, the sister colleges of the East, like their counterparts elsewhere, took on the task themselves. In the process they encouraged intimate friendships and professional networks among educated women.[14] At the same time, liberal arts and science training provided tools for women's further development, and by their examples, female teachers inspired students to use their skills creatively. As Barbara Welter noted when she first described the "Cult of True Womanhood,"[15] submissiveness was always its weakest link. Like other women's institutions, the colleges could help subvert that element of the Cult by encouraging independence in their students.

The most famous example of the impact of women's colleges may be Jane Addams's description of her experience at Rockford Seminary where she and other students were imbued with the mission of bringing their female values to bear on the entire society. While Addams later questioned the usefulness of her intellectual training in meeting the challenges of the real world, other women did build upon academic foundations when increasingly, as reformers, teachers, doctors, social workers, and in other capacities they left the home to enter public or quasi-public work. Between 1890 and 1920, the number of professional degrees granted to women increased 226 percent, at three times the rate of increase for men. Some of these professionals had attended separate female institutions such as the women's medical colleges in Philadelphia, New York, and Boston. The new female professionals often served women and children clients, in part because of the discrimination against their encroachment on men's domains, but also because they sincerely wanted to work with the traditional objects of their concern. As their skills and roles expanded, these women would demand the right to choose for themselves where and with whom they could work. This first generation of educated professional women became supporters of the suffrage movement in the early twentieth century, calling for full citizenship for women.

The process of redefining womanhood by the extension, rather than by the rejection, of the female sphere may be best illustrated by the settlement house movement. Although both men and women resided in and supported these quasi-public institutions, the high proportion of female participants and leaders (approximately three-fifths of the total), as well as the domestic structure and emphasis on service to women and children, qualify the settlements as female institutions. Mary P. Ryan has captured the link which these ventures provided between "true womanhood" and "new womanhood" in a particularly fitting metaphor: "Within the settlement houses, maternal sentiments were further sifted and leavened until they became an entirely new variety of social reform."[16] Thus did Jane Addams learn the techniques of the political world through her efforts to keep the neighborhood clean. So too did Florence Kelley of Hull House welcome appointment as chief factory inspector of Illinois, to protect women and children workers; and Julia Lathrop, another Hull House resident, entered the public sphere as director of the United States Children's Bureau; while one-time settlement resident Katherine Bement Davis moved from the superintendency of the Bedford Hills reformatory for women to become in 1914 the first female commissioner of corrections in New York City. Each of these women, and other settlement workers who moved on to professional and public office, eventually joined and often led branches of the National American Woman Suffrage Association.[17] They drew upon the networks of personal friends and professional allies that grew within separate female institutions when they waged their campaigns for social reform and for suffrage.

Separate female organizations were not limited to middle-class women. Recent histories have shown that groups hoping to bridge class lines between women existed within working-class or radical movements. In both the Women's Trade Union League and the National Consumers League, middle-class reformers strived for cooperation, rather than condescension, in their relationships with working women. Although in neither organization were they entirely successful, the Women's Trade Union League did provide valuable services in organizing women workers, many of whom were significant in its leadership. The efforts of the Consumers League, led by Florence Kelley, to improve working conditions through the use of middle-class women's buying power was probably less effective, but efforts to enact protective legislation for women workers did succeed. Members of both organizations turned to suffrage as one solution to the problems workers faced. Meanwhile, both in leftist organizations and in unions, women formed separate female organizations. Feminists within the Socialist Party met in women's groups in the early twentieth century, while within the clothing trades, women workers formed separate local unions which survived until the mid-1920s.[18]

As a final example of female institution building, I want to compare two actual buildings—the Woman's Pavillion at the 1876 Centennial Exposition in Philadelphia, analyzed recently by Judith Paine, and the Woman's Building at the 1893 World Columbian Exposition in Chicago. I think that the origins and functions of each illustrate some of the changes that occurred in the women's movement in the time interval between those two celebrations.

Originally, the managers of the 1876 Centennial had promised "a sphere for woman's action and space for her work" within the main display areas. In return women raised over $100,000 for the fair, at which point the management informed the Women's Centennial Executive Committee that there would not be any space for them in the main building. The women's response surprised the men: they raised money for a separate building, and although they hoped to find a woman architect to design it, there was no such professional at the time. From May through October, 1876, the Woman's Pavillion displayed achievements in journalism, medicine, science, art, literature, invention, teaching, business, and social work. It included a library of books by women; an office that published a newspaper for women; and an innovative kindergarten annex, the first such day school in the country. Some radical feminists, however, boycotted the building. Elizabeth Cady Stanton claimed that the pavillion "was no true exhibit of woman's art" because it did not represent the product of industrial labor or protest the inequalities of "political slavery."[19]

By 1893, there was less hesitation about the need for a woman's building and somewhat less conflict about its functions. Congress authorized the creation of a Board of Lady Managers for the Columbian Commission, and the women quickly decided on a separate Woman's Building, to be designed by a woman architect chosen by nationwide competition. Contests were also held to locate the best women sculptors, painters, and other artists to complete the designs of the building. The Lady Managers also planned and provided a Children's Building that offered nursery care for over ten thousand young visitors to the fair. At this exposition, not only were women's artistic and professional achievements heralded, but industrial organizations were "especially invited to make themselves known," and women's industrial work, as well as the conditions and wages for which they worked, were displayed. Feminists found this exhibit more agreeable; Antoinette Brown Blackwell, Julia Ward Howe, and Susan B. Anthony all attended, and Anthony read a paper written by Elizabeth Cady Stanton at one of the women's symposia. The Board of Lady Managers fought long and hard to combine their separate enterprise with participation in the rest of the fair. They demanded equal representation of women judges for the exhibitions and equal consideration of women's enterprises in all contests.[20] While they had to compromise on some goals, their efforts are noteworthy as an indication of a dual commitment to separate female institutions, but only if they had equal status within the society at large.

The Political Legacy

The separate institution building of the late nineteenth century rested on a belief in women's unique identity which had roots in the private female sphere of the early nineteenth century. Increasingly, however, as its participants entered a public female world, they adopted the more radical stance of feminists such as Stanton and Anthony who had long called for an end to political discrimination against women.

The generation that achieved suffrage, then, stood on the border of two worlds, each of which contributed to its ideology and politics. Suffragists argued that women needed the vote to perform their traditional tasks — to protect themselves as mothers and to exert their moral force on society. Yet they also argued for full citizenship and waged a successful, female-controlled political campaign to achieve it.

The suffrage movement succeeded by appealing to a broad constituency — mothers, workers, professionals, reformers — with the vision of the common concerns of womanhood. The movement failed, however, by not extending fully the political strengths of woman bonding. For one thing, the leadership allowed some members to exploit popular racist and nativist sentiments in their prosuffrage arguments, thus excluding most black and immigrant women from a potential feminist coalition. They also failed to recognize that the bonds that held the constituency together were not "natural," but social and political. The belief that women would automatically use the vote to the advantage of their sex overlooked both the class and racial lines that separated women. It underestimated the need for continued political organization so that their interests might be united and realized.

Unfortunately, the rhetoric of equality that became popular among men and women (with the exception of the National Woman's Party) just after the passage of the Suffrage Amendment in 1920 subverted the women's movement by denying the need for continued feminist organization. Of course, external factors significantly affected the movement's future, including the new Freudian views of women; the growth of a consumer economy that increasingly exploited women's sexuality; and the repression of radicalism and reform in general after World War I.[21] But at the same time, many women, seemingly oblivious that these pressures necessitated further separate organizing, insisted on striving for integration into a male world — sexually, professionally, and politically.

Examples of this integrationist approach can be found in the universities, the workplace, and politics. In contrast to an earlier generation, the women who participated in the New York World's Fair of 1937 had no separate building. Woman, the Fair Bulletin explained, "will not sit upon a pedestal, not be segregated, isolated; she will fit into the life of the Exposition as she does into life itself — never apart, always a part." The part in this World's Fair, however, consisted primarily of fashion, food, and vanity fair.[22] In the universities, the success of the first generation of female academics did not survive past the 1920s, not only because of men's resistance, but, as Rosalind Rosenberg has explained, "Success isolated women from their culture of origin and placed them in an alien and often hostile community." Many academics who cut off their ties to other women "lost their old feminine supports but had no other supports to replace them."[23]

The lessons of women's politics in the 1920s are illustrated by the life of one woman, Emily Newell Blair, who learned first hand the pitfalls of rejecting a separatist basis for feminism.[24] Blair's life exemplified the transformation of women's roles at the turn of the century. Educated at a woman's college, Goucher, this Missouri born, middle-class woman returned to her hometown to help support her family until she married and created her own home. Between 1900 and 1910 she bore two children, supported her husband's career, and joined in local women's club activities. In her spare time, Blair began writing short stories for ladies' magazines. Because she found the work, and particularly the income, satisfying, she became a free lance writer. At this point, the suffrage movement revived in Missouri, and Blair took over state publicity, editing the magazine *Missouri Woman* and doing public relations. Then, in World War I, she expanded her professional activities further by serving on the Women's Council of the U.S. Council of National Defense. These years of training in writing, feminist organizing, and public speaking served Blair well when suffrage passed and she entered politics.

In 1920, women faced three major political choices: they could become a separate feminist political force through the National Woman's Party, which few did; they could follow the moderates of the NAWSA into the newly formed, nonpartisan League of Women Voters, concentrating on citizen education and good government; or they could join the mainstream political parties. Emily Newell Blair chose the last, and rose through the Democratic Party organization to become national vice-chairman of the party in the 1920s.

Blair built her political life and her following on the belief that the vote had made women the political equals of men. Thus, the surest path to furthering women's goals was through participation in the party structure. Having helped to found the League of Women Voters, Blair then rejected nonpartisanship, while she urged women not to vote as women but as citizens. In a 1922 lecture on "What Women May Do with the Ballot," Blair argued that "reactions to political issues are not decided by sex but by intellect and emotion. . . ." Although she believed that lack of political experience and social training made women differ from men temporarily, she expected those differences to be eliminated after a few years of political activity. To hasten women's integration into the mainstream of party politics, Blair set up thirty "schools of democracy" to train the new voters during the early twenties, as well as over one thousand women's clubs. Her philosophy, she claimed, was one of "Boring from Within." Blair rejected the "sex conscious feminists" of the Woman's Party and those who wanted "woman cohesiveness." Although she favored the election of women, she wanted them to be chosen not as women but as politicians. "Give women time," she often repeated, and they would become the equals of men in politics.

By the late 1920s, however, women had not gained acceptance as men's political equals, and Blair's views changed significantly. Once she had claimed that the parties did not discriminate against women, as shown by her own powerful position. After she retired from party office in 1928, however, Blair acknowledged that the treatment of women by the parties had deteriorated since the years immediately after suffrage passed. As soon as male politicians realized that there was no strong female voting block or political organization, they refused to appoint or elect powerful women, and a "strong masculine prejudice against women in politics" surfaced. Now they chose women for party office who seemed easiest to manage or who were the wives of male officeholders.

By 1931, Blair's former optimism had turned to disillusionment. She felt herself "ineffective in politics as a feminist," a term that she began to use positively. Blair realized that women could not command political power and the respect of their male colleagues unless, like the suffrage leaders, they had a visible, vocal following. "Unfortunately for feminism," she confessed, "it was agreed to drop the sex line in politics. And it was dropped by the women." In the pages of the *Woman's Journal,* Blair called for a revival of feminism in the form of a new politics that would seek to put more women into office. Reversing her former stance, she claimed that *women* voters should back *women* candidates, and use a *women's* organization to do so. They could remain in the parties, but should form "a new organization of feminists devoted to the task of getting women into politics."

The development of Emily Newell Blair's feminist consciousness may have been unique for her time, but it is a familiar process among educated and professional women today. Having gained access to formerly male institutions, but still committed to furthering women's struggles, today's "new women" are faced with political choices not dissimilar to the generation that achieved suffrage. The bitterness of Stanton and Anthony in their advice to the younger generation in 1881, and the strategy that Emily Newell Blair presented in 1931, may serve as lessons for the present.

The Lessons of Separatism

The strength of female institutions in the late nineteenth century and the weaknesses of women's politics after the passage of the Suffrage Amendment suggest to me that the decline of feminism in the 1920s can be attributed in part to the devaluation of women's culture in general and of separate female institutions in particular. When women tried to assimilate into male-dominated institutions, without securing feminist social, economic, or political bases, they lost the momentum and the networks which had made the suffrage movement possible. Women gave up many of the strengths of the female sphere without gaining equally from the man's world they entered.

This historical record has important implications for the women's movement today. It becomes clearer, I think, why the separate, small women's group, organized either for consciousness raising or political study and action, has been effective in building a grass-roots movement over the past ten years. The groups helped to reestablish common bonds long veiled by the retreat from women's institutions into privatized families or sexually integrated, but male-dominated, institutions. The groups encouraged the reemergence of female networks and a new women's culture which in turn have given rise to female institution building — women's centers, health collectives, political unions, even new women's buildings, like the ones in Los Angeles and San Francisco.

The history of separatism also helps explain why the politics of lesbian feminism have been so important in the revival of the women's movement. Lesbian feminism, by affirming the primacy of women's relationships with each other and by providing an alternative feminist culture, forced many nonlesbians to reevaluate their relationships with men, male institutions, and male values. In the process, feminists have put to rest the myth of female dependence on men and rediscovered the significance of woman bonding. I find it personally gratifying that the lesbian feminist concept of the woman-identified woman[25] has historical roots in the female friendships, networks, and institutions of the nineteenth century. The historical sisterhood, it seems to me, can teach us a great deal about putting women first, whether as friends, lovers, or political allies.

I find two kinds of political lessons in the history of the separatist trend. In the past, one of the limitations of separate female institutions was that they were often the only places for women to pursue professional or political activities, while men's institutions retained the power over most of the society. Today it is crucial to press for feminist presence both outside and within the bastions of male dominance, such as politics, the universities, the professions, the unions. But it is equally important for the women within mixed institutions to create female interest groups and support systems. Otherwise, token women may be coopted into either traditionally deferential roles, or they will assimilate through identification with the powers that be. In the process, these women will lose touch with their feminist values and constituencies, as well as suffer the personal costs of tokenism. Thus, in universities we need both to strengthen our women's centers and women's studies programs and to form women's groups among faculty as well as students. In all of our workplaces we need women's caucuses to secure and enlarge our gains. And unlike much of the movement in the past, we need to undertake the enormous task of building coalitions of women's groups from all classes, races, and cultures.

I argue for a continuation of separatism not because the values, culture, and politics of the two sexes are biologically, irreversibly distinct, but rather because the historical and contemporary experiences that have created a unique female culture remain both salient for and compatible with the goal of sexual equality. Our common identities and heritage as women can provide enormous personal and political strength as long as we claim the power to define what women can be and what female institutions can achieve. I argue for renewed female institution building at this point in the contemporary women's movement because I fear that many feminists — faced with the isolation of personal success or dismayed by political backlash — may turn away from the separate women's politics that have achieved most of our gains in the past decade. And I argue as well for both greater respect for women's culture among political feminists and greater political engagement on the part of cultural feminists because we now face both external resistance and internal contradictions that threaten to divide our movement.

The contradictions faced by contemporary feminists are those experienced by an oppressed group — in this case, women — which needs both to affirm the value of its own culture and to reject the past oppression from which that culture in part originated.[26] To survive as a movement we must avoid two kinds of pitfalls. In this essay, I have concentrated on the dangers of rejecting our culture through individualist integration of the kind that undermined feminism after the first wave of political and educational progress. The other pitfall is that of embracing our culture too uncritically, to the point of identifying with the sources of our own oppression. Rayna Rapp has warned that "as we excavate and legitimize women's history, social organization, and cultural forms, we must not allow our own need for models of strong female collectivities to blind us to the dialectic of tradition"[27] in which women are both supported and constrained. Although we must be self-critical of women's culture and strive to use female institutions to combat inequality, not to entrench it, at the same time, we must not be self-hating of that which is female as we enter a world dominated by men. Even as women retrain in the skills that men once monopolized — in trades, professions, politics — we should not forsake, but rather we should cherish both the values and institutions that were once women's only resources. Even if the Equal Rights Amendment someday legally mandates equality, in the meantime, and for some time thereafter, the female world and separatist politics will still serve the interests of women.

Notes

Acknowledgments: I would like to thank Irene Diamond for inspiring me to write about history and strategy; Mary Felstiner for the perceptive comments she and members of the graduate seminar in women's studies at San Francisco State University offered; the members of the women's faculty group at Stanford University and the members of the history of sexuality study group for forcing me to refine my thinking; and both Yolaida Durán and John D'Emilio for support and criticism as I rewrote this essay.

1. Gayle Rubin, "The Traffic in Women: Notes on the 'Political Economy' of Sex," in *Toward an Anthropology of Women,* ed. Rayna R. Reiter (New York and London: Monthly Review Press, 1975), pp. 157–58.

2. Michelle Zimbalist Rosaldo, "Woman, Culture, and Society: A Theoretical Overview," in *Woman, Culture and Society,* eds. Michelle Zimbalist Rosaldo and Louise Lamphere (Stanford, Calif.: Stanford University Press, 1974), pp. 17–42. "Women's status will be lowest in those societies where there is a firm differentiation between domestic and public spheres of activity and

where women are isolated from one another and placed under a single man's authority in the home." For a reconsideration of her views, see M. Z. Rosaldo, "The Use and Abuse of Anthropology: Reflections on Feminism and Cross-Cultural Understanding," *Signs* 5 (1980): 39–47.

3. Rosaldo, "Woman, Culture, and Society," pp. 37–38. Rosaldo lists women's trading societies, church clubs, "or even political organizations" and cites both the Iroquois and West African societies in which "women have created fully articulated social hierarchies of their own." This strategy differs significantly from the argument that women's domestic-sphere activities are a source of power. On the recent anthropological literature on domestic and public, see Rayna Rapp, "Review Essay: Anthropology," *Signs* 4, no. 3 (Spring 1979): 505, 508–13.

4. Carroll Smith-Rosenberg, "The Female World of Love and Ritual: Relations between Women in Nineteenth-Century America," *Signs* 1, no. 1 (Autumn 1975): 1–29.

5. Nancy F. Cott, *The Bonds of Womanhood: "Women's Sphere" in New England, 1780–1835* (New Haven: Yale University Press, 1977).

6. Blanche Wiesen Cook, "Female Support Networks and Political Activism: Lillian Wald, Crystal Eastman, Emma Goldman," *Chrysalis,* no. 3 (1977): 43–61; and Nancy Sahli, "Smashing: Women's Relationships before the Fall," *Chrysalis,* no. 8 (Summer 1979): 17–27.

7. Feminist historians need clear definitions of women's culture and women's politics to avoid such divisions between the personal and political. Women's culture can exist at both private and public levels. Women's politics, too, can be personal (intrafamilial, through friendship and love, for example) as well as public (the traditional definition of politics). The question of when women's culture and politics are *feminist* has yet to be fully explored. At this time, I would suggest that any female-dominated activity that places a positive value on women's social contributions, provides personal support, and is not controlled by antifeminist leadership has feminist political potential. This is as true for the sewing circle, voluntary civic association, and women's bar as for the consciousness-raising group, coffeehouse, or women's center. Whether that potential is realized depends in part on historical circumstances, such as the overall political climate, the state of feminist ideology and leadership, and the strength of antifeminist forces. Women's culture can remain "prefeminist," as in the case of some nineteenth-century female reform associations that valued women's identity as moral guardians but did not criticize the status quo. When the group experience leads to insights about male domination, however, the reformers often become politicized as feminists. Women's culture can also become reactionary, for instance when women join together under the control of antifeminist leadership, as in the case of Nazi women's groups in prewar Germany, or right-wing movements in America today. The more autonomous the group,

the more likely it is to foster feminist political consciousness. Cott raises some of these questions for the early nineteenth century in her conclusion to *The Bonds of Womanhood*. On moral reformers, see Carroll Smith-Rosenberg, "Beauty, the Beast and the Militant Woman: A Case Study in Sex Roles and Social Stress in Jacksonian America," *American Quarterly* 23 (October 1971): 562–84; and Mary P. Ryan, "The Power of Women's Networks: A Case Study of Female Moral Reform in Antebellum America," *Feminist Studies* 5, no. 1 (Spring 1979): 66–85. Jo Freeman's discussion of the communications network as a precondition for the rebirth of feminism in the twentieth century is also relevant. See Freeman, *The Politics of Women's Liberation* (New York and London: Longman, 1975).

8. These theories are surveyed in Estelle B. Freedman, "The New Woman: Changing Views of Women in the 1920s," *Journal of American History* 61 (September 1974): 372–93.

9. Smith-Rosenberg, "The Female World of Love and Ritual." On changing ideologies of womanhood, see Mary Ryan, *Womanhood in America: From Colonial Times to the Present* (New York: Franklin Watts, 1979); and Gerda Lerner, "The Lady and the Mill Girl: Changes in the Status of Women in the Age of Jackson," *American Studies Journal* 10 (Spring 1968): 5–15.

10. See Ellen DuBois, "The Radicalism of the Woman Suffrage Movement: Notes Toward the Reconstruction of Nineteenth-Century Feminism," *Feminist Studies* 3 (Fall 1975): 63–71. On opposition to women's rights from a "traditional" woman, see Kathryn Kish Sklar, *Catherine Beecher: A Study in American Domesticity* (New Haven: Yale University Press), pp. 266–67.

11. *History of Woman Suffrage,* reprinted in *The Feminist Papers: From Adams to de Beauvoir,* ed. Alice Rossi (New York: Bantam Books, 1973), pp. 457–58. On the history of the women's rights movement, see Ellen Carol DuBois, *Feminism and Suffrage: The Emergence of an Independent Women's Movement in America, 1848–1860* (Ithaca: Cornell University Press, 1978); and Eleanor Flexner, *Century of Struggle* (New York: Atheneum, 1970).

12. William O'Neill, ed., *The Woman Movement: Feminism in the United States and England* (Chicago: Quadrangle Books, 1969), pp. 47–54; and Gerda Lerner, ed., *Black Women in White America* (New York: Vintage, 1972), chap. 8.

13. DuBois, "Radicalism," p. 69.

14. On personal networks and loving relationships in the women's colleges, see Judith Schwarz, "Yellow Clover: Katharine Lee Bates and Katharine Coman," *Frontiers* 4, no. 1 (Spring 1979); and Anna Mary Wells, *Miss Marks and Miss Woolley* (Boston: Houghton Mifflin, 1978).

15. Barbara Welter, "The Cult of True Womanhood, 1820–1860," *American Quarterly* 18 (Summer 1966): 150–74.

16. Ryan, *Womanhood in America*, p. 229.

17. For biographical data on these and other reformers, see the entries in *Notable American Women, 1607–1950,* eds. Edward T. James, Janet Wilson James, and Paul S. Boyer (Cambridge, Mass.: Harvard University Press, 1971).

18. On women in labor and radical movements, see: Nancy Schrom Dye, "Feminism or Unionism? The New York Women's Trade Union League and the Labor Movement," and Robin Miller Jacoby, "The Women's Trade Union League and American Feminism," in *Feminist Studies* 3, no. 1–2 (Fall 1975): 111–40; Allis Rosenberg Wolfe, "Women, Consumerism, and the National Consumers League in the Progressive Era, 1900–1923," *Labor History* 16 (Summer 1975), 378–92; Mary Jo Buhle, "Women and the Socialist Party, 1901–1914," *Radical America* 4, no. 2 (February 1970): 36–55; and Sherna Gluck, "The Changing Nature of Women's Participation in the American Labor Movement, 1900–1940s: Case Studies from Oral History," paper presented at the Southwest Labor History Conference, Tempe, Ariz., 5 March 1977.

19. Judith Paine, "The Women's Pavillion of 1876," *The Feminist Art Journal* 4, no. 4 (Winter 1975–76): 5–12; and *The Woman's Building, Chicago, 1893/The Woman's Building, Los Angeles, 1973* (Los Angeles, 1975).

20. Bertha Honoré Palmer, "The Growth of the Woman's Building," in *Art and Handicraft in the Woman's Building of the World's Columbian Exposition,* ed. Maud Howe Elliott (New York, 1893), pp. 11–12.

21. See Ryan, *Womanhood in America,* for an exploration of these trends.

22. The New York World's Fair Bulletin 1, no. 8 (December 1937): 20–21; the *New York City World's Fair Information Manual,* 1939, index. Amy Swerdlow kindly shared these references and quotations about the 1937 fair from her own research on women in the world's fairs.

23. Rosalind Rosenberg, "The Academic Prism: The New View of American Women," in *Women of America: A History,* eds. Carol Ruth Berkin and Mary Beth Norton (Boston: Houghton Mifflin, 1979), pp. 318–38.

24. The following account of Blair is drawn from research for a biographical essay that appeared in *The Dictionary of American Biography,* suppl., vol. 5 (New York: Charles Scribner, 1977), pp. 61–63. For examples of her writings see "What Women May Do with the Ballot" (Philadelphia, 1922); "Boring from Within," *Woman Citizen* 12 (July 1927): 49–50; "Why I Am Discouraged about Women in Politics," *Woman's Journal* 6 (January 1931): 20–22.

25. Radicalesbians, "The Woman-Identified Woman," *Notes from the Third Year: Women's Liberation* (reprinted in *Radical Feminism,* ed. Anne Koedt, Ellen Levine, and Anita Rapone [New York: Quadrangle, 1973], pp. 240–45); Lucia Valeska, "The Future of Female Separatism," *Quest* 2, no. 2 (Fall 1975): 2–16; Charlotte Bunch, "Learning from Lesbian Separatism," in *Lavender Culture,* ed. Karla Jay and Allen Young (New York: Jove Books, 1978), pp. 433–44.

26. A clear example of this contradiction is the contemporary gay subcul-

ture, which is both a product of the historical labeling of homosexuality as deviance and a source of both personal affirmation and political consciousness. I am grateful to the San Francisco Gay History Project study group for drawing this parallel between the conflicts in women's and gay politics.

27. Rapp, "Review Essay: Anthropology," p. 513.

7

Seizing the Means of Reproduction
An Illegal Feminist Abortion Collective—How and Why It Worked

Pauline B. Bart

The unique female capacity for reproduction has always been regulated. In no society and in no era have all women had control of their reproductive capacity, been free to have children or not, to contracept or not, to abort or not. Yet, everywhere and in all times, women have attempted, with varying degrees of success, to obtain such control. The history of abortion furnishes us with one dramatic example of this basic social control of women.

Jane, or the Service, began in 1969 as an abortion counseling and referral service, a work group of the Chicago Women's Liberation Union. Some of these women went on to do more than counsel and refer — they assisted the illegal abortionists. By the winter of 1971 they took over the entire process themselves. They decided to provide abortions for any woman, at any stage of her pregnancy, with or without funds.

This paper examines how and why this particular group was effective in meeting its goals. The answer lies, in part, in the nature of alternative institutions (Zald and Ash, 1964; Rothschild-Whitt, 1976, 1979; Lindenfeld and Rothschild-Whitt, 1982) in contrast to bureaucratic organizations (Michels, 1949; Weber, 1968; Simmel, 1950).

Reprinted from *Qualitative Sociology* 10 (Winter 1987): 339–57, by permission of the author and the publisher.

Method

Who Was Interviewed?

To study Jane, I interviewed thirty-two women: all the counselors who could be located plus all the women who did a task in addition to counseling (except two who moved out of the area and were not abortionists). I included in the sample women who had relocated to California; Washington, D.C.; Massachusetts; and Nebraska.

Originally the women I approached did not wish to be interviewed, because they were antiprofessional and antiacademic. However, when it became clear that I had been a feminist activist in Chicago and did not have a "professional" demeanor (a negative word in the Women's Health Movement), they agreed. Since I did not have a grant, they decided I had not been co-opted and could be trusted. Some women even requested interviews, and everyone who was asked, including women originally reluctant, ultimately was interviewed.

It was not possible to interview the women who obtained abortions unless they spontaneously spoke to me because Jane women had burned most of the records. There are conflicting stories about why this was done. When a group of records was found by some Jane women during this research, the majority of those asked decided that I could not have access so as to protect client confidentiality.

The Interview

The first interviews were unstructured. Later, I developed a focused schedule grounded in the responses I had received and issues which emerged, particularly issues on which there was disagreement (e.g., whether the Service was "really" a collective). The interviews lasted from forty-five minutes to two hours with a return visit to some of the key women.

Almost all interviews were conducted at the women's homes, furnishing additional data on their interactive styles with me, with their own and neighborhood children, with neighbors, and with other household members. Some women prepared lunch or dinner for me if the interview was at midday or in the evening. Unfortunately, when I mentioned to one of the women that "Jane women are always feeding me," she told the others — thus their feeding was no longer data on their nurturance — it was a self-fulfilling prophecy.

Women who had been interviewed earlier in the study were reinterviewed so I could ask them the added questions. Moreover, I discussed with some of the women questions raised by colleagues. I circulated drafts of papers on Jane among some of the members and included their comments and criticisms. I had promised them input into the study as part of the arrangement when they agreed to be studied. The applicability of the various dimensions of the Rothschild-Whitt model was also discussed and agreed upon by two key members of the Service. The coding categories for the interviews, like the questions themselves, emerged inductively.

Who were the Subjects and How Did They Evaluate Their Experiences with Jane?

The interviewees reported that when the Service started, the clients were mainly middle-class students, but once abortion became legal in other states, middle-class women went to those states. Since Jane would not turn anyone away for lack of funds, their clientele became "mainly poor Black women from the projects." However, women receiving abortions through Jane ranged from policewomen to Weatherwomen.

Several Jane members had abortions through the Service, both before they joined and during their tenure. With one exception, they were satisfied with the procedure. Three women (two of whom were not Jane members) disclosed they had had abortions through Jane and through legal channels, and that they preferred Jane. One of these women approached me after I had spoken about Jane at a meeting, said that she was glad the story of the Service was being publicized, and agreed to be interviewed. There were no discrepancies between her account and the interview data from Jane members.

This woman's gynecologist recommended Jane after telling her he would not perform the abortion she wanted. He told her that the women "were together and knew what they were doing." She had group counseling, which was not a "probing kind of interview," and noted that she was treated like an adult. Because of the counseling session and her physician's endorsement, she was "very comfortable" during the procedure. She paid fifty dollars and was so pleased with the experience that she recommended Jane to other women.

Some years later, at the same stage of pregnancy, she had a legal abortion in a physician's office. The legal abortion was long and painful, she received no emotional support, and was hospitalized with complications. She said she would give Jane financial support if it were necessary for the group to reorganize. And, like the Jane women, she now has less respect for physicians and demands more information from them than previously.

Obtaining an Abortion through Jane: How Woman-Controlled Abortion Worked

Let us now follow a woman through the ten steps she took to obtain an abortion from Jane.

1. A woman needing an abortion could get Jane's phone number from the Chicago Women's Liberation Union or personal networks or even Chicago police officers. She could call and leave her name and number on a message machine.

2. The messages would be collected every two hours and the call would be returned by a woman assigned to that task, called Call-back Jane. She would take a medical history and advise the woman that a counselor would call her.

3. The woman would be assigned to a counselor by the administrator "Big Jane." The counselor had the woman's medical information.

4. The counselor would see the woman either individually or in a group, depending on the counselor's preference. The purpose of counseling was to demystify the abortion process; the woman was told exactly what to expect. In a group the women could offer each other support.

5. The woman would then receive the appointment time, date, and address where she was to go.

6. The woman would go to an apartment called "the Front" with her significant other(s). The Front was set up so that nonmembers would not know where the procedures were taking place. It was described by one woman as "a mob scene" because of all the people there; another said "working the front" was a "very heavy job." Another woman said it was "like being a stewardess with a radical feminist consciousness." Some Jane women took this opportunity to politicize the women.

7. The women, but not those accompanying them, were taken by a Jane driver to an apartment where the procedure including a pap smear actually occurred.

8. They were returned by car to the Front.

9. In order to prevent complications and to treat any which occurred, the woman would phone her counselor during the following week. If she did not call, the counselor would call her, since it was important for an illegal organization like Jane to avert problems. Protection for "mistakes" available to physicians was not available to them.

10. The process for second trimester abortions varied. Leumbach Paste was inserted when available. Otherwise, the amniotic sac was ruptured or the umbilical cord was cut to induce labor. The woman was told to go to a hospital when labor started. She was given careful instructions on how to manage the hospital so that she would be admitted without the hospital calling the police. She was told her rights and what she did not have to reveal. Since women were "hassled" in spite of that information, a midwifery apartment was established with Jane women who specialized in delivering "long terms." The women aborted in that apartment.

A major logistic problem was disposal of the embryos and fetuses. At night "runs" were made to supermarket disposal bins. Sometimes this task was assumed by men who were friends, lovers or husbands of the Jane women.

Women in the collective also served as assistants, giving shots, inserting speculums and dilating cervixes. All these jobs, except abortionist, developed from the beginning of Jane's history.

Why Did It Work?

I asked the women why they thought the Service was successful, and later culled from the interview transcripts five reasons which made sense to me and the informants. With the exception of the literature on movement organizations, notably Rothschild-Whitt's (1979) germinal work, sociological theory would not have predicted the success of Jane. Moreover, the history of many similar alternative organizations (e.g., Taylor [1976] and Peterson's [1976] studies of alternative health clinics) furnishes a veritable "trail of tears"—disappointed expectations and/or cooptation.

1. *The social and historical context.* The most important reason for Jane's effectiveness was the strong, radical and feminist sentiment perva-

sive in 1969 when the Service was initiated. Police brutality vis-à-vis antiwar protestors at the Democratic Convention the year before had radicalized the liberal and radical communities, leaving them angry and disenchanted with existing institutions. Moreover, the sixties was a time of change. People were involved in political change, in changing what came to be called their lifestyles, and in seeking new experiences. (One Jane woman specifically argued that the Service would not have been possible during another time.) It was in this climate that the Women's Movement began to attain momentum in Chicago.

The first national Women's Liberation meeting was held in Chicago in November 1967. While many of the Jane women were not initially feminists and some were not "political," they wanted to do something for and with women. Such opportunities were limited at the time. Since this was their first feminist activity, it was fueled by an enormous amount of energy, faith and hope, as well as anger towards men and patriarchal institutions. One woman said "This was *our* issue. It wasn't our men's and it wasn't our kids' schools. It was ours and the energy was terrific."

In this first phase of feminist activity no one had been "burnt out" and no one questioned sisterhood. Disillusionment over differences, conflicts, and "betrayals" had not yet appeared. Thus, the women were able to devote an enormous amount of energy to Jane.

> the . . . rage was hard to deal with but it led to the making of a tremendous commitment of time and energy. It was just something that clicked because you were working with your friends and you were recruited by friendship, so there was a tremendous commitment to each other as well as to the issues and to the clients.

2. *The charisma of the leaders.*   The interviews revealed general agreement on who the leaders were and that they were effective. As one member said in response to the question of why the Service worked: "One of the things was that the four leaders that I named were really quite incredible people; they deserve a hell of a lot of credit." Another said: "It worked because it had a lot of strong personalities and they were the driving force. . . ." A third woman referred to the "inner core" as "zealots."

Not everyone liked these "sociometric stars." Some called them "manipulative." The first Jane abortionist was perceived as a very strong, talented and competent women whose only flaw was being too conscientious. She was said to feel responsible for every woman unwillingly pregnant in the entire geographic area.

Of the thirty-two women interviewed, fourteen were students at the University of Chicago, nine were housewives and eight were professionals (one occupation could not be ascertained). The original members were primarily housewives supported by their husbands and with enough free time to organize the Service before there was enough surplus money to pay them. Babysitting was performed by some childless members and also was shared. When Jane women took over the Service from the professional abortionists and created paying jobs, it allowed the participation of more women who were young, single and radical and who could devote time to the Service only if they were paid.

The presence of so many housewives was also a function of the particular historical era. Most of those women would today be in paid employment or in school. In fact, currently only one of the women previously in Jane is a housewife, while fifteen are professionals. Ironically, Jane's success may depend, in part, on the same resource that was responsible for the success of so many other volunteer organizations in the United States — women's unpaid labor.

3. *The illegality.* Although some "energy" was lost due to what women called paranoia about being infiltrated by the police or other groups who might be hostile to their goals, engaging in illegal activities made the group cohesive in the face of a common enemy. More important, the illegality of voluntarily terminating a pregnancy convinced Jane members that it was absolutely necessary to perform abortions. If Jane did not perform abortions, the pregnant woman had no satisfactory alternatives. Options were either dangerous or unavailable. One charismatic leader believed that the illegality was "the crux of it — the fact that it was illegal made it override all the other political discrepancies — swept all of us together."

Jane members followed the tradition of civil disobedience to unjust laws which they had learned through participation in the civil rights and peace movements. Although no one with whom I spoke had any moral problem violating abortion laws, an interesting array of attitudes towards illegality existed: some women were frightened, some ignored it, and some liked the danger. A few women, however, had to leave the collective because their husbands believed their own jobs would be jeopardized by their wives' participation in an illegal group.

In addition to having vocabularies of motive to justify illegal activity, the big step towards their dealing with and understanding the illegality of what they were doing was *learning that the abortionists were not physicians.* After that knowledge had been obtained and accepted, following a great deal of discussion at their meetings, it was only a small step to doing it themselves. After all, if being an M.D. was not a prerequisite for doing good abortions, why couldn't the women perform them?

Because the group was illegal, it was cohesive and efficient, according to the women. No time was spent in what they termed hassling with the licensing agencies or maintaining bureaucratic forms. When some of the women subsequently organized a legal women's health center, they found bureaucratic restrictions to be constraining.

In 1973 police raided the place where Jane had performed the abortions that day. The police were tipped off by the sister-in-law of a woman getting an abortion. The captain was new and did not understand that there was an understanding not to disturb Jane. Seven Jane women were arrested and spent the night in jail until they were bailed out. Their lawyer informed them that the police had not previously intervened since Jane provided a necessary service for policemen's wives, mistresses and daughters and for policewomen. (When a policewoman approached the Service for a needed abortion, there was some trepidation.) Further, unlike other illegal abortionists, Jane did not leave bleeding bodies in motels for the police to deal with. When charges were dropped against the seven who were arrested, the women believed that Chicago's desire to avoid another political trial shortly after the Chicago Eight conspiracy trial was responsible. Whatever the reason, the laissez-faire policy of the police exemplifies the discretion of officials in the criminal justice system. Indeed the willingness of the police to ignore Jane's illegal activities may be yet another reason why Jane worked. (Neither the interviewees nor Joyce Rothschild-Whitt mentions this factor. The women did not know the police policy, and all the groups Rothschild-Whitt studied were legal.)

Illegality is a difficult and dangerous context to duplicate, but one aspect of illegality can be consciously promoted in almost any organization: the salience of an external enemy. The more concrete, bounded, easily symbolized and evil (within the moral context of the group) the enemy, the better it will serve to promote cohesion within the group. The sanctuary movement hiding undocumented refugees from Central America meets this criterion of illegality. The dangers of distorting the reality of the enemy for purposes of promoting group solidarity may result in (1) incorrect strategies for dealing with the enemy, and (2) disaffection among participants who perceive the distortions as distortions.

4. The satisfaction of the participants.   The perceived importance of and satisfaction derived from enabling women to have abortions sustained the commitment necessary to perform the tasks. Satisfaction, in turn, is related to the necessity and utility of the work, due to the illegality of abortions. In contrast to other groups of people with equal good will, members of this group could actually solve problems — the women would walk in pregnant and leave no longer pregnant. All the members agreed on the importance of offering this solution. One woman stated "There's nothing so compelling and thus so concrete — that you get such goodies from — that's so real." Another women said:

> Whenever there were personal problems or political disagreements they were always subordinated to the job at hand, because abortion was not something one could have political disagreements about. . . . No matter how much people had different politics in their work, middle-class housewives who were members of NOW and women who were radical hippie freaks, dopers, women from the Union [the Chicago Women's Liberation Union — socialist feminists] and who knows what else. There were students and nonstudents. . . . But it could never matter because ultimately you had to do the abortion. You can argue a real lot about demonstrations, you can argue a lot about posters, you can argue a real lot about canvassing, you can argue a real lot about what you're writing in your leaflets, but you can't argue about doing an abortion. You're going to do it or you're not and if you're going to then you do it.

Indeed some women mentioned that it was the very absence of a "correct political line" except on a woman's right to have an abortion that enabled the group to survive and continue to be effective.

The quality of satisfaction deriving from Jane's unique ability to solve the woman's problem is rarely obtainable in other organizations and prevented the dissolution of the organization. In contrast, a worker in a woman's clinic said: "basically, women can get their Pap smears somewhere else and maybe it's not so nice on some fundamental level . . . but that's all." In contrast, a worker on a woman's hotline stated that there was little she could do for the battered women who called since at that time Chicago had no battered women's shelters. Discrepancy between ideal goals and real contributions leads to worker "burn out" in many organizations, forcing high expenditure of organizational resources on the recruiting and training of new members. Burn out was also a problem for women on rape crisis lines who could neither stop rape nor change the woman to an unraped status as Jane could change women to an unpregnant status. Rape counselors could only ameliorate pain and offer alternatives of varying degrees of unsatisfactoriness. An organization that can define a concrete problem and solve the problem offers members great satisfaction which, in turn, sustains the organization.

  5. *Financial self-sufficiency.* Another reason for the Service's success is that the collective supported itself and could pay salaries. Although no one was turned away for lack of funds, the average fee received was fifty dollars. While it was norm-violating for workers to be involved simply for pay, the fact that women could be paid enabled a group of women to put much time into the Service who otherwise would have had to work at what they termed "shit jobs." By earning money in productive feminist work they were able to lead totally radical feminist lives. In a movement where one tenet was "The personal is the political," that is, one's private life is relevant to one's public statements in analyzing one's behavior and achieving one's goals, the lack of contradictions in one's life was particularly valued. Financial self-sufficiency also ended the contradictions some women felt when supported by their husbands. Moreover, no energy was required for fund-raising or for grant-writing.

  Financial self-sufficiency based on client payment has rarely been adopted as a goal by alternative organizations. Such a system smacks too much of the capitalist forms of organization these organizations are trying to escape. Alternative helping organizations traditionally have preferred to dispense free services free and rely entirely on voluntary labor and donations. Only when they come close to collapse do they consider a fee scale based on the client's ability to pay. In this sense, Jane was fortunate in having to pay private abortionists at first and having to charge a small fee for that purpose. Since most clients could afford the fee, Jane workers could retain the fee in good conscience after eliminating the private practitioners.

  These five reasons sum up those suggested to me in the interviews. Unfortunately, the social and historical context of organizational success is rarely, if ever, under an organization's control. Nevertheless, an organization must pay attention to its own placement in the historical context of political feeling. In addition, a subsequent organization formed the same way and doing the same thing may fail while the first succeeded because the participants will lack the enthusiasm and excitement of being "first."

Organizational Theory

Jane displayed most of the characteristics of a collective organization as delineated by Rothschild-Whitt's (1979) theory of alternative organizations.

1. The goal of providing safe, humane abortions for every woman who needed one was not diluted by a concern for organizational survival. Classic organization theorists such as Michels (1949) and Weber (1968) claim that organizations usually come to see their own survival as their major goal. Thus, what was originally a means (the organization) becomes transformed into an end in itself. After their original goal is met, agencies and organizations survive by redefining their tasks (i.e., goal displacement). For example, the March of Dimes took as its cause the conquering of birth defects once a vaccine for polio was available (discussed in Heller et al., 1984). Indeed, some organizations have a vested interest in the continued existence or even exacerbation of their "problem" in order to justify and expand their funding. Because Jane was an alternative institution with what Rothschild-Whitt (1976) calls both a transitory and a social movement orientation, it was less likely to experience goal displacement. Rather it disbanded after the Supreme Court decision in *Roe v. Wade* which enabled the collective to decide that the need for legal abortion referral could be met by other groups.

2. Authority resides in the collectivity as a whole. The Jane women, by and large, espoused the philosophy of feminist anarchism and collective decision making. In collective organizations authority is delegated only temporarily, if at all, and is subject to recall. Individuals comply with the consensus of the collective, which is always fluid and open to negotiation. Jane's commitment to consensus meant that although they sometimes had to spend more time than they would have liked hammering out the lines of their agreement, their eventual agreement allowed them to work smoothly under pressure.

3. Minimal stipulated rules. Although Jane members followed strict rules of medical procedure—e.g., if a woman was feverish, she was given an antibiotic—they had few formal rules of collective behavior. Their openness to the ad hoc decision making of each member allowed for (1) flexibility which was crucial in dealing with a varied population in an illegal setting, and (2) a degree of autonomy for each member that helped them maintain their voluntary commitment of time and energy.

4. *Social control through homogeneity.*   In collective organizations, social controls are based primarily on personal or moralistic appeals and the selection of homogeneous personnel. Jane's membership was homogeneous: over one-half the women in Jane were between 20 and 30 years old, and all but two were white. Most were born and raised in urban areas, particularly Chicago. When the Service was operating, about one-half of its members were single and one-half married, with two divorced or separated. The ratio of Protestants to Jews was approximately 1:2, and four women were Catholic. The typical Jane worker had postgraduate education and her mother had a high school education. Fathers varied more: Although most had professional education, eleven had high school education or less.

Distressed by their own homogeneity, Jane workers, with only slight success, tried to recruit Black and Latino workers, the ethnic and racial characteristics of large segments of their clients. Although the women claimed ideological diversity, the diversity was within feminist and Left boundaries. They all agreed on the importance of abortion for women who chose it. Although they fought against it, the relative cultural homogeneity of the members of Jane was a blessing in disguise since it provided social cohesion.

5. *Social relations: the ideal of community.*   In the typical collectivist organization, ideal relations are holistic, personal, and ends in themselves. In Jane, women were "sisterly" toward the women obtaining abortions but not always sisterly towards each other. The ideal of sisterhood had two functions: it provided an effective model of interaction and it was a goal toward which the collective could strive. However, unlike the case of the free school Rothschild-Whitt studied that replaced the goal of education with the goal of community, in Jane the search for community never replaced the goal of providing safe, humane abortions. Friendship groups behaved holistically toward each other, but in the organization as a whole, relations were sometimes segmental. Little time was spent "processing" relationships because of the urgency of the task of providing abortions.

6. *Recruitment.*   In collectivist organizations, recruitment relies on friendship, shared social-political values, admired personality attributes, and informally assessed knowledge and skills. Career advancement is

not an inducement for joining the organization. The major pathway to Jane membership was through friendship networks. Some women became members after they or their friends had abortions with the Service.

Prospective members attended three meetings where they learned how to counsel first and second-trimester women, the physiology of abortion, and the organizational practices of Jane. How much was disclosed to them varied with what was termed the "paranoia" of the women presenting the information. At first some recruits were not told that the abortionists were not physicians, as implied in a pamphlet given to clients and prospective counselors (the Abortion Counseling Service, no date). When the recruits were later told that the abortionists were not physicians, and/or that the Jane women were performing the procedures themselves, they expressed some resentment at not being trusted.

New recruits were screened to locate women who both favored the availability of abortion and were willing to work illegally. Precautions were taken about disclosure, given the possibility of a hostile undercover policewoman trying to close the clinic. Recruitment procedures insured a relatively culturally and ideologically homogeneous group that could work together successfully in a condition of extreme individual autonomy. They may have also helped to select membership with a high energy level. Over one-half the informants stated that they had more energy than the people they knew, while only two said that they had less; eight said they needed six or fewer hours of sleep per night.

Transmitting Skills

All skills were learned by observing other women and performing tasks under the supervision of women with greater skill. When the male abortionist(s) had responsibility for medical procedures, the women in the Service learned to: deal with doctors and hospitals, talk to the police, buy drugs and instruments, counsel effectively, and maintain a democratic, efficient and sisterly organization. After the first eighteen months, the women evolved from counseling and referring to assisting and "finally, to doing the entire procedure":

> We learned to give shots, to take blood pressure, to take and read Pap smears for cancer. We performed abortions on pregnant eleven-year-olds and on pregnant fifty-year-olds.

Skills necessary to perform abortions are not difficult to learn. One woman said:

> The thing itself [the curettage] was real easy. It's like making canteloupe balls — the same motion with the curette. . . . The motions for the curettage themselves are not particularly delicate. They are quick and sure. The greater precision was in the handling of the dilator. You had to feel the woman's muscles through the instrument into your hand. That is a very delicate procedure. So much of what you have to learn is sensitivity to the woman's body and that is what is unlearned in medical school.

Women also learned by re-examining their own experiences:

> We learned from identifying and understanding feelings in our own bodies and then trying to relate them to another woman's problems and feelings.

They did not use the term "patient"

> . . . because patient is a word that the medical establishment uses. It implies a subject-object relation and we always tried to get away from thinking of women who came through the Service as objects we were going to do something to . . . we were all partners in the crime of demanding the freedom to control our own bodies and our own childbearing.

Birth control information was offered and all the women received copies of *Our Bodies Our Selves, The Birth Control Handbook* and the *VD Handbook*. However, counseling was considered the heart of the procedure and everyone was supposed to counsel. It was believed that you could tell by the woman's response during the abortion whether or not she had been counseled well. Women learned to counsel as they learned all the skills — primarily through an apprenticeship system in addition to the orientation sessions.

> The basic information was the description depending on how many weeks they were. You either do a description of a D&C (i.e. dilation of the cervix and scraping or curettage of the uterus) or a description of the miscarriage (i.e. euphemism for the abortion). In the long-term you had to do both because we had to do the D&C after the miscarriage.

Personal motivations and fears were not probed unless the woman seemed to need to address these issues. One key person said that it was condescending to ask the woman if she was sure she wanted an abortion. She felt it was appropriate to ask if she had told her mother or what would happen if she didn't have the abortion. I asked another counselor how she knew if a woman had abortion-related emotional problems in need of discussion. She responded, "I guess you would have to watch it and it all depended on the woman."

All Jane members counseled, whatever their other tasks, so that their work would be grounded in the woman's experiences. One abortionist did not counsel and this omission was thought to cause her inadequate performance. She was ultimately fired by a group vote.

My informants also stated that dealing with incompetence was a major problem. Emotional intensity often characterizes collective work (Rothschild-Whitt, 1979). Because intense relationships are often emotionally threatening, collective members who fear conflict tend to soften or conceal criticisms. Although this happened frequently in Jane, the importance of the work itself—including the always present possibility of serious harm to the woman who had come to have an abortion—forced the workers to acknowledge incompetence. In this way, Jane was fortunate in having a clear and serious mission that forestalled arguments for maintaining incompetent persons as is done in other collectives.

Jane's informal assessment of knowledge and skills gave a premium to those who knew how to do well that which had to be done. At the time physicians were not trained to perform abortions, although they did learn how to perform D&C's. Thus their credential was not valued in and of itself. Jane's method of assessing skill probably paid off both in terms of safety and humane procedures.

The following quote from one of the counselors demonstrates the enormous range of learning that Jane workers experienced:

> When I joined the feminist movement someone said to me, "Scratch any woman deep enough and you are going to find a feminist." And being involved in Jane, especially in the counseling part where one has to talk to many women, and being up in the Front I found that under the skin it didn't matter if you were big or Black or white or green or small or fat or rich or poor. Women had to deal with the same problems and it radicalized me. In that respect, I truly believe this now, I feel that tremendous kinship to women and I find that I seek out women as opposed to men. . . .

But the thing that was the most interesting with my husband was that he suddenly gained a better insight into this. Because when we first started, we thought that only poor Black women were going to come and he saw people coming to our house and they were all kinds of people and all ages of people and this to him was radicalizing too. . . . I also learned how my body functioned and that was, to me, one of the best things.

And I think I also learned about how to demand services from the medical profession because I knew about my body. I could now say, "Hey listen . . . what's happening, tell me . . ." and I didn't take any of this "little" crap stuff that doctors were giving, I wasn't their little girl and I don't know if this was Jane, if this was the feminist movement or being involved in NOW, I don't know. I do know, though, that it changed my whole outlook about myself.

In essence, women learned that they were competent. One woman eloquently captured the essence of the Jane experience and the philosophy of self help:

If it's necessary you can take the tools of the world in your own hands, and all that crap about how you have to be an expert to do anything, whether fixing your car or your vacuum cleaner or administering medical aid is just a ruse to make you feel incompetent in your own life. *One thing we all learned is that if you want to learn how to do something, you can do it.*

7. Incentive structure: normative, solidarity and personal growth incentives primary, material incentives secondary.   Jane's appeal was to enacting symbolic values, such as a woman's right to control her own body. Moreover, all paying jobs paid the same, and many tasks, including counseling, were not remunerated at all. This characteristic of collective organization helped members focus on the intrinsic reasons they were doing the job, and this, in turn, helped them focus on their clients as individuals.

Because the Service was illegal, no one in Jane could use their experience in the organization to further their careers. All of the members' emotional energy was concentrated on doing the present job correctly. This present-oriented psychology, in turn, made it easier to pay attention to the emotional and physical nuances of each client. This, in turn, enhanced the care.

The individual autonomy and varied work that the organization provided had a major impact on the lives and self-images of the participants. In taking care of others, the Jane women fulfilled their own potential. One woman said, "my participation in the Service grew me into the person I was meant to be" (cf. Bart and Schlesinger, 1982).

Jane women also reported sharp increases in their feelings of identification with other women. Such positive feelings towards other women were the result in part of participation in a female world, for the women's co-workers and clients were all female (cf. Smith-Rosenberg, 1975).

8. Social stratification: egalitarian. Collective organizations and subordinate groups (e.g. women) prefer equality of members, and strictly limit reward differentials. Jane had a strong commitment to equality. Consistent efforts were made to flatten the decision making and status hierarchies, especially after the paid professional abortionists were no longer present.[1] There was a hierarchy, albeit a relatively flat one. The women who performed medical procedures, particularly the abortionists, were central, unlike those who restricted their activity to counseling. Moreover, women ordinarily assisted before they performed D&C's. One interviewee who had become a medical student, clarified the link between self-growth and equality: "I will share any skill I learn with anyone who wants to learn it. If someone wants to know how to do open heart surgery and I have learned how, I will teach it to them."

9. Differentiation: minimal division of labor. In collective organizations, administration is combined with performance tasks and the usual division between intellectual and manual work is reduced. Rothschild-Whitt found that differentiation is minimized through "role rotation, teamwork, or task sharing, and the diffusion or 'demystification' of specialized knowledge through internal education." In the Service there was an additional attempt to minimize differentiation between the collective members and the clients by having the latter perform tasks during the procedure.

Moreover, collectivist organizations generalize jobs and functions, stressing holistic roles. They demystify expertise and make an ideal of the amateur. In Jane, the goal was to have every member perform every task, with the major consequences for energy and self esteem that were mentioned above. Other organizations can reduce specialization, limited only by the differential commitments of members and formal legal requirements. The Service exemplifies Marx's belief that "Only in a community with others has each individual the means of cultivating his [*sic*] gifts in all directions; only in the community therefore, is personal freedom possible" (1985, p. 83).

Conclusion

Several levels of analysis accounting for Jane's success were presented in this paper. First there were the reasons the Jane members themselves gave. Second there was the sociological conceptual scheme with which I interpreted these reasons (e.g. referring to the leaders as charismatic). Third, there is organizational theory as revised for movement organizations by Rothschild-Whitt. The relevance of this latter approach became apparent after the data had been collected. The members of Jane did not have Rothschild-Whitt's organizational principles in mind when they put their group together. Yet these principles facilitated the effectiveness of the group.

Jane illustrates both the characteristics of a successful movement organization and the possibility of making abortion a less alienating experience for the women having them and for the medical personnel involved. Roth (1974) states that for many years we have been trying to teach professionals to love their patients and have been unsuccessful. He suggests, therefore, that we teach people who already love the patients the necessary professional and technical skills. The effectiveness of Jane demonstrates the perceptiveness of this remark. To use Ehrenreich and English's phrase (1973), these women seized the "technology without buying the ideology"; that is, they used antibiotics and medical equipment but did not adopt the hierarchical system or the sense of entitlement that characterizes physicians. Since abortion has been legalized in this country, some physicians and nurses have expressed guilt over abortions they were performing. No women in Jane expressed such guilt, probably because they all had to counsel women who wanted the abortions and, therefore, knew the importance for the woman's life of not having a baby at that time. Were all personnel engaged in abortion procedures also engaged in counseling, their world would be grounded in the women's experience. The economics of the medical system, of course, make the doctor's time more expensive and valuable than that of the counselor. As a consequence, the tasks are separated which may work to the psychological disadvantage of the doctors themselves in the long run.

When this research was begun, abortion was legal and poor women received third-party payments. Lack of funds could not prevent them from terminating an unwanted pregnancy. Now, however, third-party payments for abortions are almost nonexistent and a strong lobby supporting a "human life" amendment is trying to make abortions illegal again. Perhaps knowledge of the success of Jane will do more than expand the sociology of medicine, the sociology of social movements and organizational theory. Perhaps it will enable us to seize the means of reproduction.

Notes

Acknowledgments: This is a revised version of a paper presented at the Annual Meetings of the American Sociological Association, Chicago, Illinois, 1977. I wish to thank Frances Chapman, Arlene Kaplan Daniels, Meredith Gould, Joan Huber, Carol Joffe, Kristin Luker, Patricia Miller, and three women from the abortion collective who wish to remain anonymous, for their comments. I would like to thank Jane Mansbridge and Shulamit Reinharz for their help in revising the manuscript, and Amy Siegel for editing. Rosabeth Kanter brought Joyce Rothschild-Whitt's work to my attention. Content analysis of the data on self-image was performed by Melinda Bart Schlesinger. The Boston Women's Health Book Collective generously provided funds for the coding.

1. Philosopher Kathryn Pyne Addelson (1991) examines the Service as an example of a moral revolution. Using Jane, she demonstrates the bias in traditional objective, "value free" philosophy. Participants in Jane were a subordinate group (women) and, thus, had a different perspective on morality and a stronger commitment to equality.

References

The Abortion Counseling Service. N.d. *Abortion: A Woman's Decision, a Woman's Right Pamphlet.* Chicago: Women's Liberation Movement.

Addelson, Kathryn Pyne. 1991. Moral revolution. In *Impure Thoughts: Essays on Philosophy, Feminism, and Ethics.* Philadelphia: Temple University Press.

Bart, Pauline B., and Melinda Bart Schlesinger. 1982. Collective work and self-identity. In Frank Lindenfeld and Joyce Rothschild-Whitt, *Workplace Democracy and Social Change.* Boston: Porter Sargent.

Ehrenreich, Barbara, and Deidre English. 1973. *Complaints and Disorders: The Sexual Politics of Sickness.* Old Westbury: The Feminist Press.

Heller, Ken, Richard Price, Shulamit Reinharz, Stephanie Riger, and Abraham Wandersman. 1984. *Psychology and Community Change*. Homewood, Ill.: Dorsey.

Howell, Mary (pseud. Margaret Campbell). 1973. *Why Would a Girl Go into Medicine?* Old Westbury: The Feminist Press.

Joffe, Carole. 1978. What abortion counselors want from their clients. *Social Problems* 26:112–21.

Lindenfeld, Frank, and Joyce Rothschild-Whitt. 1982. *Workplace Democracy and Social Change*. Boston: Porter Sargent.

Marx, Karl. 1985. *The German Ideology*. New York: International Press.

Michels, Robert. 1949. *Political Parties*. Glencoe, Ill.: The Free Press.

Peterson, Karen. 1976. Creating divisions of labor: A case study of nonprofessionals professing self-help. Ph.D. dissertation, Northwestern University.

Roth, J. A. 1974. Care of the sick: Professionalism vs. love. *Social Science and Medicine* 1:173–80.

Rothschild-Whitt, Joyce. 1976. Conditions facilitating participatory-democratic organizations. *Sociological Inquiry* 46(2): 75–86.

——. 1979. Collective democracy: An alternative to rational bureaucratic models of organization. *American Sociological Review* 44:519–29.

Simmel, Georg. 1950. The secret and the secret society. Pp. 307–16 in *The Sociology of Georg Simmel*. Translated, edited, and with an introduction by Kurt H. Wolff. Glencoe: The Free Press.

Smith-Rosenberg, Carroll. 1975. The female world of love and ritual: Relations between women in nineteenth-century America. *Signs* 1:1–29.

Taylor, Rosemary. 1976. Alternative medicine: Politics and organization in the free clinic movement. Ph.D. dissertation, University of California at Santa Barbara.

Tietze, Christopher. 1979. *Induced Abortion: A World Review, 1970*, 3d edition. New York: Population Council.

Weber, Max. 1968. *Economy and Society*. Edited by Guenther Roth and Claus Wittrich. New York: Bedminster Press.

Zald, Mayer N., and Roberta Ash. 1964. Social movement organizations: Growth, decay, and change. *Social Forces* 44:327–41.

8

The Furies Collective

Rita Mae Brown

Off the coast of Greece in the sixth century before Christ, feminism began as a response to patriarchy. Sappho, a revolutionary despite her wealth (or perhaps because of it), founded her school for women. We are all daughters of those distant mothers. The shrouds of centuries obscure our view. We know little of the school, nothing of its structure. We possess no portrait of its founder.

Through the upheavals, organized brutality, and stunning ignorance which has characterized male supremacy from 600 B.C. until today, there were always a few women and even fewer men, scattered across the globe, who kept the flame of female independence alive. Their names are lost but not their spirit. Their work, their very existence upon this earth makes our work possible. In the mid-1960s we, the inheritors, once again grasped the torch and set the land afire.

The fire passed to me in 1965. Up until that time I'd been rebellious and high spirited. Politics interested me, but then it's fair to say everything interested me. I had no desire to lap a track carrying the torch of revolution over my head. Even though I came from a poor background I was certain my artistic talent would see me through. I would become rich and famous, in the order of their importance, take care of my mother, bankroll my friends and gather the lights about me as did Gertrude in Paris in the 1920s.

New York City is America's Paris. I landed there on my feet but broke

Reprinted from *A Plain Brown Rapper,* by Rita Mae Brown (Oakland, Calif.: Diana Press, 1976), 9–22, by permission of the author.

in the summer of 1965. I was not in the city long, living in an abandoned car with Baby Jesus, a kitten. (She turned eleven on 14 July 1976.) One day B.J. and I walked over to St. Mark's Church in the East Village. I hadn't eaten in a few days and was lonesomer than God. There right in front of me looking quite well-fed was Candice Bergen. B.J. and I had blundered into the filming of "The Group." Candice is one year younger than I so I didn't feel distant from her as I might have from Greta Garbo. Desperately, I wanted to ask her for money for food. I felt sure she'd spring a dollar on my behalf. No matter how hungry I was I couldn't bring myself to beg. So I stood there feeling sicker and sicker as I watched my contemporary recede from me. For the first time in my life it occurred to me that I might remain poor all of my days, that people my own age and also of talent might be forever unreachable because I was too poor to get near them. Sickness transformed into rage. I wanted to go over and yank Candice out of that car she was parked in and yell, "Goddammit, I'm as good as you are. I'm not just a poor asswipe in dirty clothes. I'm an artist! I'm an important person! I'm hungry!" Instead I wandered back to University and Waverly Place because I felt dizzy and weak. The next morning I felt worse. A pizza joint on the other side of Washington Square Park threw its scraps in a garbage can placed on the sidewalk. I had noticed this a few days earlier. I managed to walk over there with B.J. I reached down in the can and picked out a pizza rind and started to eat it. Tasted delicious. The stand owner glimpsed at me and screamed. I thought he would beat me. Instead this burly Italian man dragged me inside and served both B.J. and me as though we were royal. New York did have a heart after all.

My St. Mark's revelation drove deeper than fears for my future. I knew there must be millions of people like me all over the world, young, intelligent, with a great deal to offer the societies they lived in yet who by circumstance of birth, race, sex, sex preference were unable to fully develop themselves and were unable to make friendships with those people, just like themselves, who had been born "higher." I always displayed democratic tendencies but at St. Mark's Church a revolutionary was born.

Revolutionary fervor bubbled throughout New York University in the middle sixties. Thanks to a tuition scholarship I could attend classes as well as meetings dominated by white students in beards. They bored me to tears. Surely revolution was more than hot air? I walked in peace marches and civil rights marches and thought them foolish. Why walk on the road? Why not just walk briskly into General Motors and rip hell out of the joint? If you're going to get hit over the head you might as well get hit for something real as opposed to something symbolic. I quickly understood that the white kids in the civil rights movement and the protest against Viet Nam came from one class while I came from another. Their idea of social change was at variance with my own. They were obsessed with the media which I thought way off the mark. The New Left had a national movement on the tube but no grass roots movement back home.

Giving those people any energy seemed fruitless so I marched less and concentrated more on classes with Conor Cruise O'Brien. I spent a solid year on the debate between Thomas Paine and Edmund Burke. The ideas that enraptured my generation weren't new at all. I was overwhelmed by this discovery and raced to the classics department where I devoured the writings of Sappho, Euripides, Aristophanes, anything I could lay my hands on. Every day I hit on some fantastic idea fully 2000 years old and I recall even now the marvel I experienced at the continuity of human life. These dead souls, in another language, still spoke to me as clearly as if they were in the room and surely they made more sense than the movement heavy in his workshirt. For all my material poverty, those years at New York University bore great riches. I was grounded in the cycles of Western thought. I acquired a solid education. After learning from books I graduated ready to learn from people.

Nineteen sixty-seven, the year before graduation, Martha Shelley, Stephen Donaldson, and I (and others whose names I've unfortunately forgotten) founded Student Homophile League at Columbia and at New York University. The fur flew. "Organized queers!" the administration gasped. "Capitalist decadents!" screamed the New Left. "Diseased whites!" bellowed the Black movement. By declaring our existence we managed to offend all of them. That was enough for me. I knew we were on the right track.

Political activity consumed days, months, years. I charged into the brand new feminist movement in 1968 and the straight women did their best to see I'd charge right back out again. A few diehards are still trying to purge lesbians but we are here to stay. Since then, many women have come out. The difference between feminists who became lesbians and lesbians who became feminists is that the former take great pleasure in principle while the latter make a principle of pleasure. Those women who do choose lesbianism whether by principle or pleasure are at least making that choice themselves rather than bending to relentless heterosexual propaganda.

By now, thanks to those early anti-lesbian campaigns, we've all learned to mistrust a mystique of unity which comes at the expense and silence of minority women. Women who aren't safely white aren't going to be quiet about it, nor are poor women, nor are lesbians. Lesbianism was the first issue to break ideological ground on the real meaning of multiplicity rather than conformity. Because of that initial, bitter struggle I hope the issues of class and white bias can be handled with more maturity than any of us handled the lesbian issue.

In those days I ate, breathed and slept feminism. Nothing else mattered to me. We would bring about a revolution in this nation and we would do it now. My vision of that revolution remains unchanged. However, the timetable undergoes constant revision. Change, it becomes apparent, is not a convulsion of history but the slow, steady push of people over decades.

Such burning intensity culminated in the Furies Collective. I moved to Washington, D.C., in 1970 and with the women to whom this book is dedicated* organized the Furies Collective. Though none of us were spawned in The Left's nurseries of orthodoxy we operated on a Bolshevik cell model. We lived together, shared chores equally. All clothing rested in a common room. We slept together in mattresses on the floor in the same room. We had desks together if we wanted desks. This possibility veered towards elitist individualism and Charlotte Bunch and I were forever suspect because we spent so much time at our desks. The only time you could be left alone was in the middle of the night. Consequently, Charlotte and I developed into night people out of self-defense.

We rotated jobs in the outside world except for the two of us that had decent jobs. Work for money was part time so more time could be put into Furies' projects. We created a newspaper which bore our name, a child care center, a school that taught car repair, home repair and self-defense. We also wreaked havoc in the community. Our clarity of pur-

---

A Plain Brown Rapper is dedicated to the Furies Collective. Voting members: Ginny Berson, Joan Biren, Charlotte Bunch, Tasha Petersen, Sharon Deevy, Helaine Harris, Susan Hathaway, Nancy Myron, Coletta Reid, Lee Schwing, Jennifer Woodul. Nonvoting members: Kara, Cassidy, Michelle, Charly, Frip, Baby Jesus. *Ed.*

pose frightened others. Our self-righteousness exacerbated the paranoia. Within the collective we slaved at study groups. Each woman elected a major country and a minor country. We were to report the history of that nation, the status of women, the economy and current affairs. My major country was the Soviet Union, minor Germany. I felt each in a distinct way had much in common with the U.S.A. Among us we blanketed the earth. Oddly, it didn't occur to us to study the United States until the beginning of our second year together. Precious little time was left for us to enjoy ourselves.

For all our fevers and mistakes, we learned. How we learned. We learned that cadre organizing will never work in the United States. It smacks of conspiracy to people. We learned that you can possess an accurate analysis of the political situation but that doesn't insure people will listen to it especially if you threaten them to begin with. We learned (although the other two poor kids among us already knew this) that a moral appeal will not motivate people as quickly as an appeal to gain — the gain need not be material but that mightily helps. We learned that foreign policy doesn't interest most Americans as much as domestic policy. We learned that not all women are sisters and not all men are enemies. That one was difficult. We also learned some devastating things about ourselves.

We were all white. A few of us came from lower class backgrounds. The majority were middle class. We ranged in age from 18 to 30 but eight of us were between 22 and 26. Two children were 1½ years old. One girl was 4 years old. We had social direction but few of us had personal direction. In 1971 only Charlotte and I displayed a clear sense of calling. This was to be our undoing. The other women, in time, developed career identities for themselves.

We were all lesbians at that time. As far as I know everyone still is except for two people. We shared a common feminist-socialist philosophy. We thought we knocked down all the walls. What we discovered, painfully, were the real walls that prevent effective political commitments between people.

The first and thickest barrier was that we lied to ourselves about ourselves. Individuals would not admit they were drifting or that their sense of personal identity was threatened primarily by me (devoid of all diplomacy) and secondarily by Charlotte (a diplomat but too talented to trust totally). The stronger the woman was perceived to be the greater the subterranean threat. Charlotte and I were perceived to "run" the collective yet neither Charlotte nor I felt we had any control over the group. By not defining leadership or process we made things far worse than if we'd put down rules.

Our second failing was in refusing to recognize that style is as important as content, politically and individually.

Our third failing was our dismal attempt to rectify class difference by external means only. We developed a graduated income tax according to one's past privilege and current economic status. As far as that goes it's just and effective. But we ignored the psychology of class differences. In the end, it was this issue and the issue of identity which destroyed our collective.

Women from middle class backgrounds controlled the collective's finances although, again, the rules were unclear. Unspoken assumptions about spending weighed upon us. We poor kids were much more likely to spend our pennies entertaining ourselves than our middle class sisters who needed to feel the money was being put to "good use."

The emotional directness of the poor women, particularly our anger, upset the middle class women. They came from places where communication was indirect, implied. This creates people who search for hidden meanings in your manner, who try to "read" you and then do what they think will gain your approval. Anger was perceived to be on a par with a physical threat, a shocking challenge to integrity. To us, anger was honest communication. You flared up, cooled off and that was the end of it.

Those two examples can give you some idea of the many stylistic differences we encountered. Since these differences were new to each of us, we'd never been in this situation before, we were often frustrated with one another and ourselves. We explored new territory and didn't have a language to describe it. We fell back on the language of the political Left to try and explain the dynamics within the group. As you know, this language is intellectual and corrupted. That is, oppression as a term was tossed about so loosely in the early seventies that it became devalued, useless. By the simple act of speaking in this cheapened jargon we lessened our chances to communicate and drew further apart. In this atmosphere a purge loomed inevitable. Joan Biren and Sharon Deevey were unceremoniously tossed out. Straining under the mounting tension, the two women had become moody, petty, bewildered because they felt they were missing or misreading "cues." They acted perfectly human. This was not allowed — *especially* by me.

The Furies began to create within ourselves the dynamic of a fascist state (or Stalinist, take your pick). Like many fascist states we started out on the road to a better life only to be sidetracked by personal weakness. We kept the language of the revolution but the procedure of the Inquisition. There is a difference between fascism as a political system and fascism as personal substance. I was learning this first hand plus I was forewarned because of my study selections, Russia and Germany. In this case forewarned was not forearmed.

We weren't emotionally open with one another and I take the blame for much of that. Sadness, depression, simple complaining disgusted me. I thought those emotions middle class self-indulgence. Given the physical survival battles of my early life, had I allowed myself to experience those emotions I probably would have caved in. At that time I couldn't understand the pattern of middle class women's lives. If you have food on the table, a roof over your head and clothes on your back, what's the problem? The lethal ambivalence with which middle class women live their lives was unknown to me. The only suffering I understood was physical. These women suffered emotionally. I could not fathom this. The malicious seeds of self-doubt were planted in their cribs. They sought their legitimation from others. Their revolution will be when they go cold turkey on their approval addiction and validate their own selves. Political revolution will be when we validate each other and get on with the job of winning political/economic power.

The Furies also did not reckon with the land mines of woman hatred. By becoming a feminist or a lesbian one does not automatically love women. Years of conditioning aren't wiped out so easily. I hated women, somewhat, perhaps less than most of The Furies and more than a very few. Under patriarchy a strong woman is a contradiction in terms. We were not immune from that concept. Since my gifts were more obvious at that time because of the circumstances of my life, I became dangerous. That I had gifts was sin enough. That I refused to apologize for them was unforgivable. That I blatantly enjoyed them was horrendous. The Furies purged me on March 6, 1972.

Charlotte stayed on to try and mend the fences. The Furies folded less than a month later and in the end Charlotte found herself the target.

Tasha Petersen accompanied me on my exile to 217 12th St. S.E. That was the first time in my life I was conscious of anyone standing by me. It may have happened at other times in my life and I couldn't see it. But Tasha, in the midst of our collective collapse, gave me faith. Maybe we were going at this ass-backwards — the personal bonds need to precede the obviously political.

Four years later I know The Furies Collective was a turning point as was St. Mark's a turning point. I now know many of the answers to our success rest in the penumbra of the brain, those areas we rarely see in ourselves or others, the inner life. If we can link these discoveries, psychological, to the economic, I believe we will have the basis for a strong challenge to patriarchal power. The patriarchs may not topple in our lifetime but *someone* has to brave the unknown and that is the destiny of our generation. We are the bridge generation between the desert and the promised land. If we don't build it no one gets there. Our political enemies by their colossal greed will render the earth uninhabitable. If people do not replace profit, if the land is not nourished, if simultaneity does not replace the concept of intellectual polarization, if men do not release the "feminine" within themselves and identify with women, if cooperation does not replace competition, generations hence will choke on blood and dust. World War II will look like a rehearsal. Our work will not be easy. The reward may be the work itself and your knowledge of the value of that work. As LaBelle sings to us, "The Revolution will not be televised." I learned that in The Furies.

After our break-up I saw only our failures. It took me time to realize the failure was not all our fault. It is politically impossible to create a separate, feminist "state" surrounded by an ocean of hostile patriarchs. External circumstances pulled us apart as much as we ourselves did. Most of us brokered with the outside world for menial part-time jobs to keep us alive. The clash between work and the world of the collective bore down on us. The total lack of support and outright peevishness we received from our former brothers in the New Left was no help. The ill-disguised fear of heterosexual feminists proved much harder to bear than the men's behavior. We expected more of other women. At one point the so-called radical community sank so low as to try and pit Charlotte and myself against first, Black women and second, Black men at the Institute for Policy Studies. (We both worked there.) I am happy to report that that diseased tactic flopped.

When not working for money on our jobs we worked long hours on our political projects. We didn't sleep enough and we didn't eat enough. We tried to do everything at once partly because we were so pressured and partly because we hadn't learned to organize priorities. Even if we had known how to emotionally support one another we wouldn't have had the time to act on it.

Time has greater power than any of us imagine. As months and years rolled by I could begin to see our successes. We did go into uncharted territory. Women had not lived the way we did, not that I know of. We exposed the real divisions between us. Only by understanding those differences can we overcome them. We sparked women across the country with our newspaper and we barely knew it. Intellectually we clarified lesbianism as a political issue and we began the more difficult task of clarifying class. We provided an example, however flawed, of women who were serious about power. I believe we helped other women understand that dishonesty is the ethos of the patriarchal state. The Nixon years were not an aberration.

The test of our success is the collective members themselves. Coletta Reid went to work at Diana Press, which published and printed [the book from which this essay is taken]. Nancy Myron worked there for 1½ years, before becoming art director for a D.C. firm. Ginny Berson and Jennifer Woodul along with women not in the collective founded Olivia Records. Helaine Harris and Lee Schwing started Women in Distribution. Joan Biren started a feminist filmmaking and distribution company, Moonforce Media. Sharon Deevey wrote a book called *Stat Magic* and participated in the prolonged *Washington Post* strike. Tasha Petersen and Susan Hathaway moved to North Carolina and I haven't heard from them since. Charlotte remains a Fellow at the Institute for Policy Studies and helped to guide *Quest* magazine, which she and I founded with others. She is writing her long awaited political book this year.* Kara is with her mother, Coletta. I don't know where Michelle or Cassidy are or Michelle's cat, Charly. As I write this, Baby Jesus languidly throws the completed pages on the floor because she likes to hear them rustle. Frip, one year younger, resembles a hairy hippopotamus and is happiest when eating. I wrote, so far, two novels, two books of poetry, and I'm working on another novel. I helped set up Sagaris College in 1973 then left the administration. The school did open in 1975 and I suppose it did some good but it wasn't the school I had envisioned.

The Furies taught me I have two talents, organizing and writing. Given the state of feminism I am in no danger of exercising the former. Goethe observed that the Germans would rather tolerate injustice than disorder. Feminists are able to tolerate both injustice and disorder. Our movement is still so far from political seriousness that we don't pay our workers a decent wage or compensate in some fashion. We devalue

---

*Bunch is the editor of seven books and author of *Passionate Politics: Essays, 1968–1986* (New York: St. Martin's Press, 1987). *Ed.*

women's labor to the point where we expect women to work cheap or free as in Lady Bountiful. We will only succeed politically when we build structures to keep our workers alive and when we create an organization to encompass the issues which are responses to oppression. We must go one step further and develop a plan of action so we act out upon our political enemies rather than constantly reacting to our political enemies.

So that leaves me writing. Sometimes I feel as though I'm staving off disaster with a typewriter. I'm still not rich. In fact, I make less yearly than a white man who did not graduate from high school, and I have my Ph.D. Women oppression is alive and well. I'm not the only one.

Most importantly, I am no longer tied to feminism by merely conviction or ideology. I am bound by a knot I tied over time with other women. In this circle of flesh I keep fighting not because I'm brave and certainly not because I'm saintly. I fight because I am not alone and I will never be alone again. We might hurt each other, we might feel politically out on a limb sometimes but we are no longer alone. There are too many of us and we've come too far to ever turn back.

My sisters get little glory. A few enjoy or endure fame but most of them labor under the shadow of creeping poverty and without much encouragement. Over the years I've met thousands of these women. Each one is a miracle. There are thousands more I have yet to meet. But whether I know you or whether I don't, you all keep me alive and I hope that in some way I keep you alive, too.

9

Sisterhood and Friendship as Feminist Models

María C. Lugones in collaboration with Pat Alake Rosezelle

"Sister" within a White Feminist Context, "Hermana," "Compañera"
María Lugones

Sisterhood and friendship have been proposed by feminists as *the* relationships that women need to foster or recognize among ourselves if our liberation from sexist oppression is to end. Sisterhood is thought of sometimes in feminist discourse as a metaphorical ideal and sometimes as a metaphor for the reality of relationships among women. In thinking of sisterhood as a metaphorical model, white feminists have not rethought or reconstructed the concept of sisterhood. They adopted it "as is" and extended it metaphorically to the relations among all women, not just to biological sisters. In contrast, friendship has only been thought of as a feminist ideal, not as a concept that captures actual relations among women. But when friendship, both as a concept and a relationship among women, is presented in feminist discourse it is not friendship "as is" that is being considered. Rather friendship is presented as the *product* of feminist theory and practice, both by white feminists and feminists of color.[1]

I begin this essay by explaining why sisterhood is neither an appropri-

Reprinted by permission of the author and the publisher from Kramarae, C., and Spender, D., *The Knowledge Explosion* (New York: Teachers College Press, © 1992 by Teachers College, Columbia University. All rights reserved), 406–12.

ate metaphor for the existing relations among women nor an appropriate ideal for those relations when put forth by white feminists. But we cannot narrow the investigation just to a white feminist context. The possibility of cross-cultural and cross-racial bonding depends on cross-cultural and cross-racial investigation. Thus I will also explain the meaning of "hermana" among Latinos and Latinas and contrast "hermana" and "compañera." In the next section, Pat Rosezelle will comment on the use of "sister" in the Black community. In the last section I will examine the concept of friendship and recommend a particular understanding of friendship, pluralist friendship, as a very demanding feminist ideal. Alongside this demanding ideal, I will recommend compañerismo as providing the conceptual model that will carry us through the reconstruction of ourselves towards pluralist friendship.

Sister

Sisterhood, the metaphor of kin, is about egalitarian kinship bonding. Kinship bonding itself is a kind of resilient and "unconditional"[2] bond that may, but need not, be accompanied by deep appreciation and respect. Unlike some other kinship relations, sisterhood distinguishes itself by being an egalitarian relation between women.

So understood, sisterhood is an odd model for white/Anglo-American women to adopt as the relationship to recognize or create among white/Anglo women. An odd model for several reasons. First, the white/Anglo-American family has not been known to contemporary white/Anglo feminists as an extended kinship network of support, but as a troubled and unstable relation among a few individuals. Second, the Anglo-American family has been severely scrutinized and criticized by white/Anglo feminists as an oppressive institution. Whether there are any salvageable aspects of the institution is also a matter of feminist concern. But I have not seen any analysis or defense of sisterhood in this light. That is, I have not seen any analysis or defense that places sisterhood as a relationship which is very much a part of the white/Anglo family and thus includes in the analysis the critique of the contemporary white nuclear family in the United States. Or is it that white feminists are not thinking of the white/Anglo family when proposing sisterhood as a metaphor for either the existing or ideal relationship among women?

As we will see in the next section, Pat Rosezelle understands the use of "sister" by white women as unrelated to the American white nuclear family. She sees this use as related to the Black use of "sister" which white women learned about during the Civil Rights movement. Pat's text makes even clearer the need for an analysis and defense of the use of the term "sister" by white women.

Sisterhood is not a good model to describe the *reality* of the relationship between white women and women of color in the United States given that sisterhood is an egalitarian relationship and the relationship between white/Anglo women and women of color is far from being an egalitarian one.

Sisterhood is also not a good model for white feminists to propose in describing the *ideal* relation between white women and women of color given the theory and practice of white feminism. The theory and practice of white/Anglo feminism have not succeeded in including egalitarianism across differences. Rather, they have tended to ignore differences. Sameness, not equality, has been stressed, through the exercise of what Elizabeth Spelman (1988) calls "boomerang perception": "I look at you and come right back to myself. In the United States white children like me got early training in boomerang perception when we were told by well-meaning white adults that Black people were just like us — never, however, that we were just like Blacks." Thus, white feminists are not theoretically or practically in a good position vis-à-vis women of color to propose sisterhood as a model for our relationships.

If we are to take the model seriously, then the "unconditionality" of sisterhood begins to be problematic because it is potentially burdensome to women of color. We are to stand by as sisters, no matter what, when a bond is being pressed that is conceptually but not practically inconsistent with our erasure. If the bond is unconditional, it is to be upheld even when the relationship is not egalitarian, caring, affirming. It is to be upheld even when the relationship is destructive, denying. So, though sisterhood is supposed to be egalitarian and thus conceptually inconsistent with the erasure of some of the parties to the relation, nonegalitarian practice presses the unconditional clause into service. And our erasure is precisely what we witness in most white feminist theory and practice. So, there is a significant tension between the egalitarian and the unconditional sides of sisterhood. A bond that is unconditional is not broken because the relation has ceased to be or has not yet become egalitarian. This tension creates an ambiguity when the relationship is posed as an ideal by white women without a clear inclusion of difference in their theorizing. Given the theory and practice of white feminism, women of color have every reason to believe that we are both being presented with

a true egalitarian ideal and being put in a position to honor this unconditional bond while white women are "messing up" with racism.

Hermana, Compañera

The term "hermana" (sister) is not used politically among Latinas.
The term "hermana" like the term "hermano" bear the mark of the
commitment to aid one's siblings through life in Latino extended families. It is used metaphorically in times of crisis when one wants to offer a
deep sort of empathy, sympathy and practical support. At such times one
embraces a woman and says, meaningfully, "hermana." This can be done
only by siblings and by solid, responsible, close friends. It is a litmus test
of the trueness of a close relation. It feels fake otherwise. And, of course,
there is a breach in the lack of authenticity.

The term that is used among Latinos for the sort of relation that
consists of joining forces and efforts and imagination in common political struggles is "compañera." "Compañera" does not require the depth
of emotional attachment, empathetic and sympathetic communication
that "hermana" and "amiga" (friend) require.

"Compañera" connotes egalitarianism, but the egalitarianism is one
of companionship and participation in common political struggle. The
personal is very political in this concept. The term is also used for
companionship through life, but the political tone is always there. This
extension of the term "compañera" or "compañero" to personal intimate relationships is derivative from the political use and is itself political. The relation for which it is used must be experimental and must, if
the term is to be used appropriately, stand *in contrast to* the traditional
burgeois husband-wife relation and in contrast with the traditional man-
mistress relation.

"Compañera" can be and is used within hierarchies. You can call
someone higher up in a political organization "compañera," although
there is some tension there. The term is most at home in an egalitarian
political companionship where everyone shares the rights and burdens
of political struggle. So, I am counting egalitarianism as parts of its
meaning.

It is very important that the term does not connote unconditional
bonding. The struggle is that about which the parties to the relationship
are companions. So, if someone ceases to be involved or interested in or
betrays the struggle, the relationship is at an end with respect to that
person.

I have argued so far that sisterhood is not a good model for the actual or ideal relationship among white/Anglo women or among white/Anglo women and women of color. Pat Rosezelle adds further reasons for this claim.

As Pat Rosezelle indicates below, the term "sister" has a very different and well-anchored history among Black Americans. When Black feminists use the term in the expression "Third World sisters" they are extending to all women of color a different metaphor than the one used by white feminists, a metaphor that is charged with the history of political use of the terms "brother" and "sister" in the Black community.

"Sister"
Pat Alake Rosezelle

"Sister," "my Sister," "Sister-love," "the sister," "Sister-friend," "a Sister," "Sister outsider." Terms of endearment, a name as title/authority, a greeting as acknowledgment of being and respect. "Sister," the word as conveyer. "Sister." Two syllables that have the ability to instantly establish a sense of community, status, and affection. "Sister," a people's history, struggles, victories and power. "Sister," a sense of familial tie where there is no blood, women trusting, celebrating, loving and being bound to other women. All this and more is the legacy of "Sister" in the African-American community.

The slave experience is the beginning of "sister" and "brother." When a people are bastardized, raped, and fragmented from their families, they have to create family. Then it is a political act to call those who are not your blood, but who are your people "brother" and "sister." It is a political act to call "brother" and "sister" the very people who are given no respect out of racism and out of racism are called by names you would call children or by service names. In a society where whites call Black men and women "uncle" or "aunt" instead of "Mr." or "Mrs.," it is a political act for Blacks to call each other "brother" or "sister." It is a political act of saying "I am connected to you." When I think of Black women who gave birth at the same time that a white mistress was giving birth and they had to nurse a white child and sometimes watch their own children die of starvation and I think that they then would be called "auntie," I see that name as the epitome of a vile insult. In this context, "brother" and "sister" become a way of redeeming, of respect, of resistance.

The church is the other way that "brother" and "sister" get used. I think there is a connection. There is a cross fertilization between the resistant slave and how "sister" and "brother" are used in the church, in the conscious church as opposed to the colluding church. "Brother" and "sister" become respect as someone of authority, someone who is an elder, someone who has something to give. In a lot of ways, "brother" and "sister" are code for what "Mr." and "Mrs." are in the larger society.

And then "sister" takes on another meaning, which separates it from "brother." "Sister" as saying respect for this female, not buying into the racism that says that she is loose, lewd or promiscuous because she has been raped in a rape that as a slave she had no control over. And so, "sister" is maintained in a way that even when Black men are not called "brothers," a Black man will show his respect by saying to this strange female that he is just meeting, "sister." This is all part of Black community.

In *Personal Politics,* Sara Evans made a wonderful political decision as a feminist. She decided that she couldn't talk about white feminism in this country without talking about white women in the Civil Rights movement and the problems: women with white skin privilege reclaiming themselves as females and at the same time being in the contradiction of being abusive of their racist privilege. Where else can a white woman go in the late 1960s and receive the kind of respect and support that white women got in the Civil Rights movement because she was an ally in a brutally dangerous situation? But at the same time all the issues around Black men and sexism were there.

White women shared this experience with the Black community, an experience that was very freeing spiritually as well as politically for them. They began to try and use the language of this experience. But when they would call "sister" to Black women, Black women were angry because there was also the issue of these white women with Black men. The issue was whether when you reach out to me and call me "sister," you are reaching to me or reaching past me to my Black man.

When white women left the movement or were expelled — because both things happened — they felt politically and spiritually encompassed in this community of resistance. That meant that when they moved on to begin to organize other white women around issues of sexism, sisterhood was the only experience they had, not alien, away from the white male. It was the only model they had of what the community looked like, people resisting and fighting. And so they took it. I don't believe that they took it as thieves. I believe they took it to try and connect. But at the same time there was something oppressive. In fighting sexism white women only dealt with what was like them.[3]

When Sara Evans writes, it is clear that the connection she took from the Civil Rights movement is sisterhood. But that connection becomes lost in the history of the women's movement. The movement develops a racism all its own and white women don't even know that the root of their white feminism comes out of the Civil Rights movement. And so "sisterhood" has no meaning into the second generation of white women who were not part of the Civil Rights movement. Those women who were involved were taking with them the one thing that made sense as resistance against the white male structure.

So, "sisterhood," a term that arose out of resistance to enslavement and racism, comes to be used by white women as a way of resisting the white male domination. White women learned from the Black community to use the term in resistance of white male domination, but they did not unlearn their racism and so they came to misuse the term. White women forgot what they learned and began using the term "sister" as if all women were alike; they began to erase Black women. White women came to embrace the racism that they were fighting when they learned to call each other "sister."

Pluralist Friendship
María Lugones

There has been little political use of the term "friend" and not much theoretical examination of the concept in the history of thought, feminist or otherwise. I find friendship interesting in the building of a feminist ethos because I am interested in bonding among women across differences. Friendship is a kind of practical love that commits one to perceptual changes in the knowledge of other persons. The commitment is there because understanding the other is central to the possibility of loving the other person practically. Practical love is an emotion that involves a commitment to make decisions or act in ways that take the well-being of the other person into account. Because I think a commitment to perceptual changes is central to the possibility of bonding across differences and the commitment is part of friendship, I think that friendship is a good concept to start the radical theoretical and practical reconstruction of the relations among women.

Unlike "sister," which presupposes the institution of the family and takes as a model a particular relation within the institution of the family, friendship is not an institutional relationship. It does not have any legal or other institutional components. Friendship is not a normal relation.

There are no rules specifying the duties and rights of friends. Rather, in friendship, one is guided by a concern for the friend in her particularity. This is an aspect of friendship that cannot be up for reconstruction without losing the concept, as one would lose the concept of sisterhood if one were to think it *apart* from family. But there is a lot of room for making feminist sense of the meaning of the well-being of the friend in all her particularity.

We cannot propose unconditional love among women as a model at a time when there is so much abuse among women across class and racial lines. Unconditionality is not necessarily a good thing. This is another reason for the adoption of friendship as a feminist ideal: the bond of friendship is not unconditional. In friendship there are failures of friendship that would terminate the relation. Friendship is practical and wholly individuated love that is not unconditional. Friendship as a political vision points to a very different understanding of human organization *because* the particularities of each person are so important, the love is wholly individuated. That is why it is an anarchist ideal.

In the remaining paragraphs, I will add to the concept of friendship an element that is the result of my understanding of the varied realities, worlds, of women. The element is plurality. Not all of the worlds we inhabit construct us as oppressed and one does not find white/Anglo values, norms, and institutions as dominant in all of them. If reality is complex, plural, then our bonding must honor this plurality. If our bonding misses the complexity of reality, then it will necessarily erase some of us. It will only be the illusion of bonding as it will be among women given some construction of them that falsifies them. To put it another way: if you remake me in your image, then the bonding between us is not really between us but between you and your double. You confuse me with your double and that confusion erases and harms me. White women have tended to engage in this falsification and denial *because* racism demands a simplification of reality. White women have tended to remake women of color in their own image. Racism demands that the world as told by whites be all there is to the world. (Think of Adrienne Rich's 1979 account of white solipsism.)

So, if there is more than one way of understanding reality or more than one reality,[4] and friendship is significantly constituted by understanding of the other — friendship, that is, is not love that misses the point — then friendship must embrace this plurality. Pluralist friendship must carry with it a commitment to an understanding of the realities of the friend. One needs to understand the logic of these different realities. In becoming conversant with these realities one comes to see oneself as constructed in that reality in ways different from the ways one is constructed in the reality one started from (see María Lugones, 1991). Thus pluralist friendship enhances self-knowledge.

Because I do think that reality and our selves in it are plural (María Lugones, in press), I describe a friendship that takes plurality into account. I think that different positions in the racist, ethnocentric state define different realities with their own logic and their own semantics. We also exist in the worlds of those who are differently positioned than ourselves in the racist, ethnocentric state. Thus, each one of us is many selves. Pluralist friendship is a kind of practical love that includes a multivocal communication, a dialogue among multiple selves. A dialogue among people who are fluent in the ways of their own position in the racist and ethnocentric state and in the ways of people who are differently positioned than themselves.

Friendship across positions of inequality has to be worked for rather than discovered or found. One needs to shift the focus of one's attention in ways that are epistemically very demanding. The shift in focus requires a dislodging of the centrality of one's position in the racist, ethnocentric, capitalist, patriarchal state in one's own self-concept. This entails a profound transformation of one's self.

As we have seen this is a very ambitious ideal, a political relation. One of its difficulties lies in its depending on understanding the subtleties of racism in ways that many white/Anglo women may not. In this regard, women of color have an epistemic advantage, they have access to knowledge that white/Anglo women lack.[5] From this epistemic advantage, we can posit feminist pluralism. White women can justify their adoption of this ideal through their acceptance of our epistemic privilege. But such acceptance cannot be very helpful as a guide in their relations to women of color. Rather white/Anglo women need to come to understand our varied realities.

Though pluralist friendship is part of my vision of feminist community, I think we are very far from this ideal. We are very far apart *epistemically*, in a way that makes the ideal hard to grasp for white/Anglo women. I don't think this ideal can carry us through the destruction of the capitalist, patriarchal, racist, ethnocentric state. Therefore, I suggest the term "compañera" for the political relation that can carry women through the destruction of racism and racist ethnocentrism.

Notes

1. Sisterhood is a frequent metaphor in feminist discourse. So, here I am not just referring to the use of "sisterhood" in the literature of the movement. Even though Robin Morgan's *Sisterhood Is Powerful* (1970) was an early work, the use of sisterhood is still common in feminist discussions. "Friendship" is less used. It is used most often in lesbian and/or anarchist feminism. See, for example, Janice Raymond's *A Passion for Friends* (1986) and María Lugones and Elizabeth Spelman's "Have we got a theory for you!" (1983).

2. The "unconditionality" of the bond has very unclear limits. Gays and lesbians are a common and interesting example of the limits of kinship as people who often find themselves without kin, disowned.

3. This again reminds us of "boomerang perception" and its power. As Bernice Johnson Reagon (1983) says, "You don't really want Black folks, you are just looking for yourself with a little color to it."

4. Think here of bell hooks's *Feminist Theory: From Margin to Center* (1984), where margin and center are either two realities or two aspects of one reality known only to people of color and proletarians. The white bourgeoisie only knows the center. Think also of Nancy Hartsock's (1983) two levels of reality, both of which are real: the reality of the managers, capitalists, patriarchs and the reality of women — proletarians. Think also of my own "worlds" in "Playfulness, 'world'-traveling, and loving perception" (1987).

5. There is quite a bit of work that attributes epistemic privilege to women of color. Uma Narayan's "Working together across difference" (1988), bell hooks's *Feminist Theory: From Margin to Center* (1984), and Alison Jaggar's *Feminist Politics and Human Nature* (1983) are examples.

References

Evans, Sara. 1979. *Personal Politics: The Roots of Women's Liberation in the Civil Rights Movement and the New Left.* New York: Knopf.

hooks, bell. 1984. *Feminist Theory: From Margin to Center.* Boston: South End Press.

Hartsock, Nancy. 1983. The feminist standpoint: Developing the ground for a specifically feminist historical materialism. In Sandra Harding and Merrill Hintikka, eds., *Discovering Reality: Feminist Perspectives on Epistemology, Metaphysics, Methodology, and Philosophy of Science.* New York: Dordrecht & Reidel.

Jaggar, Alison. 1983. *Feminist Politics and Human Nature.* Totowa, N.J.: Rowman & Allanheld.

Lugones, María. 1987. Playfulness, "world"-traveling, and loving perception. *Hypatia* 2(2): 3–19.

Lugones, María. 1991. On the logic of pluralist feminism. In Claudia Card, ed., *Feminist Ethics*. Lawrence: University Press of Kansas.

———. In press. *Pilgrimages/Peregrinajes: Essays in Pluralist Feminism*. Albany, N.Y.: State University of New York Press.

Lugones, María, and Elizabeth Spelman. 1983. Have we got a theory for you! *Hypatia* 1 [special issue], *Women's Studies International Forum* 6, 573–81.

Morgan, Robin. 1970. *Sisterhood Is Powerful: An Anthology of Writings from the Women's Liberation Movement*. New York: Random House.

Narayan, Uma. 1988, Summer. Working together across difference. *Hypatia* 3(2).

Raymond, Janice. 1986. *A Passion for Friends*. Boston: Beacon Press.

Reagon, Bernice Johnson. 1983. Coalition politics: Turning the century. In Barbara Smith (ed.), *Home Girls: A Black Feminist Anthology*. New York: Kitchen Table/Women of Color Press.

Rich, Adrienne. 1979. Disloyal to civilization. In *On Lies, Secrets, and Silence*. New York: W. W. Norton.

Spelman, Elizabeth. 1988. *Inessential Woman*. Boston: Beacon Press.

10

Breathing Life into Ourselves

The Evolution of the National Black Women's Health Project

Byllye Y. Avery

I got involved in women's health in the 1970s around the issue of abortion. There were three of us at the University of Florida, in Gainesville, who just seemed to get picked out by women who needed abortions. They came to us. I didn't know anything about abortions. In my life that word couldn't even be mentioned without having somebody look at you crazy. Then someone's talking to me about abortion. It seemed unreal. But as more women came (and at first they were mostly white women), we found out this New York number we could give them, and they could catch a plane and go there for their abortions. But then a black woman came and we gave her the number, and she looked at us in awe: "I can't get to New York. . . ." We realized we needed a different plan of action, so in May 1974 we opened up the Gainesville Women's Health Center.

As we learned more about abortions and gynecological care, we immediately started to look at birth, and to realize that we are women with a total reproductive cycle. We might have to make different decisions about our lives, but whatever the decision, we deserved the best services available. So, in 1978, we opened up Birthplace, an alternative birthing center. It was exhilarating work; I assisted in probably around two hundred births. I understood life, and working in birth, I understood

Reprinted from *The Black Women's Health Book*, ed. Evelyn C. White (Seattle: Seal Pr.-Feminist, 1990), by permission of the author.

death, too. I certainly learned what's missing in prenatal care and why so many of our babies die.

Through my work at Birthplace, I learned the importance of being involved in our own health. We have to create environments that say "yes." Birthplace was a wonderful space. It was a big, old turn-of-the-century house that we decorated with antiques. We went to people's houses and, if we liked something, we begged for it — things off their walls, furniture, rugs. We fixed the place so that when women walked in, they would say, "Byllye, I was excited when I got up today because this was my day to come to Birthplace." That's how prenatal care needs to be given — so that people are excited when they come. It's about eight and a half or nine months that a woman comes on a continuous basis. That is the time to start affecting her life so that she can start making meaningful lifestyle changes. So you see, health provides us with all sorts of opportunities for empowerment.

Through Birthplace, I came to understand the importance of our attitudes about birthing. Many women don't get the exquisite care they deserve. They go to these large facilities, and they don't understand the importance of prenatal care. They ask, "Why is it so important for me to get in here and go through all this hassle?" We have to work around that.

Through the work of Birthplace, we have created a prenatal caring program that provides each woman who comes for care with a support group. She enters the group when she arrives, leaves the group to go for her physical checkup, and then returns to the group when she is finished. She doesn't sit in a waiting room for two hours. Most of these women have nobody to talk to. No one listens to them; no one helps them plan. They're asking: "Who's going to get me to the hospital if I go into labor in the middle of the night, or the middle of the day, for that matter? Who's going to help me get out of this abusive relationship? Who's going to make sure I have the food I need to eat?" Infant mortality is not a medical problem; it's a social problem.

One of the things that black women have started talking about regarding infant mortality is that many of us are like empty wells; we give a lot, but we don't get much back. We're asked to be strong. I have said, "If one more person says to me that black women are strong I'm going to scream in their face." I am so tired of that stuff. What are you going to do — just lay down and die? We have to do what's necessary to survive. It's just a part of living. But most of us are empty wells that never really get replenished. Most of us are dead inside. We are walking around dead.

That's why we end up in relationships that reinforce that particular thought. So you're talking about a baby being alive inside of a dead person; it just won't work.

We need to stop letting doctors get away with piling up all this money, buying all these little machines. They can keep the tiniest little piece of protoplasm alive, and then it goes home and dies. All this foolishness with putting all this money back into their pockets on that end of the care and not on the other end has to stop. When are we going to wake up?

The National Black Women's Health Project

I left the birthing center around 1980 or '81, mostly because we needed more midwives and I wasn't willing to go to nursing school. But an important thing had happened for me in 1979. I began looking at myself as a black woman. Before that I had been looking at myself as a woman. When I left the birthing center, I went to work in a Comprehensive Employment Training Program (CETA) job at a community college and it brought me face-to-face with my sisters and face-to-face with myself. Just by the nature of the program and the population that I worked with, I had, for the first time in my life, a chance to ask a nineteen-year-old why — please give me the reason why — you have four babies and you're only nineteen years old. And I was able to listen, and bring these sisters together to talk about their lives. It was there that I started to understand the lives of black women and to realize that we live in a conspiracy of silence. It was hearing these women's stories that led me to start conceptualizing the National Black Women's Health Project.

First I wanted to do an hour-long presentation on black women's health issues, so I started doing research. I got all the books, and I was shocked at what I saw. I was angry — angry that the people who wrote these books didn't put it into a format that made sense to us, angry that nobody was saying anything to black women or to black men. I was so angry I threw one book across the room and it stayed there for three or four days, because I knew I had just seen the tip of the iceberg, but I also knew enough to know that I couldn't go back. I had opened my eyes, and I had to go on and look.

Instead of an hour-long presentation we had a conference. It didn't happen until 1983, but when it did, 2,000 women came. But I knew we couldn't just have a conference. From the health statistics I saw, I knew that there was a deeper problem. People needed to be able to work individually, and on a daily basis. So we got the idea of self-help groups. The first group we formed was in a rural area outside of Gainesville, with twenty-one women who were severely obese. I thought, "Oh this is a piece of cake. Obviously these sisters don't have any information. I'll go in there and talk to them about losing weight, talk to them about high blood pressure, talk to them about diabetes — it'll be easy."

Little did I know that when I got there, they would be able to tell me everything that went into a 1200-calorie-a-day diet. They all had been to Weight Watchers at least five or six times; they all had blood-pressure-reading machines in their homes as well as medications they were on. And when we sat down to talk, they said, "We know all that information, but what we also know is that living in the world that we are in, we feel like we are absolutely nothing." One woman said to me, "I work for General Electric making batteries, and, from the stuff they suit me up in, I know it's killing me." She said, "My home life is not working. My old man is an alcoholic. My kids got babies. Things are not well with me. And the one thing I know I can do when I come home is cook me a pot of food and sit down in front of the TV and eat it. And you can't take that away from me until you're ready to give me something in its place."

So that made me start to think that there was some other piece to this health puzzle that had been missing, that it's not just about giving information; people need something else. We just spent a lot of time talking. And while we were talking, we were planning the 1983 conference, so I took the information back to the planning committee. Lillie Allen (a trainer who works with NBWHP) was there. We worked with her to understand that we are dying inside. That unless we are able to go inside of ourselves and touch and breathe fire, breathe life into ourselves, that, of course, we couldn't be healthy. Lillie started working on a workshop that we named "Black and Female: What is the Reality?" This is a workshop that terrifies us all. And we are also terrified not to have it, because the conspiracy of silence is killing us.

Stopping Violence

As we started to talk, I looked at those health statistics in a new way. Now, I'm not saying that we are not suffering from the things we die from — that's what the statistics give us. But what causes all this sickness? Like cardiovascular disease — it's the number one killer. What causes all that heart pain? When sisters take their shoes off and start talking about what's happening, the first thing we cry about is violence. The violence in our lives. And if you look in statistics books, they mention violence in one paragraph. They don't even give numbers, because they can't count it: the violence is too pervasive.

The number one issue for most of our sisters is violence — battering, sexual abuse. Same thing for their daughters, whether they are twelve or four. We have to look at how violence is used, how violence and sexism go hand in hand, and how it affects the sexual response of females. We have to stop it, because violence is the training ground for us.

When you talk to young people about being pregnant, you find out a lot of things. Number one is that most of these girls did not get pregnant by teenage boys; most of them got pregnant by their mother's boyfriends or their brothers or their daddies. We've been sitting on that. We can't just tell our daughters, "just say no." What do they do about all those feelings running around their bodies? And we need to talk to our brothers. We need to tell them, the incest makes us crazy. It's something that stays on our minds all the time. We need the men to know that. And they need to know that when they hurt us, they hurt themselves. Because we are their mothers, their sisters, their wives; we are their allies on this planet. They can't just damage one part of it without damaging themselves. We need men to stop giving consent, by their silence, to rape, to sexual abuse, to violence. You need to talk to your boyfriends, your husbands, your sons, whatever males you have around you — talk to them about talking to other men. When they are sitting around womanizing, talking bad about women, make sure you have somebody stand up and be your ally and help stop this. For future generations, this has got to stop somewhere.

Mothers and Daughters

If violence is the number one thing women talk about, the next is being mothers too early and too long. We've developed a documentary called "On Becoming a Woman: Mothers and Daughters Talking Together." It's eight mothers and eight daughters — sixteen ordinary people talking about extraordinary things.

The idea of the film came out of my own experience with my daughter. When Sonja turned eleven, I started bemoaning that there were no rituals left; there was nothing to let a girl know that once you get your period your life can totally change, nothing to celebrate that something wonderful is happening. So I got a cake that said, "Happy Birthday! Happy Menstruation!" It had white icing with red writing. I talked about the importance of becoming a woman, and, out of that, I developed a workshop for mothers and daughters for the public schools. I did the workshops in Gainesville, and, when we came to Atlanta, I started doing them there. The film took ten years, from the first glimmer of an idea to completion.

The film is in three parts. In the first part all the mothers talk about when we got our periods. Then the daughters who have their periods talk about getting theirs, and the ones who are still waiting talk about that. The second part of the film deals with contraception, birth control, anatomy and physiology. This part of the film is animated, so it keeps the kids' attention. It's funny. It shows all the anxiety: passing around condoms, hating it, saying, "Oh no, we don't want to do this."

The third part of the film is the hardest. We worked on communication with the mothers and daughters. We feel that the key to birth control and to controlling reproduction is the nature of the relationship between the parents and their young people. And what's happening is that everybody is willing to beat up on the young kids, asking, "Why did you get pregnant? Why did you do this?" No one is saying to the parents, "Do you need some help with learning how to talk to your young person? Do you want someone to sit with you? Do you want to see what it feels like?" We don't have all the answers. In this film, you see us struggling.

What we created, which was hard for the parents, is a safe space where everybody can say anything they need to say. And if you think about that, as parents, we have that relationship with our kids: we can ask them anything. But when we talk about sex, it's special to be in a space where the kids can ask *us,* "Mama, what do you do when you start feeling funny all in your body?" What the kids want to know is, what about lust? What do we do about it? And that's the very information that we don't want to give up. That's "our business." But they want to hear it from us, because they can trust us. And we have to struggle with how we do that: How do we share that information? How do we deal with our feelings?

Realizing the Dream

The National Black Women's Health Project has ninety-six self-help groups in twenty-two states, six groups in Kenya, and a group in Barbados and in Belize. In addition, we were just funded by the W. K. Kellogg Foundation to do some work in three housing projects in Atlanta. We received $1,032,000 for a three-year period to set up three community centers. Our plan is to do health screening and referral for adolescents and women, and in addition to hook them up with whatever social services they need — to help cut through the red tape. There will be computerized learning programs and individualized tutorial programs to help young women get their General Equivalency Degrees (GED), along with a panel from the community who will be working on job readiness skills. And we'll be doing our self-help groups — talking about who we are, examining, looking at ourselves.

We hope this will be a model program that can be duplicated anywhere. And we're excited about it. Folks in Atlanta thought it was a big deal for a group of black women to get a million dollars. We thought it was pretty good, too. Our time is coming.

11

Lesbian Community

Heterodox Congregation

Marilyn Frye

(On Saturday, April 29, 1989, at the Mountainmoving Coffeehouse in Chicago, I was a member of a panel of nine lesbians who had contributed to the new anthology *For Lesbians Only,* a collection of lesbian separatist writings.[1] Each of us did a reading or made a short presentation. This is the statement I composed and read for the occasion.)

I live in Lansing, Michigan. I have lived there for almost fifteen years. There's a lesbian community there which I, along with many others, have worked to create, grow, and maintain. This community has been shaped in many ways by lesbians who are separatist — though being separatist does not mean the same thing to all of us. I'm proud of the lesbian community in the town I live in. I move in that community with a strong and satisfying sense of shared accomplishments. I want to talk a bit about that community tonight.

Two things have happened recently in my community that have generated a lot of feeling and a lot of talk. The two things weren't causally connected with each other; they just happened to happen close to each other. About a week ago, a lesbian in my town committed suicide. She did it decisively and deliberately. The other thing is that Sarah Hoag-

Reprinted from *Willful Virgin: Essays in Feminism, 1976–1992,* by Marilyn Frye (Freedom, Calif.: Crossing Press, 1992), 12–23, by kind permission of the author. First published, under the title "The Possibility of Lesbian Community," in *Lesbian Ethics* 4 (Spring 1990): 84–87. © 1990 by Marilyn Frye.

land's recent presentation in Lansing triggered open conflict about the value of twelve-step programs to individual dykes and as an influence in the community. Both of these things, the suicide and the conflict, focused my attention on lesbian community — what it is, how it works, what kind of glue holds it together.

Probably the most obvious thing about what makes this community a community is that it is *not* that we agree on everything. There is, in fact, much disagreement on practically everything. Here's a list of some things there is *not* agreement on in my community:

- we do not agree on the importance of recycling jars and paper, or on whether it's OK to have christmas trees;
- we do not agree about what the priority is on working against U.S. imperialism in Central America or on working against nuclear power and nuclear weapons, or on working for legal and available abortions;
- we do not agree on whether the practice of friendship requires remaining supportive, or even civil, to lesbians who go straight, or requires active support of lesbians who have male babies;
- we all say that we are against racism, but we do not agree at all about what it is or what to do about it;
- we don't agree about whether it's OK to wear skirts and dresses, to shave our legs, to get permanents, to wear make-up; we don't agree about whether twelve-step programs are wholesome for dykes, or whether it's OK to practice or to purchase therapy;
- we do not agree about how much of the Lesbian Alliance's funds should be donated to the Sharon Kowalski fund, or about whether the Lesbian Alliance and the Ambitious Amazons should try to work together more;
- we don't agree about what kinds of behavior between lovers are OK and what kinds are terrible;
- we do not agree about whether there is still any such thing women's music or about whether the Olivia Caribbean cruises are absurd;
- we don't agree about how important it is to have events, activities, and homes accessible to wheelchair users, or about whether it's OK to drink alcohol, to go to weddings, to like your father or brother, to de-dyke your house when your parents visit, to get a hot-tub or a nice car if you can afford it, to watch tv, or to go to a male dentist;
- we do not agree about hamburgers.

And this is only a few of the things we don't all agree about in my community. I'm sure I don't even know what some of the things are that we don't agree about.

You might suppose that there is agreement among us on some other level, and I supposed it too. But the issues about 12-step programs have made me doubt it. I thought that in spite of all our differences about specific actions and practices, what held us together was something some of us have called "ethical compatibility" — some deep likeness of ethical and political intuition. I have thought something like that underlay our *lesbianism,* our *desire* for each other. But now I'm thinking that within my community there is not even a significant likeness of basic ethical and political intuition.

So what *is* there? What holds us in community? The answer seems to be either (1) nothing holds us in community, or (2) I've asked the wrong question. I opt for (2).

What I'm getting at here is that it's the natural normal thing for women to be connected and sustained in community with each other, and it has nothing in particular to do with agreeing about anything, or even liking each other. It certainly doesn't have anything in particular to do with approving of each other. Instead of looking for something like common values to account for what holds us together, we should consider whatever kept us apart or works to keep us apart . . . And this brings me to the topic of separatism.

Heteropatriarchal forms of social organization keep women apart from women, separate women from women. And that, I would say, is unnatural. I spoke at the beginning of creating and maintaining lesbian community. But when I think about the actual activities and behaviors we do, what they mostly add up to is not *building* something, but just *clearing space* for something. Almost all the organizing adds up to nothing more than making space and getting a whole bunch of lesbians in that space all at once. That is, we separate lesbians from separation from each other and then community happens. It is anarchic, often strife-ridden and stressful, not always fun, not always affirming of whatever we think about things or about ourselves, but it's also just the normal thing for women — to be in lesbian connection with each other. It doesn't have to be explained.

Now, what about the suicide? It is terribly sad and awful, and I grieve for the life that might have been. It makes everyone wonder what we could or should have done to make living tolerable, not to mention joyful, for that woman. But one of my friends (with whom I disagree about some very important things) noted that in the almost fifteen years we've known this community of many hundreds of lesbians, this is only the second suicide she knew of (only the first that I had known of). Before the current era of lesbian feminist consciousness and gay rights, suicide was epidemic among lesbians, so my older friends have told me. But it is not, among us. In the time I have known this community, we have fought and quarreled, and trashed, and bashed, and made love and made hate, had parties and played and flowed through shifting patterns of affiliation and ostracism, and had powerful feelings of solidarity and powerful feelings of alienation from each other, and put out a zillion newsletters and fliers and organized fund-raisers and gossiped, and felt great and felt terrible. And lesbians in my community have survived in large numbers.

What I'm saying is that lesbian community is possible — a community that is "separate" in the sense that there is a lesbian center of gravity (or of hilarity, perhaps), a force field, in which natural lesbian connection happens, which sustains and protects lesbians in many ways and varying degrees from the ravages of misogyny and heterosexualism, even, for some and in some ways from the violences of racism and poverty.

In my community, lesbians don't agree about anything and *lesbians survive in droves.*

Note

1. *For Lesbians Only: A Separatist Anthology,* edited by Julia Penelope and Sarah Lucia Hoagland (London: Onlywomen Press, 1988).

III

Feminist Communitarianism

12

Feminism and Communitarianism
Comparing Critiques of Liberalism

Penny A. Weiss

Why, when there is so much interest in community among feminists, is there so little interest in feminism among communitarians? In terms of their philosophical assumptions and political ideals, there exists enough common ground between feminism and communitarianism that the cool relationship between them is somewhat curious. Both emphasize context, care, and community, and both reject central features of liberalism. Yet from Plato to Sandel communitarians display, at best, an aloofness from the issues that inform feminism, and today some feminists explicitly warn against alliances with communitarians. It seems that whatever the extent to which communitarian theorists might be said to be egalitarian, inegalitarian threads also connect them — threads that, variously throughout history, define women out of certain communities, downplay the negative effects of women's domestication, exclude women in conceptions and calculations of the "common" good, refuse to address sexual differentiation and inequality as obstacles to personal and political bonds, and advocate patriarchal principles, values, and structures to guide their communities.

To understand why feminists and communitarians have not been, are not, and perhaps cannot or should not be more consistent allies, I compare the contemporary feminist and communitarian critiques of liberal-

Reprinted from *Gendered Community: Rousseau, Sex, and Politics* (New York: New York University Press, 1993): 121–48 and 172–74, by permission of the author and the publisher.

ism's conceptions of the self, social relations, and political community. Regarding each of these, I consider central aspects of: (a) how communitarians and feminists understand the liberal view, (b) what each finds problematic in it and, at least briefly, (c) what alternatives each endorses.

It is important to see precisely where (nonfeminist) communitarians diverge from (even communitarian) feminists. I argue here that contemporary communitarians fail to offer a critique of liberalism that gives voice to concerns heard in feminist critiques of liberalism, even when those feminist critiques are informed by a commitment to community. Feminists thus cannot "choose" between alignment with liberals or with communitarians, cannot choose one side of an old battle in which women's interests, at best, are secondary. Instead, we need to reconfigure the recurring debate between liberals and communitarians into one that includes what might be called communitarian feminism, or, perhaps better, the communitarian strain of numerous feminisms. For feminism challenges the terms of both liberalism and communitarianism in ways that neither does of the other.

While both communitarianism and feminism are almost astonishingly diverse in theory and practice, focusing only on their critiques of liberalism allows me to talk about each in something resembling a generic form. I treat writings by a number of feminist and communitarian thinkers without attempting systematically to analyze any particular individual, since my aim is more general. Nor does it matter whether these feminists and communitarians have perceived liberalism correctly, whatever that might mean. In fact, several writers contend that aspects of liberalism criticized by feminists and communitarians are not integral to liberalism. For the purpose of understanding where feminism and communitarianism part ways, what matters is their perceptions of liberalism and its limitations.

Not all feminists are strong communitarians. Feminist opposition to community exists, for example, among liberal feminists wary of politicizing the private out of fear of government power, among postmodern feminists wary of the fate and status of differences in a unified community, and among those feminists dissatisfied with facile glorification of "the feminine" as a model of community. Even among feminists committed to community debate is ongoing, including, for example, questions about how much feminists can or should adopt from traditional women's communities and about what practices and structures nurture both community and individuality.

The warnings issued by feminists about community (which, to avoid confusion, are distinct from warnings about feminist alliance with non-feminist communitarianism) are valid and important to address. But all feminisms, including liberal feminism, challenge aspects of classic liberalism from a position that is less individualistic and more communitarian than classical liberalism,[1] and of concern here are the grounds on which feminism does challenge liberalism. Despite the fact that there are feminist visions very much more and less informed by community, generic feminism, or "feminism unmodified," still opposes central ideas and practices of classic liberalism. Yet the critiques of liberalism by contemporary communitarians and feminists are not based upon and do not lead to similar understandings or visions of politics.

Conceptions of the Self

Understanding Liberalism

Communitarianism	Feminism
The dispute between communitarians and liberals hinges on opposing conceptions of the self. Where liberals conceive of the self as essentially unencumbered and free to choose among a wide range of alternatives, communitarians insist that the self is situated in and constituted by tradition, membership in a historically rooted community.[2]	Abstract individualism considers individual human beings as social atoms, abstracted from their social contexts, and disregards the role of social relationships and human community in constituting the very identity and nature of individual human beings.[5]
[For liberals] Individuals . . . are primary and society secondary, and the identification of individual interests is prior to, and independent of, the construction of any moral or social bonds between them.[3]	Although it would be mistaken to suggest that all liberal theorists conceive of human nature as being egoistic, most do argue that people tend naturally in this direction and must work to develop moral capacities to counter their basic selfish, acquisitive inclinations.[6]
[Liberalism's] atomism posits that as physical beings, humans are	[Abstract individualism is] the assumption that the essential human characteristics are properties

separate, integral, self-contained, unitary particles or atoms.[4]

of individuals and are given independently of any particular social context . . . [It] takes human nature as a presocial system.[7]

Both feminists and communitarians find in liberalism the notion of a presocial, solitary subject with "natural" rights. Both see as a central feature of liberalism its belief that individual interests exist before or independent of social relationships, moral bonds, a social context, or the human community. Liberalism, it is said, views individual selves as having identities apart from their ends. The liberal self is also one who can and should be free — an individual whose relations, attachments, and goals are chosen from a wide range of alternatives and are detachable, independent of the self.[8] Liberal theory starts with the individual outside of society, fully developed, in possession of "natural" rights and duties, and unable to live very well with other basically self-concerned individuals, the guidance of "natural" law notwithstanding.

To the extent that the independent self of liberalism is given content, the substance is in terms of tendencies, motivations, and capacities. The individual of liberal theory is thought, for example, to tend to be self-interested; to be motivated by profit, pleasure, and pride; and to be capable of rationality, usually equated with prudential reasoning. That toward which one moves is undetermined: what gives pleasure, what profits, and what inspires one to reason instrumentally are individual variables and not essential or social features.

While contemporary feminist and communitarian understandings of liberalism's view of the self have much in common with each other, and while it may be "a commonplace amongst communitarians, socialists and feminists that liberalism is to be rejected for its excessive 'individualism' or 'atomism' " (Kymlicka 181), their grounds for rejecting it are not identical. And this is true despite the fact that each understands the implications of their critique to undercut everything from the liberal conception of freedom as noninterference to the liberal justification of the state as fulfilling the interests of its citizens.

Critiques of the Liberal View

Communitarianism

Feminism

[For the] right to exist prior to the good it would be necessary for the

Feminist theorists argue that the vision of the atomic, "unencum-

subject to exist independently of his/her intentions and his/her ends. Such a conception requires therefore a subject who can have an identity defined prior to the values and objectives that he/she chooses. It is, in effect, the capacity to choose, not the choices that he makes, that defines such a subject. He can never have ends which are constitutive of his identity and this denies him the possibility of participation in a community where it is the very definition of who he is that is in question.[9]

[T]he peculiarly modern self, the emotivist self, in acquiring sovereignty in its own realm lost its traditional boundaries provided by a social identity and a view of human life as ordered to a given end. (MacIntyre 32)

bered self," criticized by communitarians, is a male one, since the degree of separateness and independence it postulates among individuals has never been the case for women. . . . Indeed, her individuality has been sacrificed to the "constitutive definitions" of her identity. . . . If unencumbered males have difficulties in recognizing those social relations constitutive of their ego identity, situated females often find it impossible to recognize their true selves amidst the constitutive roles that attach to their persons.[10]

[A]t each moment of our lives our every thought, value, and act — from the most mundane to the most lofty — takes its meaning and purpose from the wider political and social reality that constitutes and conditions us. (Dietz 1)

Communitarians and feminists both reject the liberal notion of an isolated self with rights, interests, values, and ends independent of a social context. They do so, however, for different reasons. I discuss three differences in the communitarian and feminist critiques of liberalism's conception of the self, looking both to describe the differences and to give some account of their origins and implications. The three differences concern sources of identity, the extent of socialization, and evaluations of traditional societies.

First, in discussing the range of social forces that influence the formation of the self, Sandel talks of the "family or community or nation or people,"[11] and MacIntyre includes families, neighborhoods, cities, guilds, professions, clans, tribes, and nations (MacIntyre 204–5). The factors left out of such accounts are often precisely the ones with which feminists are critically concerned. From a feminist perspective, most centrally affecting the formation of the self are factors such as sex, age, race, sexuality, and class. Yet about such things most nonfeminist communitarians are peculiarly hushed. Despite communitarian interest in "traditions" and "practices," their notion of social context seems to be somewhat narrowly conceived. While including certain well-defined groups and communities, it omits such traditions and practices as sexism and racism, practices that may have a larger role in forming the self and determining one's social place than do cities or neighborhoods, not least because the former are more pervasive, constant, intimate, and unconscious. Such forces as sexism and homophobia, for example, not only often create distinct communities ("the lesbian community," Boy Scouts, etc.) but also establish relations that pervade and structure all communities, including ones that seem to have nothing to do with gender, race, sexuality, or class.

According to feminists, communitarian language and theory are falsely universalized; communitarians challenge liberalism's pronouncements without noting how their accuracy varies according to the race, class, gender, or sexuality of individuals and groups. Without attention to such factors it is difficult to assess the accuracy of liberalism's descriptions. For example, communitarians fail to note that the separated self of liberalism reflects the reality of men more than women. Liberalism's portrait may also be more reflective in many Western cultures of those who are white and/or heterosexual than of those who are Black and/or homosexual, for as oppressed minorities the latter have bound together in "subcultures." In the communitarian critique there is some wavering about whether the picture of the self drawn by liberalism is descriptively accurate but normatively undesirable, or both inaccurate and undesirable (see Walzer). Such wavering may be a consequence of a misguided attempt to universalize what sexism and other forces of social domination render incapable of universalization. Liberalism's descriptions of social identity are more apt in some areas than in others, and in most areas vary according to factors ignored by communitarians.

In their critiques of liberalism's view of the self feminists not only recognize a broader range of social forces that influence identities than do communitarians, but they also find that these forces have a deeper impact than is generally acknowledged by communitarians. For example, while communitarians are most likely to consider the social nature of individual interests and ends, feminists stress how social context affects everything from individual characteristics, emotions, beliefs, capacities, and motives to human nature itself.[12] This difference may be attributed to the fact that feminists have always had to engage in debate over whether women and men have different natures. Feminists from Christine de Pizan and Harriet Taylor to Simone de Beauvoir and bell hooks have understood the differences between the sexes to be caused at least in large part by their different social experiences, their different social contexts. It would seem that one of the earliest and most consistent sources of feminist rejection of abstract individualism is the understanding of how strongly desires, physiques, interests, values, emotions, and other traits depend on a social context, and how rejection of this truth historically led to lies about the natures of the sexes, lies that were claimed to provide evidence for the naturalness and inevitability of male supremacy. Perhaps, then, the absence of this political history is what permits communitarians to see the impact of social context as both narrower and shallower than it is seen by feminists.

A third difference in the feminist and communitarian critiques of liberalism's view of the self is the standpoint from which they are leveled. As the earlier quotes show, the contrast can sometimes be stark: communitarians are concerned with the *loss* of "traditional boundaries," while feminists are concerned with the *costs* of those boundaries, especially for women. Nostalgia for communities of the past almost forces nonfeminist communitarians to gloss over or ignore those social forces and structures that have allowed and justified exclusion, oppression, and hierarchy. Feminism's defining commitment to ending oppression directs it at precisely those structures and practices communitarianism so often denies or marginalizes.

The difference in standpoints does not mean that the communitarian critique is apolitical, as evidenced by MacIntyre's concern, for example, with social decay and dislocation. But communitarian criticism often remains politically vague and abstract. It is not clear, for example, who feels dislocated and why, and who, perhaps, does not. It could be the case, for example, that the women's movement and the Black civil rights movement have raised uncomfortable questions about "place" for white men and that the emergence of such questions contributes positively to society. The vagueness of the communitarian critique tends in practice to reinforce conservative, inegalitarian politics.

Alternatives to the Liberal View

Communitarianism

Feminism

[I]t is through his or her member-ship in a variety of social groups that the individual identifies him-self or herself and is identified by

[W]hereas communitarians em-phasize the situatedness of the dis-embedded self in a network of re-lations and narratives, feminists

others. I am brother, cousin and grandson, member of this household, that village, this tribe. These are not characteristics that belong to human beings accidentally, to be stripped away in order to discover "the real me." They are part of my substance, defining partially at least and sometimes wholly my obligations and my duties. Individuals inherit a particular space within an interlocking set of social relationships; lacking that space, they are nobody, or at best a stranger or an outcast. (MacIntyre 32)

also begin with the situated self but view the *renegotiation* of our psychosexual identities, and their *autonomous reconstitution* by individuals as essential to women's and human liberation. . . . The simple identification of the subject with its social roles reinstates the very logic of identity that feminists have sought to critique in their examinations of the psychosexual constitution of gender. (Benhabib and Cornell 12–13)

As may already be clear, what communitarians prefer to liberalism is an Aristotelian understanding of the self as fundamentally political, realizing itself only in a given historical setting, a particular social context. The Aristotelian understanding views the self as embedded in and constituted by particular communal commitments and values. It sees participation in a value-defining community as giving the self a conception of right and justice. It understands that by and large the forces that constitute one's self — family, nation, etc. — are outside of one's free choosing. Finally, this view is preferred by communitarianism because of its ability to "locate" people, to give them an identity that delineates their obligations and determines the contours of their relationships, thereby providing personal and political stability, limits, and order.

Feminists do not deny that "through his or her membership in a variety of social groups . . . the individual identifies himself or herself and is identified by others." It would be most surprising, even impossible, for those with the political understanding feminists have of gender "socialization" or "conditioning" (to use terms that for some reason sound almost quaint today) to think otherwise. To say that socialization, or embeddedness, is inevitable, however, is only a modest beginning. The process of identity formation within and between cultures takes a wide range of forms that lead to distinctly different ways of living and living together. Feminists are more interested than are communitarians in understanding *how* social selves are constituted, toward what ends, and with what costs and benefits for various individuals, groups, and relations. Given the experience of gender oppression, feminists are likely to work for understandings of the self that acknowledge human interdependence, social responsibility, and an end to "gender obsession." Further, knowledge of the historical reality of social change and the present need for it tempers a possible resignation by showing that the individual can constructively gain some distance from the community, can critique and evaluate, and can work to create alternative cultures that will foster individuals with new concepts of themselves and others. Such choice and critical distance are viewed differently by feminists and communitarians because of their different evaluations of how fragile and destructive bonds are perceived as being.

The political challenge made by feminists to abstract individualism rejects the communitarian vision. Liberalism's ideal is criticized for encouraging people to think of themselves first, for fostering egoism and rewarding selfishness, and for drawing a picture of the self that is incomplete where it is not inaccurate. But the complacent communitarian reliance on "place" and inattention to the *problems* of social identity are also rejected for failing to address, and therefore to solve, the issues at the heart of feminism.

Grounded in women's experiences, feminist argument does not see the self as so unconnected as to make individual autonomy dangerous, so rapacious as to make meeting material needs an impossible means for encouraging solidarity, or so asocial as to make chosen communities untenable.

Social Relations

Understanding Liberalism

Communitarianism

[According to liberalism] the social world [is] nothing but a meeting place for individual wills, each with its own set of attitudes and preferences and who understand that world solely as an arena for

Feminism

Western liberal democratic thought has been built on the concept of the "individual" seen as a theoretically isolatable entity. This entity can assert interests, have rights, and enter into conthe achievement of their own satisfaction. (MacIntyre 24)

[T]hel liberal portrait of human nature . . . construe[s] the human essence as radically individual and solitary, as hedonistic and prudential, and as social only to the extent required by the quest for preservation and liberty in an adversary world of scarcity. (Barber 213)

[For individualists] No binding obligations and no wider social understanding justify a relationship. It exists only as the expression of the choices of the free selves who make it up. And should it no longer meet their needs, it must end.[13]

tractual relations with other entities. But this individual is not seen as related to other individuals in inextricable or intrinsic ways. This individual is assumed to be motivated primarily by a desire to pursue his own interest, though he can recognize the need to agree to contractual restraints on the ways everyone may pursue their interests.[14]

According to both feminists and communitarians, the liberal vision of interpersonal relations follows from its atomism: the boundaries of human relations are drawn by the nature of the self, understood in liberalism as competitive, privatistic, hedonistic, prudential, isolated, and self-interested. Liberal assumptions theoretically limit the potential bonds that can and should be created between people to ones that are voluntary, self-interested, instrumental, and contractual. Parties to contracts, however, like their interests, remain essentially separate. According to feminist and communitarian portraits of liberal theory, people see themselves, rightly, not primarily as members of a group with a common good and shared values, but as individuals with independent identities and separate, often opposed interests. Relationships are more akin to "mere associations" than to full-fledged communities because they are based solely on "congruent private interests" and are not capable of progressing beyond this base (Buchanan 856–57). That social world which does exist is minimal, because the individual of liberal theory does not seem to want, to need, or to be able to form deep connections with others; in fact, in a world perceived to be in a condition of scarcity, others may even be enemies, clashing in what is aptly called the social "arena."

Self-interest both forces individuals into a social setting and restricts how social that setting can be.

While there seems to be no significant difference in the communitarian and feminist understandings of the liberal view of social relationships, such harmony once again abruptly ends when they critique it. To the extent that it is true that "[t]he central issue for political theory is not the constitution of the self but the connection of constituted selves, the pattern of social relations" (Walzer 21), differences here may reflect fundamentally different political perspectives.

Critiques of the Liberal View

Communitarianism

[O]ur great modern free world is all too often a world in which men and women do not exist for others; . . . in which altruistic behavior is discouraged in the name of bargaining efficiency and utility accounting. . . . In this world, there can be no fraternal feeling, no general will, no selfless act, no mutuality, no species identity, no gift relationship, no disinterested obligation, no social empathy, no love or belief or commitment that is not wholly private. (Barber 71–72)

Liberal theory . . . deprives us of any ready access to our own experience of communal embeddedness. . . . It explains our inability to form cohesive solidarities, stable movements and parties that might make our deep convictions visible and effective in the world. (Walzer 10)

Feminism

To see contractual relations between self-interested or mutually disinterested individuals as constituting a paradigm of human relations is to take a certain historically specific conception of "economic man" as representative of humanity. And it is, many feminists are beginning to agree, to overlook or to discount in very fundamental ways the experience of women. . . . To the extent that some of our relations should be seen as contractual, we should recognize how essentially limited rather than general such relations are. (Held 113, 115)

Atomism cannot . . . represent nonpeer relationships like those of parent and child, teacher and student, or any where one person takes care of the interest of another.[15]

Communitarians find at least two things troubling in the liberal account of human relations. First, because the relations between people are portrayed as superficial, extrinsic, and utilitarian, individuals remain essentially alone, private. Altruism, fraternity [*sic*], mutuality, and empathy are discouraged, penalized, or dissolved by liberal ideology and social and economic structures, while narrowly self-interested acts are encouraged and rewarded. Consequently, "[u]nder such conditions many individuals will be incapable of achieving genuine community, either because the pressures to live the life of an autonomous chooser of ends will undermine their own attempts at commitment, or because they will be unable to rely upon the commitments of others" (Buchanan 866). The loss or absence of community, whether caused by or reflected in the philosophy of liberalism, is seen as both real and regrettable.

A second, and generally incompatible, communitarian critique of the liberal approach to human relations recognizes within liberal societies the existence and especially the validity of nonvoluntary, noncontractual relations and obligations — familial, communal, and national — and faults liberalism for inadequately accounting for them. The problem with liberalism in this reading is not the actual absence of community but the theoretical misrepresentation or neglect of concrete communal experiences. The incompleteness of liberal theory affects action and understanding, leaving people with motives too weak to protect communities, models too meager to assist efforts in creating and maintaining communities, and doubts too serious about the trustworthiness and altruism of others to support communal political activism.

The differences between the feminist and communitarian critiques here seem to be ones of emphasis and specificity. While this sounds like a relatively minor divergence, the differences, when examined, reveal very distinct political agendas.

The stress in feminist analysis is on how very few actual relations the liberal account covers, rather than on the actual lack of noncompetitive, other-concerned, interdependent relations in society. Positive relations of dependency, of care, of cooperation, and between unequals all exist but are omitted in varying ways in the liberal account, despite the fact that these are relations in which we spend most of our lives: as children or parents, teachers or students, clients or helpers, employers or employees.

This criticism, which thus far is very similar to at least one strain of the communitarian commentary, is more precise in naming what and who is left out. Feminists argue that what liberal analysis most systematically neglects are the experiences of women and children and of the private realm with which they are primarily identified. Given the earlier feminist argument that the supposedly neutral, abstract individual of liberal theory is, to the extent there is reality to the model, a (privileged) male, it follows that the social relations of liberal theory are, to the extent they reflect reality, those between men or seen from a (privileged) male perspective. "If the epitome of what it is to be human is thought to be a disposition to be a rational contractor, human persons creating other human persons through the processes of human mothering are overlooked. And human children developing human personhood are not recognized as engaged in a most obviously human activity" (Held 120). The recognition this neglect generally receives from (nonfeminist) communitarians is minimal, and thus its importance is minimized: "it is an interesting question, *not addressed here*, whether this first [Marxist] communitarian critique speaks to the experience of women: Are necessity and private interest their only bonds with one another?" (Walzer 8; emphasis added).

Further, feminists point out that this omission of women, children, and the private is an "oversight" with real costs. For example, "it is a great distortion of the [traditional] place of married women to see them as self-interested, autonomous beings competing for the satisfaction of their interests. This way of viewing them will not lead to a recognition of the real needs such women have" (Wolgast 155–56).

This feminist attention to women's lives can be connected to another point made by feminists and not found, or not emphasized, in the communitarian literature. Not only is it argued that narrowly self-interested relations should be understood as one limited variety of human experience, but liberalism's very understanding of self-interest is challenged as too restricted: "when people think about what they want, they think about more than just their narrow self-interest. When they define their own interests and when they act to pursue those interests, they often give great weight both to their moral principles and to the interests of others."[16]

There is more in the communitarian critique that feminists find deeply troubling. In considering nonvoluntary, noncontractual relations, communitarians tend to speak of "the family" as a universal, unproblematical, and undifferentiated unit and to link it with political community and nation. By lumping the familial with the political, communitarians make it too easy to assume that the two do or should serve the same ends and consist of similar relationships. Yet analogies such as these have brought particular harm to women, by providing, for example, "evidence" of the need for a (male) head of household and by turning childrearing into the task of "republican motherhood." By neglecting to differentiate the relations *within* families, communitarians render invisible power differences correlated with age and gender, as well as many of the problems to which they contribute, including the numerous forms of domestic violence. By not discussing varieties of family structures across time and from culture to culture communitarians implicitly leave the heterosexual, patriarchal family as *the* norm. The family of communitarian theory is too often that which serves male advantage. Thus, while feminists, like communitarians, do take issue with liberalism for its neglect of the family, feminists are more interested in bringing the familial experiences of women and children into the conversation, and the attention they want paid to the family is far more critical.

Alternatives to Liberalism

Communitarianism

Feminism

So to see ourselves as deontology would see us is to deprive us of those qualities of character, reflectiveness, and friendship that depend on the possibility of constitutive projects and attachments. And to see ourselves as given to commitments such as these is to admit a deeper commonality than benevolence describes, a commonality of shared self-understanding as well as "enlarged affection." As the independent self finds its limits in those aims and attachments from which it cannot stand apart, so justice finds its limits in those forms of community that engage the identity as well as the interests of the participants. (Sandel 181–82)

Instead of importing into the household principles derived from the marketplace, perhaps we should export to the wider society the relations suitable for mothering persons and children . . . relations . . . characterized by more care and concern and openness and trust and human feeling than are the contractual bargains that have developed so far in political and economic life, or even that are aspired to in contractarian prescriptions. (Held 122)

We need a model that allows for organic connections, some more fundamental than others, among people, connections of dependency and interdependency of many kinds. (Wolgast 147)

The model of interpersonal relationships preferred by feminists to that of liberalism is not unitary, but "acknowledges many kinds of relations among people, and many kinds of social roles, and other kinds of interest than self-interest. . . . competition will be only one of the relations among people where determinations of justice apply." A model such as this acknowledges the diversity of human beings and human relationships, and that alone accords it superiority over liberalism's, which, as we have seen, especially ignores traditional women, children, and the relationships in which they are involved. Women will "fit in [this new model] in a variety of ways and roles" (Wolgast 156–57) because relationships between males will not be taken as the norm at the outset, because the complexity of human connections will not be reduced to a unitary ideal, and because it will be assumed that as sexism has differentiated the lives of the sexes, women have lessons to teach about relationships.

One of the questions with which feminist political theory concerns itself is how to resolve the tension, most felt by women, between care for and obligations to others and care for and obligations to one's self. It is necessary to "envision a society that grants each of us our 'individual dignity' but does not allow us to lose sight of our connections to each other."[17] Women's roles have frequently meant obliteration and sacrifice of the self, or redefinition of one's self and self-interest predominantly in terms of and in relation to others. The communitarian solution to liberalism's impoverished social life fails, however, to solve or even seriously address this enforced self-abnegation. Because communitarians see the social problem as fragmentation, their answer is connection. They favor tradition and applaud mores, because they offer place, security, coherence, and stability. But the problem for women has not been solitude and lack of commitment, and the feminist alternative is neither simply connection nor simply separation. A feminist vision also necessarily entails critical reevaluation and restructuring of such engendered institutions and practices as the family, the sexual division of labor, and the connections between private and public. Contemporary communitarians do not see sexual differentiation as particularly problematic; in fact, it is often held up as a cure to *other* (read: important) social ills. At that point feminists and communitarians truly part ways.

Political Community

Understanding Liberalism

Communitarianism	Feminism
For liberal individualism a community is simply an arena in	[L]iberal philosophers seek to develop a political theory that is in

which individuals each pursue their own self-chosen conception of the good life, and political institutions exist to provide that degree of order which makes such self-determined activity possible. Government and law are, or ought to be, neutral between rival conceptions of the good life for man, and hence, although it is the task of government to promote law-abidingness, it is in the liberal view no part of the legitimate function of government to inculcate any one moral outlook. (MacIntyre 182)

dependent of any substantive claims about the nature of the good life or of human happiness or fulfillment. Individuals are entitled to set their own ends. . . . They see the state as the neutral arbiter of conflicting social interests, whose task is to protect individual rights and so to defend against the tyranny of any individual or group. (Jaggar 174, 200)

What liberalism professes to offer, according to communitarians and feminists, is a limited, neutral state that provides the conditions of "liberty" and "protection" in which individuals can pursue their private interests and goods as they define them. MacIntyre agrees with Ronald Dworkin that "the central doctrine of modern liberalism is the thesis that questions about the *good life for man* or the ends of human life are to be regarded from the public standpoint as systematically unsettlable. . . . The rules of morality and law hence are not to be derived from or justified in terms of some more fundamental conception of the good for man" (MacIntyre 112; emphasis in original). This is also Sandel's conceptualization of "deontological liberalism": "society, being composed of a plurality of persons, each with his own aims, interests, and conceptions of the good, is best arranged when it is governed by principles that do not *themselves* presuppose any particular conception of the good" (Sandel 1; emphasis in original). Individuals have rights, and equal rights at that, and the task of the liberal state is to preserve them. It does this by protecting individuals from one another, and by itself not interfering with what is properly an individual's private concern.

This political posture follows, as does the liberal view of social relations, from liberalism's atomism: separate, self-interested individuals demand a politics that imposes no ends but enables the fulfillment of the individual's independently chosen ones. "The standard liberal argument for neutrality is an induction from social fragmentation. Since dissociated individuals will never agree on the good life, the state must allow them to live as they think best, subject only to John Stuart Mill's harm principle, without endorsing or sponsoring any particular understanding of what 'best' means" (Walzer 16).

Just as there is considerable agreement between feminist and communitarian understandings of liberalism's perspectives on the self and on social relations, so is there considerable agreement between them concerning liberalism's concept of political community. Perhaps most importantly, both note that liberalism accepts a politics of conflict that leads to the need for government as mediator. There are, however, some differences in emphasis among the portrayals of liberalism that will become significant. The aspect of liberal politics that gets most attention from feminists is the gap between neutrality in theory and partiality in practice, itself related to the larger problem of liberalism's public-private distinction and the role of government in each. The aspect of the liberal state that gets most attention from communitarians is government's misguided role as a neutral "referee" of values.

Critiques of Liberalism

Communitarianism

Feminism

Liberal democracy may not be a theory of political community at all. It does not so much provide a justification for politics as it offers a politics that justifies individual rights. It is concerned more to promote individual liberty than to secure public justice, to advance interests rather than to discover goods, and to keep men safely apart rather than to bring them fruitfully together. As a consequence, it is capable of fiercely resisting every assault on the individual — his privacy, his property, his interests, and his rights — but is far less effective in resisting as-

Liberal theory does not provide the language or concepts to help us understand the various kinds of human interdependence which are part of the life of both families and polities, nor to articulate a feminist vision of "the good life."[18]

[R]ights oversimplify complex power relations . . . [T]he resort to rights can be effectively countered by the resort to competing rights . . . [R]ights formulated to protect the individual against the state, or the weak against the strong, may be appropriated by the more powerful.[19]

saults on community or justice or citizenship or participation. (Barber 4)

[T]he liberal notion of "the private" has included what has been called "woman's sphere" as "male property" and sought not only to preserve it from the interference of the public realm but also to keep those who "belong" in that realm — women — from the life of the public. (Dietz 4)

For communitarians, the liberal political world, in which all that people share is protection from one another by an impartial state, leaves people without a common moral anchor, requires of them morally nothing higher than law-abidingness, and abdicates its responsibility for moral education. "Liberalism teaches respect for the distance of self and ends. . . . By putting the self beyond the reach of politics, it makes human agency an article of faith rather than an object of continuing attention and concern, a premise of politics rather than its precarious achievement. This misses the pathos of politics and also its most inspiring possibilities" (Sandel 183). According to communitarians, liberal politics follows from and reinforces atomistic individualism. The successes of the liberal state concern only its ability to protect the self-interested and isolated self, via structures and practices such as property rights, privacy claims, and interest-group politics. Social skills and feelings are not consciously cultivated, deeply restricting the style and substance of political life.

While communitarians find liberalism's politics inadequate, feminists find it at times mythical and at times positively injurious to women. More fully, communitarians speak as if liberalism were basically good at doing what it set out to do, but argue that it does not set out to do the right things. While feminists, too, question whether liberal principles can or should be the ones guiding the state, they also challenge liberalism for its failure in practice to do for both sexes what in principle it sets out to do.

Feminists evaluate liberalism's politics from a vantage point that reveals dynamics not attended to by communitarians. Catherine MacKinnon discusses how "liberal neutrality" in fact amounts to "substantive misogyny."[20] In the face of existing sexual inequality, a politics that, in the name of neutrality, refuses to take sides is in reality taking sides with the more powerful, men, allowing them to maintain their dominance through state policy of noninterference. Feminist critiques of liberal politics challenge its pretense to (gender) neutrality in a second way: feminists wonder how a state can be considered neutral that has upheld sexual segregation in employment, continues in public policy to prefer the nuclear heterosexual family over all other familial arrangements, considers affirmative action reverse discrimination, and refuses, on "privacy" grounds, to "interfere" in cases of domestic abuse, even while it outlaws "private" sexual acts between consenting adult members of the same sex.

Further, granting "rights" to the less powerful, a time-honored liberal solution, receives mixed reviews from feminists. True, gaining rights is a victory over those who would prefer little restraint on the potential exploitation of women.[21] But problems remain: private (male) power is often untouched by and impervious to (women's) formal rights; social and economic factors can limit the exercise of women's rights; and appeals to rights tend to treat the sexes (and individuals generally) as adversaries, thus reinforcing a problematical politics.

As Marxist feminists might prefer, liberal rights are fictitious cover-ups veiling the class rule of men. "Marxist feminists would have us recognize that a system of economics and gender rooted in capitalist, male-dominated structures underlies much of liberal ideology, from the notion of independent rational man to the conception of separate private and public realms, from the value of individualism to the equation of freedom with free trade" (Dietz 8). In fact, many feminists present a view of the liberal state as male-dominated, a concept parallel to the Marxist notion of a class-dominated state. One understanding of the destructiveness of the patriarchal liberal state, not subscribed to only by Marxist feminists, is offered by Hartsock:

> The masculine gender carried by power intensifies the tensions of community and leads to the construction of an even more conflictual and false community than that formed by means of exchange. It is a community both in theory and in fact obsessed with revenge and structured by conquest and domination. . . . These dynamics of conquest and domination mean that the gain of one participant can come only at the expense of the other's submission, humiliation, or even death.[22]

Because it is infused with patriarchal principles and processes, feminists would necessarily insist not on a state that reasserts *its* rights in the moral domain, as communitarians desire, but one that reassesses its own ethics.

Feminists and communitarians share a deep concern about the social and political consequences of a polity based on individual advantage. Many communitarians see the rise of self-interest as causally connected to the fall of a common moral sense in political communities and thus look to a resurrection of the latter as a solution to the problems of liberal politics. Feminists see the consequences of the liberal state as significantly different for the two sexes and urge attention to women's communities and networks for both insight into liberalism and ideas for alternatives to self-interested individualism. Here it becomes clear how criticisms of liberalism that are "gender-blind" are also "gender-biased"; the problems of liberalism most specific to women are ignored in the gender-blind critiques, and the call for a return to "a common moral vision" or, more common today, to "traditional values," is a gender-biased solution that does not speak from or to the lives of many women.

Alternatives to the Liberal View

Communitarianism

The application of that measure [of goodness] in a community whose shared aim is the realization of the human good presupposes . . . a wide range of agreement in that community on goods and virtues, and it is this agreement which makes possible the kind of bond between citizens which, on Aristotle's view, constitutes a *polis*. That bond is the bond of friendship. . . . Indeed from an Aristotelian point of view a modern liberal political society can appear only as a collection of citizens of nowhere who have banded together for their common protection. They possess at best that inferior form of friendship which is founded on mutual advantage. . . . They have abandoned the moral unity of Aristotelianism. (MacIntyre 146)

Feminism

A valuable alternative conception of politics . . . is perhaps best called the democratic one, and it takes politics to be the collective and participatory engagement of citizens in the determination of the affairs of their community. The community may be the neighborhood, the city, the state, the region, or the nation itself. What counts is that all matters relating to the community are undertaken as "the people's affair." (Dietz 14)

[T]he conception of power as dominance is partial and misleading . . . one must not take the question of who rules whom to be the most critical political issue. (Hartsock 224)

There are so many visions of political community that perhaps it is impossible to represent them fairly here. Communitarian schemes range from MacIntyre's conventionalist Aristotelianism and Sandel's revitalized civic republicanism to Barber's Rousseauean participatory democracy. Feminist visions run the gamut from Sara Ruddick's maternal politics to Marge Piercy's small-town, ecologically minded democracies and Alison Jaggar's socialist feminist state. There is overlap as well as diversity among these theorists, most obvious in their frequent advocacy of democratic and socialist communities. Too often, however, the overlap is merely nominal. Focusing only on the common ground of democracy or socialism may conceal the different and often incompatible sets of political concerns and arrangements behind feminist and communitarian versions of each. One illustration of how feminists and communitarians diverge in their visions of community is the striking contrast in their attitudes toward ancient Greece.

MacIntyre's *After Virtue* devotes three chapters exclusively to ancient Greece. It is fair to say that his picture of community is very strongly and positively affected by the ancient Greek polities, even if he does not accept them as flawless. (There is, however, precious little evidence of his finding fault with them.)

These "heroic societies," as MacIntyre calls them, are marked by certain "key features": "Every individual has a given role and status within a well-defined and highly determinate system of roles and statuses." "[T]here is for each status a prescribed set of duties and privileges. There is also a clear understanding of what actions are required to perform these and what actions fall short" (MacIntyre 115).

As Okin notes, "one is left with the impression that it is [MacIntyre's] conscious intention to make the reader forget about the exclusionary nature of Aristotle's views about who could lead 'the good life for a human being,'" or who was capable of Aristotle's highest form of friendship. "[H]is benign interpretation de-emphasizes both the social hierarchy of heroic societies and the heavy sanctions that reinforced it."[23] Once again, then, the gloss painted on a picture of hierarchy, exclusion, and degradation by MacIntyre comes at precisely those points where feminists would scour the surface and reveal all the undercoats. In this case the difference is so striking that feminists seem quite justified in their lack of enthusiasm for communitarianism.

[T]he Greek understanding of politics and power rested more directly and explicitly than ours on the division between women

and men, between the household, a private and apolitical space,
and the *polis,* a public and political space. This division was,
moreover, a division between a realm of necessity and a realm of
freedom, a realm held to be characterized by inequality and a realm
seen as populated by equals, a realm described as dominated by the
body and a realm where the soul or intellect was held to be
dominant. All of this both rested on and reinforced a profound
misogyny. (Hartsock 187)

Feminists should be wary of communitarian calls for moral unity. Such
calls may signal a readiness to accept grave social inequalities and an
insensitivity to the enriching power of differences.

Conclusion

The writers explored here all prefer a more communal theory and practice than is found in liberalism. A final, more subterranean, issue helps
explain the distance between feminist and communitarian thought: their
motives for rejecting liberalism.

MacIntyre's *After Virtue* is informed by the "grave disorder" of moral
anomie, which "perhaps . . . a very few — recognised as a catastrophe"
(MacIntyre 2, 3). The concerns at the center of his enterprise seem most
directly to involve and be felt by moral theorists — truly a "very few."
The "catastrophe" is that there is "no rational way of securing moral
agreement in our culture" (MacIntyre 6). That we are experiencing a
moral decline is shown by our "complacency" with "moral pluralism,"
when what we really have is "an unharmonious melange of ill-assorted
fragments" of viewpoints (MacIntyre 10). Given the cultural power of
"emotivism," we are quite comfortable with the view that "all moral
judgments are *nothing but* expressions of preference, expressions of attitude or feeling," despite the fact that this "Weberian vision of the world
cannot be rationally sustained" (MacIntyre 19, 11, 103; emphasis in
original). MacIntyre's concern is with "modern moral theorists" who are
faced with "insoluble problems . . . [by] modern moral utterance and
practice" (MacIntyre 104–5), who are searching for "impersonal . . .
standards of justice or generosity or duty" (MacIntyre 9). It is not clear
that MacIntyre's problem is necessarily so remote from the political
concerns that inform feminism, but the inference from his writing is that
feminist issues are not necessarily relevant to a search for justice or

virtue. Immoral misogynist behavior must, again, take a back seat, this time to moral agreement in theory. It is then unsurprising that his "vindication" of Aristotlean ethics and politics and the "way of life" they entail (MacIntyre 111) seem so politically uncritical from a feminist perspective.

Much the same can be said of Michael Sandel's *Liberalism and the Limits of Justice*. He tells us at the outset that the limits of (liberal) justice he argues for "are not practical but conceptual" (Sandel 1). His enterprise of showing the incoherence of a "concept of a subject given prior to and independent of its objects" has as its end the refutation of the liberal "claim for the primacy of justice" (Sandel 7). Feminists are not necessarily unconcerned about the theoretical consistency of liberalism or whether the right is prior to the good. But, unlike Sandel, feminists find the limits of liberal justice most dramatically visible in the "practical" world; little would be gained, from a feminist perspective, if liberalism were made more tidy conceptually and left as dirty in practice.

Finally, the authors of *Habits of the Heart* speak thus of the "tensions" analyzed in their text: "We strongly assert the value of our self-reliance and autonomy. We deeply feel the emptiness of a life without sustaining social commitments. Yet we are hesitant to articulate our sense that we need one another as much as we need to stand alone, for fear that if we did we would lose our independence altogether" (Bellah et al. 151). The standpoint from which this passage is written is that of the traditional male, endless usages of "we" and "our" notwithstanding. This is the male who is more comfortable asserting his autonomy than acknowledging his need for or debt to others, most fearful of all of losing what he calls his independence. Traditional woman's starting point is the opposite: she is more comfortable acknowledging her need for others than asserting her autonomy, most fearful of losing her connections to others. Indeed, the individual stories in *Habits of the Heart* show this to be true, and still the point is missed. The authors continue to treat the male experience as the norm, rendering women's experiences invisible, outside the mainstream of supposedly universal human experience. That which could be learned from women's unique experiences with community, positive and negative, is lost.

It is astonishing that in the long lists of modern woes cited by communitarians one almost never finds items such as the feminization of illiteracy and poverty (by the year 2000 virtually all "officially" poor people in the United States will be women or children), rape (perpetrated on perhaps one of every four women, compromising the freedom of all women), domestic violence (half of all married women can expect at least one violent episode at the hands of their mate), pornography (an $8 billion a year industry in the United States alone), reproductive issues from compulsory motherhood to forced sterilization, inadequate and unaffordable child care, prostitution, child abuse, sexual harassment, or undervaluing of women's labor. If any one of these is mentioned, it is too often as a mere symptom of a "real" or "bigger" problem that has nothing to do with male domination.

Given the sexism, racism, and homophobia pervasive in most cultures, educational systems, workplaces, and political practices, unless people start out explicitly committed *not* to discriminate, they usually end up discriminating. This understanding of how oppression is maintained is, of course, the basis of affirmative action policies. Communitarianism lacks feminist consciousness and commitment to resolving problems of gender hierarchy. Thus, it usually ignores and therefore perpetuates those problems: it ends up with a white male vision, as "unintentional" and as thorough as that found anywhere. Feminists do indeed find a "perilous ally" (Friedman 277) in communitarianism, whether it is Plato's, Rousseau's, or MacIntyre's, and will continue to as long as communitarianism is isolationist in its politics.

We are in the midst of what Michael Walzer calls "a recurrent [communitarian] critique" of liberalism (Walzer 6). The disciplines at least of philosophy and political theory are awash in communitarian attacks upon liberals and responding defenses of liberalism. Walzer sees such debate as useful even if, likely, never-ending. A constant feature of the recurring debate that Walzer neglects to note, however, is the absence of concern by both sides about sexual equality. To the extent that the communitarian-liberal debate continues to command so much attention from social and political theorists, feminism continues to be relatively ignored. Antifeminism and communitarianism have a "tradition" of coexistence and cooperation, and we learn more about both by studying them together. Because patriarchal values and institutions continue to pervade communitarian visions, feminists most definitely must persist in developing full-fledged communitarian visions of our own.

Notes

1. The best text on this is probably Zillah Eisenstein's *The Radical Future of Liberal Feminism* (New York: Longman, 1981).

2. Christopher Lasch, "The Communitarian Critics of Liberalism," in *Community in America: The Challenge of Habits of the Heart,* edited by Charles Reynolds and Ralph Norman (Berkeley: University of California Press, 1988), 175.

3. Alasdair MacIntyre, *After Virtue: A Study in Moral Theory* (Notre Dame, Ind.: University of Notre Dame Press, 1981), 232–33.

4. Benjamin Barber, *Strong Democracy: Participatory Politics for a New Age* (Berkeley: University of California Press, 1984), 33.

5. Marilyn Friedman, "Feminism and Modern Friendship: Dislocating the Community," *Ethics* 99 (January 1989): 275.

6. Mary Dietz, "Context Is All: Feminism and Theories of Citizenship," *Daedalus* 116 (Fall 1987): 5.

7. Alison Jaggar, *Feminist Politics and Human Nature* (Totowa, N.J.: Rowman and Allanheld, 1983), 42.

8. Not everyone agrees that these features of the self are necessarily part of liberalism. There is a significant effort to counter the charges against liberalism made by communitarians, in particular. See, for example, Michael Walzer, "The Communitarian Critique of Liberalism," *Political Theory* 18 (February 1990): 173–84; Will Kymlicka, "Liberalism and Communitarianism," *Canadian Journal of Philosophy* 18 (June 1988): 181–95; and Allen Buchanan, "Assessing the Communitarian Critique of Liberalism," *Ethics* 99 (July 1989). Also see Susan Wendell, "A (Qualified) Defense of Liberal Feminism," *Hypatia: A Journal of Feminist Philosophy* 2 (Summer 1987): 65–94.

9. Chantal Mouffe, "American Liberalism and Its Critics: Rawls, Taylor, Sandel and Walzer," *Praxis International* 8 (July 1988): 198.

10. Seyla Benhabib and Drucilla Cornell, "Introduction: Beyond the Politics of Gender," *Feminism as Critique,* ed. Benhabib and Cornell (Minneapolis: University of Minnesota Press, 1987), 12.

11. Michael J. Sandel, *Liberalism and the Limits of Justice* (Cambridge: Cambridge University Press, 1982), 179.

12. Good examples of this include Naomi Scheman, "Individualism and the Objects of Psychology," in *Discovering Reality: Feminist Perspectives on Epistemology, Metaphysics, Methodology and the Philosophy of Science,* ed. S. Harding and M. Hintikka (Dordrecht: Reidel, 1983); Sara Ruddick, "Maternal Thinking," *Feminist Studies* 6 (Summer 1980): 342–67; and Nancy Holmstrom, "Do Women Have a Distinct Nature?" in *Women and Values: Readings in Recent Feminist Philosophy,* ed. Marilyn Pearsall (Belmont, Calif.: Wadsworth, 1986), 15.

13. Robert Bellah, Richard Madsen, William Sullivan, Ann Swidler, and Steven Tipton, *Habits of the Heart: Individualism and Commitment in American Life* (Berkeley: University of California Press, 1985), 107.

14. Virginia Held, "Non-Contractual Society: A Feminist View," *Canadian Journal of Philosophy* Supplementary 13 (1987): 124–25.

15. Elizabeth Wolgast, *Equality and the Rights of Women* (Ithaca: Cornell University Press, 1980), 154.

16. Jane Mansbridge, *Beyond Self-Interest* (Chicago: University of Chicago Press, 1990), ix.

17. M. Elizabeth Albert, "In the Interest of the Public Good? New Questions for Feminism," in *Community in America: The Challenge of Habits of the Heart,* edited by Charles H. Reynolds and Ralph V. Norman (Berkeley and Los Angeles: University of California Press, 1988), 88.

18. Mary Lyndon Shanley, "Marital Slavery and Friendship," *Political Theory* 8 (May 1980): 360.

19. Carol Smart, *Feminism and the Power of the Law* (New York: Routledge, 1989), 144–45.

20. Catherine MacKinnon, *Feminism Unmodified: Discourses on Life and Law* (Cambridge: Harvard University Press, 1987), 15.

21. Patricia Williams, *The Alchemy of Race and Rights* (Cambridge: Harvard University Press, 1991).

22. Nancy Hartsock, *Money, Sex and Power: Toward a Feminist Historical Materialism* (Boston: Northeastern University Press, 1983), 177.

23. Susan Moller Okin, *Justice, Gender, and the Family* (New York: Basic Books, 1989), 45 and 49.

13

Feminism and Modern Friendship
Dislocating the Community

Marilyn Friedman

A predominant theme of much recent feminist thought is the criticism
of the abstract individualism that underlies some important versions
of liberal political theory.[1] Abstract individualism considers individual
human beings as social atoms, abstracted from their social contexts, and
disregards the role of social relationships and human community in
constituting the very identity and nature of individual human beings.
Sometimes the individuals of abstract individualism are posited as rationally self-interested utility-maximizers.[2] Sometimes, also, they are
theorized to form communities based fundamentally on competition and
conflict among persons vying for scarce resources, communities that
represent no deeper social bond than that of instrumental relations based
on calculated self-interest.[3]

Against this abstractive individualist view of the self and of human
community, many feminists assert a conception of the self as inherently
social. This conception acknowledges the fundamental role of social
relationships and human community in constituting both self-identity
and the nature and meaning of the particulars of individual lives.[4] The

Reprinted from *What Are Friends For? Feminist Perspectives on Personal Relationships and Moral Theory* (Ithaca, N.Y.: Cornell University Press, 1993). First
published in *Ethics* 99 (January 1989): 275–90 and reprinted by permission of
the author and the publisher. © 1989 by The University of Chicago. All rights
reserved.

modified conception of the self carries with it an altered conception of community. Conflict and competition are no longer considered to be the basic human relationships; instead they are being replaced by alternative visions of the foundation of human society derived from nurturance, caring attachment, and mutual interestedness.[5] Some feminists, for example, urge that the mother-child relationship be recognized as central to human society, and they project major changes in moral theory from such a revised focus.[6]

Some of these anti-individualist developments emerging from feminist thought are strikingly similar to other theoretical developments which are not specifically feminist. Thus, the "new communitarians," to borrow Amy Gutmann's term,[7] have also reacted critically to various aspects of modern liberal thought, including abstract individualism, rational egoism, and an instrumental conception of social relationships. The communitarian self, or subject, is also not a social atom but is instead a being constituted and defined by its attachments, including the particularities of its social relationships, community ties, and historical context. Its identity cannot be abstracted from community or social relationships.

With the recent feminist attention to values of care, nurturance, and relatedness — values that psychologists call "communal"[8] and which have been amply associated with women and women's moral reasoning[9] — one might anticipate that communitarian theory would offer important insights for feminist reflection. There is considerable power to the model of the self as deriving its identity and nature from its social relationships, from the way it is intersubjectively apprehended, from the norms of the community in which it is embedded.

However, communitarian philosophy as a whole is a perilous ally for feminist theory. Communitarians invoke a model of community that is focused particularly on families, neighborhoods, and nations. These sorts of communities have harbored numerous social roles and structures that lead to the subordination of women, as much recent research has shown. Communitarians, however, seem oblivious to those difficulties and manifest a troubling complacency about the moral authority claimed or presupposed by those communities in regard to their members. By building on uncritical references to those sorts of communities, communitarian philosophy can lead in directions feminists should not wish to follow.

This discussion is an effort to redirect communitarian thought so as to avoid some of the pitfalls it poses, in its present form, for feminist theory and feminist practice. In the first section, I develop some feminist-inspired criticisms of communitarian philosophy as it is found in writings of Michael Sandel and Alasdair MacIntyre.[10] My brief critique of communitarian thought has the aim of showing that communitarian theory, in the form in which it condones or tolerates traditional communal norms of gender subordination, is unacceptable from any standpoint enlightened by feminist analysis. This does not preclude agreeing with certain specific communitarian views, for example, the broad metaphysical conception of the individual, self, or subject as constituted by its social relationships and communal ties, or the assumption that traditional communities have some value. But my aim in section 1 is critical: to focus on the communitarian disregard of gender-related problems with the norms and practices of traditional communities.

In the second section, I delve more deeply into the nature of certain sorts of communities and social relationship that communitarians largely disregard. I suggest that modern friendships, on the one hand, and urban relationships and communities, on the other, offer an important clue for developing a model of community that usefully counterbalances the family-neighborhood-nation complex favored by communitarians. With that model in view, we can begin to transform the communitarian vision of self and community into a more congenial ally for feminist theory.

1. The Social Self, in Communitarian Perspective

Communitarians share with most feminist theorists a rejection of the abstractly individualist conception of self and society so prominent in modern liberal thought.[11] This self—atomistic, pre-social, empty of all metaphysical content except abstract reason and will—is allegedly able to stand back from all the contingent moral commitments and norms of its particular historical context and assess each of them in the light of impartial and universal criteria of reason. The self who achieves a substantial measure of such reflective reconsideration of the moral particulars of her life has achieved autonomy, a widely esteemed liberal value.

In contrast to this vision of the self, the new communitarians pose the conception of a self whose identity and nature are defined by her contingent and particular social attachments. Communitarians extol the communities and social relationships, including family and nation, that comprise the typical social context in which the self emerges to self-consciousness. Thus, Michael Sandel speaks warmly of "those loyalties and convictions whose moral force consists partly in the fact that living by them is inseparable from understanding ourselves as the particular persons we are — as members of this family or community or nation or people, as bearers of this history, as sons and daughters of that revolution, as citizens of this republic."[12] Sandel continues:

> Allegiances such as these are more than values I happen to have or aims I "espouse at any given time." They go beyond the obligations I voluntarily incur and the "natural duties" I owe to human beings as such. They allow that to some I owe more than justice requires or even permits, not by reason of agreements I have made but instead in virtue of those more or less enduring attachments and commitments which taken together partly *define the person I am.*[13]

Voicing similar sentiments, Alasdair MacIntyre writes:

> We all approach our own circumstances as bearers of a particular social identity. I am someone's son or daughter, someone else's cousin or uncle; I am a citizen of this or that city, a member of this or that guild or profession; I belong to this clan, that tribe, this nation. Hence what is good for me has to be the good for one who inhabits these roles. As such, I inherit from the past of my family, my city, my tribe, my nation, a variety of debts, inheritances, rightful expectations and obligations. These constitute the given of my life, my moral starting point. This is in part what gives my life its own moral particularity.[14]

It is remarkable that neither writer mentions sex or gender as a determinant of particular identity. Perhaps this glaring omission derives not from a failure to realize the fundamental importance of gender in personal identity — could anyone really miss that? — but rather from the aim to emphasize what social relationships and communities contribute to identity, along with the inability to conceive that gender is a social relationship or that it constitutes communities.

For communitarians, at any rate, these social relationships and communities have a kind of morally normative legitimacy; they define the "moral starting points," to use MacIntyre's phrase, of each individual life. The traditions, practices, and conventions of our communities have at least a prima facie legitimate moral claim upon us. MacIntyre does qualify the latter point by conceding that "the fact that the self has to find its moral identity in and through its membership in communities such as those of the family, the neighborhood, the city and the tribe does not entail that the self has to accept the moral *limitations* of the particularity of those forms of community."[15] Nevertheless, according to MacIntyre, one's moral quests must begin by "moving forward from such particularity," for it "can never be simply left behind or obliterated."[16]

Despite feminist sympathy for a conception of the self as social and an emphasis on the importance of social relationships, at least three features of the communitarian version of these notions are troubling from a feminist standpoint. First, the communitarian's metaphysical conception of an inherently social self has little usefulness for normative analysis; in particular, it will not support a specifically feminist critique of individualist personality. Second, communitarian theory pays insufficient regard to the illegitimate moral claims that communities make on their members, linked, for example, to hierarchies of domination and subordination. Third, the specific communities of family, neighborhood, and nation so commonly invoked by communitarians are troubling paradigms of social relationship and communal life. I discuss each of these points in turn.

First, the communitarian's metaphysical conception of the social self does not support feminist critiques of ruggedly individualist personality or its associated attributes: the avoidance of intimacy, non-nurturance, social distancing, aggression, and violence. Feminist theorists have often been interested in developing a critique of our cultural norm of the highly individualistic, competitive, aggressive personality type, seeing that personality type as more characteristically male than female and as an important part of the foundation for male domination throughout society and culture.

Largely following the work of Nancy Chodorow, Dorothy Dinnerstein, and, more recently, Carol Gilligan,[17] many feminists have theorized that the processes of psycho-gender development, in a society in which early infant care is the primary responsibility of women but not men, result in a radical distinction between the genders in the extent to which the self is constituted by, and identifies with, its relational connections to others. Males are theorized to seek and value autonomy, individuation, separation, and the moral ideals of rights and justice that are thought to depend on a highly individuated conception of persons. By contrast, females are theorized to seek and value connection, sociality, inclusion, and moral ideals of care and nurturance.

Highly individuated selves seem to be a problem. They appear incapable of human attachments based on mutuality and trust, unresponsive to human needs, approaching social relationships merely as rationally self-interested utility maximizers, thriving on separation and competition, and creating social institutions that tolerate, even legitimize, violence and aggression.

However, a metaphysical view that all human selves are constituted by their social and communal relationships does not itself entail a critique of these highly individualistic selves or yield any indication of what degree of psychological attachment to others is desirable. On metaphysical grounds alone, there is no reason to suppose that caring, nurturant, relational, sociable selves are better than more autonomous, individualistic, and independent selves. According to a conception of selves as inherently social, all selves, whatever their personality or character, are equivalently constituted as social at a metaphysical level.

On this view, abstract individualism's failure is not that it has produced asocial selves, for, on the communitarian view, such beings are metaphysically impossible. Rather, the mistake in abstract individualism is simply to have failed theoretically to *acknowledge* that selves are inherently social. On the basis of a metaphysical conception of the self as social, it follows that autonomy, independence, and separateness are merely alternative ways of being socially constituted, no worse or better than heteronomy, dependence, and connectedness.

The communitarian conception of the social self, if it is simply a metaphysical view about the constitution of the self (which is what it seems to be), thus provides no basis for regarding nurturant, relational selves as morally superior to those who are highly individualistic. For that reason, it appears to be of no assistance to feminist theorists seeking a normative account of what might be wrong or excessive about competitive self-seeking behaviors or aggressively individualistic character traits. The communitarian social self, indeed, any merely metaphysical account of the self as inherently social, is largely irrelevant to the array of normative tasks that many feminist thinkers have set for a conception of the self.

My second concern about communitarian philosophy has to do with the legitimacy of the communal norms and traditions that are supposed to define the moral starting points of community members. As a matter of moral psychology, it is certainly common for people to take for granted the moral legitimacy of the norms, traditions, and practices of their communities. However, this point about moral psychology does not entail that those norms and practices really are morally legitimate. It leaves open the question of whether, and to what extent, those claims might really be morally binding. Unfortunately, the new communitarians seem sometimes to go beyond the point of moral psychology to a stronger view, namely, that the moral claims of communities really are morally binding, at least as "moral starting points." MacIntyre refers to the "debts, inheritances, *rightful* expectations and obligations"[18] that we "inherit" from family, nation and so forth.

But such inheritances are enormously varied. In light of this variety, MacIntyre's normative complacency is quite troubling. Many communities practice the disturbing exclusion and suppression of non-group members, especially outsiders defined by ethnicity and sexual orientation.[19] In addition, there surely are "rightful expectations and obligations" that cross community lines, some of them involving the rectification of past wrongs that also crossed community lines. Did Jews, Gypsies, Poles, Czechoslovakians, among others, not have "rightful expectations" that Germany would not practice military conquest and unimaginable genocide? Did Germany not owe reparations to non-Germans for those same genocidal practices? If the new communitarians do not recognize legitimate "debts, inheritances, rightful expectations and obligations" across community lines, then their views also have diminished relevance for our radically heterogeneous modern society. Our society intermixes an array of smaller communities which often retain a substantial degree of cohesive separation from the rest. If there are intercommunity obligations that override communal norms and practices, then moral particularity is not accounted for by communal norms alone. In that case, the community as such, that is, the relatively bounded and local network of relationships which forms a subject's primary social setting, would not singularly determine the legitimate moral values or requirements that rightfully constitute the self's moral commitments or self-definition.

Besides excluding or suppressing outsiders, the practices and traditions of numerous communities are exploitative and oppressive toward many of their own members. This problem is of special relevance to women. The traditions and practices that create, promote, emphasize, or rely on gender differentiation often lead to the subordination, exploitation, or abuse of women. Many of these traditions are located in the sorts of communities invoked uncritically by communitarians, for example, family practices and national political traditions. The communitarian emphasis on communities unfortunately dovetails too well with the current emphasis on that mythic idealization known as "the family." It harkens back to the world of what some sociologists call communities of "place," the world of family, neighborhood, school, and church, which rested on a morally troubling politics of gender. Any political theory that lends support to the cultural hegemony of such communities and that supports them in a position of unquestioned moral authority must be viewed with grave suspicion. I will come back to this issue when I turn to my third objection to communitarian philosophy.

It is eminently plausible to admit into our descriptive notion of the self the important constitutive role played by social and communal relationships. It does not thereby follow, however, that the moral claims made by a community on any particular subject who is a member or who identifies herself in its terms are necessarily morally authoritative for her. The moral claims of her constitutive community. To evaluate the moral someone are not morally binding on her simply in virtue of being the moral claims of her constitutive communities. To evaluate the moral identities conferred by communities on their members, we need a theory of communities, of their interrelationships, of the structures of power, dominance, and oppression within and among them. Only such a theory would allow us to assess the legitimacy of the claims made by communities upon their members by way of their traditions, practices, and conventions of "debts, inheritances, . . . expectations, and obligations."

The communitarian approach appears to celebrate the attachments in which any person finds herself unavoidably embedded, the familial ties and so forth. Even apart from the questionable moral authority of communities, the issue of communal loyalty is not so easily decided. In our heterogeneous society, we may find ourselves embedded in several communities simultaneously. Some communities and relationships compete with others, and some relationships provide standpoints from which other relationships appear threatening or dangerous to oneself, one's integrity, or one's well-being. In such cases, simple formulas about the value of community provide no guidance. The problem is not simply to appreciate community per se but rather to reconcile the conflicting claims, demands, and identity-defining influences of the variety of communities of which one is a part.

It is worth recalling that liberalism has always condemned, in principle if not in practice, the norms of social hierarchy and political subordination based on inherited or ascribed status. While liberals historically have usually applied this tenet only to the public realm of civic relationships,[20] feminism seeks to extend it more radically to the "private" realm of family and other communities of place. In particular, those norms and claims of local communities that sustain hierarchies based on gender have no intrinsic legitimacy from a feminist standpoint. A feminist interest in community aims for social institutions and relational structures that diminish and, finally, erase gender subordination.

Reflections such as these characterize the concerns of the modern self, the self who acknowledges no a priori loyalty to any feature of situation or role and who claims the right to question the moral legitimacy of any contingent moral claim.[21] We can agree with the communitarians that it would be impossible for the self to question all her contingencies at once, but at the same time, unlike the communitarians, still emphasize the critical importance of morally questioning various particular communal norms and circumstances one at a time.

A third problem with communitarian philosophy has to do with the sorts of communities evidently endorsed by communitarian theorists. Human beings participate in a variety of communities and social relationships, not only across time but at any one time. However, when people think of community, the examples they commonly call to mind are primarily those of family, neighborhood, school, and church.[22] These paradigms of community are also the ones most commonly invoked by Sandel and MacIntyre. These most familiar examples of community fall largely into two groups. First, there are political, or government-based, communities which constitute our civic and national identities in a public world of nation-states. MacIntyre mentions city and nation, while Sandel writes of "nation or people, . . . bearers of this history, . . . sons and daughters of that revolution, . . . citizens of this republic."[23] Second, there are local communities centered around families and neighborhood, which some sociologists call "communities of place." MacIntyre and Sandel both emphasize family, and MacIntyre also cites neighborhood along with clan and tribe.[24]

But where, one might ask, is the International Ladies Garment Workers' Union, the Teamsters, the Democratic party, Alcoholics Anonymous, or the National Organization for Women? Although MacIntyre does mention professions and, rather archaically, "guilds,"[25] these references are anomalous in his work, which, for the most part, ignores such communities as trade unions, political action groups, and even associations of hobbyists.

Some of the communities cited by MacIntyre and Sandel have indeed figured prominently in the historical experiences of women, especially the inclusive communities of family and neighborhood. By contrast, political communities form a particularly suspect class from a woman's perspective. We all recall how political communities have, until only recently in recorded history, excluded the legitimate participation of women. It would seem to follow that they have accordingly *not* historically constituted the identities of women in profound ways. As "daughters" of an American revolution spawned parthenogenetically by the "fathers" of our country, we find that our political community has denied us the self-identifying heritage of our cultural mothers. In general, the contribution made to the identities of various groups of people by political communities is quite uneven, given that they are communities to which many are subject but in which far fewer actively participate.

At any rate, there is an underlying commonality to most of the communities that MacIntyre and Sandel cite as constitutive of self-identity and definitive of our moral starting points. Sandel himself explicates this commonality when he writes that, for people "bound by a sense of community," the notion of community describes *"not a relationship they choose (as in a voluntary association) but an attachment they discover,* not merely an attribute but a constituent of their identity" (italics mine).[26] Not voluntary, but "discovered," relationships and communities are what Sandel takes to define subjective identity for those who are bound by a "sense of community." The communities to which we are involuntarily bound are those to which Sandel accords metaphysical pride of place in the constitution of subjectivity. What are important are not simply the "associations" in which people "co-operate" but the "communities" in which people "participate," for these latter "describe a form of life in which the members find themselves commonly situated 'to begin with,' their commonality consisting less in relationships they have entered than in attachments they have found."[27] Thus, the social relationships one finds, the attachments that are discovered and not chosen, become the points of reference for self-definition by the communitarian subject.

For the child maturing to self-consciousness in her community of origin, typically a complex of family, neighborhood, school, and church, it seems uncontroversial that "the" community is found, not entered; discovered, not created. But this need not be true of an adult's communities of mature self-identification. Many communities are, for at least some of their members, communities of choice to a significant extent: labor unions, philanthropic associations, political coalitions, and, if one has ever moved or migrated, even the communities of neighborhood, church, city, or nation-state may have been chosen to an important extent. One need not have simply discovered oneself to be embedded in them in order for one's identity or the moral particulars of one's life to be defined by them. Sandel is right to indicate the role of found communities in constituting the unreflective, "given" identity that the self discovers when first beginning to reflect on herself. But for mature self-identity, we should also recognize a legitimate role for communities of choice, supplementing, if not displacing, the communities and attachments that are merely found.

Moreover, the discovered identity constituted by one's original community of place may be fraught with ambivalences and ambiguities. Our communities of origin do not necessarily constitute us as selves who agree or comply with the norms that unify those communities. Some of us are constituted as deviants and resisters by our communities of origin, and our defiance may well run to the foundational social norms that ground the most basic social roles and relationships upon which those communities rest.

Poet Adrienne Rich writes about her experiences growing up with a Christian mother, a Jewish father who suppressed his ethnicity, and a family community that taught Rich contempt for all that was identified with Jewishness. In 1946, while still a high school student, Rich saw, for the first time, a film about the Allied liberation of Nazi concentration camps. Writing about this experience in 1982, she brooded: "I feel belated rage that I was so impoverished by the family and social worlds I lived in, that I had to try to figure out by myself what this did indeed mean for me. That I had never been taught about resistance, only about passing. That I had no language for anti-Semitism itself."[28] As a student at Radcliffe in the late forties, Rich met "real" Jewish women who inducted her into the lore of Jewish background and customs, holidays and foods, names and noses. She plunged in despite her trepidation: "I felt I was testing a forbidden current, that there was danger in these revelations. I bought a reproduction of a Chagall portrait of a rabbi in striped prayer shawl and hung it on the wall of my room. I was admittedly young and trying to educate myself, but I was also doing something that *is* dangerous: I was flirting with identity."[29] Most important, Rich was consolidating her identity while separated, both geographically and psychologically, from the family community in which her ambiguous ethnicity originated.

For Sandel, Rich's lifelong troubled reflections on her ethnic identity might seem compatible with his theory. In his view, the subject discovers the attachments that are constitutive of her subjectivity through reflection on a multitude of values and aims, differentiating what is self from what is not self. He might say that Rich discriminated among the many loyalties and projects which defined who she was in her original community, that is, her family, and discerned that her Jewishness appeared "essential"[30] to who she was. But it is not obvious, without question begging, that her original community really defined her as essentially Jewish. Indeed, her family endeavored to suppress loyalties and attachments to all things Jewish. Thus, one of Rich's quests in life, so evidently not inspired by her community of origin alone, was to reexamine the identity found in that original context. The communitarian view that found communities and social attachments constitute self-identity does not, by itself, explicate the processes by which we reconsider and revise, often through tortured struggles, our originally given identities. It seems more illuminating to say that Rich's identity became, in part, "chosen," that it had to do with social relationships and attachments she sought out rather than merely found, created as well as discovered.

Communities of place are relatively nonvoluntary; one's extended family of origin, for instance, is given or ascribed, and the relationships are found as one grows. The commitments and loyalties of our found communities, our communities of origin, may harbor ambiguities, ambivalences, contradictions, and oppressions that complicate as well as constitute identity and that have to be sorted out, critically scrutinized. In these undertakings, we are likely to use resources and skills derived from various communities and relationships, both those that are chosen or created and those that are found or discovered. Thus, our theories of community should recognize that resources and skills derived from communities that are not merely found or discovered may equally well contribute to the constitution of identity. The constitution of identity and moral particularity, for the modern self, may well require the contribution of radically different communities from those invoked by communitarians.

The whole tenor of communitarian thinking would change if we opened up the conception of the social self to encompass chosen communities, especially those that lie beyond the typical original community of family-neighborhood-school-church. No longer would communitarian thought present a seemingly conservative complacency about the private and local communities of place which have so effectively circumscribed, in particular, the lives of most women.

In the next section I explore more fully the role of communities and relationships of choice, which point the way toward a notion of community more congenial to feminist aspirations.

2. Modern Friendship, Urban Community, and Beyond

My goals are twofold: to retain the communitarian insights about the descriptive contribution of communities and social relationships to self-identity, yet open up for critical reflection the moral particulars imparted by those communities and identify the sorts of communities that provide nonoppressive and enriched lives for women.

Toward these ends, it will be helpful to consider models of human relationship and community that contrast with those cited by communitarians. I believe that modern friendship and urban community can offer us crucial insights into the social nature of the modern self. It is in moving forward from these relationships that we have the best chance of reconciling the communitarian conception of the social self with the longed-for communities of feminist aspiration.

Modern friendship and the stereotypical urban community share an important feature that is either neglected or deliberately avoided in communitarian conceptions of human relationship. From a liberal, or Enlightenment, or modernist standpoint, this feature would be characterized as voluntariness: these relationships are based partly on choice.

Let's first consider friendship as it is understood in this culture. Friends are supposed to be people one chooses on one's own to share activities and intimacies. No particular people are assigned by custom or tradition to be a person's friends. From among the larger number of one's acquaintances, one moves toward closer and more friendlike relationships with some of them, motivated by one's own needs, values, and attractions. No consanguineal or legal connections formally establish or maintain ties of friendship. As this relationship is widely understood in our culture, its basis lies in voluntary choice.

In this context, "voluntary choice" refers to motivations arising out of one's own needs, desires, interests, values, and attractions, in contrast to motivations arising from what is socially assigned, ascribed, demanded, or coercively imposed. Because of its basis in voluntary choice, friendship is more likely than many other relationships, such as those of family and neighborhood, to be grounded and sustained by shared interests and values, mutual affection, and possibilities for generating reciprocal respect and esteem.

Friendship is more likely than many other relationships to provide social support for people who are idiosyncratic, whose unconventional values and deviant life-styles make them victims of intolerance from family members and others who are unwillingly related to them. In this regard, friendship has socially disruptive possibilities. Out of the unconventional living it helps to sustain there often arise influential forces for social change. Friendship has had an obvious importance to feminist aspirations as the basis of the bond that is (ironically) called "sisterhood."[31] Friendship among women has been the cement not only of the various historical waves of the feminist movement but also of numerous communities of women throughout history who defied the local conventions for their gender and lived lives of creative disorder.[32] In all these cases, women moved out of their given or found communities into new attachments with other women by their own choice, that is, motivated by their own needs, desires, attractions, and fears, rather than, and often in opposition to, the expectations and ascribed roles of their found communities.

Like friendship, many urban relationships are also based more on choice than on socially ascribed roles, biological connections, or other nonvoluntary ties. Urban communities include numerous voluntary associations, such as political action groups, support groups, associations of cohobbyists, and so on. Yet friendship is almost universally extolled, while urban communities and relationships have been theorized in wildly contradictory ways. Cities have sometimes been taken as "harbingers" of modern culture per se[33] and have been particularly associated with the major social trends of modern life, such as industrialization and bureaucratization.[34] The results of these trends are often thought to have been a fragmentation of real community and the widely lamented alienation of modern urban life: people seldom know their neighbors; population concentration generates massive psychic overload;[35] fear and mutual distrust, even outright hostility, generated by the dangers of urban life may dominate most daily associations. Under such circumstances, meaningful relationships are often theorized to be rare, if even possible.

Does this portrait of urban life sufficiently represent what cities offer their residents? It is probably true, in urban areas, that communities of *place* are diminished in importance; neighborhood plays a much less significant role in constituting community than it does in nonurban areas.[36] This does not entail, however, that the social networks and communities of urban dwellers are inferior to those of nonurban residents.

Much evidence suggests that urban settings do not, as commonly stereotyped, promote only alienation, isolation, and psychic breakdown. The communities available to urban dwellers are different from those available to nonurban dwellers but not necessarily less gratifying or fulfilling.[37] Sociological research has shown that urban dwellers tend to form their social networks, their communities, from people who come together for reasons other than geographical proximity. Voluntary associations, such as political action groups, support groups, and so on, are a common part of modern urban life, with its large population centers and the greater availability of critical masses of people with special interests or needs. Communities of place, centered around family-neighborhood-church-school are more likely, for urban dwellers, to be supplanted by other sorts of communities, resulting in what sociologist Melvin Webber calls "community without propinquity."[38] As the sociologist Claude Fischer states, in urban areas, "population concentration stimulates allegiances to subcultures based on more significant social traits" than common locality or neighborhood.[39] But most important for our purposes, these are still often genuine communities and not the cesspools of Rum, Romanism, and Rebellion sometimes depicted by antiurbanists.

Literature reveals that women writers have been both repelled and inspired by urban communities. The city, as a concentrated center of male political and economic power, seems to exclude women altogether.[40] The city, however, can provide women with jobs, education, and the cultural tools with which to escape imposed gender roles, familial demands, and domestic servitude. The city can also bring women together, in work or in leisure, and lay the basis for bonds of sisterhood.[41] The quests of women who journey to cities leaving behind men, home, and family are subversive, writes literary critic Blanche Gelfant, and may well be perceived by others "as assaults upon society."[42] Cities open up for women possibilities of supplanting communities of place with relationships and communities of choice. Thus, urban communities of choice can provide the resources for women to surmount those moral particularities of family and place that define and limit their moral starting points.

Social theorists have long decried the interpersonal estrangement of urban life, an observation that seems predominantly inspired by the public world of conflict between various subcultural groups. Urbanism does not create interpersonal estrangement within subcultures but, rather, tends to promote social involvement.[43] This is especially true for people with special backgrounds and interests, for people who are members of small minorities, and for ethnic groups. Fischer has found that social relationships in urban centers are more "culturally specialized: urbanites were relatively involved with associates in the social world they considered most important and relatively uninvolved with associates, if any, in other worlds."[44] As Fischer summarizes it, "Urbanism . . . fosters social involvement in the subculture(s) of *choice,* rather than the subculture(s) of circumstances."[45] This is doubtless reinforced by the historically recent, and sometimes militant, expression of group values and demands for rights and respect by urban subcultural minorities.

We might describe urban relationships as being characteristically "modern" to signal their relatively greater voluntary basis. We find in these relationships and the social networks formed of them, not a necessary loss of community, but often an increase in importance of community of a different sort from that of family-neighborhood-church-school complexes. Yet these more voluntary communities may be as deeply constitutive of the identities and particulars of the individuals who participate in them as the communities of place so warmly invoked by communitarians.

Perhaps it is more illuminating to say that communities of choice foster not so much the constitution of subjects as their reconstitution. We seek out such communities as contexts in which to relocate and renegotiate the various constituents of our identities, as Adrienne Rich sought out Jewish community in her college years. While people in a community of choice may not share a common history, their shared values or interests are likely to manifest backgrounds of similar experiences, as, for example, among the members of a lesbian community. The modern self may seek new communities whose norms and relationships stimulate and develop her identity and self-understanding more adequately than her unchosen community of origin, her original community of place.

In case it is chosen communities that help us to define ourselves, the project of self-definition would not arise from communities in which we merely found or discovered our immersion. It is likely that chosen communities, lesbian communities, for example, attract us in the first place because they appeal to features of ourselves which, though perhaps merely found or discovered, were inadequately or ambivalently sustained by our *un*chosen families, neighborhoods, schools, or churches. Unchosen communities of origin can provide us with deeply troubled identities, perhaps severely lacking in self-esteem or basic self-respect. Thus, unchosen communities are sometimes communities we can and should leave, to search elsewhere for the resources to help us discern who we really are. Such a search is not a quest for a timeless essence but, rather, for a vital and potentially evolving self-concept that one currently affirms.

A community of choice may be a community of people who share a common oppression. This is particularly critical in those cases in which the shared oppression is not concentrated within certain communities of place, as with ethnic minorities, but, rather, is focused on people who are distributed throughout social and ethnic groupings and who do not themselves comprise a traditional community of place. Unlike the communities of ethnic minorities, women are a paradigm example of such a distributed group and do not comprise a traditional community of place. Women's communities are seldom the original, nonvoluntary, found communities of their members.

To be sure, communities of choice range widely, from benign associations of hobbyists, gardening clubs, for example, to more hateful and deadly associations such as the Ku Klux Klan. Regrettably, these treacherous communities of choice may define the personal identities of their members as decisively and as profoundly as do the most virtuous of affiliations. In this respect, even the most loathsome of voluntary associations exemplifies the communitarian's metaphysical conception of social selfhood. Such communities serve to remind us of my earlier call to conjoin the communitarian metaphysical account of the origins of moral identity with a critical perspective on communal traditions and practices. I contended above that the normative traditions of communities of place should not be regarded unquestioningly as morally authoritative. That caution must obviously extend as well to communities of choice.

It must also be remembered that nonvoluntary communities of place are not without value. Most lives contain mixtures of relationships and communities, some given/found/discovered and some chosen/created. Most people probably are ineradicably constituted, to some extent, by their communities of place, their original families, neighborhoods, schools, churches, and nations. It is crucial that dependent children, elderly persons, and all other individuals whose lives and well-being are at great risk be supported by communities or social relationships whose other members do not or cannot choose arbitrarily to leave. Recent philosophical reflection on communities and relationships not founded or sustained by choice has brought out the importance of these social networks for the constitution of social life.[46] But these insights should not obscure the additional need for communities of choice to counter oppressive and abusive relational structures in those nonvoluntary communities by providing models of alternative social relationships and standpoints for critical reflection on self and community.

If one has already attained a critically reflective stance toward one's communities of origin, one's community of place, toward family, neighborhood, church, school, and nation, then one has probably at the same time already begun to question and distance oneself from aspects of one's identity in that community and, therefore, to have embarked on the path of personal redefinition. From such a perspective, the uncritical invocation of communities of place by communitarians appears deeply problematic. We can concede the influence of those communities without needing unreflectively to endorse it. We must develop communitarian thought beyond its complacent regard for the communities in which we merely find ourselves toward (and beyond) an awareness of the crucial importance of "dislocated" communities, communities of choice.

Notes

1. See Carole Pateman, *The Problem of Political Obligation: A Critique of Liberal Theory* (Berkeley: University of California Press, 1979); Zillah Eisenstein, *The Radical Future of Liberal Feminism* (New York: Longman, 1981); Nancy C. M. Hartsock, *Money, Sex, and Power* (Boston: Northeastern University Press, 1983); Alison M. Jaggar, *Feminist Politics and Human Nature* (Totowa, N.J.: Rowman & Allanheld, 1983); Naomi Scheman, "Individualism and the Objects of Psychology," in Sandra Harding and Merrill B. Hintikka, eds., *Discovering Reality* (Dordrecht: D. Reidel, 1983), pp. 225–44; Jane Flax, "Political Philosophy and the Patriarchal Unconscious: A Psychoanalytic Perspective on Epistemology and Metaphysics," in Harding and Hintikka, *Discovering Reality,* pp. 245–81; and Seyla Benhabib, "The Generalized and the Concrete Other: The Kohlberg-Gilligan Controversy and Moral Theory," in Eva Feder Kittay and Diana T. Meyers, eds., *Women and Moral Theory* (Totowa, N.J.: Rowman & Littlefield, 1987), pp. 154–77.

2. See David Gauthier, *Morals by Agreement* (Oxford: Oxford University Press, 1986).

3. See George Homans, *Social Behavior: Its Elementary Forms* (New York:

Harcourt, Brace and World, 1961); and Peter Blau, *Exchange and Power in Social Life* (New York: Wiley, 1974).

4. See Drucilla Cornell, "Toward a Modern/Postmodern Reconstruction of Ethics," *University of Pennsylvania Law Review* 133 (January 1985): 291–380.

5. See Annette Baier, "Trust and Antitrust," *Ethics* 96, no. 2 (1986): 231–60; and Owen Flanagan and Kathryn Jackson, "Justice, Care, and Gender: The Kohlberg-Gilligan Debate Revisited," *Ethics* 97, no. 3 (1987): 622–37.

6. See Hartsock, *Money, Sex, and Power,* pp. 41–42; and Virginia Held, "Non-Contractual Society: A Feminist View," in Marsha Hanen and Kai Nielsen, eds., *Science Morality, and Feminist Theory, Canadian Journal of Philosophy* suppl. vol. 13 (1987): 111–38.

7. Amy Gutmann, "Communitarian Critics of Liberalism," *Philosophy and Public Affairs* 14 (Summer 1985): 308–22.

8. See Alice H. Eagly and Valerie J. Steffen, "Gender Stereotypes Stem from the Distribution of Women and Men into Social Roles," *Journal of Personality and Social Psychology* 46 (1984): 735–54.

9. See Carol Gilligan, *In a Different Voice* (Cambridge: Harvard University Press, 1982).

10. In particular, Michael Sandel, *Liberalism and the Limits of Justice* (Cambridge: Cambridge University Press, 1982); and Alasdair MacIntyre, *After Virtue* (Notre Dame, Ind.: University of Notre Dame Press, 1981).

11. Contemporary liberals do not regard the communitarians' metaphysical claims (discussed later in the text) as a threat to liberal theory. The liberal concept of the self as abstracted from social relationships and historical context is now treated, not as a metaphysical presupposition, but, rather, as a vehicle for evoking a pluralistic political society whose members disagree about the good for human life. With this device, liberalism seeks a theory of political process that aims to avoid relying on any human particularities that might presuppose parochial human goods or purposes. See John Rawls, "Justice as Fairness: Political Not Metaphysical," *Philosophy and Public Affairs* 14, no. 3 (1985): 223–51; and Joel Feinberg, "Liberalism, Community, and Tradition," excerpted from *Harmless Wrongdoing,* vol. 4 of *The Moral Limits of the Criminal Law* (Oxford: Oxford University Press, 1988).

12. *Liberalism and the Limits of Justice,* p. 179.

13. Ibid.; italics mine.

14. *After Virtue,* pp. 204–5.

15. Ibid., p. 205.

16. Ibid.

17. Dorothy Dinnerstein, *The Mermaid and the Minotaur: Sexual Arrangements and Human Malaise* (New York: Harper & Row, 1976); Nancy Chodorow, *The Reproduction of Mothering* (Berkeley: University of California Press, 1978); and Gilligan, *In a Different Voice.*

18. *After Virtue,* p. 205; italics mine.

19. A similar point is made by Iris Young in "The Ideal of Community and the Politics of Difference," *Social Theory and Practice* 12 (Spring 1986): 12–13.

20. John Stuart Mill's *Subjection of Women* is a noteworthy exception. My thanks to L. W. Sumner for reminding me of the relevance of this work to my discussion.

21. See Cornell, "Toward a Modern/Postmodern Reconstruction of Ethics," p. 323. Such reflections among feminists often reflect a postmodern, rather than modern, standpoint. Fortunately, that topic exceeds the scope of this essay.

22. This point is made by Young in "Ideal of Community," p. 12.

23. MacIntyre, *After Virtue,* p. 204; Sandel, *Liberalism and the Limits of Justice,* p. 179.

24. MacIntyre, *After Virtue,* p. 204; Sandel, *Liberalism and the Limits of Justice,* p. 179.

25. MacIntyre, *After Virtue,* p. 204.

26. Sandel, *Liberalism and the Limits of Justice,* p. 150.

27. Ibid., pp. 151–52.

28. "Split at the Root: An Essay on Jewish Identity," in Adrienne Rich, *Blood, Bread, and Poetry* (New York: W. W. Norton, 1986), p. 107.

29. Ibid., p. 108.

30. This term is used by Sandel in *Liberalism and the Limits of Justice,* p. 180.

31. Martha Ackelsberg points out the ironic and misleading nature of this use of the term "sisterhood" in "Sisters' or 'Comrades'? The Politics of Friends and Families," in Irene Diamond, ed., *Families, Politics, and Public Policy* (New York: Longman, 1983), pp. 339–56.

32. See Janice Raymond, *A Passion for Friends* (Boston: Beacon Press, 1986), esp. chaps. 2 and 3.

33. Claude Fischer, *To Dwell among Friends* (Chicago: University of Chicago Press, 1982), p. 1.

34. See Richard Sennett, "An Introduction," in Richard Sennett, ed., *Classic Essays on the Culture of Cities* (New York: Appleton-Century-Crofts, 1969), pp. 3–22.

35. See Stanley Milgram, "The Experience of Living in Cities," *Science* 167 (1970): 1461–68.

36. Fischer, *To Dwell among Friends,* pp. 97–103.

37. Ibid., pp. 193–232. Urban communities of place vary widely along numerous dimensions, one of the most important and thorniest of which is socioeconomic status. High-income urban dwellers are more involved with those not their kin than are low-income urban dwellers (pp. 91–93). Obviously, very poor urban dwellers do not have access to anything like the range of voluntary communal urban opportunities that wealthy urban dwellers do. The generalized observations presented in the text are not intended to deny these differences, but

rather to emphasize features of urban community that contrast most strongly with communitarian models.

38. "Order in Diversity: Community without Propinquity," in R. Gutman and D. Popenoe, eds., *Neighborhood, City, and Metropolis* (New York: Random House, 1970), pp. 792–811.

39. Fischer, *To Dwell among Friends,* p. 273.

40. See the essays in Catharine Stimpson et al., eds., *Women and the American City* (Chicago: University of Chicago Press, 1980, 1981); and the special issue on "Women in the City," *Urban Resources* 3 (Winter 1986).

41. This is pointed out in Susan Merrill Squier, ed., *Women Writers and the City* (Knoxville: University of Tennessee Press, 1984), "Introduction," esp. pp. 3–10.

42. Blanche Gelfant, "Sister to Faust: The City's 'Hungry' Woman as Heroine," in ibid., p. 267.

43. Fischer, *To Dwell among Friends,* pp. 247–48.

44. Ibid., p. 230.

45. Ibid.

46. See Baier, "Trust and Antitrust"; Held, "Non-Contractual Society"; and Pateman, *Problem of Political Obligation.*

14

Non-Contractual Society

A Feminist View

Virginia Held

Contemporary society is in the grip of contractual thinking. Realities are interpreted in contractual terms, and goals are formulated in terms of rational contracts. The leading current conceptions of rationality begin with assumptions that human beings are independent, self-interested or mutually disinterested, individuals; they then typically argue that it is often rational for human beings to enter into contractual relationships with each other.

On the side of description, assumptions characteristic of a contractual view of human relations underlie the dominant attempts to view social realities through the lenses of the social sciences.[1] They also underlie the principles upon which most persons in contemporary Western society claim their most powerful institutions to be founded. We are told that modern democratic states rest on a social contract,[2] that their economies should be thought of as a free market where producers and consumers, employers and employees make contractual agreements.[3] And we should even, it is suggested, interpret our culture as a free market of ideas.[4]

On the side of prescription, leading theories of justice and equality such as those of Rawls, Nozick, and Dworkin, suggest what social arrangements should be like to more fully reflect the requirements of contractual rationality.[5] And various philosophers claim that even mo-

Reprinted from *Canadian Journal of Philosophy,* suppl. vol. 13 (1987): 111–37, by permission of the author and the publisher.

rality itself is best understood in contractual terms.[6] The vast domain of rational choice theory, supposedly applicable to the whole range of human activity and experience, makes the same basic assumptions about individuals, contractual relations, and rationality, as are by now familiar in the social contract tradition.[7] And contractual solutions are increasingly suggested for problems which arise in areas not hitherto thought of in contractual terms, such as in dealing with unruly patients in treatment contexts, in controlling inmates in prisons, and even in bringing up children.

When subjected to examination, the assumptions and conceptions of contractual thinking seem highly questionable. As descriptions of reality they can be seriously misleading. Actual societies are the results of war, exploitation, racism, and patriarchy far more than of social contracts. Economic and political realities are the outcomes of economic strength triumphing over economic weakness more than of a free market. And rather than a free market of ideas, we have a culture in which the loudspeakers that are the mass media drown out the soft voices of free expression. As expressions of normative concern, moreover, contractual theories hold out an impoverished view of human aspiration.

To see contractual relations between self-interested or mutually disinterested individuals as constituting a paradigm of human relations is to take a certain historically specific conception of "economic man" as representative of humanity. And it is, many feminists are beginning to agree, to overlook or to discount in very fundamental ways the experience of women.

I shall try in this paper to look at society from a thoroughly different point of view than that of economic man. I shall take the point of view of women, and especially of mothers, as the basis for trying to rethink society and its possible goals. Certainly there is no single point of view of women; the perspectives of women are potentially as diverse as those of men. But since the perspectives of women have all been to a large extent discounted, across the spectrum, I shall not try to deal here with diversity among such views, but rather to give voice to one possible feminist outlook.

The social contract tradition and bourgeois conceptions of rationality have already been criticized for some time from Marxian and other continental perspectives. These perspectives, however, usually leave out the perspective of mothers as fully as do those they criticize, so I shall not try to deal here with these alternatives either. I shall try instead to imagine what society would look like, for both descriptive and prescriptive purposes, if we replaced the paradigm of "economic man" and substituted for it the paradigm of mother and child. I shall try to explore how society and our goals for it might appear if, instead of thinking of human relations as contractual, we thought of them as *like* relations between mothers and children. What would social relations look like? What would society look like if we would take the relation between mother and child as not just one relation among many, but as the *primary* social relation? And what sorts of aspirations might we have for such a society?

On the face of it, it seems plausible to take the relation between mother and child as *the* primary social relation, since before there could have been any self-sufficient, independent men in a hypothetical state of nature, there would have had to have been mothers, and the children these men would have had to have been. And the argument could be developed in terms of a conceptual as well as a causal primacy. However, let me anticipate a likely reaction and say before I begin this exploration that I doubt that the view I am going to present is the one we should end up with. I doubt that we should take any one relation as paradigmatic for all the others. And I doubt that morality should be based on any one type of human relation. In my recent book *Rights and Goods* I argue for different moral approaches for different contexts, and try to map out which approaches are suitable for which contexts.[8] Perhaps this book will turn out to be a mere stage in my thinking, and I will eventually suppose that relations between mothers and children should be thought of as primary, and as the sort of human relation all other human relations should resemble or reflect. But I am inclined at this point to think that we will continue to need conceptions of different types of relations for different domains, such as the domains of law, of economic activity, and of the family.

To think of relations between mothers and children as paradigmatic, however, may be an important stage to go through in reconstructing a view of human relationships that will be adequate from a feminist point of view. Since the image of rational economic man in contractual relations is pervasive in this society, and expanding constantly, it may be a useful endeavor to try to see everything in this different way, as if the primary social relation is that between mother and child, and as if all the others could and should be made over in the image of this one, or be embedded in a framework of such relations. In any case, if we pay attention to this neglected relation between mother and child, perhaps we can put a stop to the imperialism of the model of economic man, and assert with conviction that at least there are some or perhaps many domains where this model is definitely not appropriate. And perhaps we can show that morality must be as relevant to, and moral theory as appropriately based on, the context of mothering as the context of contracting. To the extent that some of our relations should be seen as contractual, we should recognize how essentially limited rather than general such relations are. And to the extent that some of morality should be understood in terms of what national contractors would agree to, we should recognize that such a morality can only be suitable for a particular domain of human relations, and should not be supposed to be a model for morality in general.

Rational choice theorists point out that their theories are formulated for just those situations where individuals do seek to maximize their own interests and are uninterested in each others' interests. Their theories, they suggest, are not intended to deal with people in love. But the questions I am trying to raise in this paper have to do with how we ought to treat, conceptually, a great variety of human relations. Of course we *can,* theoretically, treat them *as* contractual, but *should* we do so? Is it plausible to do so? And when we ask these questions we can see that of course it is not only in special cases that persons can be and perhaps should be and often are bound together in social ties of a non-contractual kind.

To see society in terms of family rather than marketplace relationships is not new. Feudal conceptions, for instance, drew analogies between monarchs and the heads of households. But these were views based on relations between patriarchal fathers and their wives and children, not views of society seen in terms of mothering. To explore the latter is not to suggest a return to pre-contractual society, but to consider what further progress is needed.

Since it is the practice of mothering with which I shall be concerned in what follows, rather than with women in the biological sense, I shall use the term "mothering person" rather than "mother." A "mothering person" can be male or female. So I shall speak of "mothering persons" in the same gender-neutral way that various writers now try to speak of "rational contractors." If men feel uncomfortable being referred to as, or even more so in being, "mothering persons," this may possibly mirror the discomfort many mothers feel adapting to the norms and practices, and language, of "economic man."

It is important to emphasize that I shall look at the practice of mothering not as it has in fact existed in any patriarchal society, but in terms of what the characteristic features of this practice would be without patriarchal domination. In method this may be comparable to what has been done in developing a concept of rational contracting. This concept of course developed while large segments of society were in fact still feudal, and of course actual human beings are not in fact fully rational. These realities have not prevented the contractual relation from being taken as paradigmatic.

Furthermore, it may well be that the concept of the mother/child relation that I shall develop is somewhat historically specific. But perhaps no concept can avoid being that. My aim is only to have the conception I shall try to develop capable of being considered an alternative to the conception of economic man in contractual relations, that is, of being no more historically limited, and contextually dependent, than that. To the extent that the mother/child relation will be an idealization, I hope it will not be more severely idealized than the relation between rational contractors that it is to replace; for the purposes of my exploration, it does not need to be less of an idealization.

I. Women and Family

A first point to note in trying to imagine society from the point of view of women is that the contractual model was hardly ever applied, as either description or ideal, to women or to relations within the family. The family was imagined to be "outside" the polis and "outside" the market in a "private" domain. This private domain was contrasted with the public domain, and with what, by the time of Hobbes and Locke, was thought of as the contractual domain of citizen and state and tradesman and market. Although women have always worked, and although both women and children were later pressed into work in factories, they were still thought of as outside the domain in which the contractual models of "equal men" were developed. Women were not expected to demand equal rights either in the public domain or at home. Women were not expected to be "economic men." And children were simply excluded from the realm of what was being interpreted in contractual terms as distinctively human.

The clearest example of the extraordinary bias to which such views can lead can be seen in the writings of Rousseau. Moral principles were to be applied to men and to women in ways thoroughly inconsistent with each other. Rousseau argued that in the polity no man should surrender his freedom. He thought that government could be based on a social contract in which citizens under law will be as free as in the state of nature because they will give the law to themselves.[9] But, he argued, within the household, the man must rule and the woman must submit to this rule.[10] Rousseau maintained that women must be trained from the beginning to serve and to submit to men. Since the essence of being fully human was for Rousseau being free from submission to the will of another, women were to be denied the essential condition for being fully human. And he thought that if women were accorded equality with men in the household (which was the only domain to be open to them) this would bring about the dissolution of society. Human society, Rousseau thought, was incompatible with extending the principles of contractual society to women and the family.

The contrast, in this view, is total: complete freedom and equality in the exclusively male polity; absolute male authority and female submission in the household. And Rousseau seems not to have considered the implications of such a view. If one really believes that two persons in a household, with ties of affection and time for discussion, can never reach decisions by consensus, or by taking turns at deciding, but must always have one person in full authority to have the final word, what hope could there possibly be for the larger democratic, participatory, consensual political life Rousseau so eloquently advocated? On the other hand, if decisions in the political realm *can* be arrived at in such a way that the will of no man needs to be overpowered, as Rousseau thought, why cannot such concern for avoiding coercion be extended to relations between men and women in the family?

One way in which the dominant patterns of thought have managed to overlook such inconsistencies has been to see women as primarily mothers, and mothering as a primarily biological function. Then it has been supposed that while contracting is a specifically human activity, women are engaged in an activity which is not specifically human. Women have accordingly been thought to be closer to nature than men, to be enmeshed in a biological function involving processes more like those in which other animals are involved than like the rational contracting of distinctively human "economic man." The total or relative exclusion of women from the domain of voluntary contracting has then been thought to be either inevitable or appropriate.

The view that women are more governed by biology than are men is still prevalent. It is as questionable as many other traditional misinterpretations of women's experience. Human mothering is an extremely different activity from the mothering engaged in by other animals. It is as different from the mothering of other animals as is the work and speech of men different from the "work" and "speech" of other animals. Since humans are also animals, one should not exaggerate the differences between humans and other animals. But to whatever extent it is appropriate to recognize a difference between "man" and other animals, so would it be appropriate to recognize a comparable difference between human mothering and the mothering of other animals.

Human mothering shapes language and culture, and forms human social personhood. Human mothering develops morality, it does not merely transmit techniques of survival; impressive as the latter can be, they do not have built into them the aims of morality. Human mothering teaches consideration for others based on moral concern; it does not merely follow and bring the child to follow instinctive tendency. Human mothering creates autonomous persons; it does not merely propagate a species. It can be fully as creative an activity as most other human activities; to create *new* persons, and new types of *persons,* is surely as creative as to make new objects, products, or institutions. Human mothering is no more "natural" than any other human activity. It may include many dull and repetitive tasks, as does farming, industrial production, banking, and work in a laboratory. But degree of dullness has nothing to do with degree of "naturalness." In sum, human mothering is as different from animal mothering as humans are from animals.

On a variety of grounds there are good reasons to have mothering become an activity performed by men as well as by women.[11] We may wish to continue to use the term "mothering" to designate the activity, in recognition of the fact that it has been overwhelmingly women who have engaged in this activity,[12] and because for the foreseeable future it is the point of view of women, including women engaged in mothering, which should be called on to provide a contrast with the point of view of men. A time may come when a term such as "the nurturing of children" would be preferable to "mothering."[13]

Clearly, the view that contractual relations are a model for human relations generally is especially unsuitable for considering the relations between mothering persons and children. It stretches credulity even further than most philosophers can tolerate to imagine babies as little rational calculators contracting with their mothers for care. Of course the fundamental contracts have always been thought of as hypothetical rather than real. But one cannot imagine hypothetical babies contracting either. And mothering persons, in their care of children, demonstrate hardly any of the "trucking" or trading instinct claimed by Adam Smith to be the *most* characteristic aspect of human nature.[14] If the epitome of what it is to be human is thought to be a disposition to be a rational contractor, human persons creating other human persons through the processes of human mothering are overlooked. And human children developing human personhood are not recognized as engaged in a most obviously human activity.

David Hume, whom some admire for having moral views more compatible with "women's moral sense" than most philosophers have had,[15] had the following to say about the passion of avarice: "Avarice, or the desire of gain, is a universal passion which operates at all times, in all places, and upon all persons."[16] Surely we can note that in the relation between mothering person and child, not only as it should be but often enough as it is, avarice is hard to find. One can uncover very many emotions in the relation, but the avarice that fuels the model of "economic man" with his rational interest is not prominent among them.

There is an exchange in Charlotte Perkins Gilman's *Herland* that illustrates the contrast between the motives ascribed to rational economic man building contractual society, and those central to the practice of mothering. Herland is an imaginary society composed entirely of women. They reproduce by parthenogenesis, and there are only mothers and daughters in the society. Everything is arranged to benefit the next generation and the society has existed peacefully for hundreds of years, with a high level of technological advancement but without any conception of a "survival of the fittest" ethic. Three young men from twentieth century America manage to get to Herland. They acknowledge that in Herland there are no wars, no kings, no priests, no aristocracies, that the women are all like sisters to each other and work together not by competition but by united action. But they argue that things are much better at home. In one exchange they try to explain how important it is to have competition. One of them expounds on the advantages of competition, on how it develops fine qualities, saying that "without it there would be 'no stimulus to industry.' "[17] He says competition is necessary to provide an incentive to work; "competition," he explains, "is the motor power" of society.

The women of Herland are genuinely curious and good-naturedly skeptical, as they so often are in Gilman's novel. "Do you mean," they ask, "that no mother would work for her children without the stimulus of competition?" In Herland, the entire, industrious society works on the strong motivation of making the society better for the children. As one woman explains, "The children in this country are the one center and focus of all our thoughts. Every step of our advance is always considered in its effects on them . . . You see, we are *Mothers*."[18]

Of course, this is an idealized picture of mothering. But I am contrasting it with an idealized picture of rationally contracting. Quite probably we would not want a society devoted entirely to mothering. But then we might not want a society devoted entirely to better bargains either. In developing these suggestions, it is instructive to see what is most seriously overlooked by a contractual view of society, and to see how important what is overlooked is.

II. Family and Society

In recent years, many feminists have demanded that the principles of justice and freedom and equality on which it is claimed that democracy rests be extended to women and the family. They have demanded that women be treated as equals in the polity, in the workplace, and, finally, at home. They have demanded, in short, to be accorded full rights to enter freely the contractual relations of modern society. They have asked that these be extended to take in the family.

But some feminists are now considering whether the arguments should perhaps, instead, run the other way. Instead of importing into the household principles derived from the marketplace, perhaps we should export to the wider society the relations suitable for mothering persons and children. This approach suggests that just as relations between persons within the family should be based on concern and caring, rather than on egoistic or non-tuistic contracts,* so various relations in the wider society should be characterized by more care and concern and

---

*"Non-tuism" is a term David Gauthier imported into philosophical discussions from the work of P. H. Wicksteed. It means mutual unconcern or mutual disinterest, and it is used by Gauthier as a requirement for his version of the "original position" from which people are supposed to consider socially contracting. It is his version of Rawls's requirement of mutual disinterest. See Gauthier, *Morals by Agreement* (Oxford: Clarendon Press, 1986) and Wicksteed, *The Common Sense of Political Economy and Selected Papers and Reviews on Economic Theory,* ed. L. Robbins, 2 vols. (London, 1933). *Ed.*

openness and trust and human feeling than are the contractual bargains that have developed so far in political and economic life, or even than are aspired to in contractarian prescriptions. Then, the household instead of the marketplace might provide a model for society. Of course what we would mean by the household would not be the patriarchal household which was, before the rise of contractual thinking, also thought of as a model of society. We would now mean the relations between mothering persons and children *without* the patriarch. We would take our conception of the *post*-patriarchal family as a model.

The model of the social contract was certainly an improvement over that of political patriarchy. Locke's prescriptions for political order are so clearly better than Filmer's that almost no one still reads the arguments made by philosophers such as Filmer, whose views were completely dominant until replaced by those of contractualists like Locke. Filmer thought that political authority should be based on correct inheritance: God gave the world to Adam, and authority to govern was transferred from Adam through the ancient patriarchs to the legitimate monarchs of any historical period. Democracy, to Filmer, was dangerous nonsense. Of course no feminist would wish to go back to such views as Filmer's, nor to those of Aristotle if interpreted as holding that the polity should be a version on a grander scale of the patriarchal household. But to consider whether we should generalize the relation between mothering person and child to any regions beyond the home is to consider generalizing a quite different relation from that which has existed within the patriarchal household, even between mothers and children within patriarchal society. It is to explore what relations between mothering persons and children should be in non-patriarchal societies, and to consider how a transformed household might contribute to a transformed society.

These questions lead us to focus on the family as a social institution of the utmost importance. The family is a set of relations creating human persons. Societies are composed of families. And a family is a small society. The family is undergoing profound change at the present time, and the attendant upheavals in the personal lives of many persons hold out the promise of remarkable social change, quite possibly for the better.

The family is only beginning to receive the central attention from feminists that it deserves, partly because feminist theory is still in such exploratory stages, trying to understand all at once the multiplicity of forces — social, economic, political, legal, psychological, sexual, biological, and cultural — that affect women. Multiple causes shape the sex/gender structures within which human females and males develop feminine and masculine characteristics and come to occupy the roles that existing societies designate as female and male. We need to understand empirically how this happens. We also need normative theories of the family. Jane Flax, surveying recent feminist writing on the family, writes that to develop alternatives to the oppressive relations that now prevail, we need to think through

> what kinds of child care are best for parents and children; what family structures are best for persons at various stages of the life cycle . . . ; how the state and political processes should affect families; and how work and the organization of production should be transformed to support whatever family forms are preferred.[19]

It is an enormous task, but recent years have provided more new thought on these subjects than many previous decades.[20]

The major question remains: what are the possibilities of remaking society by remaking what have been thought of as "personal" relations? Societies are composed of persons in relation to one another. The "personal" relations among persons are the most affective and influential in many ways. But the extent to which they are central to wider social relations, or could possibly provide a model for social and political relations of a kind that has been thought of as "public," remains an open question.

Western liberal democratic thought has been built on the concept of the "individual" seen as a theoretically isolatable entity. This entity can assert interests, have rights, and enter into contractual relations with other entities. But this individual is not seen as related to other individuals in inextricable or intrinsic ways. This individual is assumed to be motivated primarily by a desire to pursue his own interests, though he can recognize the need to agree to contractual restraints on the ways everyone may pursue their interests. To the extent that groups have been dealt with at all, they have been treated *as* individuals.

The difficulties of developing trust and cooperation and society itself on the sands of self-interested individuals pursuing their own gain are extreme.[21] Contractual society is society perpetually in danger of breaking down. Perhaps what are needed for even adequate levels of social cohesion are persons tied together by relations of concern and caring and empathy and trust rather than merely by contracts it may be in their interests to disregard. Any enforcement mechanisms put in place to keep persons to their contracts will be as subject to disintegration as the contracts themselves; at some point contracts must be embedded in social relations that are non-contractual.

The relation between mothering person and child, hardly understandable in contractual terms, may be a more fundamental human relation, and a more promising one on which to build our recommendations for the future, than is any relation between rational contractors. Perhaps we should look to the relation between mothering person and child for suggestions of how better to describe such society as we now have. And perhaps we should look to it especially for a view of a future more fit for our children than a global battleground for rational, egoistic entities trying, somehow, to restrain their antagonisms by fragile contracts.

The Marxian view of the relations between human beings is in various ways more satisfactory than the contractual one and more capable of accounting for social relations in general. However, the Marxian view of our history split into classes and driven by economic forces, is hardly more capable of encompassing, and does not lend itself to reflecting, the experience of the relation between mothering person and child either. So I will continue to develop here the contrast between the relation between mothering person and child on the one hand, and the contractual exchanges of "economic man" on the other.

III. The Mother/Child Relation

Let us examine in more detail the relation between mothering person and child. A first aspect of the relation that we can note is the extent to which it is not voluntary and, for this reason among others, not contractual. The ties that bind mothering person and child are affectional and solicitous on the one hand, and emotional and dependent on the other. The degree to which bearing and caring for children has been voluntary for most mothers throughout most of history has been extremely limited; it is still quite limited for most mothering persons. The relation *should* be voluntary for the mothering person but it cannot possibly be voluntary for the young child, and it can only become, gradually, slightly more voluntary.

A woman can have decided voluntarily to have a child, but once that decision has been made, she will never again be unaffected by the fact that she has brought this particular child into existence. And even if the decision to have a child is voluntary, the decision to have this particular child, for either parent, cannot be. Technological developments can continue to reduce the uncertainties of childbirth, but unpredictable aspects are likely to remain great for most parents. Unlike that contract where buyer and seller can know what is being exchanged, and which is void if the participants cannot know what they are agreeing to, a parent cannot know what a particular child will be like. And children are totally unable to choose their parents and, for many years, any of their caretakers.

The recognition of how limited are the aspects of voluntariness in the relation between mothering person and child may help us to gain a closer approximation to reality in our understanding of most human relations, especially at a global level, than we can gain from imagining the purely voluntary trades entered into by rational economic contractors to be characteristic of human relations in other domains.

Society may impose certain reciprocal obligations: on parents to care for children when the children are young, and on children to care for parents when the parents are old. But if there is any element of a bargain in the relation between mothering person and child, it is very different from the bargain supposedly characteristic of the marketplace. If a parent thinks "I'll take care of you now so you'll take care of me when I'm old," it must be based, unlike the contracts of political and economic bargains, on enormous trust and on a virtual absence of enforcement.[22] And few mothering persons have any such exchange in mind when they engage in the activities of mothering. At least the bargain would only be resorted to when the callousness or poverty of the society made the plight of the old person desperate. This is demonstrated in survey after survey; old persons certainly hope not to have to be a burden on their children.[23] And they prefer social arrangements that will allow them to refuse to cash in on any such bargain. So the intention and goal of mothering is to give of one's care without obtaining a return of a self-interested kind. The emotional satisfaction of a mothering person is a satisfaction in the well-being and happiness of another human being, and a satisfaction in the health of the relation between the two persons, not the gain that results from an egoistic bargain. The motive behind the activity of mothering is thus entirely different from that behind a market transaction. And so is, perhaps even more clearly, the motive behind the child's project of growth and development.

A second aspect of the contrast between market relations and relations between mothering person and child is found in the qualities of permanence and non-replaceability. The market makes of everything, even human labor and artistic expression and sexual desire, a commodity to be bought and sold, with one unit of economic value replaceable by any other of equivalent value. To the extent that political life reflects these aspects of the market, politicians are replaceable and political influence is bought and sold. Though rights may be thought of as outside the economic market, in contractual thinking they are seen as inside the wider market of the social contract, and can be traded against each other. But the ties between parents and children are permanent ties, however stained or slack they become at times. And no person within a family should be a commodity to any other. Although various persons may participate in mothering a given child, and a given person may mother many children, still no child and no mothering person is to the other a merely replaceable commodity. The extent to which more of our attitudes, for instance toward our society's cultural productions, should be thought of in these terms rather than in the terms of the marketplace, should be considered.

A third aspect of the relation between mothering person and child that may be of interest is the insight it provides for our notions of equality. It shows us unmistakably that equality is not equivalent to having equal legal rights. All feminists are committed to equality and to equal rights in contexts where rights are what are appropriately at issue. But in many contexts, concerns other than rights are more salient and appropriate. And the equality that is at issue in the relation between mothering person and child is the equal consideration of persons, not a legal or contractual notion of equal rights.

Parents and children should not have equal rights in the sense that what they are entitled to decide or to do or to have should be the same. A family of several small children, an adult or two, and an aged parent should not, for instance, make its decisions by majority vote in most cases.[24] But every member of a family is worthy of equal respect and consideration. Each person in a family is as important as a person as every other.

Sometimes the interests of children have been thought in some sense to count for more, justifying "sacrificing for the children." Certainly, the interests of mothers have often counted for less than those of either fathers or children. Increasingly, we may come to think that the interests of all should count equally, but we should recognize that this claim is appropriately invoked only if the issue should be thought of as one of interest. Often, it should not. Much of the time we can see that calculations of interest, and of equal interests, are as out of place as are determinations of equal rights. Both the rights and the interests of individuals seen as separate entities, and equality between them all, should not exhaust our moral concerns. The flourishing of shared joy, of mutual affection, of bonds of trust and hope between mothering persons and children can illustrate this as clearly as anything can. Harmony, love, and cooperation cannot be broken down into individual benefits or burdens. They are goals we ought to share and relations *between* persons. And although the degree of their intensity may be different, many and various relations *between* persons are important also at the level of communities or societies. We can consider, of a society, whether the relations between its members are trusting and mutually supportive, or suspicious and hostile. To focus only on contractual relations and the gains and losses of individuals obscures these often more important relational aspects of societies.

A fourth important feature of the relation between mothering person and child is that we obviously do not fulfil our obligations by merely leaving people alone. If one leaves an infant alone he will starve. If one leaves a two-year old alone she will rapidly harm herself. The whole tradition that sees respecting others as constituted by non-interference with them is most effectively shown up as inadequate. It assumes that people can fend for themselves and provide through their own initiatives and efforts what they need. This Robinson Crusoe image of "economic man" is false for almost everyone, but it is totally and obviously false in the case of infants and children, and recognizing this can be salutary. It can lead us to see very vividly how unsatisfactory are those prevalent political views according to which we fulfil our obligations merely by refraining from interference. We ought to acknowledge that our fellow citizens, and fellow inhabitants of the globe, have moral rights to what they need to live—to the food, shelter, and medical care that are the necessary conditions of living and growing—and that when the resources exist for honoring such rights there are few excuses for not doing so. Such rights are not rights to be left to starve unimpeded. Seeing how unsatisfactory rights merely to be left alone are as an interpretation of the rights of children may help us to recognize a similar truth about other persons. And the arguments—though appropriately in a different form—can be repeated for interests as distinct from rights.[25]

A fifth interesting feature of the relation between mothering person and child is the very different view it provides of privacy. We come to see that to be in a position where others are *not* making demands on us is a rare luxury, not a normal state. To be a mothering person is to be subjected to the continual demands and needs of others. And to be a child is to be subjected to the continual demands and expectations of others. Both mothering persons and children need to extricate themselves from the thick and heavy social fabric in which they are entwined in order to enjoy any pockets of privacy at all.

Here the picture we form of our individuality and the concept we form of a "self" is entirely different from the one we get if we start with the self-sufficient individual of the "state of nature." If we begin with the picture of rational contractor entering into agreements with others, the "natural" condition is seen as one of individuality and privacy, and the problem is the building of society and government. From the point of view of the relation between mothering person and child, on the other hand, the problem is the reverse. The starting condition is an enveloping tie, and the problem is individuating oneself. The task is to carve out a gradually increasing measure of privacy in ways appropriate to a constantly shifting interdependency. For the child, the problem is to become gradually more independent. For the mothering person, the problem is to free oneself from an all-consuming involvement. For both, the progression is from society to greater individuality rather than from self-sufficient individuality to contractual ties.

Psychology and psychoanalysis have long been interested in the process by which children develop and individuate themselves. Especially relevant now are feminist explorations of the different development of a sense of self in boys and in girls, and of a possibly different moral sense. Philosophers are just beginning to consider the normative issues involved. And social philosophers are just beginning to consider what we should think about social relations if we take women as our starting point. That we need not start with the patriarchal family in forming our concepts of society has been recognized for several centuries, ever since Locke won out over Filmer. That it might be instructive to begin with the point of view of women, and within that with the relation between mothering person and child, to try to reconceptualize society and our goals for better societies, is a new idea. A new concept of the "self" may be at the heart of such reconceptualizations. And we should expect that a new concept of "self" or "person" should have as much significance for our views of politics and society, and for our conceptualizations of the supposedly "impersonal" and "public" domain distinct from the supposedly "personal" and "private" sphere of the family, as has the concept of the self as rational calculator and the conceptualization of society as contractual. The same real "persons" can act in and inhabit both marketplace and household contexts. It is open to them to decide what sorts of institutions to encourage for the sake of what sorts of persons.

A sixth aspect of the relation between mothering person and child which is noteworthy is the very different view of power it provides. We are accustomed to thinking of power as something that can be wielded by one person over another, as a means by which one person can bend another to his will. An ideal has been to equalize power so that agreements can be forged and conflicts defused. But consider now the very different view of power in the relation between mothering person and child. The superior power of the mothering person over the child is relatively useless for most of what the mothering person aims to achieve in bringing up the child. The mothering person seeks to *empower* the child to act responsibly, she neither wants to "wield" power nor to defend herself against the power "wielded" by the child. The relative powerlessness of the child is largely irrelevant to most of the project of growing up. When the child is physically weakest, as in infancy and illness, the child can "command" the greatest amount of attention and care from the mothering person because of the seriousness of the child's needs.

The mothering person's stance is characteristically one of caring, of being vulnerable to the needs and pains of the child, and of fearing the loss of the child before the child is ready for independence. It is not characteristically a stance of domination. The child's project is one of developing, of gaining ever greater control over his or her own life, of relying on the mothering person rather than of submitting to superior strength. Of course the relation may in a degenerate form be one of domination and submission, but this only indicates that the relation is not what it should be. In a form in which the relation between mothering person and child is even adequately exemplified, the conceptions of power with which we are familiar, from Hobbes and Locke to Hegel and Marx, are of little use for understanding the aspects of power involved in the relation.[26] The power of a mothering person to empower others, to foster transformative growth, is a different sort of power than that of a stronger sword or dominant will. And the power of a child to call forth tenderness and care is perhaps more different still.

IV. Mothering and Moral Theory

A final aspect of the relation between mothering person and child about which I would like to speculate is what a focus on this relation might imply for our views of morality itself, and of ethical theory itself.

Hobbes thought we could build society on the equal vulnerability of every man to the sword of his fellows. Women have never fit into that picture. We are more vulnerable to the sword. And yet the sword is powerless to create new wielders of it. Only the power of mothers can in the long run triumph. But the power of mothers is continually being eclipsed by the power of children.

The vulnerability of men may bring them to seek peace and to covenant against violence. We can hope for whatever progress can be made in curbing the murderous conflicts, tempered by truces and treaties, to which this has led, though our expectations under current conditions must realistically be very modest.

But let us speculate about a different vulnerability and a different development. Mothering persons are vulnerable to the demands and needs of children. We do not know if this is instinctive or innate, or not. Some claim that women lack a mothering instinct. Others claim that the experiences of carrying a child, of laboring and suffering to give birth, of suckling, inevitably cause mothers to be especially sensitive to the cries and needs of a child. Others claim that fathers, placed in the position of being the only persons capable of responding to the needs of a child, develop similar responsiveness. Whatever the truth, one can admit that no one can become a mothering person without becoming sensitive to the needs of relatively helpless or less powerful others. And to become thus sensitive is to become vulnerable. If the vulnerability is chosen, so much the better. Mothering persons become in this way vulnerable to the claims of morality.

It is not, however, the morality of following abstract, universal rules so much as the morality of being responsive to the needs of actual, particular others in relations with us. The traditional view, reasserted in the psychological studies of Lawrence Kohlberg, that women are less likely than men to be guided by the highest forms of morality, would only be plausible if morality were no more than the abstract and rational rules of pure and perfect principle.[27] For traditional morality, increasingly recognizable as developed from a male point of view, there seems to be either the pure principle of the rational law-giver, or the self-interest of the individual contractor. There is the unreal universality of *all*, or the real *self* of individual interest.

Both views, however, lose sight of acting *for* particular others in actual contexts. Mothering persons cannot lose sight of the particularity of the child being mothered nor of the actuality of the circumstances in which the activity is taking place. Mothering persons may tend to resist harming or sacrificing those particular others for the sake of abstract principles or total faith; on the other hand, it is for the sake of *others*, or for the sake of relationships between persons, rather than to further their own interests, that such resistance is presented by mothering persons. Morality, for mothering persons, must guide us in our relations with actual, particular children, enabling them to develop their own lives and commitments. For mothering persons, morality can never seem adequate if it offers no more than ideal rules for hypothetical situations: morality must connect with the actual context of real, particular others in need. At the same time, morality, for mothering persons, cannot possibly be a mere bargain between rational contractors. That morality in this context could not be based on self-interest or mutual disinterest directly is obvious; that a contractual escape is unavailable or inappropriate is clear enough.

The morality that could offer guidance for those engaged in mothering might be a superior morality to those available at present. It would be a morality based on caring and concern for actual human others, and it would have to recognize the limitations of both egoism and perfect justice.[28] When we would turn to the social and political theories that would be compatible with such a view of morality, we would see that they would have to be very different not only from the patriarchial models of pre-contractual conceptions, but also from the contractual models that so dominate current thinking. Contractual relations would not be ruled out, but they would cease to seem paradigmatic of human relations, and the regions within which they could be thought to be justified would be greatly reduced.

V. The Child's Perspective

What about the point of view of the child? A most salient characteristic of the relation between mothering person and child is the child's relative powerlessness. The child cannot possibly rely on the Hobbesian safeguard of the equal vulnerability of the caretaker. Not even when the caretaker is asleep is she vulnerable to the sword of the small child, and it will be years, if ever, before the child can match the caretaker in even physical strength, let alone social and economic and psychological power. Whatever claims the child makes against a mothering person must be based on something else than superior strength, and the child should come to trust the restraint of one who could but does not wish to cause the child harm.

The child in relation to the mothering person is permanently in the best possible position from which to recognize that right is *not* equivalent to might, that power, including the power to teach and enforce a given morality, is not equivalent to morality itself. Becoming a person is not so much learning a morality that is being taught as it is developing the ability to decide for oneself what morality requires of one. Children characteristically go beyond the mothering persons in their lives, becoming autonomous beings. They do not characteristically then respond to the mothering persons they leave behind with proposals for better bargains for themselves now that they have the power to enforce their terms. The relation between mothering person and child is such that disparities of power are given. Though the positions may reverse themselves, unequal power is almost everpresent. But it is often also irrelevant to the relation.

When young men are invited to enter the public realm of contractual relations they are encouraged to forget their past lack of power and to assume a position of equality or superiority. But we should probably none of us ever forget what it is like to lack power. Taking the relation between child and mothering person as the primary social relation might encourage us to remember the point of view of those who cannot rely on the power of arms to uphold their moral claims. It might remind us of the distinction between the morality that, as developed autonomous persons, we come to construct for ourselves, and the moral injunctions which those with superior force can hold us to. Though I cannot develop these suggestions further in this particular paper, *much* more needs to be felt from the point of view of children.

VI. Models for Society

In an earlier paper called "Marx, Sex, and the Transformation of Society,"[29] I looked at the relation between man and woman, if it could be transformed by love into a relation of mutual concern and respect, as a possible model for transformed relations in the wider society. It now seems to me that the relation between man and woman, especially as transformed in the way I suggested, is more special and more limited, as well as far more distant and uncertain, than the relation between mothering person and child. The latter relation seems especially worth exploring to see what implications and insights it might suggest for a transformed society.

There are good reasons to believe that a society resting on no more than bargains between self-interested or mutually disinterested individuals will not be able to withstand the forces of egoism and dissolution pulling such societies apart. Although there may be some limited domains in which rational contracts are the appropriate form of social relations, as a foundation for the fundamental ties which ought to bind human beings together, they are clearly inadequate. Perhaps we can learn from a non-patriarchal household better than from further searching in the marketplace what the sources might be for justifiable trust, cooperation, and caring.

On the first occasion when I spoke about considering the relation between mothering person and child as the primary social relation, a young man in the audience asked: but in society, by which he meant society outside the family, who are the mothers and who are the children? It was meant as a hostile question, but it is actually a very good question. The very difficulty so many persons have in imagining an answer may indicate how distorted are the traditional contractual conceptions. Such persons can imagine human society on the model of "economic man," society built on a contract between rationally self-interested persons, because these are the theories they have been brought up with. But they cannot imagine society resembling a group of persons tied together by on-going relations of caring and trust between persons in positions such as those of mothers and children where, as adults, we would sometimes be one and sometimes the other. Suppose now we ask: in the relation between mothering person and child, who are the contractors? Where is the rational self-interest? The model of "economic man" makes no sense in this context. Anyone in the social contract tradition who has noticed the relation of mothering person and child at all has supposed it to belong to some domain outside the realm of the "free market" and outside the "public" realm of politics and the law. Such theorists have supposed the context of mothering to be of much less significance for human history and of much less relevance for moral theory than the realms of trade and government, or they have imagined mothers and children as somehow outside human society altogether in a region labeled "nature," and engaged wholly in "reproduction." But mothering is at the heart of human society.

If the dynamic relation between mothering person and child is taken as the primary social relation, then it is the model of "economic man" that can be seen to be deficient as a model for society and morality, and unsuitable for all but a special context. A domain such as law, if built on no more than contractual foundations, can then be recognized as one limited domain among others; law protects some moral rights when people are too immoral or weak to respect them without the force of law. But it is hardly a majestic edifice that can serve as a model for morality. Neither can the domain of politics, if built on no more than self-interest or mutual disinterest, provide us with a model with which to understand and improve society and morality. And neither, even more clearly, can the market itself.

When we explore the implications of these speculations we may come to realize that instead of seeing the family as an anomalous island in a sea of rational contracts composing economic and political and social life, perhaps it is instead "economic man" who belongs on a relatively small island surrounded by social ties of a less hostile, cold, and precarious kind.

Notes

Acknowledgments: This essay was first presented at a conference at Loyola University on April 18, 1983. It has also been discussed at philosophy department or women's studies colloquia at Hamilton and Dartmouth, at a conference on feminist theory at the University of Cincinnati, and at a conference on contractarianism at the University of Western Ontario. I am grateful to the many persons who have commented on the paper on these occasions, and also to Elise Boulding, Marsha Hanen, Kai Nielsen, Carole Pateman, Elizabeth Potter, and Sara Ruddick for additional comments.

1. As Carole Pateman writes, "One of the most striking features of the past two decades is the extent to which the assumptions of liberal individualism have permeated the whole of social life." Carole Pateman, *The Problem of Political Obligation: A Critique of Liberal Theory* (Berkeley: University of California Press, 1985), 182–83. All those fields influenced by rational choice theory — and that includes most of the social sciences — thus "hark back to classical liberal

contract doctrines," Pateman writes, "and claims that social order is founded on the interactions of self-interested, utility-maximizing individuals, protecting and enlarging their property in the capitalist market" (183).

2. For example, Thomas Hobbes, *Leviathan,* C. B. Macpherson, ed. (Baltimore: Penguin, 1971); John Locke, *Two Treatises of Government,* Peter Laslett, ed. (New York: Mentor, 1965); Jean-Jacques Rousseau, *The Social Contract,* Charles Frankel, ed. (New York: Hafner, 1947); the U.S. Declaration of Independence; and of course a literature too vast to mention. As Carole Pateman writes of this tradition, "a corollary of the liberal view . . . is that social contract theory is central to liberalism. Paradigmatically, contract is the act through which two free and equal individuals create social bonds, or a collection of such individuals creates the state" (180).

3. For example, Adam Smith, *The Wealth of Nations,* M. Lerner, ed. (New York: Random House, 1937) and virtually the whole of classical and neoclassical economics.

4. The phrase has been entrenched in judicial and social discussion since Oliver Wendell Holmes used it in *Abrams v. United States* (250 U.S. 616, 630 [1919]).

5. For example John Rawls, *A Theory of Justice* (Cambridge, Mass.: Harvard University Press, 1971); Robert Nozick, *Anarchy, State, and Utopia* (New York: Basic Books, 1974); and Ronald Dworkin, *Taking Rights Seriously* (Cambridge, Mass.: Harvard University Press, 1977).

6. For example, David A. J. Richards, *A Theory of Reasons for Action* (New York: Oxford University Press, 1971); and David Gauthier, *Morals by Agreement* (New York: Oxford University Press, 1986).

7. For a sample, see the symposium "Explanation and Justification in Social Theory," in *Ethics* 97, no. 1.

8. Virginia Held, *Rights and Goods: Justifying Social Action* (New York: Free Press/Macmillan, 1984).

9. J.-J. Rousseau, *The Social Contract.*

10. J.-J. Rousseau, *Emile,* trans. B. Foxley (New York: Dutton, 1911).

11. See especially Nancy Chodorow, *The Reproduction of Mothering: Psychoanalysis and the Sociology of Gender* (Berkeley, Calif.: University of California Press, 1978); and Joyce Trebilcot, ed., *Mothering: Essays in Feminist Theory* (Totowa, N.J.: Rowman and Allanheld, 1984).

12. See, e.g., Susan Peterson, "Against 'Parenting,'" in Trebilcot, *Mothering.*

13. By then "parenting" might also be acceptable to those who find it presently misleading.

14. Adam Smith, *Wealth of Nations,* book 1, chap. 2.

15. See, e.g., Annette Baier, "Hume: The Women's Moral Theorist?" in *Women and Moral Theory,* Eva Kittay and Diana Meyers, eds. (Totowa, N.J.: Rowman and Littlefield, 1986).

16. David Hume, *Essays Moral, Political, and Literary,* vol. 1, Green and T. H. Grose, eds. (London: Longmans, 1898), 176.

17. Charlotte Perkins Gilman, *Herland* (New York: Pantheon, 1979), 60; originally publ. 1915.

18. Ibid., 66.

19. Jane Flax, "The Family in Contemporary Feminist Thought: A Critical Review," in *The Family in Political Thought,* Jean Bethke Elshtain, ed. (Amherst: University of Massachusetts Press, 1982), 252.

20. The collection of readings in Barrie Thorne, ed., *Rethinking the Family* (New York: Longmans, 1982) is a useful source. Joyce Trebilcot's *Mothering* is another helpful collection. And among the best sources of suggestions are feminist utopian novels, e.g., Marge Piercy's *Woman on the Edge of Time* (New York: Fawcett, 1976).

21. See especially Virginia Held, *Rights and Goods,* chapter 5.

22. In some societies, social pressures to conform with the norms of reciprocal care — of children by parents and later of parents by children — can be very great. But these societies are usually of a kind which are thought to be at a stage of development antecedent to that of contractual society.

23. The gerontologist Elaine Brody says about old people that "what we hear over and over again — and I'm talking gross numbers of 80 to 90 percent in survey after survey — is 'I don't want to be a burden on my children.'" Interview by Lindsy Van Gelder, *Ms.* Magazine, January 1986, 48.

24. For a different view see Howard Cohen, *Equal Rights for Children* (Totowa, N.J.: Littlefield, Adams, 1980).

25. See Virginia Held, *Rights and Goods.*

26. For related discussions, see Nancy Hartsock, *Money, Sex, and Power: Toward a Feminist Historical Materialism* (New York: Longmans, 1983); and Sara Ruddick, "Maternal Thinking," in Trebilcot, *Mothering.*

27. For examples of the view that women are more deficient than men in understanding morality and acting morally, see e.g. Mary Mahowald, ed., *Philosophy of Woman: Classical to Current Concepts* (Indianapolis: Hackett, 1978). See also Lawrence Kohlberg, *The Philosophy of Moral Development* (San Francisco: Harper and Row, 1981), and L. Kohlberg and R. Kramer, "Continuities and Discontinuities in Child and Adult Moral Development," *Human Development* 12 (1969): 93–120.

28. For further discussion, see Virginia Held, "Feminism and Moral Theory," in *Women and Moral Theory,* Eva Kittay and Diana Meyers, eds. (Totowa, N.J.: Rowman & Littlefield, 1987).

29. Virginia Held, "Marx, Sex, and the Transformation of Society," *The Philosophical Forum* 5, no. 1–2 (Fall–Winter 1973–74).

15

The Ideal of Community
and the Politics of Difference

Iris Marion Young

Radical theorists and activists often appeal to an ideal of community as an alternative to the oppression and exploitation they argue characterize capitalist patriarchal society. Such appeals often do not explicitly articulate the meaning of the concept of community, but rather tend to evoke an affective value. Even more rarely do those who invoke an ideal of community as an alternative to capitalist patriarchal society ask what it presupposes or implies, or what it means concretely to institute a society that embodies community. I raise a number of critical questions about the meaning, presuppositions, implications and practical import of the ideal of community.

As in all conceptual reflection, in this case there is no universally shared concept of community, but only particular articulations that overlap, complement, or sit at acute angles to one another.[1] I shall rely on the definitions and expositions of a number of writers for examples of conceptualizations about community as a political ideal. All these writers share a critique of liberal individualist social ontology, and most think democratic socialism is the best principle of social organization. I claim acceptance for my analysis only within this general field of political discourse, though I suspect that much of the conceptual structure I identify applies to an ideal of community that might be appealed to by more conservative or liberal writers.

Reprinted from *Social Theory and Practice* 12 (Spring 1986): 1–26, by permission of the author and the publisher.

I criticize the notion of community on both philosophical and practical grounds. I argue that the ideal of community participates in what Derrida calls the metaphysics of presence or Adorno calls the logic of identity, a metaphysics that denies difference. The ideal of community presumes subjects who are present to themselves and presumes subjects can understand one another as they understand themselves. It thus denies the difference between subjects. The desire for community relies on the same desire for social wholeness and identification that underlies racism and ethnic chauvinism, on the one hand, and political sectarianism on the other.

Insofar as the ideal of community entails promoting a model of face-to-face relations as best, it devalues and denies difference in the form of temporal and spatial distancing. The ideal of a society consisting of decentralized face-to-face communities is undesirably utopian in several ways. It fails to see that alienation and violence are not a function of mediation of social relations, but can and do exist in face-to-face relations. It implausibly proposes a society without the city. It fails to address the political question of the relations among face-to-face communities.

The ideal of community, finally, totalizes and detemporalizes its conception of social life by setting up an opposition between authentic and inauthentic social relations. It also detemporalizes its understanding of social change by positing the desired society as the complete negation of existing society. It thus provides no understanding of the move from here to there that would be rooted in an understanding of the contradictions and possibilities of existing society.

I propose that instead of community as the normative ideal of political emancipation, that radicals should develop a politics of difference. A model of the unoppressive city offers an understanding of social relations without domination in which persons live together in relations of mediation among strangers with whom they are not in community.

1. The Metaphysics of Presence

Western conceptualization, as expressed both in philosophical writing, other theoretical writing, and quite often everyday speech as well, exhibits what Derrida calls a metaphysics of presence and what Adorno calls a logic of identity.[2] This metaphysics consists in a desire to think things together in a unity, to formulate a representation of a whole, a totality. It seeks the unity of the thinking subject with the object thought, that the object would be a grasping of the real. This urge to unity seeks to think everything that is as a whole, or to describe some ontological region, such as social life, as a whole, a system. Such totalization need not be restricted to synchronic conceptualization, moreover. The conceptualization of a process teleologically also exhibits the logic of identity, inasmuch as the end conceptually organizes the process into a unity.

The desire to bring things into unity generates a logic of hierarchical opposition. Any move to define an identity, a closed totality, always depends on excluding some elements, separating the pure from the impure. Bringing particular things under a universal essence, for example, depends on determining some attribute of particulars as accidental, lying outside the essence. Any definition or category creates an inside/outside distinction, and the logic of identity seeks to keep those borders firmly drawn. In the history of Western thought the metaphysics of presence has created a vast number of such mutually exclusive oppositions that structure whole philosophies: subject/object, mind/body, culture/nature, male/female. In the metaphysical tradition the first of these is elevated over the second because it designates the unified, the self-identical, whereas the second side lies outside the unified, the chaotic, unformed, transforming. Metaphysical thinking makes distinctions and formulates accounts by relying on such oppositions, where one side designates the pure, authentic, good, and the other the impure, inauthentic, bad.

The logic of identity also seeks to understand the subject, the person, as a self-identical unity. Beginning with Descartes, modern philosophy is particularly preoccupied with the unity of consciousness and its immediate presence to itself. The tradition of transcendental philosophy from Descartes through Kant to Husserl conceives the subject as a unity and an origin, the self-same starting point of thought and meaning, whose signification is never out of its grasp.

There are two sorts of criticisms Derrida, Adorno, Kristeva and others make of the metaphysics of presence. First, its effort to bring things into unity is doomed to failure. The claim to totality asserted by this metaphysics is incoherent, because, as I have already discussed, the process of totalizing itself expels some aspects of the entities. Some of the experienced particulars are expelled to an unaccounted for, "accidental" realm, what Derrida calls the supplement and Adorno calls the addendum. The move to create totality, as the logic of hierarchical opposition shows, creates not one, but two: inside and outside. The identity or essence sought receives its meaning and purity only by its relation to its outside. What Derrida calls the method of deconstruction consists in showing how with a concept or category what it claims to exclude is implicated in it. Dialectical logic, of course, makes a similar claim. The method of deconstruction, or what Adorno calls negative dialectic, however, rejects the Hegelian method of dialectic. For Hegelian dialectic is the ultimate totalizer, bringing the oppositions generated by metaphysical logic into ultimate unity within a totality.

Second, the metaphysics of presence represses or denies difference. This term has come to carry a great deal of meaning in these philosophical accounts. As I understand it, difference means the irreducible particularity of entities, which makes it impossible to reduce them to commonness or bring them into unity without remainder. Such particularity derives from the contextuality of existence, the being of a thing and what is said about it is a function of its contextual relation to other things. Adorno in particular contrasts the logic of identity with entities in their particularity, which for him also means their materiality. Idealism, which Adorno thinks exhibits the logic of identity, withdraws from such particularity and constructs unreal essences.[3]

Derrida defines difference primarily in terms of the functioning of language, expressing the irreducible spatio-temporality of language. The sign signifies, has meaning, by its place in the chain of signs, by differing from other signs. Any moment of signification also defers, holds in abeyance, any completion of its meaning. Any utterance has a multiplicity of meanings and directions of interpretation and development in which it can be taken. For Derrida, the metaphysics of presence seeks to detemporalize and despatialize this signifying process, inventing the illusion of pure present meaning which eliminates the referential relation. This is idealism: conceiving the being and truth of things as lying outside time and change.[4]

Kristeva more often uses the term "heterogeneity" than difference, but like Derrida and Adorno suggests that a logic of identity represses heterogeneity, which she associates with the body as well as language. She too focuses on language and the process of signification, especially the speaking subject. The subject is never a unity, but always in process, for Kristeva, producing meaning through the play between the literal and figurative, representational and musical aspects that any speech simultaneously carries.[5]

Along with such writers as Anthony Giddens and Fred Dallmayr, I think the critique of the metaphysics of presence and the claim that we need to attend to the irreducibility of difference have important implications for social philosophy and social theory.[6] I shall argue that the ideal of community exhibits the desire for unity these writers find in the metaphysics of presence. Community usually appears as one side of a dichotomy in which individualism is the opposite pole, but as with any such opposition, each side is determined by its relation to the other. I argue that the ideal of community exhibits a totalizing impulse and denies difference in two primary ways. First, it denies the difference within and between subjects. Second, in privileging face to face relations it seeks a model of social relations that are not mediated by space and time distancing. In radically opposing the inauthentic social relations of alienated society with the authentic social relations of community, moreover, it detemporalizes the process of social change into a static before and after structure.

2. The Opposition between Individualism and Community

Critics of liberalism frequently invoke a conception of community to project an alternative to the individualism and abstract formalism they attribute to liberalism.[7] This alternative social ontology rejects the image of persons as separate and self-contained atoms, each with the same formal rights, the rights to keep others out, separate. In the idea of community, critics of liberalism find a social ontology which sees the attributes of a person as coeval with the society in which he or she lives.

For such writers, the ideal of community evokes the absence of the self-interested competitiveness of modern society. In this ideal of community, critics of liberalism find an alternative to the abstract, formal methodology of liberalism. Existing in community with others entails more than merely respecting their rights, but rather attending to and sharing in the particularity of their needs and interests.

For example, in his critique of Rawls, Michael Sandel argues that liberalism's emphasis on the primacy of justice presupposes a self as an antecedent unity existing prior to its desires and goals, whole unto itself, separated and bounded. This is an unreal and incoherent conception of the self, he argues, better replaced by a constitutive conception of self as the product of an identity it shares with others, all of whom mutually understand and affirm one another. This constitutive conception of self is expressed by the concept of community.

And insofar as our constitutive self-understandings comprehend a wider subject than the individual alone, whether a family or a tribe or a city or class or nation or people, to this extent they define a community in the constitutive sense. And what marks such a community is not merely a spirit of benevolence, or the prevalence of communitarian values, or even certain "shared final ends" alone, but a common vocabulary of discourse and a background of implicit practices and understandings within which the opacity of persons is reduced if never finally dissolved. Insofar as justice depends for its pre-eminence on the separatedness and boundedness of persons in the cognitive sense, its priority would diminish as that opacity faded and those community values deepened.[8]

In contemporary political discussion, for the most part, the ideal of community arises in this way as a response to the individualism perceived as the prevailing theoretical position, and the alienation and fragmentation perceived as the prevailing condition of society. Community appears, that is, as part of an opposition, individualism/community, separated self/shared self. In this opposition each term comes to be defined by its negative relation to the other, thus existing in a logical dependency. I suggest that this opposition, however, is integral to modern political theory, and is not an alternative to it.

The opposition individualism/community receives one of its expressions in bourgeois culture in the opposition between masculinity and femininity. The culture identifies masculinity with the values associated with individualism — self-sufficiency, competition, separation, the formal equality of rights. The culture identifies femininity, on the other hand, with the values associated with community — affective relations of care, mutual aid, and cooperation.

Carol Gilligan has posed this opposition between masculine and feminine in terms of the opposition between two orientations on moral reasoning.[9] The "ethic of rights" that Gilligan takes to be typical of masculine thinking emphasizes the separation of selves and the sense of fair play necessary to mediate the competition among such separated selves. The "ethic of care," on the other hand, which she takes to be typical of feminine thinking, emphasizes relatedness among persons, is an ethic of sympathy and affective attention to particular needs, rather than formal measuring of each according to universal rules. This ethic of care expresses the relatedness of the ideal of community as opposed to the atomistic formalism of liberal individualism.

The opposition between individualism and community, then, is homologous with and often implies the oppositions masculine/feminine, public/private, calculative/affective, instrumental/aesthetic, which are also present in modern political thinking.[10] This thinking has always valued the first side of these oppositions more highly than the second, and provided them with a dominant institutional expression in the society. For that reason asserting the value of community over individualism, the feminine over the masculine, the aesthetic over the instrumental, the relational over the competitive, does have some critical force with respect to the dominant ideology and social relations. The oppositions themselves, however, arise from and belong to bourgeois culture, and for that reason merely reversing their valuation does not constitute a genuine alternative to capitalist patriarchal society.

Like most such oppositions, moreover, individualism and community have a common logic underlying their polarity, which makes it possible for them to define each other negatively. Each entails a denial of difference and desire to bring multiplicity and heterogeneity into unity, though in opposing ways. Liberal individualism denies difference by positing the self as a solid, self-sufficient unity, not defined by or in need of anything or anyone other than itself. Its formalistic ethic of rights denies difference by leveling all such separated individuals under a common measure of rights. Community, on the other hand, denies difference by positing fusion rather than separation as the social ideal. Community proponents conceive the social subject as a relation of unity composed by identification and symmetry among individuals within a totality. As Sandel puts it, the opacity of persons tends to dissolve as ends, vocabulary, and practices become identical. This represents an urge to see persons in unity with each other in a shared whole.

As is the case with many dichotomies, in this one the possibilities for social ontology and social relations appear to be exhausted in the two categories. For many writers, the rejection of individualism logically entails asserting community, and conversely any rejection of community entails that one necessarily supports individualism. In their discussion of the debate between Elshtain and Ehrenreich, for example, Sara Evans and Harry Boyte claim that Ehrenreich promotes individualism because she rejects the appeal to community that Elshtain makes.[11] The possibility that there could be other conceptions of social organization does not appear because all possibilities have been reduced to the mutually exclusive opposition between individualism and community.

Ultimately, however, for most radical theorists the hard opposition of individualism and community breaks down. Unlike reactionary appeals to community which consistently assert the subordination of individual aims and values to the collective, most radical theorists assert that community itself consists in the respect for and fulfillment of individual aims and capacities. The neat distinction between individualism and community thus generates a dialectic in which each is a condition for the other.

3. Denying Difference within and between Subjects

In her interpretation of Marx's social ontology, Carol Gould formulates such a dialectical conception of community as the transcended synthesis of sociality and individuality. This ideal society of the future is realized as the third stage of a process of social evolution. The first stage is a communal society in which the individual is subjected to the collective and the second is the individualist society of capitalist alienation.

> The separate subjects who were related to each other only as objects, namely, as beings for another, now recognize themselves in these objects, or recognize these objects as like themselves. Therefore they recognize each other as subjects, and the unity between subjects and objects is reestablished in this recognition. The subjects are then related to each other not as alien external others, but as aspects of a common species subject. The relations are therefore internal, since they are the interrelations within this common or communal subject which is now no longer made up of discrete individuals in external relations, but rather of individuals who are unified in their common subjectivity. . . . The subjects are therefore mutually interdependent and the relations between them are internal because each subject is what it is — a subject — through its relation to the other, namely, through being recognized as a subject by the other. These individuals therefore form a communal but differentiated subject that expresses itself in and through each individual. The whole or unity that is reconstituted in these internal relations among the individuals is thus mediated or differentiated by their individuality, but unified by their commonality.[12]

According to Derrida, dialectical logic represses difference not by bringing multiplicity under a simple universal, but by putting closure on the process of exteriorization. This closure emerges in the concept of a whole or totality within which opposites, differences, are reconciled and balanced.[13] Like many other expressions of this ideal of community, Gould's conception of community works on and through a totalizing desire to reconcile the differences of subjects.

This communitarian ideal participates in the metaphysics of presence because it conceives that subjects no longer need be exterior to one another. They need no longer outrun one another in directions they do not mutually understand and affirm. The ideal, moreover, extends this mutuality to its conception of the good society as a telos, an end to the conflict and violence of human interaction. Community here is conceived as a totality, in two ways. It has no ontological exterior, since it realizes the unity of general will and individual subjectivity. It also has no historical exterior, for there is no further stage to travel.

While she does not specifically speak of her ideal as community, Seyla Benhabib expresses a similar ideal of persons relating to one another through reciprocal recognition of subjectivities as a particular standpoint of moral autonomy. Liberalism holds a conception of moral autonomy she calls the "standpoint of the generalized other," which abstracts from the difference, desires and feeling among persons, to regard all as sharing a common set of formal rights and duties. In contrast, what Benhabib calls the "standpoint of the concrete other" views each person in his or her concrete individuality.

> In assuming this standpoint, we abstract from what constitutes our commonality and seek to understand the other as he/she understands him/herself. We seek to comprehend the needs of the other, their motivations, what they search for and what they desire. Our relation to the other is governed by the norm of *complementary reciprocity:* each is entitled to expect and assume from the other forms of behavior through which the other feels recognized and confirmed as a concrete, individual being with specific needs, talents and capacities. Our differences in this case complement rather than exclude one another.[14]

Benhabib's notion of the standpoint of the concrete other expresses community as the mutual and reciprocal understanding of persons, relating internally, as Gould puts it, rather than externally. Many other writers express a similar ideal of relating to other persons internally, understanding them from their point of view. In the quotation previously cited, Sandel poses the elimination of the opacity of other persons as the ideal for community. Isaac Balbus represents the goal of radical politics and the establishment of community as the overcoming of the "otherness" of others in reciprocal recognition.[15] Roberto Unger articulates the ideal of community as the political alternative to personal love. In community persons relate to one another as concrete individuals who recognize themselves in each other because they have shared purposes. The conflict between the demands of individuality and the demands of sociability disappears in mutual sympathy.[16] Dorothy Allison proposes an ideal of community for feminists that is characterized by a "shared feeling of belonging and merging," with an "ecstatic sense of oneness."[17]

All these formulations seek to understand community as a unification of particular persons through the sharing of subjectivities: persons will cease to be opaque, other, not understood, and instead become fused, mutually sympathetic, understanding one another as they understand themselves. Such an ideal of shared subjectivity, or the transparency of subjects to one another, denies difference in the sense of the basic asymmetry of subjects. As Hegel first brought to focus and Sartre's analysis deepened, persons necessarily transcend each other because subjectivity is negativity. The regard of the other upon me is always objectifying. Other persons never see the world from my perspective, and I am always faced with an experience of myself I do not have in witnessing the other's objective grasp of my body, actions and words.

This mutual intersubjective transcendence, of course, makes sharing between us possible, a fact that Sartre notices less than Hegel. The sharing, however, is never complete mutual understanding and reciprocity. Sharing, moreover, is fragile. The other person may at the next moment understand my words differently from the way I meant them, or carry my actions to consequences I do not intend. The same difference that makes sharing between us possible also makes misunderstanding, rejection, withdrawal, and conflict always possible conditions of social being.

The notion that each person can understand the other as he or she understands himself or herself, moreover, that persons can know other subjects in their concrete needs and desires, presupposes that a subject can know himself or herself and express that knowledge accurately and unambiguously to others. Such a concept of self-knowledge retains the Cartesian understanding of subjectivity basic to the modern metaphysics of presence. The idea of the self as a unified subject of desire and need and an origin of assertion and action has been powerfully called into question by contemporary philosophers.[18] I will rely on my reading of Julia Kristeva.

Without elaborating the linguistic detail in which she couches her notion of the subject-in-process, I will summarize briefly the general idea. Kristeva relies on a psychoanalytic notion of the unconscious to assert that subjectivity is heterogeneous, decentered. Consciousness, meaning and intention are only possible because the subject-in-process slips and surpasses its intentions and meanings. Any utterance, for example, not only has a literal meaning, but is laden with ambiguities, embodied in gesture, tone of voice, rhythm, that all contribute to the heterogeneity of its meaning without being intended. So it is with actions and interactions with other persons. What I say and do always has a multiplicity of meanings, ambiguities, plays, and these are not always coherent.[19]

Because the subject is not a unity, it cannot be present to itself, know itself. I do not always know what I mean, need, want, desire, because these do not arise from some ego as origin. Often I express my desire in gesture or tone of voice, without meaning to do so. Consciousness, speech, expressiveness, are possible only if the subject always surpasses itself, and is thus necessarily unable to comprehend itself. Subjects all have multiple desires that do not cohere, they attach layers of meanings to objects without always being aware of each layer or their connections. Consequently, any individual subject is a play of differences that cannot be comprehended.

If the subject is heterogeneous process, unable to be present to itself, then it follows that subjects cannot make themselves transparent, wholly present to one another. If each subject escapes its own comprehension and for that reason cannot fully express to another its needs and desires, then necessarily each subject also escapes sympathetic comprehension by others. I cannot understand another as he or she understands himself or herself, because he or she does not completely understand himself or herself. Indeed, because other people's expression to me may outrun their own awareness or intention, I may understand certain aspects of them more fully than they.

Gould appeals to such an ideal of "common subjectivity" as an alternative to the commodification of persons she finds characteristic of capitalist domination. Her conceptualization suggests that only if persons understood one another "internally," as she puts it, would such domination be eliminated. While I certainly do not wish to deny that current social relations are full of domination and exploitation, conceiving the elimination of these conditions in terms of an impossible ideal of shared subjectivity can tend to deflect attention from more concrete analysis of the conditions of their elimination.

Not only does this ideal of shared subjectivity express an impossibility, but it has undesirable political implications. Political theorists and activists should distrust this desire for reciprocal recognition and identification with others, I suggest, because it denies difference in the concrete sense of making it difficult for people to respect those with whom they do not identify. I suggest that the desire for mutual understanding and reciprocity underlying the ideal of community is similar to the desire for identification that underlies racial and ethnic chauvinism.

In ordinary speech for most people in the U.S., the term community refers to the people with whom I identify in a locale. It refers to neighborhood, church, schools. It also carries connotations of ethnicity or race. For most people in the U.S., insofar as they consider themselves members of communities at all, a community is a group that shares a specific heritage, a common self-identification, a common culture and set of norms. In the U.S. today, identification as a member of such a community also often occurs as an oppositional differentiation from other groups, who are feared, or at best devalued. Persons identify only with some other persons, feel in community only with those, and fear the difference others confront them with because they identify with a different culture, history and point of view on the world.

Racism, ethnic chauvinism, and class devaluation, I suggest, grow partly from a desire for community; that is, from the desire to understand others as they understand themselves and from the desire to be understood as I understand myself. Practically speaking, such mutual understanding can be approximated only within a homogeneous group that defines itself by common attributes. Such common identification, however, entails reference also to those excluded.[20] In the dynamics of racism and ethnic chauvinism in the U.S. today, the positive identification of some groups is often achieved by first defining other groups as the Other, the devalued semi-human. I do not claim that appeal to the ideal of community is itself racist. Rather, my claim is that such appeals, within the context of a racist and chauvinistic society, can validate the impulses that reproduce racist and ethnically chauvinistic identification.

The striving for mutual identification and shared understanding among those who seek to foster a radical and progressive politics, moreover, can and has led to denying or suppressing differences within political groups or movements. Many feminist groups, for example, have sought to foster relations of equality and reciprocity of understanding in such a way that disagreement, difference and deviation have been interpreted as a breech of sisterhood, the destruction of personal relatedness and community. There has often been strong pressure within women's groups for members to share the same understanding of the world and the same lifestyle, in addition to distributing tasks equally and rotating leadership. Such pressure has often led to group and even movement homogeneity — primarily straight, or primarily lesbian, primarily white, or primarily academic.[21] In recent years feminists, perhaps more seriously than any other progressive political groups, have discussed how their organizations and movement might become more heterogeneous and recognize difference. A continuing desire for mutual identification and reciprocity, however, hampers the implementation of a principled call for heterogeneity.

In a racist, sexist, homophobic society that has despised and devalued certain groups, it is necessary and desirable for members of those groups to adhere with one another and celebrate a common culture, heritage and experience. Even within such separatist movements, however, too strong a desire for unity can lead to repressing the differences within the group, or forcing some out: gays and lesbians from black nationalist groups, for example, or feminists from native American groups, and so on.

Many other progressive political organizations and movements founder on the same desire for community. Too often people in political groups take mutual friendship to be a goal of the group, and thus find themselves wanting as a group when they do not achieve such commonality.[22] Such a desire for community often channels energy away from the political goals of the group, and also produces a clique atmosphere which keeps groups small and turns potential members away. A more acceptable politics would acknowledge that members of an organization do not understand one another as they understand themselves, and would accept this distance without closing it into exclusion.

4. Denial of Difference as Time and Space Distancing

Many political theorists who put forward an ideal of community specify small group, face-to-face relations as essential to the realization of that ideal. Peter Manicas expresses a version of the ideal of community that includes this face-to-face specification.

Consider an association in which persons are in face-to-face contact, but where the relations of persons are not mediated by "authorities," sanctified rules, reified bureaucracies or commodities. Each is prepared to absorb the attitudes, reasoning and ideas of others and each is in a position to do so. Their relations, thus, are open, immediate and reciprocal. Further, the total conditions of their social lives are to be conjointly determined with each having an equal voice and equal power. When these conditions are satisfied and when as a result, the consequences and fruits of their associated and independent activities are perceived and consciously become an object of individual desire and effort, then there is a democratic community.[23]

Roberto Unger argues that community requires face-to-face interaction among members within a plurality of contexts. To understand other people and to be understood by them in our concrete individuality, we must not only work together, but play together, take care of children together, grieve together, and so on.[24] Christian Bay envisions the good society as founded upon small face-to-face communities of direct democracy and many-sided interaction.[25] Michael Taylor specifies that in a community relations among members must be direct and many-sided. Like Manicas, he asserts that relations are direct only when they are unmediated by representatives, leaders, bureaucrats, state institutions or codes.[26] While Gould does not specify face-to-face relations as necessary for community, some of her language suggests that community can only be realized in such face-to-face relations. In the institutionalization of democratic socialism, she says, "social combination now becomes the *immediate* subjective relations of mutuality among individuals. The relations again become *personal* relations as in the pre-capitalist stage, but no longer relations of domination and no longer mediated, as in the second stage, by external objects."[27]

I take there to be several problems with the privileging of face-to-face relations by theorists of community. It presumes an illusory ideal of unmediated social relations, and wrongly identifies mediation with alienation. It denies difference in the sense of time and space distancing. It implies a model of the good society as consisting of decentralized small units which is both unrealistic and politically undesirable. And finally, it avoids the political question of the relation among the decentralized communities.

All the writers cited above give primacy to face-to-face presence because they claim that only under those conditions can the social relations be *immediate*. I understand them to mean several things by social relations that are immediate. They are direct, personal relations, in which each understands the other in her or his individuality. This is an extension of the ideal of mutual understanding I have criticized in the previous section. Immediacy also here means relations of co-presence in which persons experience a simultaneity of speaking and hearing, and are in the same space, that is, have the possibility to move close enough to touch.[28]

This ideal of the immediate presence of subjects to one another, however, is a metaphysical illusion. Even a face-to-face relation between two is mediated by voice and gesture, spacing and temporality. As soon as a third person enters the interaction the possibility arises of the relation between the first two being mediated through the third, and so on. The mediation of relations among persons by the speech and actions of still other persons is a fundamental condition of sociality. The richness, creativity, diversity and potential of a society expand with growth in the scope and means of its media, linking persons across time and distance. The greater the time and distance, however, the greater the number of persons who stand between other persons.

The normative privileging of face-to-face relations in the ideal of community seeks to suppress difference in the sense of the time and space distancing of social processes, which material media facilitate and enlarge. Such an ideal dematerializes its conception of interaction and institutions. For all social interaction takes place over time and across space. Social desire consists in the urge to carry meaning, agency, and the effects of agency, beyond the moment and beyond the place. As laboring subjects we separate the moment of production from the moment of consumption. Even societies confined to a limited territory with few institutions and a small population devise means of their members communicating with one another over distances, means of maintaining their social relationships even though they are not face to face. Societies occupy wider and wider territorial fields and increasingly differentiate their activity in both space, time and function, a movement that of course accelerates and takes on qualitatively specific form in modern industrial societies.[29]

I suggest that there are no conceptual grounds for considering face-to-face relations more pure, authentic social relations than relations mediated across time and distance. For both face-to-face and non-face-to-face relations are mediated relations, and in both there is as much the possibility of separation and violence as there is communication and consensus. Theorists of community are inclined to privilege face-to-face relations, I suggest, because they wrongly identify mediation and alienation.

By alienation, I mean a situation in which persons do not have control either over their actions, the conditions of their action, or the consequences of their action, due to the intervention of other agents.[30] Social mediation is a condition for the possibility of alienation in this sense; media make possible the intervention of agents between the conditions of a subject's action and the action, or between a subject's action and its consequences. Thus media make domination and exploitation possible. In modern society the primary structures creating alienation and domination are bureaucracy and commodification of all aspects of human activity, including and especially labor. Both bureaucracy and commodification of social relations depend on complex structures of mediation among a large number of persons.

That mediation is a necessary condition of alienation, however, does not entail the reverse implication: that only by eliminating structures of mediation do we eliminate alienation. If temporal and spatial distancing are basic to social processes, and if persons always mediate between other persons to generate social networks, then a society of immediacy is impossible. While mediation may be a necessary condition for alienation, it is not sufficient. Alienation is that specific process of mediation in which the actions of some serve the ends of others without reciprocation and without being explicit, and this requires coercion and domination.

By positing a society of immediate face-to-face relations as ideal, community theorists generate a dichotomy between the "authentic" society of the future and the "inauthentic" society we live in, which is characterized only by alienation, bureaucratization, and degradation. Such a dichotomization between the inauthentic society we have and the authentic society of community, however, detemporalizes our understanding of social change. On this understanding social change, revolution, consists in the complete negation of this society and the establishment of the truly good society. In her scheme of social evolution, Gould conceives of "the society of the future" as the negated sublation of capitalist society. This understands history not as temporal process, but as divided into two static structures: the before of alienated society and the after of community.

The projection of the ideal of community as the radical other of existing society denies difference in the sense of the contradictions and ambiguities of social life. Instead of dichotomizing the pure and the impure into two stages of history or two kinds of social relations, a liberating politics should conceive the social process in which we move as a multiplicity of actions and structures which cohere and contradict, some of them exploitative and some of them liberating. The polarization between the impure, inauthentic society we live in and the pure, authentic society we seek to institute, detemporalizes the process of change, because it fails to articulate how we move from one to the other. If institutional change is possible at all, it must begin from intervening in the contradictions and tensions of existing society. No telos of the final society exists, moreover; society understood as a moving and contradictory process implies that change for the better is always possible and always necessary.

The requirement that genuine community embody face-to-face relations, when taken as a model of the good society, carries a specific vision of social organization. Since the ideal of community demands that relations between members be direct and many-sided, the ideal society is composed of small locales, populated by a small enough number of persons so that each can be personally acquainted with all the others. For most writers this implies that the ideal social organization is decentralized, with small-scale industry and local markets. Each community aims for economic self-sufficiency, and each democratically makes its own decisions about how to organize its working and playing life.

I do not doubt the desirability of small groups in which individuals have personal acquaintance with one another and interact in a plurality of contexts. Just as the intimacy of living with a few others in the same household has unique dimensions that are humanly valuable, so existing with others in communities of mutual friendship has specific characteristics of warmth and sharing that are humanly valuable. Furthermore, there is no question that capitalist patriarchal society discourages and destroys such communities of mutual friendship, just as it squeezes and fragments families. In our vision of the good society we surely wish to include institutional arrangements that would nurture the specific experience of mutual friendship which only relatively small groups interacting in a plurality of contexts can produce. Recognizing the specific value of such face-to-face relations, however, is quite a different matter from proposing them as the organizing principle of a whole society.

Such a model of the good society as composed of decentralized, economically self-sufficient face-to-face communities functioning as autonomous political entities is both wildly utopian and undesirable. To bring it into being would require dismantling the urban character of modern society, a gargantuan physical overhaul of living space, workplaces, places of trade and commerce. A model of a transformed better society must in some concrete sense begin from the concrete material structures that are given to us at this time in history, and in the United States these are large-scale industry and urban centers. The model of society composed of small communities is not desirable, at least in the eyes of many. If we take seriously the way many people live their lives today, it appears that people enjoy cities, that is, places where strangers are thrown together.

One final problem arises from the model of face-to-face community taken as a political goal. This model of the good society as usually articulated leaves completely unaddressed the question of how such small communities are to relate to one another. Frequently the ideal projects a level of self-sufficiency and decentralization which suggests that proponents envision few relations among the decentralized communities except those of friendly visits. But surely it is unrealistic to assume that such decentralized communities need not engage in extensive relations of exchange of resources, goods and culture. Even if one accepts the notion that a radical restructuring of society in the direction of a just and humane society entails people living in small democratically organized units of work and neighborhood, this has not addressed the important political question: how will the relations among these communities be organized so as to foster justice and prevent domination? When we raise this political question the philosophical and practical importance of mediation reemerges. Once again politics must be conceived as a relationship of strangers who do not understand one another in a subjective and immediate sense, relating across time and distance.

5. City Life and the Politics of Difference

I have claimed that radical politics must begin from historical givens, and conceive radical change not as the negation of the given, but rather as making something good from many elements of the given. The city, as a vastly populated area with large-scale industry and places of mass assembly, is for us a historical given, and radical politics must begin from the existence of modern urban life. The material surroundings and structures available to us define and presuppose urban relationships. The very size of populations in our society and most other nations of the world, coupled with a continuing sense of national or ethnic identity with millions of other people, all support the conclusion that a vision of dismantling the city is hopelessly utopian.

Starting from the given of modern urban life is not simply necessary, moreover, it is desirable. Even for many of those who decry the alienation, massification and bureaucratization of capitalist patriarchal society, city life exerts a powerful attraction. Modern literature, art and film have celebrated city life, its energy, cultural diversity, technological complexity, and the multiplicity of its activities. Even many of the most staunch proponents of decentralized community love to show visiting friends around the Boston, or San Francisco or New York in which they live, climbing up towers to see the glitter of lights and sampling the fare at the best ethnic restaurants. For many people deemed deviant in the closeness of the face-to-face community in which they lived, whether "independent" women or socialists or gay men and lesbians, the city has often offered a welcome anonymity and some measure of freedom.[31] To be sure, the liberatory possibilities of capitalist cities have been fraught with ambiguity.

Yet I suggest that instead of the ideal of community we begin from our positive experience of city life to form a vision of the good society. Our political ideal is the unoppressive city. In sketching this ideal, I assume some material premises. We will assume a productivity level in the society that can meet everyone's needs, and a physical urban environment that is cleaned up and renovated. We will assume, too, that everyone who can work has meaningful work and those who cannot are provided for with dignity. In sketching this ideal of city life, I am concerned to describe the city as a *kind of relationship* of people to one another, to their own history and one another's history. Thus by "city" I am not referring only to those huge metropolises that we call cities in the U.S. The kinds of relationship I describe obtain also ideally in those places we call "towns," where perhaps 10 or 20 thousand people live.

As a process of people's relating to one another, city life embodies difference in all the senses I have discussed in this essay. The city obviously exhibits the temporal and spatial distancing and differentiation I have argued the ideal of community seeks to collapse. On the face of the city environment lies its history and the history of the individuals and groups that have dwelt within it. Such physical historicity, as well as the functions and groups that live in the city at any given time, create its spatial differentiation. The city as a network and sedimentation of discretely understood places, such as particular buildings, parks, neighborhoods, and as a physical environment offers changes and surprises in transition from one place to another.

The temporal and spatial differentiation that mark the physical environment of the city produce an experience of aesthetic *inexhaustibility*. Buildings, squares, the twists and turns of streets and alleys, offer an inexhaustible store of individual spaces and things, each with unique aesthetic characteristics. The juxtaposition of incongruous styles and functions that usually emerge after a long time in city places contributes to this pleasure in detail and surprise. This is an experience of difference in the sense of always being inserted. The modern city is without walls; it is not planned and coherent. Dwelling in the city means always having a sense of beyond, that there is much human life beyond my experience going on in or near these spaces, and I can never grasp the city as a whole.

City life thus also embodies difference as the contrary of the face-to-face ideal expressed by most assertions of community. City life is the "being-together" of strangers. Strangers encounter one another, either face to face or through media, often remaining strangers and yet acknowledging their contiguity in living and the contributions each makes to the others. In such encountering people are not "internally" related, as the community theorists would have it, and do not understand one another from within their own perspective. They are externally related, they experience each other as other, different, from different groups, histories, professions, cultures, which they do not understand.

The public spaces of the city are both an image of the total relationships of city life and a primary way those relationships are enacted and experienced. A public space is a place accessible to anyone, where people engage in activity as individuals or in small groups. In public spaces people are aware of each other's presence and even at times attend to it. In a city there are a multitude of such public spaces, streets, restaurants, concert halls, parks. In such public spaces the diversity of the city's residents come together and dwell side by side, sometimes appreciating one another, entertaining one another, or just chatting, always to go off again as strangers. City parks as we now experience them often have this character.

City life implies a social inexhaustibility quite different from the ideal of the face-to-face community in which there is mutual understanding and group identification and loyalty. The city consists in a great diversity of people and groups, with a multitude of subcultures and differentiated activities and functions, whose lives and movements mingle and overlap in public spaces. People belong to distinct groups or cultures, and interact in neighborhoods and workplaces. They venture out from these locales, however, to public places of entertainment, consumption and politics. They witness one another's cultures and functions in such public interaction, without adopting them as their own. The appreciation of ethnic foods or professional musicians, for example, consists in the recognition that these transcend the familiar everyday world of my life.

In the city strangers live side by side in public places, giving to and receiving from one another social and aesthetic products, often mediated by a huge chain of interactions. This instantiates social relations as difference in the sense of an understanding of groups and cultures that are different, with exchanging and overlapping interactions that do not issue in community, yet which prevent them from being outside of one another. The social differentiation of the city also provides a positive inexhaustibility of human relations. The possibility always exists of becoming acquainted with new and different people, with different cultural and social experience; the possibility always exists for new groups to form or emerge around specific interests.

The unoppressive city is thus defined as openness to unassimilated otherness. Of course, we do not have such openness to difference in our current social relations. I am asserting an ideal, which consists in a politics of difference. Assuming that group differentiation is a given of social life for us, how can the relationships of group identities embody justice, respect and the absence of oppression? The relationship among group identities and cultures in our society is blotted by racism, sexism, xenophobia, homophobia, suspicion and mockery. A politics of difference lays down institutional and ideological means for recognizing and affirming differently identifying groups in two basic senses: giving political representation to group interests and celebrating the distinctive cultures and characteristics of different groups.[32]

Many questions arise in proposing a politics of difference. What defines a group that deserves recognition and celebration? How does one provide representation to group interests that avoids the mere pluralism of liberal interest groups? What are institutional forms by which the mediations of the city and the representation of its groups in decision making can be made democratic? These questions, as well as many others, confront the ideal of the unoppressive city. They are not dissimilar from questions of the relationships that ought to exist among communities. They are questions, however, which appeal to community as the ideal of social life appears to repress or ignore. Some might claim that a politics of difference does express what the ideal of community ought to express, despite the meaning that many writers give the concept of community. Fred Dallmayr, for example, reserves the term community for just this openness toward unassimilated otherness, designating the more totalistic understandings of social relations I have criticized as either "communalism" or "movement."

> As opposed to the homogeneity deliberately fostered in the movement, the communitarian mode cultivates diversity — but without encouraging willful segregation or the repressive preponderance of one of the social subsectors. . . . Community may be the only form of social aggregation which reflects upon, and makes room for, otherness or the reverse side of subjectivity (and inter-subjectivity) and thus for the play of difference — the difference between ego and Other and between man and nature.[33]

In the end it may be a matter of stipulation whether one chooses to call such politics as play of difference "community." Because most articulations of the ideal of community carry the urge to unity I have criticized, however, I think it is less confusing to use a term other than community rather than to redefine the term. Whatever the label, the concept of social relations that embody openness to unassimilated otherness with justice and appreciation needs to be developed. Radical politics, moreover, must develop discourse and institutions for bringing differently identified groups together without suppressing or subsuming the differences.

Notes

Acknowledgments: I am grateful to David Alexander, Ann Ferguson, Roger Gottlieb, Peter Manicas, Peter Onuf, Lucius Outlaw, Michael Ryan, Richard Schmitt, Ruth Smith, Tom Wartenburg, and Hugh Wilder for helpful comments on earlier versions of this essay.

1. I examine community specifically as a normative ideal designating how social relations ought to be organized. There are various non-normative uses of

the term "community" to which my analysis does not apply. Sociologists engaged in community studies, for example, usually use the term to mean something like "small town" or "neighborhood," and use the term primarily in a descriptive sense. The questions raised apply to community understood only as a normative model of ideal social organization. See Jessie Bernard, *The Sociology of Community* (Glenview: Scott, Foresman and Co., 1973), for a summary of different sociological theories of community in its non-normative senses.

2. The texts of these authors I am relying on primarily are, Derrida, *Of Grammatology* (Baltimore: Johns Hopkins University Press, 1976); Adorno, *Negative Dialectics* (New York: Continuum Publishing Company, 1973); Kristeva, *Polylogue* (Paris: Editions du Seuil, 1977). These three writers have a similar critique of Western metaphysics. Several writers have noted similarities between Adorno and Derrida in this regard. See Fred Dallmayr, *Twilight of Subjectivity: Contributions to a Post-Structuralist Theory of Politics* (Amherst: University of Massachusetts Press, 1981), pp. 107–14, pp. 127–36; and Michael Ryan, *Marxism and Deconstruction* (Baltimore: Johns Hopkins University Press, 1982), pp. 73–81. For an account that draws some parallel between Kristeva and Adorno in this respect, see Drucilla Cornell and Adam Thurschwell, "Feminism, Negativity and Intersubjectivity," *Praxis International* (1986). My account of metaphysics of presence is based on my reading of these three writers, but I do not claim to be "representing" what they say. Nor in this paper am I claiming to appropriate all these writers say for social theory. While I do regard the critique of the ideal of community I engage in here loosely as a deconstructive critique along the lines of Derrida's method. I part ways with him and some of the other poststructuralists insofar as I think that it is both possible and necessary to pose alternative conceptualizations. Doing so is, of course, always a positing, and hence excludes and demarks, thus always itself open to the possibility of deconstructive critique.

3. See Adorno, *Negative Dialectics,* part 2, pp. 134–210.

4. Derrida, *Of Grammatology,* pp. 12–87.

5. Kristeva, *Polylogue,* "Le sujet en procès," pp. 55–106; "L'experience et la pratique," pp. 107–36; "Matière, sense, dialectique," pp. 263–86.

6. Anthony Giddens, *Central Problems in Social Theory* (Berkeley: University of California Press, 1979), pp. 28–40; Dallmayr, *Twilight of Subjectivity,* pp. 107–15.

7. See R. P. Wolff, *The Poverty of Liberalism* (Boston: Beacon Press, 1978), chapter 5.

8. Michael Sandel, *Liberalism and the Limits of Justice* (Cambridge: Cambridge University Press, 1982), pp. 172–73.

9. Carol Gilligan, *In a Different Voice* (Cambridge: Harvard University Press, 1981).

10. I develop more thoroughly the implications of these oppositions in mod-

ern political theory and practice and a practical vision of their unsettling in my paper "Impartiality and the Civic Public: Some Implications of Feminist Critics of Modern Political Theory," *Praxis International* 5 (1986): 381–401.

11. Harry C. Boyte and Sara M. Evans, "Strategies in Search of America: Cultural Radicalism, Populism, and Democratic Culture," *Socialist Review* (May to August 1984): 73–100.

12. Carol Gould, *Marx's Social Ontology* (Cambridge, Mass.: MIT Press, 1978), p. 9.

13. Michael Ryan, *Marxism and Deconstruction,* pp. 65–71.

14. Seyla Benhabib, "Communicative Ethics and Moral Autonomy," presented at a meeting of the American Philosophical Association, Eastern Division, December 1982; see also "The Generalized and the Concrete Other: Toward a Feminist Critique of Substitutionalist Universalism," *Praxis International* 5 (1986): 402–24.

15. Isaac Balbus, *Marxism and Domination* (Princeton: Princeton University Press, 1983).

16. Roberto Mangabeira Unger, *Knowledge and Politics* (New York: The Free Press, 1975), pp. 220–22.

17. Dorothy Alison, "Weaving the Web of Community," *Quest: A Feminist Quarterly* 4 (1978): 79.

18. Michael Sandel, in the work already cited, levels a powerful critique against Rawls by arguing that his theory of justice presupposes a self as separated from and prior to the actions it undertakes, as its unified origin. Sandel gives several arguments showing the incoherence of such a conception of the unified self prior to the context of action.

19. Kristeva, "Le sujet en procès," *Polylogue,* pp. 55–106.

20. Sartre's *Critique of Dialectical Reason* is a classic statement on this dynamic of inclusion and exclusion. For another statement referring specifically to the exclusionary aspects of attempts to found communities, see Rosabeth Moss Kanter, *Commitment and Community: Communes and Utopias in Sociological Perspective* (Cambridge: Harvard University Press, 1972), pp. 52–53.

21. See Francine Rainone, "Community, Politics and Spirituality," paper presented at a conference on Feminism and Psychology, Boston, Mass., February 1984; Jana Sawicki, "Foucault and Feminism: Towards a Politics of Difference," *Hypatia: A Journal of Feminist Philosophy* 1 (1986): 23–36.

See also Audre Lorde, essays in *Sister Outsider* (Trumansburg, N.Y.: Crossing Press, 1984), especially "The Master's Tools Will Never Dismantle the Master's House," and "Age, Race, Class and Sex: Women Redefining Difference."

22. Wini Breines documents this urge to mutual friendship and some of the disappointments that followed from it in the student movement in the 1960s. See *Community and Organization in the New Left: 1962–68* (South Hadley, Mass.: J. F. Bergin Publishers, 1982), especially chapter 4.

23. Peter Manicas, *The Death of the State* (New York: C. P. Putnam and Sons, 1974), p. 247.

24. Unger, *Knowledge and Politics,* pp. 262–63.

25. Christian Bay, *Strategies of Political Emancipation* (South Bend: University of Notre Dame Press, 1981), chapters 5 and 6.

26. Michael Taylor, *Community, Anarchy and Liberty* (Cambridge: Cambridge University Press, 1982), pp. 27–28.

27. Gould, *Marx's Social Ontology,* p. 26.

28. Derrida discusses the illusory character of this ideal of immediate presence of subjects to one another in community in his discussions of Lévi-Strauss and Rousseau. See *Of Grammatology,* pp. 101–40.

29. See Anthony Giddens, *Central Problems in Social Theory,* pp. 198–233.

30. For a useful account of alienation, see Richard Schmitt, *Alienation and Class* (Cambridge, Mass.: Schenkman Publishing Co., 1983), especially chapter 5. In this book Schmitt, like many other of the writers I have cited, takes community to stand as the negation of the society of alienation. Unlike those writers discussed in this section, however, he does not take face-to-face relations as a condition of community. To the degree that he makes a pure/impure distinction, and exhibits the desire for unity I have criticized, however, the critique articulated here applies to Schmitt's appeal to the ideal of community.

31. Marshall Berman presents a fascinating account of the attractions of city life in *All That Is Solid Melts Into Air,* (New York: Simon and Schuster, 1982). George Shulman points to the open-endedness of city life as contrasted with the pastoral vision of community in "The Pastoral Idyll of *Democracy,*" in *Democracy* 3 (1983): 43–54; for a similar critique, see David Plotke, "Democracy, Modernization, and *Democracy,*" *Socialist Review* 14 (March–April 1984): 31–56.

32. In my previously cited essay, "Impartiality and the Civic Public," I formulate some ideals of a heterogeneous public life; I have developed further some principles of a politics of difference in "Elements of a Politics of Difference," paper presented at the North American Society for Social Philosophy, Colorado Springs, August 1985.

33. Dallmayr, *Twilight of Subjectivity,* pp. 142–43.

16

Feminism, Family, and Community

Jean Bethke Elshtain

I must write a piece on feminism, family, and community. I write as someone who has been involved in the politics of the feminist movement since the early 1960s, someone who characterizes her own work as made possible in part by the intellectual ferment feminism has generated. But, as I begin, I find that the image of a strong woman, my grandmother, supplants all other visions, wipes out abstract ideologies and theoretical models. I see her instructing her grandchildren in the crafts that create things of beauty and utility to provide envelopes for our bodies, warmth for our beds, and food for our tables. I mark her pride and her intensity, her conviction that she has lived a good and a productive life. I know that what keeps the fires of her life burning is the drive to pass her heritage of wisdom, piety, and goodness on to her great-grandchildren. That my grandmother's image emerges so powerfully is appropriate. For the need to write this piece derives from my discontent with the way "the family" has been treated in much feminist and radical argumentation since the 1960s, and with the way "community," while celebrated, has remained mostly an empty term — for there is no way to create real communities out of an aggregate of "freely" choosing adults.

The term my grandmother uses to describe her people is *unsere Leute*, "our people," a people without a country but with an authentic historic identity, the Volga Germans. She could never see herself through the lens of some abstract universalism like "class"; for her, always, "people-

Reprinted from *Dissent* 29 (Fall 1982): 442–49, by permission of the author and the publisher.

hood" was paramount. To Marx and his orthodox followers she and her people are "rural idiots," for they formed a peasant society and most of them remain farmers. Yet the tradition that ties these people to the land also makes them profoundly suspicious of the "progressive" force represented by capitalism. "Our people's" way of life was threaded through and through by a populist pietism—a deeply rooted animus against experts ("big shots" to my grandma), the too powerful ("Pride goeth before the fall, and some of them guys are gonna fall hard, just you wait"), and the too rich ("It is easier for a camel to go through the eye of a needle than for a rich man to enter the Kingdom of God"). This pietism cautioned against judging things by appearances only, stressed responsibility to and for one's life as a social life lived among others, advocated going the "extra mile" (the Good Samaritan parable) and tempering justice with mercy (the Prodigal Son).

None of the values of "our people" mesh neatly with the "needs" of capitalism, nor with market images of human beings; they clash at nearly every point. Yet the ties of such organic communities have been seen by those progressive movements that grew out of Enlightenment rationalism and liberal myths of historic progress as precisely what we all need to be "liberated from." The hard truth we have now come up against is, simply, this: to the extent that reformers and radicals see family and traditional community as reactionary by definition and repressive by nature, to that extent they have bought into a one-dimensional image of human beings. This is a serious charge and I intend to defend it.

First, a few reminders of the way in which the family was singled out by powerful voices within middle-class movements for social change—feminist, radical, "psychological"—as *the* institution most deeply implicated in the oppression of all people but of women in particular. Calls for "smashing" the family, or its dramatic transformation in order to bring it in line with a feminist or left-wing revolution abstractly conceived, helped to invite the reaction we now face. The right has been able to portray itself as the defender of family life in part because of the early and dramatic hostility of many, though not all, feminists and radicals to all traditional social forms.

The right's portrayal of feminist and radical antifamilialism is of course drastically overdrawn, but there is just enough truth to make the charges seem plausible. Most American citizens see themselves, first and foremost, as family men and women and members of communities, and much of their energy is devoted to keeping these families and communities alive. Thus far feminists and radicals have failed to provide a compelling vision of an alternative society to grip the imagination and gain the adherence of these citizens. It may be that none of this commitment to family and traditional community *should* persist, not in 1982, not according to certain ideologies. But, to repeat one of Freud's favorite quotations, "*La théorie c'est bon, mais ça n'empêche d'exister.*" (Theory is good, but it doesn't prevent things from existing.) I shall argue that things that exist — such as the family — incorporate values that implicitly challenge corporate power and antidemocratic, managerial elites, and that this potential can be strengthened.

It would be tedious to repeat in detail all the charges against the family, but a reminder is necessary. Unless we recall at least some of these charges, we will fail to appreciate the complex interaction between protest and reaction. My now-yellowed copy of *Women and Revolution,* a "newspaper of revolutionary women's liberation," dated May–June 1971, outlines in bold letters its "program" on family, education, and production:

> The institution of the family is inherently reactionary and helps to maintain the capitalist system. The family, as a socioeconomic unit, is oppressive to its members. Women are especially oppressed by the family. . . . Each nuclear family exists in isolation from the rest of society and, thus, weakens the class consciousness of the workers.

In a widely circulated essay by Laurel Limpus on "Liberation of Women: Sexual Repression and the Family," the family was declared "the central agent of repression," inculcating "both the subservience of women and sexual taboos." Married women were called dishonest "prostitutes" for, unlike real prostitutes, they were in bad faith about what they were up to. Another manifesto depicted the new mother as a pitiful creature descending into a condition of terminal social decay, imprisoned in the home, which "is perhaps the basis of all evil." The editors of *No More Fun and Games* reduced childbearing and rearing to terms of crude possession. A woman choosing motherhood signifies that she has not "achieved sufficient maturity and autonomy and is seeking a hopeless fulfillment through neurotic channels."

There were, of course, always feminists who had deep reservations about these arguments, but they were made by such influential theorists as Kate Millett, for whom the entire society was but the oppressive, patriarchal family writ large, with women cast as universal victims and an oppressed class, or by Germaine Greer, who enjoined women who would be "free" to leave their homes and families in pursuit of the untrammeled life. Orthodox Marxist feminism, according to Jane Humphries, in her critical essay "The Working-Class Family: A Marxist Perspective,"[1] views the family through a lens labeled "functional requisites of capital" and depicts mothering as a kind of hapless mimicry of production, the "reproduction of a future commodity labor power."

True, there were, and are, feminists of all sorts who refused to jump on the antifamilial bandwagon. But this should not obscure the fact that a major thrust of early feminist rhetoric was a dramatic insistence that the family was "the enemy." Even a liberal feminist such as Betty Friedan, in her "first-stage" incarnation, referred to the home as a "comfortable concentration camp" and celebrated, as an alternative to suburban housewifery, not a transformed vision of the human community but women's absorption into the exciting world of those "able, ambitious" men who went off to the city and "kept on growing."

Feminist critics of family life were joined by a variety of (mostly male) cultural radicals. Counterculture protesters sought escape from their uptight families in drug experimentation and communal living that soon ran ashoal on its own inner contradiction — a simultaneous commitment to individual freedom (to "do your own thing") and total community. Psychological radicals found in R. D. Laing a guru who proclaimed that all human beings, having been raised in families, were "half-crazed creatures." Familial love and parental concern got redescribed by Laing as devious forms of violence. "From the moment of birth," he declared, "when the Stone Age baby confronts the twentieth-century mother, the baby is subjected to these forces of violence called love. . . ." Families were a bunch of "gangsters" and homes were sites of "reciprocal terrorism." Mocking the efforts of parents to provide security for their children, often under such difficult conditions as those depicted by Sennett and Cobb in *The Hidden Injuries of Class,* Laing denounced parental action as a debased "protection racket."

In retrospect, much of this criticism has the air of "hit and run" and is made by radicals who refused to acknowledge any of the legitimate human needs for intimacy and security imbedded and answered, however imperfectly, within the traditional family. Already weakened by market forces that eroded community ties and severed work from community life, the American family, by the 1960s, was a vulnerable target for social criticism and personal-political protest. But family critics failed to come through on what should have been an essential part of their agenda: they did not articulate viable, humane alternatives to replace what they proposed to reform or "smash." Instead, they tended to reiterate as dogma the notion that if people were no longer dependent on families, they would get together to demand radical social change.

The unhappy history of the past several decades tells a different story. What oozed into the vacuum created by the breakup of community and the breakdown of families were the forces of right-wing reaction and a bewildering smorgasbord of cults, human-potential movements, and therapeutic options for those who could afford them. The most widespread reaction to the crisis of the family is the embattled retreat embodied in such groups as the Moral Majority.* It is important to remember that militant right-wing reaction did not create our current troubles; instead, human beings who were frightened by a world increasingly out of their effective control, concerned to preserve what they saw as traditional values imperiled by liberals and radicals, got caught up in an ideology that sought to return to some imagined Good Old Days when men were men, women knew their place, children kept their place, and all was well.

It would be inaccurate, and self-serving, for feminists and radicals to see all this as no more than thousands of Americans being manipulated by the right around such issues as the family. Conservatives addressed themselves forcefully (though often dishonestly) to those cultural issues posed most dramatically in the 1960s. So far, feminists and other social critics have failed to tackle the moral issues posed by the crisis in American institutions, most importantly in the family.

Another frequently sinister alternative to family and community is presented by dozens of cults and cultlike groups. The Jim Joneses of this world prey on persons who have fallen into despair or confusion.** Cults moved into the vacuum created by the "thinning-out" of community and family ties, even as they further eroded those ties to preclude any

---

*The Moral Majority was a multi-issue, conservative evangelical group founded in 1979. It became the popular symbol of the new Christian Right. *Ed.*

**Jim Jones was minister of the People's Temple, which emigrated from the United States to Guyana and self-destructed there in November 1978 in a mass suicide of over nine hundred members. *Ed.*

outside locus for human relations. In an argument that eerily replicates radical claims that attachment to the family vitiates commitment to "the Cause," Jim Jones rejected a request by two members of his doomed cult for a Thanksgiving visit to the family of one of them in these words: "It's time for you to cut your family ties. . . . Blood ties are dangerous because they prevent people from being totally dedicated to the Cause." "Families are a part of the enemy system," one of Jones's henchmen declared. "They do not love you. . . . They don't understand this Cause, and therefore you cannot trust them."

Those who find *any* analytic comparison between certain sorts of radical protest and the theory and practice of cults unsavory, should reflect for a moment on the similarities between the views of the family propounded in each instance — that it is part of an oppressive structure inimical to liberation and the Cause; that it inhibits wholehearted political and social commitment; that it exists to perpetuate an "enemy" system. Then it is worth pondering the proposed solutions: creating some unspecified "higher form" of the family; forming a cult, a commune, or a postrevolutionary society, in which no one has an "exclusive" relationship with anybody; the absorption of childrearing "functions" by everybody, or by a public bureaucracy, or by a private sector whose enlightened entrepreneurs would meet a social need and garner a profit by going into what one Marxist critic nicely dubbed the "Kentucky Fried Children" business.

Ordinary citizens see in all this yet another assault on those social forms that help their lives make sense. The presumptions that in order to have a revolutionary or feminist consciousness one must disconnect oneself from particular ties, from what Jane Addams called "the family claim," are correctly perceived by members of working-class and traditional communities as destructive of their way of life. They sometimes even recognize in such views an extension of those market forces that have nearly annihilated older forms of social existence and replaced them by atomistic ways of life. The standpoint of "possessive individualism" — a term I owe to the political theorist C. B. Macpherson — dovetails perfectly with markets and fails to consider the emotional and social needs the family continues, however fitfully, to fulfill.

For my grandmother, the "I" of the self was always a "we," located within a dense web of human ties. She could no more think of herself outside the tissue of *"unsere Leute"* than she could fly. These ties of community were altered forever by the twin forces of liberalism and capitalism, emerging historically in tandem and realizing, in practice, awesome possibilities for both good and ill unthinkable in older social formations. For women, the promises of liberalism were slow to come, including their incorporation into the reigning definition of "the person" as a being with an identity separable from that of others — whether one's spouse, one's family, or one's community. Liberal society opened up possibilities for persons to "relocate" themselves, as civil society grew more open-textured, to move away from older ties and constraints toward personal identities that are self-defined and chosen.

The ideal was that free individuals, in pursuit of self-interest, would also be mindful of higher duties as citizens of a political community. Unfortunately, the prevailing norm for public identity in liberal America has become almost indistinguishable from its predatory variant of "possessive individualism." The terms under which individuals act in the public world are thoroughly permeated by market values that undermine possibilities for a shared life of civic virtue. This free-market model, translated into feminist protest and cultural revolt, becomes either the ideology of the "how to get yours" versions of feminism or, more "radically," the ideology that proclaims all constraints on individual expression to be coercive.

So we get an ideal of nonbinding commitments, with particular appeal to the upper-middle class, the mobile, and the well-educated, served up as a radical repast. The overall effect of all this "actualizing" of selves is supposed to be a wider good, for modes of radical protest indebted to classical liberalism implicitly embrace a notion of an "invisible hand," operating to transform self-interest and personal freedom into a social benefit.

But this will not do, finally, for there is no way to make a community out of "possessive individuals." Within this frame, where the individuals are "free" only insofar as each is the sole "proprietor" of self, the only acceptable human relations are those calculated to yield maximum utility. Within such a perspective, all human ties, including marriage, must be construed as starkly contractual — supplanting marriage and communities as social compacts.

The social compact is a different notion from that of contract. It is inseparable from ideals of civic virtue and retains a hold on working-class, religious, and rural culture. A compact is no contingent agreement but a solemn commitment to create something "new" out of disparate elements — a family, a community, a polity — whose individual members do not remain "as before" once they become part of this social mode of existence. Within the social compact, community members, ideally, share values that are sustained by moral suasion, not enforced by coercion. Unlike social-contract theories, the compact ideal revolves around the varying needs of human beings over the span of their life cycle. Contract theory is a static view: it presents a picture of consenting, rational adults — a world in which no one is born and no one dies. Children, old people, ill and dying people who need care are nowhere to be seen.

Now, in practice, contractual society remains linked, in ways that go unacknowledged, to older notions of the social compact. In Michael Walzer's words, "What made liberalism endurable for all these years was the fact that the individualism it generated was imperfect, tempered by older restraints and loyalties, by stable patterns of local, ethnic, religious, or class relationships. An untempered liberalism would be unendurable." But that is precisely what feminist and radical protest grounded in "possessive individualism" refuses to recognize; this protest has failed to demonstrate convincingly how intimate social relations are to be sustained if individualism continues to erode the social foundations upon which individuals are nourished in the first place.

"My body, my self" is a necessary corrective when communities overwhelm the individual or stifle dissent. But the obsession with "self" that is one hallmark of much radical protest offers no opposition to the terms of market society. As more and more areas of social life are subjected to decisions made along the lines of a narrowly construed theory of policy science, it is families and the remnants of traditional communities that can preserve meanings and embody relations that cannot be settled by impersonal standards. And this is why notions of a social compact that are different from the dominant public ideology in a bureaucratic state, whether capitalist or communist, hold out the possibility of radical critique. Those feminists and radicals who have faced the fact that they have failed to gain allegiance to their cause from the very people in whose behalf their struggle is ostensibly being waged should consider this world and understand its potential for social opposition.

In the concluding section of this essay I shall draw feminism and traditional notions of family life into a mutual relation in a manner that does not see earlier terms of women's oppression as the only way to restore family life. Instead, I shall embrace a revitalized form of family life and community as one way to break the destructive hold of market images on feminist protest. If we fail in this effort, we are likely to see more of the defensive reactions of right-wing movements and the destructive possibilities of cults. My aim is to contest, not to abandon, the grounds of tradition, a terrain thus far handed over to the right.

Feminists who reject the terms of our society are in the best position emphatically to assay the powerful symbols that inspire familial, religious, and community loyalties. Harry Boyte observes that "the basic theory that saw revolutionary consciousness as an abstract universalism, a rootless cosmopolitanism, and that saw anticapitalist insurgency as growing from radical deracination continues to hold sway over the left." But this world view remains willfully blind to the phenomenon, documented by social historians, that anticapitalist struggles have been waged by human beings determined to defend their particular historic identities, not by "homeless" masses in the grip of such notions as "sex-class." The Solidarity movement in Poland is animated by profoundly communal and religious values;* so was Martin Luther King's Southern Christian Leadership Conference with its base in Southern black churches. And we could cite many other examples.

To recover what Simone Weil called our "need for roots," we must first give up the hollow notion that all families or religious institutions reinforce the ideology of the wider society. Only then can we set about recasting a vision of the family as central to any humane way of life. By "family" I mean the widely accepted, popular understanding of the term as having its basis in marriage and kinship, involving links between particular persons that cannot be reduced to instrumental terms. This family stands as one barrier between human beings and the flattening out of their social world under the demands of untrammeled self-interest.

Feminist protest that sought the elimination of this sphere of traditional femininity was understandable when it was a response by women to conditions of their identities that had grown problematic under the pressures of modernization and capitalism. But the end-point of this feminist argumentation, whether radical or liberal, is ironically self-

---

*Solidarity was born in Poland from thirty-six regional independent unions. Solidarity was seen as a threat by Poland's Communist Party and the Warsaw Pact. It defied government imposition of martial law in 1981 by continuing to strike and to pursue its economic and social agenda. *Ed.*

defeating, for it requires that women, in the name of feminism, embrace the terms of a public life that was created by men who had rejected or devalued the world of the traditionally "feminine" with its "softer" virtues. Behold, the new woman as the old man!

An alternative to the feminist protest that seeks women's full absorption within the market society must make contact with women's traditional social sphere. Women's world arose on a template of concern and care for others. Any viable human community must have, in its ranks, an important segment devoted to the protection of vulnerable human life. That, historically, has been the mission of women. The pity is not that women reflect an ethic of social responsibility but that the public world has, for the most part, repudiated such an ethic. Rather than denying women the meaning their traditional world provided, even under conditions of male domination, feminists should move to challenge a society that downgrades female-created and -sustained values.

If it is the case, as Carol Gilligan has argued, that women have a distinctive moral "voice," emphasizing concern and responsibility for others, feminists should be among the first to preserve the sphere that makes this morality possible and to determine how best to extend its imperatives to serve a less-than-humane public world. If Gilligan learns that women now have a greater ability to identify with others, to sustain a variety of personal relationships, and locates those qualities and capacities in women's involvement with children, friends, and communities, feminists must think about what would be lost if we gave up this realm altogether in the name of an abstract ideal of liberation.

Right-wing defenses of the family can only be countered by a feminism that agrees that the family is a prerequisite for any form of social life and that a particular ideal of the family is imperative to create a more humane society. One sign of hope is the attempt by many men and women, not all of them professionals, both to sustain strong family ties and simultaneously to struggle toward more egalitarian relations between husband and wife.

The feminism I have in mind bears little resemblance to that "major shift" in thinking on the family some claim has taken place in Betty Friedan's *The Second Stage*. Friedan's vision of the family embodies an accommodation with the corporate and political structures most deeply implicated in the breakdown of family ties in the first place. The kind of family arrangement Friedan celebrates as exemplary (dual-career professionals on flexi-time, but often requiring paid help) is possible, at best, for the top 10–15 percent of the American population. For the remaining 85 percent we get the reiteration of a pretty standard liberal agenda — more day care, more reliance on social-engineering "experts," and, *mirabile dictu,* the final "transcendence" of any conflict between "self-realization" and "social good." Such sleight of hand blunts the edges of conflict and diffuses political debate. If, finally, the aims of a feminism guided by the values of current society, the needs of individuals for long-time intimate ties, and the attainment of some notion of the social good are all compatible, what has all the fuss been about?

My version of a feminist perspective that makes a case for family ties, unlike Friedan's, refuses to build either familial or feminist alternatives on the shaky sand of accommodation to the status quo. In defining the family simply as the place "you come home to," Friedan defines it out of existence. Her logic dictates that she put on a par with one another the swinging single in an "adult residential village"; the young couple struggling to raise their family and to make ends meet in an inflationary recession; the husband and wife, now grandparents, who have spent 40 years of their lives together; the single parent exhausted by the double responsibility for home and a job; and the four college kids who have rented a house together for the fall semester.

If a feminist case for the family is to bear any critical weight, important conflicts between popular understanding of the family and attempts by a variety of groups to redefine it in a way that accepts nearly any social arrangement human beings conjure up as "families" must not be evaded. To throw the honorable mantle "family" over every ad hoc collection of persons who happen to be under one roof at the same time is to diminish the genuine achievements of family men and women who have retained their commitments to and for one another. Feminism of the sort I propose recognizes that there is no final resolution to the twin goals of individual freedom and social good. To skip over these matters by celebrating widespread social breakdown as evidence of vital social change is to trivialize profoundly important questions.

Within the family of which I write the nourishment of humanity takes place at every point in the life cycle. This family concerns itself with those who have gone before and those who are to come after. But responsibilities for children are paramount. We know — the evidence on this score is overwhelming — that children incur an assault to their humanity if they suffer from neglect, from the uprootedness that comes from being "cared for" by no one in particular. The evidence we have of what happens to children deprived of attachments to specific adults bears out that we are talking about a prerequisite for authentic human existence.

In their understandable preoccupation with the status and role of women, feminists, until recently, were too little concerned with the impact of social change on whole families. Social feminism of the sort I propose places children in the center of its concern — children surrounded, as they need to be, by parents or their permanent, not temporary, substitutes. Unless or until this happens, the right will retain a powerful opening wedge into popular consciousness, for ordinary people love and fear for their children. The feminism I seek is not reducible to a clever strategic move; it is, instead, the reaffirmation of moral imperatives and their insertion into the heart of feminist politics.

This is a recognition Antonio Gramsci seems to have come to toward the end of his life when he wrote, in a passage of exquisite pathos:

> How many times have I wondered if it is really possible to forge links with a mass of people when one has never had strong feelings for anyone, not even one's parents; if it is possible to love a collectivity when one has not been deeply loved oneself, by individual human creatures. Hasn't this had some effect on my life as a militant, has it not tended to make me sterile and reduce my quality as a revolutionary by making everything a matter of intellect, of mere magical calculation?

My call, finally, is for a rethinking of terms that have tended to overschematize the world as one of either/ors: either traditional family life or careerism, and so on. The vision I propose opens the way to a transformed notion of community that repudiates the unacceptable poles of narcissistic self-absorption, on the one hand, and single-minded, overweening commitment to "the Cause" on the other. It sees human beings as social but not as so oversocialized that they emerge as passive reactors to external stimuli. In affirming the dignity of the human subject, beginning with the needs of children, social feminism challenges irresponsible corporate power and a politics of group self-interest, for both run roughshod over the needs of families. It indicts an economic system that denies families a living, family wage and that forces both parents into the labor force, often against the will of the woman who would prefer to be with her children but must, instead, work at a low-pay, dead-end job just to make "ends meet." The solution to this dilemma is not to join Friedan's chorus for more day care, which implicitly accepts an economic system that cannot provide decently for its families, but to challenge that system. Nor is this an argument against day care; it is a refusal to embrace the standard liberal agenda of more provision of social services to ameliorate the destructive effects of a socially irresponsible corporate structure.

If we dare to hope for a future, one coherent way is to articulate a vision of feminism and a radical politics that does not require that either feminism or radicalism be feared or despised by decent, ordinary people. "American history and tradition," writes Boyte,

> like that of any nation, embodies contradictions between rapaciously individualist, democratic, and authoritarian elements. To reclaim the best in America's traditions and history is to rediscover the popular democratic heritage: our nation's civic idealism, our practices of mutual aid and self-help, our religious wellsprings of social justice.

I began these reflections on feminism, family, and community by honoring the integrity of my grandmother, recalling, as I did, Virginia Woolf's prescient cry to the women of her generation that the education of their uneducated mothers and grandmothers must have had "great virtues as well as defects" and that "we should be extremely foolish if we threw away the results of that education or gave up the knowledge that we have obtained from it for any bribe or decoration whatever." A second luminescent image also asks that I "attend" to it. Several months ago, I read a remarkable book by a moral philosopher, Philip Hallie, who told the story of the village of Le Chambon-sur-Lignon and the "goodness" that happened there during one of the darkest moments in Western history. The entire community committed itself to resist the Nazi occupation of France by rescuing Jews, giving them food, shelter, and safety at risk to their own lives, providing them with false identity cards and helping them escape into neutral Switzerland. It was a quiet struggle. There were no macho heroes, no Maquis members engaged in guerrilla tactics. There was instead, waged by these pietists, many of them pacifist, a struggle that "began and ended in the privacy of people's homes." Decisions that were turning points in the struggle took place in kitchens. Males did not dictate these decisions; women and children were centrally involved. "A kitchen is a private, intimate place; in it there are no uniforms, no buttons or badges symbolizing public duty and public support," writes Hallie. Yet through this "kitchen struggle" a few thousand human beings were changed, irrevocably, by their resistance, as they spared hundreds the ultimate terror of nazism.

Orthodoxies holding that this village and its families, like all villages and families, are merely performing decreed functions for the larger social order cannot explain Le Chambon. For there, and at great risk to themselves, Le Chambon's men, women, and children did just the opposite. Let Freud have the final word: "La théorie c'est bon, mais ça n'empêche d'exister."

Note

1. Humphries' essay appears in *The Family in Political Thought,* ed. Jean Bethke Elshtain (Amherst: University of Massachusetts Press, 1982), pp. 197–222. The book includes an extensive bibliography of political treatments of the family.

17

Separating from Heterosexualism

Sarah Lucia Hoagland

Significantly, just as traditional ethics does not recognize moral revolution, so it does not acknowledge separation as an option for moral agents. Withdrawal or separation is not perceived as an option when the game played appears to be the only game in town and so is taken for reality. In a sense the game is reality, but its continued existence is not a matter of fact so much as a matter of agreement. The game is an agreement in value which players breathe life into. And this suggests that participation in the system at some level — support, reform, rebellion — must be an unquestioned norm and hence not itself perceived as a choice.[1]

Consider, again, that shelters for women who have been beaten by their husbands lose funding if shelter workers are suspected of encouraging those seeking refuge to withdraw or separate from the particular batterer or from marriage or from heterosexuality in general. Ethical considerations forced on most women whom men beat involve how to maintain the family unit, how to work with their husband's problems, how to restore his "dignity," how to help the children adjust — in short, how to go on as a (heterosexual) woman. Such judgments hold in place the feminine, in this case feminine virtue, and the function of such judgments is not to encourage the integrity of the individual in her choices. It is rather to maintain the social order and specific relationships and avenues of hierarchy within it.

I want to suggest that it is crucial to acknowledge withdrawal, separa-

Reprinted from *Lesbian Ethics,* by Sara Lucia Hoagland (Palo Alto: Institute of Lesbian Studies, 1988), 54–68, by permission of the author. Available from Institute of Lesbian Studies, P.O. Box 25568, Chicago, IL 60625.

tism, as an option if we are to engage in moral revolution. Separation is a central option both as a political strategy and as a consideration in individual relationships. We may withdraw from a particular situation when it threatens to dissolve into a relationship of dominance and subordination. And we may withdraw from a system of dominance and subordination in order to engage in moral revolution.

To withdraw from a system, a conceptual framework, or a particular situation is to refuse to act according to its rules. A system can only function if there are participants. A king can direct his domain only if most everyone else acknowledges him as king, if the couriers carry his messages.[2] If the messengers dump their messages and go on to something else, not only is the king's communication interrupted, so is his status, for the couriers are no longer focused on him and are therefore declaring themselves no longer couriers. If enough couriers lay down their messages, the king will not be able to amass sufficient power to force those messengers to again focus on him.

When we separate, when we withdraw from someone's game plan, the game becomes meaningless, at least to some extent, ceasing to exist for lack of acknowledgment. Of course if a tree falls in the forest, there are sound waves, whether or not there are human or other animal ears, or whether there are any other sorts of mechanisms in addition to the king's own ears to detect them. But if the listeners, the messengers, have withdrawn, then the sound waves can't be translated or even acknowledged. Thus the messages of the king in a certain respect make no sense, and in a certain respect have ceased to exist. So has the king . . . as a king.

Separation is a legitimate moral and political choice. (I mean by saying it is legitimate that it has a political and moral function.) That is, to engage in a situation or a system in order to try to change it is one choice. To withdraw from it, particularly in order to render it meaningless, is another choice. Within a given situation or at a given moment there are often good reasons for either choice. Further, both choices involve considerable risk; neither one comes with guarantees: while directly challenging something can validate it, withdrawing may allow it to continue essentially unhampered.

What is significant to me is that the choice to separate is not *acknowledged* as a legitimate ethical choice. There are considerable prohibitions in all quarters against withdrawal. Depending on various factors, including the location within the power hierarchy of the perceiver, the choice to withdraw is judged to be (a) functionally equivalent to collaborating with the enemy, (b) cowardly hiding from the situation and foolishly hoping it will go away, (c) an indication of dull-wittedness or an admission of defeat, (d) a refusal to be politically responsible, or (e) a denial of reality, indicating insanity.

For example, during a war — that is, a struggle over who will dominate — those in power regard draft dodgers and even conscientious objectors not as moral challengers but as immoral quitters, not significantly different from those who collaborate with the enemy. In time of war this moral equation is drawn because, to be successful, those who wage war must have grand-scale cooperation in order to defeat the enemy. And when social organization must be very tight, those who dissent and withdraw are perceived as no different from those who attack. (To some degree, this is an accurate perception.)

Those who withdraw may be perceived by their peers as cowardly hiding from the situation and hoping it will go away or as foolishly ignoring reality. For example, one who withdraws from a fight will often be considered a coward. Such labeling, of course, is an attempt to coerce participation. Alternatively, some who have opposed united states draft dodgers and conscientious objectors charge them with failing to recognize that if the enemy won, they would no longer have the right to dissent. And because of our (at least partial) withdrawal from the institution of heterosexuality, lesbians are accused of foolishly ignoring half the human race and hence of denying reality.

Certainly, there are those who believe problems will just go away. But I am concerned with the choice to withdraw as a political strategy. For example, the danes refused to cooperate with the nazi policy of identifying jews. This was a refusal to participate in the debate over who should be saved, and as a result it rendered the nazi effort at "purification" meaningless. Pacifism, too, is a withdrawal. And during world war ii, pacifists were perceived as cowards. In fact, the label "passive resistance" itself a contradiction of terms, is an attempt to discredit the actions of those who refuse to play the games of dominance and subordination — Gandhi's strategy was hardly passive.

Political activists will often perceive withdrawing or separating as simply being politically irresponsible. For example, many will show overt hostility toward those who refuse to participate in the u.s. election process, even though they themselves are horrified by what passes for candidates, campaigning, and voting in this country. Those who refuse to vote, on the other hand, refuse to participate in the illusion. As one female nonvoter stated, "Oh, I never vote, it encourages them so."[3]

Lesbian separatists, too, are perceived as not caring about or wanting to end injustice. Separatists are often judged by liberals, socialists, and coalitionists as almost more morally reprehensible than those who control the system.[4] As a result, lesbian separatists are scapegoated.

In certain respects, to engage, to participate, in a situation or in a system is to affirm its central values. This is true whether we actively uphold the system, attempt to change it through designated avenues of reform, or rebel against it through designated avenues of rebellion (act in ways named evil or bad within the system). For in acting in any of these capacities, we are operating within the system's parameters and are thus giving the system meaning by helping to hold its axis (what goes unquestioned) in place.

While a great deal is accomplished through reform, the change that occurs must fit within the (usually unacknowledged) parameters of the system. Thus "votes for women" was achieved only when women's suffrage was generally perceived as not altering the structure and value of patriarchal, heterosexual society. As Kate Millett points out in *Sexual Politics,* the first wave of the feminist movement failed to challenge the institution of the family, thereby ending in reform rather than revolution. She argues that without radical change in value, that which reformers found most offensive — "the economic disabilities of women, the double standard, prostitution, venereal disease, coercive marital unions and involuntary parenthood" — could not be eradicated.[5] Reform perpetuates existing value.

In the first place, feminist reform forces women to focus on men and address men's conceptions of women rather than creating and developing women's values about themselves. It forces women to focus on men's reactions and mass media stereotypes of women; it forces women to respond by means of apology to masculinist depictions of witches, manhaters, lesbians, and amazons. It forces women to prove that men's fears are unfounded — to prove that women, or "real" women, are not lesbians or manhaters. It forces women to appear feminine and prove they are not threatening. Feminist reform forces women to attend male fantasies and validate masculinist value. As a result men are invited to act out and are given even greater license to project their insecurities on women, while women must soothe and tend male egos. In other words, reform keeps women focused on finding ways of seducing men. I want a moral revolution.

Secondly, feminist reform makes the actual success of women's efforts depend on the intelligence, willingness, and benevolence of the men they're seeking to convince to enact reform. Efforts in this regard may at times gain relief for women, relief which is badly needed even if selective. But it is a relief of symptoms, not a removal of causes.[6] In this respect reform forces the reformer to restrict her imagination and efforts to the limits of those she's trying to convince. A feminist striving for change by working for reform within the dominant/subordinate framework is like a starving person seeking nourishment in junk food.

Finally, feminist reform sets up women to value change in men more highly than change in women.[7] It makes any failure a failure of effort on women's part, not a refusal on men's part. And it sets up women to fear risking any small gain they might have gotten. As a result, to avoid offending men, they promote lesbian erasure, thereby reinforcing heterosexualism.[8] This is one of the reasons some french-speaking radical lesbians insist that feminism is the last stronghold of patriarchy.[9]

Aside from reform, there are also serious problems with rebellion, particularly when that rebellion fits the parameters of what counts as rebellion from the dominant perspective. For example, a young woman might rebel against her family by getting pregnant, or a high school student might rebel by becoming addicted to heroin. These actions, while not in conformity with what is called good in society, nevertheless support and uphold it; though they are designated as evil within the system, they are not real threats to it. Further, as I have suggested above, there are serious dangers involved in sabotage when a movement is afoot, when a group is interacting in ways which begin to challenge the consensus which made the individual act of sabotage plausible for the saboteurs.

Another form of rebellion — the male pornographic rebellion against the establishment — has been challenged by Mary Daly, Susan Griffin, Catharine A. MacKinnon, and Andrea Dworkin, each in her own way. For while pornographic sons rebel against church fathers, they nevertheless operate out of the same conceptual framework — a framework which gives rise to necrophilic hatred of the body.[10] Far from undermining the system, they infuse it with meaning. And when things get too far out of hand, protectors can target pornographers, launching a crusade to clean up our minds, all the while polluting our minds with church imagery which gives rise to pornography.

Significantly, the so-called sexual "revolution" is hardly a revolution of values but simply a reversal of certain polarities within the same value system. Thus, rather than being a "proper lady," a woman is now a "hot mama." Either way her sexual subordination to men remains unchallenged. The "sexual revolution" has displaced the women's movement in the media.

Advocates of sadomasochism also claim to be rebelling against the system, yet they are neither resisting it nor striving for change. In emulating nazi/jew or master/slave scenes, for example, sadomasochists contribute to the context which allows such institutions to flourish, thereby validating them. And rather than shock us into political awareness, as can a parody, such practices lull us into acceptance and resignation.[11]

In general, the system of the fathers designates as evil what it can tolerate and uses it as a safety valve. When things threaten to get out of hand, those in power can then scapegoat that which they designate as evil to explain why that which they designate as good — marriage, business, education, religion, medicine, for example — isn't working. And this suggests that withdrawal from and change in central values, rather than evil, are the real threats to the traditional framework of ethics and politics.

Upon examining the system, we may find we actually agree with the underlying value and structure. Alternatively, we may find we disagree significantly with it but judge that it is the best structure around or that the existing structure is better than no structure or better than the risk involved in creating a new one. We might even feel that a new structure would be preferable but that the current situation is a crisis which needs immediate relief, even though this results in incomplete solution and cooptation. After all, working to create a new value system hardly solves an immediate problem of starvation.

But what is missing from the focus of traditional ethics as well as from lesbian community ethics is acknowledgment that these choices involve agreement with the system in certain key ways, acknowledgment that such agreement is a choice, and acknowledgment that there is another choice. What is missing from traditional ethics is acknowledgment that there are ethical choices at this level, that participation is one of those choices, and that separation — at the very least from the belief system — is another.

Now beyond noting that withdrawal or separation is a crucial moral option, I want to suggest that such a choice is central to lesbian moral agency. What I am calling separation or withdrawal is not a set of rules we live up to, particularly in an attempt to be purists. It is rather a general approach to the world which involves various choices in various circumstances, choices which depend on various factors but which are choices from a lesbian center.

In her history and analysis of *Lavender Woman,* a chicago lesbian newspaper published between 1971 and 1976, Michal Brody offers a basic definition of separatism which, while apparently clear-cut, invited "universes of interpretation":

> The fundamental core of separation was separation of women from men. This was desirable for two basic reasons: 1) there was too much frustration and aggravation involved in trying to work or deal with men. Sexism, once perceived, became intolerable, and 2) it became urgent to understand the meaning and essence of womanhood as only we could define it for ourselves.[12]

I named myself separatist in 1976 in lincoln, nebraska, a little over a year after I came out and while teaching at the university of nebraska, as the result of a very simple statement from Julia Penelope [Stanley]. I had just returned from the second national women's music festival, where I observed Meg Christian and Holly Near defend women-only concerts and Holly Near participate in a group discussion on the issue. I was confused. They were all talking about separating from men, yet all they seemed to talk about was men. I, too, knew about men, but I didn't comprehend what the big issue was. Standing at her kitchen sink peeling potatoes, Julia said, quite simply, "Power." This made sense to me. Since that time, how and why I conceive and enact separatism has developed. What follows are those aspects of separatism I consider central to the continuing creation of lesbian community and meaning.

Separatism is, first, a way of pulling back from the existing conceptual framework, noting its patterns, and understanding their function regardless of the mythology espoused within the framework. For example, within the framework it is said that women don't resist male domination. However, by stepping out of the framework, we can detect quite another story. Separatism is a matter of deconstructing and revaluing existing perceptions and judgments.

In this way, withdrawing or separating is not the opposite of participating; rather, it is a form of engagement. While it is important for survival to stay in touch with what is going on, by becoming detached from belief in heterosexual values, we can move through the system in very different ways, noting very different things.[13]

Secondly, separatism is a way of undermining heterosexual patterns. As Marilyn Frye argues, feminist separation is

> separation of various sorts or modes from men and from institutions, roles and activities which are male-defined, male-dominated and operating for the benefit of males and the maintenance of male privilege—this separation being initiated or maintained, at will, *by women.*

The point of this is to undermine male parasitism:

> that is, generally speaking, the strength, energy, inspiration and nurturance of women that keeps men going, and not the strength, aggression, spirituality and hunting of men that keeps women going.[14]

Marilyn Frye goes on to argue that male parasitism means males must have access to females, that total power is unconditional access, that the first act of challenging this must be denying access in order to create a power shift, and that such a denial of access is also to claim the power of naming for oneself: "The slave who excludes the master from her hut thereby declares herself *not a slave.*"[15]

Thirdly, separatism is "paring away the layers of false selves from the Self," as Mary Daly suggests.[16] What draws us to each other, I believe, is a sense of female agency, a sense of inner strength. Separatism allows us to expand our imaginations and hence our risks beyond the boundaries of heterosexualism. It allows us an ethical option to the de-moralization that results when we resign ourselves to the categories of the fathers and lose each other.[17] Thus, it allows us the possibility of developing female agency outside the master/slave virtues of heterosexualism.

Consequently, fourthly, lesbian separatism is a withdrawal from heterosexualism. Following Simone de Beauvoir's perception that we are not born women, Monique Wittig announces that lesbians are not women.[18] She argues:

> The refusal to become (or to remain) heterosexual always meant to refuse to become a man or a woman, consciously or not. For a lesbian this goes further than the refusal of the *role* "woman." It is the refusal of the economic, ideological, and political power of a man.[19]

And she concludes:

Lesbianism is the only concept I know of which is beyond the categories of sex (woman and man), because the designated subject (lesbian) is *not* a woman, either economically, or politically, or ideologically. For what makes a woman is a specific social relation to a man, a relation that we have previously called servitude . . . a relation which implies personal and physical obligation as well as economic obligation ("forced residence,"[20] domestic corvée, conjugal duties, unlimited production of children, etc.), a relation which lesbians escape by refusing to become or stay heterosexual.[21]

Withdrawal or separatism is a refusal to participate in the heterosexual social construction of reality; to practice separatism is to deconstruct the dominant/subordinate relationship of men and women.

Monique Wittig goes on to argue that our task is to define oppression in materialist terms:

to make it evident that women are a class, which is to say that the category "woman" as well as the category "man" are political and economic categories not eternal ones.[22]

She suggests that our strategy must be to

suppress men as a class, not through a genocidal, but a political struggle. Once the class "men" disappears, "women" as a class will disappear as well, for there are no slaves without masters.[23]

Thus she does not advocate resisting male domination by trying to oppose men as men have opposed women, as Simone de Beauvoir seems to imply women must do if women are to resist male sovereignty. However, neither is her strategy a separatist one. She anticipates a struggle between men and women similar to a class struggle, a struggle in which gender categories will finally disappear, thereby ending the economic, political, and ideological order which perpetuates the dominance and subordination of heterosexualism:

The class struggle is precisely that which resolves the contradictions between two opposed classes by abolishing them at the same time it constitutes them as classes. The class struggle between women and men, which should be undertaken by all women, is that which resolves the contradictions between the sexes, abolishing them at the same time as it makes them understood.[24]

Once this struggle breaks out, the violence of the categories (dominant/suppressed, male/female) becomes apparent, and what was considered natural differences now can be understood as material opposition.

While I agree that heterosexualism is a violent opposition between men and women, my focus is different. I agree with the goal of deconstructing heterosexualism and the categories "man" and "woman." But in my opinion there can be slaves without masters, there can be women without men. Thus, even though "lesbian" is a concept beyond the categories of sex, nevertheless we tend to embrace the existing categories both in assimilation and in resistance. More often than not, we embrace the values of dominance and subordination.

We tend to seek meaning by subordinating ourselves to a higher order or system because we seek the semblance of security in something constructed outside of us in which we can participate. Heterosexualism is such a system. In another context Marilyn Frye writes of the "mortal dread of being outside the field of vision of the arrogant eye":

> We fear that if we are not in that web of meaning there will be no meaning: our work will be meaningless, our lives of no value, our accomplishments empty, our identities illusory.[25]

My concern is involved with the sense in which it is true that there are no "masters" without "slaves," for in that same sense there are no "men" without "women." A king cannot be king without his messengers attending him. And patriarchy cannot persist without female complicity, regardless of how that complicity is commandeered, complicity that persists as women and lesbians back away from our power to invent.[26] My concern in pursuing withdrawal or separation, both ethically and politically, involves pursuing lesbian agency outside the dominant/subordinate values of heterosexualism. To separate, withdraw, refocus, is to cease attending to the existing system. As Alice Molloy wrote:

> return no thing to evil, that is the basis of separatism. give it no energy, no time, no attention. no nourishment.[27]

The no-saying and the struggle are essential, but so is the ability to withdraw from the existing ground of meaning. If we remain riveted on their categories, we will not succeed in creating new ones.

Thus, separatism is, most importantly, a refocusing, a focusing on lesbians and a lesbian conceptual framework. Through our focus, our attention, we determine what is significant and what is not. Attending is active and creative. And by focusing on ourselves and each other as lesbians in all our diversity, we determine, not that we exist in relation to a dominant other, but rather that we can create new value, lesbian meaning. By focusing on ourselves and each other, we make lesbianism possible. In calling for withdrawal from the existing heterosexual value system, I am calling for a moral revolution.

Now, beginning with the first aspect of separatism, by withdrawing or separating from the conceptual framework of heterosexualism we can understand a number of things central to lesbian moral agency and the creation of new value. We can realize male domination persists through both predation and protection. We can realize that what it means to be a woman is a creation of the patriarchy, and that "femininity" makes male domination appear natural. We can realize that what men call "difference" is actually "opposition," and that women have resisted male domination, though not necessarily by challenging heterosexualism. We can perceive women as moral agents, making choices as best they can within the framework of heterosexualism. And we can also understand that lesbians have made other choices, choices not among the designated options.

Describing her first trip to a gay bar, Judy Grahn writes:

> Nothing distinguished the Rendezvous Bar from any of the others except that its reputation among queers was that it was "ours." . . . In those days homosexuality was so closely guarded and so heavily punished that it might as well have been illegal just to gather in a bar together. . . . But the sleazy Rendezvous was where we bottom-of-the-world overt Gay people could go and be "ourselves."
>
> I went there one night with another Lesbian I had met in the service; I remember the fear I felt on the bus ride downtown. The bus passed through a dark tunnel and the driver had a black curtain wrapped around his seat. I felt I was on a journey to hell and had to laugh at my young self for undertaking such a perilous journey. There would be no turning back for me once I had entered such a place; I knew very distinctly that I had "crossed over."
>
> From the minute I entered the doors of the Rendezvous . . . and gaped in thrilled shock at the self-assured, proud Lesbians in pants and the men in makeup and sculptured, displayed, eerily beautiful faces, I saw myself as part of a group that included some very peculiar characters and characteristics. I ceased then to be a nice

white Protestant girl with a tomboy nature who had once had a secret and very loving Lesbian relationship with another nice girl who was attending college to become a teacher. That definition no longer applied as I stepped into my first Gay bar to become a full-fledged dike, a more-than-a-Lesbian.[28]

The choice to act on lesbianism was a solitary one, as Audre Lorde describes:

There were no mothers, no sisters, no heroes. We had to do it alone, like our sister Amazons, the riders on the loneliest outposts of the kingdom of Dahomey. We, young and Black and fine and gay, sweated out our first heartbreaks with no school nor office chums to share that confidence over lunch hour. Just as there were no rings to make tangible the reason for our happy secret smiles, there were no names nor reason given or shared for the tears that messed up the lab reports or the library bills.[29]

The choice was based on lives that went before, as Elana Dykewomon writes:

These women, I think, are my true foremothers. They became strong and independent in isolation. They may seem to me all caught up in roles, they may never agree with me about what's important, what a political act it is within the state to be a lesbian, an act of defiance — nevertheless, they committed that act and gave me the courage to commit mine. I love them for it.[30]

And it was a central choice, as Caryl Bentley describes, one involving integrity:

I think coming out is a life-long process. It consists for me of connecting feelings, ideas, and experiences to my identity as a Lesbian through naming and perhaps acting on them. In the mid-1950s, when I, like other Lesbians my age, was alone, claiming my Lesbianism meant recognizing and owning my feelings of love for one other woman. Refusing to bury and deny my feelings was a matter of integrity to me; this stubborn claiming is something I still respect myself for.[31]

But it was also not without consequences. From Beth Brant:

The word *lesbian*. Lesbian. The word that makes them panic, makes them afraid, makes them destroy children. The word that dares them. Lesbian. *I am one.* Even for Patricia, even for her, *I will not cease to be!* As I kneel amidst the colorful scraps, Raggedy Anns smiling up at me, my chest gives a sigh. My heart slows to its normal speech. I feel the blood pumping outward to my veins, carrying nourishment and life.[32]

It was a revolutionary choice, as Cheryl Clarke notes:

> For a woman to be a lesbian in a male-supremist, capitalist, misogynist, racist, homophobic, imperialist culture, such as that of North America, is an act of resistance. . . . The lesbian has decolonized her body. She has rejected a life of servitude implicit in Western, heterosexual relationships and has accepted the potential of mutuality in a lesbian relationship — *roles* notwithstanding.[33]

Yes, these were political choices. In her essay on butch-fem relationships in the 1950s in the u.s., Joan Nestle articulates the political nature of many lesbians' choices:

> In the 1950s this courage to feel comfortable with arousing another woman became a political act.
>
> Butch-fem was an erotic partnership, serving both as a conspicuous flag of rebellion and as an intimate exploration of women's sexuality.[34]

In reply to the charge that lesbians were merely copying heterosexual choices, Joan Nestle argues:

> Since at times fems dressed similarly to their butch lovers, the aping of heterosexual roles was not visually apparent, yet the sight of us was enraging. My understanding of why we angered straight spectators so is not that they saw us modeling ourselves after them, but just the opposite — that we were a symbol of women's erotic autonomy, a sexual accomplishment that did not include them. The physical attacks were a direct attempt to break into this self-sufficient, erotic partnership. The most frequently shouted taunt was: "Which one of you is the man?" This was not a reflection of our Lesbian experience as much as it was a testimony to the lack of erotic categories in straight culture.[35]

In other words, lesbian relationships of the 1950s were a challenge to existing values. Lillian Faderman adds that

> there were in several eras and places many instances of women who were known to engage in lesbian sex, and they did so with

impunity. As long as they appeared feminine, their sexual behavior would be viewed as an activity in which women indulged when men were unavailable or as an apprenticeship or appetite-whetter to heterosexual sex. But if one or both of the pair demanded masculine privileges, the illusion of lesbianism as *faute de mieux* behavior was destroyed. At the base was not the sexual aspect of lesbianism as much as the attempted usurpation of male prerogative by women who behaved like men that many societies appeared to find most disturbing.[36]

Of course, to claim the prerogative of men is not necessarily to try to become men. Judy Grahn argues that the point was not to be men but to be butch and get away with it:

We always kept something back: a high-pitched voice, a slant of the head, or a limpness of hand gestures, something that was clearly labeled female. I believe our statement was "Here is another way of being a woman," not "Here is a woman trying to be taken for a man."[37]

Joan Nestle adds:

The irony of social change has made a radical, sexual, political statement of the 1950s appear today as a reactionary, non-feminist experience.[38]

Nevertheless, there has been copying of heterosexual roles. Some lesbians worked to become like man and wife; some even became trans-sexual men. And that is to say that the choice to affirm lesbianism does not make lesbians immune to heterosexual social organization. Further, the choice to affirm lesbianism does not make lesbians immune to racism. As Audre Lorde writes:

Being gay-girls without set roles was the one difference we allowed ourselves to see and to bind us to each other. We were not of that *other* world and we wanted to believe that, by definition, we were therefore free of that *other* world's problems of capitalism, greed, racism, classism, etc. This was not so. But we continued to visit each other and eat together, and in general, share our lives and resources, as if it were.[39]

Nor are lesbians immune to deeply internalizing heterosexual value, the value of dominance and subordination, as Julia Penelope notes:

Just as I based my own sense of power on making love to other wimmin, I perceived their willingness to let me make love to them as a "giving up" of power. When they yielded to me, surrendered themselves to me passionately, made themselves "vulnerable" to me, I became powerful. I was absorbed by the anticipatory thrills of the "chase," and my sexuality was dependent on the sexual charge I experienced when I made a new "conquest." By identifying my own sexuality with power, and making satisfaction dependent on controlling another Lesbian's body, I'd bound myself to the constant need to rekindle that "charge" over and over again. Because I saw sex as a way of empowering myself, I saw the wimmin I made love to as giving up *their* power to me, and it was never long before I had to find another "conquest." If I was "getting" power, then my lover of the moment must be "losing" power, and I would begin to disengage myself from a Lesbian I'd begun to despise because I perceived her as "powerless" and "weak." The very "femininity," the softness, that had first drawn me to her would now repulse me, and I would refuse to make love to her. My refusal, like my previous love-making, became an assertion of my "power over" her.[40]

The need to control and be controlled in relationships is central to the dominant/subordinate values of heterosexualism, and, as I will argue, it is central to the values of the anglo-european tradition of ethics.

Through all of this, I am not trying to argue that heterosexualism is the "cause" of oppression. I do mean to suggest, however, that any revolution which does not challenge it will be incomplete and will eventually revert to the values of oppression. Heterosexualism is the form of social organization through which other forms of oppression, at times more vicious forms, become credible, palatable, even desirable. Heterosexualism — that is, the balance between masculine predation upon and masculine protection of a feminine object of masculine attention — de-skills a woman, makes her emotionally, socially, and economically dependent, and allows another to dominate her "for her own good" all in the name of "love." In no other situation[41] are people expected to love, identify with, and become other to those who dominate them to the extent that women are supposed to love, identify with, and become other to men.[42]

It is heterosexualism which makes us feel that it is possible to dominate another for her own good, that one who resists such domination is abnormal or doesn't understand what is good for her, and that one who refuses to participate in dominant/subordinate relationships doesn't exist. And once we accept all this, imperialism, colonialism, and ethnocentrism, for example, while existing all along, become more socially tolerable in liberal thought. They become less a matter of exercising overt force and more a matter of the natural function of (a) social order.

Heterosexualism is a conceptual framework within which the concept of "moral agency" independent of the master/slave virtues cannot find fertile ground. And it combines with ethical judgments to create a value whose primary function is not the moral development of individuals but rather the preservation of a patriarchal social control. This will require a discussion of the feminine virtues of altruism, self-sacrifice, and vulnerability, and how we use them to gain control in relationships.

In discussing what I call Lesbian Ethics, I do not claim that lesbians haven't made many of the choices (heterosexual) women have made or that lesbians haven't participated in the consensus of straight thinking or that lesbians have withdrawn from the value of dominance and subordination and the security of established meaning we can find therein. I am not claiming that lesbians have lived under different conceptual or material conditions. I am claiming, however, that lesbian choice holds certain possibilities. It is a matter of further choice whether we go on to develop these possibilities or whether instead we try to fit into the existing heterosexual framework in any one of a number of ways.

Thus I am claiming that the conceptual category "lesbian" — unlike the category "woman" — is not irretrievably tied up with dominance and subordination as norms of behavior. And I am claiming that by attending each other, we may find the possibility of ethical values appropriate to lesbian existence, values we can choose as moral agents to give meaning to our lives as lesbians. In calling for withdrawal from the existing heterosexual value system, I am calling for a moral revolution, a revolution of lesbianism.

Notes

1. I do not mean to suggest that governments have not forced people into other options, for example, emigration from oppressive conditions or exile. But this has occurred precisely because such people have been considered not part of the moral community. Nor do I mean to suggest there have been no separatists. There have been many, many different groups of separatists. What I am suggest-

ing in this section is that the tradition tends not to recognize separation as a choice among those considered moral agents because it cannot afford to acknowledge that participation is a choice.

2. I've adapted this idea from Franz Kafka, "Couriers," in *Parables*, trans. Willa and Edwin Muir (New York: Schocken Books, 1946), pp. 268–78; however, Kafka's point is not about change, and his parable contains no king to begin with.

3. Reported to me by Juana María Paz and Bette S. Tallen.

4. For example, it is argued in the community that separatism is racist. . . . [T]his statement was made by Barbara Smith at a panel on racism, "Racism and the Lesbian Community," at the National Women's Studies Association conference, Storrs, Conn., June 1981. In my opinion, that accusation has functioned to bury a form of what might be called a socialist/anarchist debate. . . . [See my] "Introduction" in *For Lesbians Only*, edited by Sarah Hoagland and Julia Penelope (Only-women Press, London); a shortened version was published as "Lesbian Separatism: An Empowering Reality," in *Gossip* 6: 24–36, and in *Sinister Wisdom* 34 (Spring 1988): 23–33.

5. Kate Millett, *Sexual Politics* (New York: Ballantine, 1978), p. 157.

6. Communication, Marilyn Frye.

7. For example, many women's studies faculty value a male entering a women's studies class more highly than a female, take female students' presence for granted, and try to figure out how to increase male participation rather than focusing on how to get more women to investigate feminism — and more heterosexual women of color and lesbians of all colors to enroll.

8. It is heterosexualism which keeps women believing that, for one reason or another, the agreement of men is necessary to women's efforts to change society. Yet whenever men are included, the goals and focus of women's projects transform into men's goals and focus. For example, once men entered Josephine Butler's campaign against the contagious diseases acts, male perceptions and values undermined the women's goals. (Kathleen Barry, "Josephine Butler: The First Wave of Protest," *Female Sexual Slavery* (Englewood Cliffs, N.J.: Prentice-Hall, 1979), pp. 12–32.) Further, I would argue that the most effective changes in black-white relations emerged from the black power movement when blacks ceased focusing on whites. While whites ultimately played a part in the change that occurred, the change did not occur as a result of blacks catering to or waiting on whites' agreement.

9. Conversation, Ariane Brunet.

10. Susan Griffin, "Sacred Images," in *Pornography and Silence* (New York: Harper & Row, 1981), pp. 8–81; Mary Daly, *Gyn/Ecology* (Boston: Beacon Press, 1978); Catharine A. MacKinnon, *Feminism Unmodified: Discourse on Life and Law* (Cambridge, Mass.: Harvard University Press, 1987); Andrea Dworkin, *Pornography* (New York: G. P. Putnam's Sons, 1979).

11. For an earlier development of this argument note Sarah Lucia Hoagland, "Sadism, Masochism, and Lesbian-Feminism," in *Against Sadomasochism: A Radical Feminist Analysis,* ed. Robin Ruth Linden, Darlene R. Pagano, Diana E. H. Russell, and Susan Leigh Star (East Palo Alto, Calif.: Frog in the Well, 1982), pp. 153–63.

12. Michal Brody, *Are We There Yet? A Continuing History of 'Lavender Woman': A Chicago Lesbian Newspaper, 1971–1976* (Iowa City: Aunt Lute Book Co., 1985; now Spinsters/Aunt Lute, San Francisco), p. 184.

13. Communication, Claudia Card.

14. Marilyn Frye, "Some Reflections on Separatism and Power," in *Politics of Reality* (Trumansburg, N.Y.: The Crossing Press, 1983), pp. 96, 98–99.

15. Ibid., pp. 103–5.

16. Mary Daly, *Gyn/Ecology,* p. 381.

17. Resignation is one of the plastic passions Mary Daly names in *Pure Lust* (Boston: Beacon Press, 1984), pp. 200–226.

18. Monique Wittig, "The Straight Mind," *Feminist Issues* 1, no. 1 (Summer 1980): 110.

19. Monique Wittig, "One Is Not Born a Woman," *Feminist Issues* 1, no. 2 (Winter 1981): 49.

20. Christiane Rochefort, *Les Stances à Sophie* (Paris: Grasset, 1963) as cited by Monique Wittig, "One Is Not Born a Woman."

21. Monique Wittig, "One is Not Born a Woman," p. 53.

22. Ibid., p. 50.

23. Ibid.; note also Monique Wittig, "The Category of Sex," *Feminist Issues* 2, no. 2 (Fall 1982): 64.

24. Monique Wittig, "Category of Sex," p. 64.

25. Marilyn Frye, "In and Out of Harm's Way," *Politics of Reality,* p. 80.

26. Conversation, Harriet Ellenberger.

27. Alice Molloy, *In Other Words,* p. 39.

28. Judy Grahn, *Another Mother Tongue: Gay Words, Gay Worlds* (Boston: Beacon Press, 1984), pp. 29–30.

29. Audre Lorde, *Zami: A New Spelling of My Name* (Watertown, Mass.: Persephone Press, 1982, now published by the Crossing Press, Freedom, Calif.), p. 176.

30. Elana Nachman [Dykewomon], *Riverfinger Women* (Plainfield, Vt.: Daughters, Inc., 1974), p. 174.

31. Caryl B. Bentley, "My Third Coming Out At Last Has My Own Name," in *The Coming Out Stories,* ed. Julia Penelope Stanley and Susan J. Wolfe (Watertown, Mass.: Persephone Press, 1980), pp. 79–88.

32. Beth Brant, *Mohawk Trail* (Ithaca, N.Y.: Firebrand Books, 1985), p. 85.

33. Cheryl Clarke, "Lesbianism: An Act of Resistance," in *This Bridge Called My Back: Writings by Radical Women of Color,* ed. Cherríe Moraga and

Gloria Anzaldúa (Watertown, Mass.: Persephone Press, 1981), now published by Kitchen Table: Women of Color Press, p. 128.

34. Joan Nestle, "Butch-Fem Relationships: Sexual Courage in the 1950's," *Heresies* 3, no. 4, issue 12 (1981): 21; reprinted in *A Restricted Country* (Ithaca, N.Y.: Firebrand Books, 1987), pp. 100–109.

35. Ibid., p. 22.

36. Lillian Faderman, *Surpassing the Love of Men: Romantic Friendship and Love between Women from the Renaissance to the Present* (New York: William Morrow & Co., 1981), p. 17.

37. Judy Grahn, *Another Mother Tongue*, p. 31.

38. Joan Nestle, "Butch-Fem Relationships," p. 22.

39. Audre Lorde, *Zami*, p. 205.

40. Julia Penelope, "Whose Past Are We Reclaiming?" *Common Lives/Lesbian Lives* 13 (Autumn 1984): 27.

41. The situation of the mammy is similar. Racism and the politics of property intervened, however, to keep her from being quite so close to the master or mistress as woman is to man. Nevertheless, this did not make her situation any more palatable, and in many respects, it was worse.

42. This point has been made many times before; for example note Shulamith Firestone, *The Dialectic of Sex: The Case for Feminist Revolution* (New York: Bantam/William Morrow & Co., 1972), chapter 6; Ti-Grace Atkinson, *Amazon Odyssey* (New York: Links Books, 1974), p. 43; and more recently, noting the reverse — namely, that in "no other form of slavery are those in power called upon to love those whom they have found to be inferior and despicable" — Kathleen Barry, *Female Sexual Slavery*, p. 136.

18

Sisterhood
Political Solidarity between Women

bell hooks

Women are the group most victimized by sexist oppression. As with other forms of group oppression, sexism is perpetuated by institutional and social structures; by the individuals who dominate, exploit, or oppress; and by the victims themselves who are socialized to behave in ways that make them act in complicity with the status quo. Male supremacist ideology encourages women to believe we are valueless and obtain value only by relating to or bonding with men. We are taught that our relationships with one another diminish rather than enrich our experience. We are taught that women are "natural" enemies, that solidarity will never exist between us because we cannot, should not, and do not bond with one another. We have learned these lessons well. We must unlearn them if we are to build a sustained feminist movement. We must learn to live and work in solidarity. We must learn the true meaning and value of Sisterhood.

Although contemporary feminist movement should have provided a training ground for women to learn about political solidarity, Sisterhood was not viewed as a revolutionary accomplishment women would work and struggle to obtain. The vision of Sisterhood evoked by women's liberationists was based on the idea of common oppression. Needless to say, it was primarily bourgeois white women, both liberal and radical in

Reprinted from *Feminist Theory: From Margin to Center* (Boston: South End Press, 1984): 43–65, by permission of the publisher.

perspective, who professed belief in the notion of common oppression. The idea of "common oppression" was a false and corrupt platform disguising and mystifying the true nature of women's varied and complex social reality. Women are divided by sexist attitudes, racism, class privilege, and a host of other prejudices. Sustained woman bonding can occur only when these divisions are confronted and the necessary steps are taken to eliminate them. Divisions will not be eliminated by wishful thinking or romantic reverie about common oppression despite the value of highlighting experiences all women share.

In recent years Sisterhood as slogan, motto, rallying cry no longer evokes the spirit of power in unity. Some feminists now seem to feel that unity between women is impossible given our differences. Abandoning the idea of Sisterhood as an expression of political solidarity weakens and diminishes feminist movement. Solidarity strengthens resistance struggle. There can be no mass-based feminist movement to end sexist oppression without a united front—women must take the initiative and demonstrate the power of solidarity. Unless we can show that barriers separating women can be eliminated, that solidarity can exist, we cannot hope to change and transform society as a whole. The shift away from an emphasis on Sisterhood has occurred because many women, angered by the insistence on "common oppression," shared identity, sameness, criticized or dismissed feminist movement altogether. The emphasis on Sisterhood was often seen as the emotional appeal masking the opportunism of manipulative bourgeois white women. It was seen as a cover-up hiding the fact that many women exploit and oppress other women. Black woman activist lawyer Florynce Kennedy wrote an essay, published in the anthology *Sisterhood Is Powerful,* voicing her suspicions about the existence of solidarity between women as early as 1970:

> It is for this reason that I have considerable difficulty with the sisterhood mystique: "We are sisters," "Don't criticize a 'sister' publicly," etc. When a female judge asks my client where the bruises are when she complains about being assaulted by her husband (as did Family Court Judge Sylvia Jaffin Liese), and makes smart remarks about her being overweight, and when another female judge is so hostile that she disqualifies herself but refuses to order a combative husband out of the house (even though he owns property elsewhere with suitable living quarters)—these judges are not my sisters.[1]

Women were wise to reject a false Sisterhood based on shallow notions of bonding. We are mistaken if we allow these distortions or the women who created them (many of whom now tell us bonding between women is unimportant) to lead us to devalue Sisterhood.[2]

Women are enriched when we bond with one another but we cannot develop sustaining ties or political solidarity using the model of Sisterhood created by bourgeois women's liberationists. According to their analysis, the basis for bonding was shared victimization, hence the emphasis on common oppression. This concept of bonding directly reflects male supremacist thinking. Sexist ideology teaches women that to be female is to be a victim. Rather than repudiate this equation (which mystifies female experience — in their daily lives most women are not continually passive, helpless, or powerless "victims"), women's liberationists embraced it, making shared victimization the basis for woman bonding. This meant that women had to conceive of themselves as "victims" in order to feel that feminist movement was relevant to their lives. Bonding as victims created a situation in which assertive, self-affirming women were often seen as having no place in feminist movement. It was this logic that led white women activists (along with black men) to suggest that black women were so "strong" they did not need to be active in feminist movement. It was this logic that led many white women activists to abandon feminist movement when they no longer embraced the victim identity. Ironically, the women who were most eager to be seen as "victims," who overwhelmingly stressed the role of victim, were more privileged and powerful than the vast majority of women in our society. An example of this tendency is some writing about violence against women. Women who are exploited and oppressed daily cannot afford to relinquish the belief that they exercise some measure of control, however relative, over their lives. They cannot afford to see themselves solely as "victims" because their survival depends on continued exercise of whatever personal powers they possess. It would be psychologically demoralizing for these women to bond with other women on the basis of shared victimization. They bond with other women on the basis of shared strengths and resources. This is the woman bonding feminist movement should encourage. It is this type of bonding that is the essence of Sisterhood.

Bonding as "victims," white women liberationists were not required to assume responsibility for confronting the complexity of their own experience. They were not challenging one another to examine their sexist attitudes towards women unlike themselves or exploring the impact of race and class privilege on their relationships to women outside their race/class groups. Identifying as "victims," they could abdicate responsibility for their role in the maintenance and perpetuation of sexism, racism, and classism, which they did by insisting that only men were the enemy. They did not acknowledge and confront the enemy within. They were not prepared to forego privilege and do the "dirty work" (the struggle and confrontation necessary to build political awareness as well as the many tedious tasks to be accomplished in day-to-day organizing) that is necessary in the development of radical political consciousness. . . . [white women activists] were seeking to avoid self-awareness. Sisterhood became yet another shield against reality, another support system. Their version of Sisterhood was informed by racist and classist assumptions about white womanhood, that the white "lady" (that is to say bourgeois woman) should be protected from all that might upset or discomfort her and shielded from negative realities that might lead to confrontation. Their version of Sisterhood dictated that sisters were to "unconditionally" love one another; that they were to avoid conflict and minimize disagreement; that they were not to criticize one other, especially in public. For a time these mandates created an illusion of unity suppressing the competition, hostility, perpetual disagreement, and abusive criticism (trashing) that was often the norm in feminist groups. Today many splinter groups who share common identities (WASP working class, white academic faculty women, anarchist feminists, etc.) use this same model of Sisterhood, but participants in these groups endeavor to support, affirm, and protect one another while demonstrating hostility (usually through excessive trashing) towards women outside the chosen sphere. Bonding between a chosen circle of women who strengthen their ties by excluding and devaluing women outside their group closely resembles the type of personal bonding between women that has always occurred under patriarchy: the one difference being the interest in feminism.

To develop political solidarity between women, feminist activists cannot bond on the terms set by the dominant ideology of the culture. We must define our own terms. Rather than bond on the basis of shared victimization or in response to a false sense of a common enemy, we can bond on the basis of our political commitment to a feminist movement that aims to end sexist oppression. Given such a commitment, our energies would not be concentrated on the issue of equality with men or solely on the struggle to resist male domination. We would no longer accept a simplistic good girls/bad boys account of the structure of sexist oppression. Before we can resist male domination we must break our attachment to sexism; we must work to transform female consciousness. Working together to expose, examine, and eliminate sexist socialization within ourselves, women would strengthen and affirm one another and build a solid foundation for developing political solidarity.[3]

Between women and men, sexism is most often expressed in the form of male domination which leads to discrimination, exploitation, or oppression. Between women, male supremacist values are expressed through suspicious, defensive, competitive behavior. It is sexism that leads women to feel threatened by one another without cause. While sexism teaches women to be sex objects for men, it is also manifest when women who have repudiated this role feel contemptuous and superior in relation to those women who have not. Sexism leads women to devalue parenting work while inflating the value of jobs and careers. Acceptance of sexist ideology is indicated when women teach children that there are only two possible behavior patterns: the role of dominant or of submissive being. Sexism teaches women woman-hating, and both consciously and unconsciously we act out this hatred in our daily contact with one another.

Although contemporary feminist activists, especially radical feminists, called attention to women's absorption in sexist ideology, ways that women who are advocates of patriarchy, as well as women who uncritically accept sexist assumptions, could unlearn that socialization were not stressed. It was often assumed that to support feminism was synonymous with repudiation of sexism in all its forms. Taking on the label "feminist" was accepted as a sign of personal transformation; as a consequence, the process by which values were altered was either ignored or could not be spelled out because no fundamental change had occurred. Sometimes consciousness-raising groups provided space for women to explore their sexism. This examination of attitudes towards themselves and other women was often a catalyst for transformation. Describing the function of rap groups in *The Politics of Women's Liberation,* Jo Freeman explains:

> Women came together in small groups to share personal experiences, problems, and feelings. From this public sharing comes the realization that what was thought to be individual is in fact com-

mon: that what was thought to be a personal problem has a social cause and a political solution. The rap group attacks the effects of psychological oppression and helps women to put it into a feminist context. Women learn to see how social structures and attitudes have molded them from birth and limited their opportunities. They ascertain the extent to which women have been denigrated in this society and how they have developed prejudices against themselves and other women. They learn to develop self-esteem and to appreciate the value of group solidarity.[4]

As consciousness-raising groups lost their popularity new groups were not formed to fulfill similar functions. Women produced a large quantity of feminist writing but placed little emphasis on ways to unlearn sexism.

Since we live in a society that promotes faddism and temporary superficial adaptation of different values, we are easily convinced that changes have occurred in arenas where there has been little or no change. Women's sexist attitudes towards one another are one such arena. All over the United States, women spend hours of their time daily verbally abusing other women, usually through malicious gossip (not to be confused with gossip as positive communication). Television soap operas and nighttime dramas continually portray woman-to-woman relationships as characterized by aggression, contempt, and competitiveness. In feminist circles sexism towards women is expressed by abusive trashing, total disregard and lack of concern or interest in women who have not joined feminist movement. This is especially evident at university campuses where feminist studies is often seen as a discipline or program having no relationship to feminist movement. In her commencement address at Barnard College in May 1979, black woman writer Toni Morrison told her audience:

> I want not to ask you but to tell you not to participate in the oppression of your sisters. Mothers who abuse their children are women, and another woman, not an agency, has to be willing to stay their hands. Mothers who set fire to school buses are women, and another woman, not an agency, has to tell them to stay their hands. Women who stop the promotion of other women in careers are women, and another woman must come to the victim's aid. Social and welfare workers who humiliate their clients may be women, and other women colleagues have to deflect their anger.
>
> I am alarmed by the violence that women do to each other: professional violence, competitive violence, emotional violence. I am

alarmed by the willingness of women to enslave other women. I am alarmed by a growing absence of decency on the killing floor of professional women's worlds.[5]

To build a politicized, mass-based feminist movement, women must work harder to overcome the alienation from one another that exists when sexist socialization has not been unlearned, for example, homophobia, judging by appearance, conflicts between women with diverse sexual practices. So far, feminist movement has not transformed woman-to-woman relationships, especially between women who are strangers to one another or from different backgrounds, even though it has been the occasion for bonding between individuals and groups of women. We must renew our efforts to help women unlearn sexism if we are to develop affirming personal relationships as well as political unity.

Racism is another barrier to solidarity between women. The ideology of Sisterhood as expressed by contemporary feminist activists indicated no acknowledgement that racist discrimination, exploitation, and oppression of multi-ethnic women by white women had made it impossible for the two groups to feel they shared common interests or political concerns. Also the existence of totally different cultural backgrounds can make communication difficult. This has been especially true of black and white female relationships. Historically, many black women experienced white women as the white supremacist group who most directly exercised power over them, often in a manner far more brutal and dehumanizing than that of racist white men. Today, despite predominant rule by white supremacist patriarchs, black women often work in situations where the immediate supervisor, boss, or authority figure is a white woman. Conscious of the privileges white men as well as white women gain as a consequence of racial domination, black women were quick to react to the feminist call for Sisterhood by pointing to the contradiction — that we should join with women who exploit us to help liberate them. The call for Sisterhood was heard by many black women as a plea for help and support for a movement that did not address us. As Toni Morrison explains in her article "What the Black Woman Thinks about Women's Lib," many black women do not respect bourgeois white women and could not imagine supporting a cause that would be for their benefit.

> Black women have been able to envy white women (their looks, their easy life, the attention they seem to get from their men); they could fear them (for the economic control they have had over black

women's lives); and even love them (as mammies and domestic workers can); but black women have found it impossible to respect white women. . . . Black women have no abiding admiration of white women as competent, complete people, whether vying with them for the few professional slots available to women in general, or moving their dirt from one place to another, they regarded them as willful children, pretty children, mean children, but never as real adults capable of handling the real problems of the world.

White women were ignorant of the facts of life — perhaps by choice, perhaps with the assistance of men, but ignorant anyway. They were totally dependent on marriage or male support (emotionally and economically). They confronted their sexuality with furtiveness, complete abandon, or repression. Those who could afford it gave over the management of the house and the rearing of children to others. (It is a source of amusement even now to black women to listen to feminist talk of liberation while somebody's nice black grandmother shoulders the daily responsibility of child rearing and floor mopping, and the liberated one comes home to examine the housekeeping, correct it, and be entertained by the children.) If Women's Lib needs those grandmothers to thrive, it has a serious flaw.[6]

Many perceived that women's liberation movement as outlined by bourgeois white women would serve their interests at the expense of poor and working class women, many of whom are black. Certainly this was not a basis for Sisterhood and black women would have been politically naive had we joined such a movement. However, given the struggles of black women's participation historically and currently in political organizing, the emphasis could have been on the development and clarification of the nature of political solidarity.

White females discriminate against and exploit black women while simultaneously being envious and competitive in their interactions with them. Neither process of interaction creates conditions wherein trust and mutually reciprocal relationships can develop. After constructing feminist theory and praxis in such a way as to omit focus on racism, white women shifted the responsibility for calling attention to race onto others. They did not have to take the initiative in discussions of racism or race privilege but could listen and respond to nonwhite women discussing racism without changing in any way the structure of feminist movement, without losing their hegemonic hold. They could then show their concern with having more women of color in feminist organizations by encouraging greater participation. They were not confronting racism. In more recent years, racism has become an accepted topic in feminist discussions not as a result of black women calling attention to it (this was done at the very onset of the movement), but as a result of white female input validating such discussions, a process which is indicative of how racism works. Commenting on this tendency in her essay "The Incompatible Menage à Trois: Marxism, Feminism, and Racism," Gloria Joseph states:

> To date feminists have not concretely demonstrated the potential or capacity to become involved in fighting racism on an equal footing with sexism. Adrienne Rich's recent article on feminism and racism is an exemplary one on this topic. She reiterates much that has been voiced by black female writers, but the acclaim given her article shows again that it takes whiteness to give even Blackness validity.[7]

Focus on racism in feminist circles is usually directed at legitimating the "as is" structure of feminist theory and praxis. Like other affirmative action agendas in white supremacist capitalist patriarchy, lengthy discussions of racism or lip service to its importance tend to call attention to the "political correctness" of current feminist movement; they are not directed at an overall struggle to resist racist oppression in our society (not just racism in feminist movement). Discussions of racism have been implicitly sexist because of the focus on guilt and personal behavior. Racism is not an issue simply because white women activists are individually racist. They represent a small percentage of women in this society. They could have all been anti-racist from the outset but eliminating racism would still need to be a central feminist issue. Racism is fundamentally a feminist issue because it is so interconnected with sexist oppression. In the West, the philosophical foundations of racist and sexist ideology are similar. Although ethnocentric white values have led feminist theorists to argue the priority of sexism over racism, they do so in the context of attempting to create an evolutionary notion of culture, which in no way corresponds to our lived experience. In the United States, maintaining white supremacy has always been as great if not a greater priority than maintaining strict sex role divisions. It is no mere coincidence that interest in white women's rights is kindled whenever there is mass-based anti-racist protest. Even the most politically naive person can comprehend that a white supremacist state, asked to respond to the needs of oppressed black people and/or the needs of white women (particularly those from the bourgeois classes), will find it in its interest to respond to whites. Radical movement to end racism (a struggle that many have died to advance) is far more threatening than a women's movement shaped to meet the class needs of upwardly mobile white women.

It does not in any way diminish the value of or the need for feminist movement to recognize the significance of anti-racist struggle. Feminist theory would have much to offer if it showed women ways in which racism and sexism are immutably connected rather than pitting one struggle against the other or blatantly dismissing racism. A central issue for feminist activists has been the struggle to obtain for women the right to control their bodies. The very concept of white supremacy relies on the perpetuation of a white race. It is in the interest of continued white racist domination of the planet for white patriarchy to maintain control over all women's bodies. Any white female activist who works daily to help women gain control over their bodies and is racist negates and undermines her own effort. When white women attack white supremacy they are simultaneously participating in the struggle to end sexist oppression. This is just one example of the intersecting, complementary nature of racist and sexist oppression. There are many others that need to be examined by feminist theorists.

Racism allows white women to construct feminist theory and praxis in such a way that it is far removed from anything resembling radical struggle. Racist socialization teaches bourgeois white women to think they are necessarily more capable of leading masses of women than other groups of women. Time and time again, they have shown that they do not want to be part of feminist movement — they want to lead it. Even though bourgeois white women liberationists probably know less about grassroots organizing than many poor and working class women, they were certain of their leadership ability, as well as confident that theirs should be the dominant role in shaping theory and praxis. Racism teaches an inflated sense of importance and value, especially when coupled with class privilege. Most poor and working class women or even individual bourgeois nonwhite women would not have assumed that they could launch a feminist movement without first having the support and participation of diverse groups of women. Elizabeth Spelman stresses this impact of racism in her essay "Theories of Race and Gender: The Erasure of Black Women":

This is a racist society, and part of what this means is that, generally, the self-esteem of white people is deeply influenced by their difference from and supposed superiority to black people. White people may not think of themselves as racists, because they do not own slaves or hate blacks, but that does not mean that much of what props up white people's sense of self-esteem is not based on the racism which unfairly distributes benefits and burdens to whites and blacks.[8]

One reason white women active in feminist movement were unwilling to confront racism was their arrogant assumption that their call for Sisterhood was a nonracist gesture. Many white women have said to me, "we wanted black women and other nonwhite women to join the movement," totally unaware of their perception that they somehow "own" the movement, that they are the "hosts" inviting us as "guests."

Despite current focus on eliminating racism in feminist movement, there has been little change in the direction of theory and praxis. While white feminist activists now include writings by women of color on course outlines, or hire one woman of color to teach a class about her ethnic group, or make sure one or more women of color are represented in feminist organizations (even though this contribution of women of color is needed and valuable), more often than not they are attempting to cover up the fact that they are totally unwilling to surrender their hegemonic dominance of theory and praxis, a dominance which they would not have established were this not a white supremacist, capitalist state. Their attempts to manipulate women of color, a component of the process of dehumanization, do not always go unnoticed. In the July 1983 issue of *In These Times,* a letter written by Theresa Funiciello was published on the subject of poor women and the women's movement which shows the nature of racism within feminist movement:

Prior to a conference some time ago on the Urban Woman sponsored by the New York City chapter of NOW, I received a phone call from a NOW representative (whose name I have forgotten) asking for a welfare speaker with special qualifications. I was asked that she not be white — she might be "too articulate" — (i.e., not me), that she not be black, she might be "too angry." Perhaps she could be Puerto Rican? She should not say anything political or analytical but confine herself to the subject of "what the women's movement has done for me."

Funiciello responded to this situation by organizing a multiracial women's takeover of the conference. This type of action shows the spirit of Sisterhood.

Another response to racism has been the establishment of unlearning racism workshops, which are often led by white women. These workshops are important, yet they tend to focus primarily on cathartic individual psychological acknowledgement of personal prejudice without stressing the need for corresponding change in political commitment and action. A woman who attends an unlearning racism workshop and learns to acknowledge that she is racist is no less a threat than one who does not. Acknowledgement of racism is significant when it leads to transformation. More research, writing, and practical implementation of findings must be done on ways to unlearn racist socialization. Many white women who daily exercise race privilege lack awareness that they are doing so (which explains the emphasis on confession in unlearning racism workshops). They may not have conscious understanding of the ideology of white supremacy and the extent to which it shapes their behavior and attitudes towards women unlike themselves. Often, white women bond on the basis of shared racial identity without conscious awareness of the significance of their actions. This unconscious maintenance and perpetuation of white supremacy is dangerous because none of us can struggle to change racist attitudes if we do not recognize that they exist. For example, a group of white feminist activists who do not know one another may be present at a meeting to discuss feminist theory. They may feel they are bonded on the basis of shared womanhood, but the atmosphere will noticeably change when a woman of color enters the room. The white women will become tense, no longer relaxed, no longer celebratory. Unconsciously, they felt close to one another because they shared racial identity. The "whiteness" that bonds them together is a racial identity that is directly related to the experience of nonwhite people as "other" and as a "threat." Often when I speak to white women about racial bonding, they deny that it exists; it is not unlike sexist men denying their sexism. Until white supremacy is understood and attacked by white women there can be no bonding between them and multi-ethnic groups of women.

Women will know that white feminist activists have begun to confront racism in a serious and revolutionary manner when they are not simply acknowledging racism in feminist movement or calling attention to personal prejudice, but are actively struggling to resist racist oppression in our society. Women will know they have made a political commitment to eliminating racism when they help change the direction of feminist movement, when they work to unlearn racist socialization prior to assuming positions of leadership or shaping theory or making contact with women of color so that they will not perpetuate and maintain racial oppression or, unconsciously or consciously, abuse and hurt nonwhite women. These are the truly radical gestures that create a foundation for the experience of political solidarity between white women and women of color.

White women are not the only group who must confront racism if Sisterhood is to emerge. Women of color must confront our absorption of white supremacist beliefs, "internalized racism," which may lead us to feel self-hate, to vent anger and rage at injustice at one another rather than at oppressive forces, to hurt and abuse one another, or to lead one ethnic group to make no effort to communicate with another. Often women of color from varied ethnic groups have learned to resent and hate one another, or to be competitive with one another. Often Asian, Latina, or Native American Indian groups find they can bond with whites by hating blacks. Black people respond to this by perpetuating racist stereotypes and images of these ethnic groups. It becomes a vicious cycle. Divisions between women of color will not be eliminated until we assume rsponsibility for uniting (not solely on the basis of resisting racism) to learn about our cultures, to share our knowledge and skills, and to gain strength from our diversity. We need to do more research and writing about the barriers that separate us and the ways we can overcome such separation. Often the men in our ethnic groups have greater contact with one another than we do. Women often assume so many job-related and domestic responsibilities that we lack the time or do not make the time to get to know women outside our group or community. Language differences often prevent us from communicating; we can change this by encouraging one another to learn to speak Spanish, English, Japanese, Chinese, etc.

One factor that makes interaction between multi-ethnic groups of women difficult and sometimes impossible is our failure to recognize that a behavior pattern in one culture may be unacceptable in another, that it may have different signification cross-culturally. Through repeated teaching of a course titled "Third World Women in the United States," I have learned the importance of learning what we called one another's cultural codes. An Asian-American student, of Japanese heritage, explained her reluctance to participate in feminist organizations by calling attention to the tendency among feminist activists to speak rapidly without pause, to be quick on the uptake, always ready with a response. She had been raised to pause and think before speaking, to consider the impact of one's words, a characteristic which she felt was particularly true of Asian-Americans. She expressed feelings of inadequacy on the various occasions she was present in feminist groups. In our class, we learned to allow pauses and appreciate them. By sharing this cultural code, we created an atmosphere in the classroom that allowed for different communication patterns. This particular class was peopled primarily by black women. Several white women students complained that the atmosphere in the class was "too hostile." They cited the noise level and direct confrontations that took place in the room prior to class starting as an example of this hostility. Our response was to explain that what they perceived as hostility and aggression, we considered playful teasing and affectionate expressions of our pleasure at being together. Our tendency to talk loudly we saw as a consequence of being in a room with many people speaking as well as cultural background: many of us were raised in families where individuals speak loudly. In their upbringing as white, middle-class females, the complaining students had been taught to identify loud and direct speech with anger. We explained that we did not identify loud or blunt speech in this way, and encouraged them to switch codes, to think of it as an affirming gesture. Once they switched codes, they not only began to have a more creative, joyful experience in the class, but they also learned that silence and quiet speech can in some cultures indicate hostility and aggression. By learning one another's cultural codes and respecting our differences, we felt a sense of community, of Sisterhood. Respecting diversity does not mean uniformity or sameness.[9]

A crucial concern in these multi-racial classroom settings was recognition and acknowledgement of our differences and the extent to which they determine how we will be perceived by others. We had to continually remind one another to appreciate difference since many of us were raised to fear it. We talked about the need to acknowledge that we all suffer in some way but that we are not all oppressed nor equally oppressed. Many of us feared that our experiences were irrelevant because they were not as oppressive or as exploited as the experience of others. We discovered that we had a greater feeling of unity when people focused truthfully on their own experiences without comparing them with those of others in a competitive way. One student, Isabel Yrigoyei, wrote:

> We are not equally oppressed. There is no joy in this. We must speak from within us, our own experiences, our own oppressions — taking someone else's oppression is nothing to feel proud of. We should never speak for that which we have not felt.

When we began our communication by focusing on individual experiences, we found them to be varied even among those of us who shared common ethnic backgrounds. We learned that these differences mean we have no monolithic experiences that we can identify as "Chicana experience," "Black experience," etc. A Chicana growing up in a rural environment in a Spanish-speaking home has a life experience that differs from that of a Chicana raised in an English-speaking family in a bourgeois, predominantly white New Jersey suburb. These two women will not automatically feel solidarity. Even though they are from the same ethnic group, they must work to develop Sisterhood. Seeing these types of differences, we also confronted our tendency to value some experiences over others. We might see the Spanish-speaking Chicana as being more "politically correct" than her English-speaking peer. By no longer passively accepting the learned tendency to compare and judge, we could see value in each experience. We could also see that our different experiences often meant that we had different needs, that there was no one strategy or formula for the development of political consciousness. By mapping out various strategies, we affirmed our diversity while working towards solidarity. Women must explore various ways to communicate with one another cross-culturally if we are to develop political solidarity. When women of color strive to learn with and about one another we take responsibility for building Sisterhood. We need not rely on white women to lead the way to solidarity; all too often opportunistic concerns point them in other directions. We can establish unity among ourselves with anti-racist women. We can stand together united in political solidarity, in feminist movement. We can restore to the idea of Sisterhood its true meaning and value.

Cutting across racial lines, class is a serious political division between women. It was often suggested in early feminist literature that class would not be so important if more poor and working class women would join the movement. Such thinking was both a denial of the existence of class privilege gained through exploitation as well as a denial of class struggle. To build Sisterhood, women must criticize and repudiate class exploitation. The bourgeois woman who takes a less privileged "sister" to lunch or dinner at a fancy restaurant may be acknowledging class but she is not repudiating class privilege — she is exercising it. Wearing secondhand clothing and living in low-cost housing in a poor neighborhood while buying stock is not a gesture of solidarity with those who are deprived or underprivileged. As in the case of racism in feminist movement, the emphasis on class has been focused on individual status and change. Until women accept the need for redistribution of wealth and resources in the United States and work towards the achievement of that end, there will be no bonding between women that transcends class.

It is terribly apparent that feminist movement so far has primarily served the class interests of bourgeois white women and men. The great majority of women from middle-class situations who recently entered the labor force (an entry encouraged and promoted by feminist movement) helped strengthen the economy of the 1970s. In *The Two-Paycheck Marriage,* Caroline Bird emphasizes the extent to which these women (most of whom are white) helped bolster a waning economy:

> Working wives helped families maintain that standard of living through inflation. The Bureau of Labor Statistics has concluded that between 1973 and 1974 the real purchasing power of single-earner families dropped 3 percent compared with only 1 percent for families in which the wife was working. . . . Women especially will put themselves out to defend a standard of living they see threatened.
>
> Women did more than maintain standards. Working women lifted millions of families into middle class life. Her pay meant the difference between an apartment and a house, or college for the children. . . .
>
> Working wives were beginning to create a new kind of rich — and . . . a new kind of poor.[10]

More than ten years later, it is evident that large numbers of individual white women (especially those from middle-class backgrounds) have made economic strides in the wake of feminist movement support of careerism, and affirmative action programs in many professions. However, the masses of women are as poor as ever, or poorer. To the bourgeois "feminist," the million-dollar salary granted newscaster Barbara

Walters represents a victory for women. To working class women who make less than the minimum wage and receive few if any benefits, it means continued class exploitation.

Leah Fritz's *Dreamers and Dealers* is a fine example of the liberal woman's attempt to gloss over the fact that class privilege is based on exploitation, that rich women support and condone that exploitation, that the people who suffer most are poor, underprivileged women and children. Fritz attempts to evoke sympathy for all upper class women by stressing their psychological suffering, their victimization at the hands of men. She concludes her chapter "Rich Women" with the statement:

> Feminism belongs as much to the rich woman as to the poor woman. It can help her to understand that her own interests are linked with the advancement of all womankind; that comfort in dependency is a trap; that the golden cage has bars, too; and that, rich and poor, we are all wounded in the service of the patriarchy, although our scars are different. The inner turmoil that sends her to a psychoanalyst can generate energy for the movement which alone may heal her, by setting her free.[11]

Fritz conveniently ignores that domination and exploitation are necessary if there are to be rich women who may experience sexist discrimination or exploitation. She conveniently ignores class struggle.

Women from lower class groups had no difficulty recognizing that the social equality women's liberationists talked about equated careerism and class mobility with liberation. They also knew who would be exploited in the service of this liberation. Daily confronting class exploitation, they cannot conveniently ignore class struggle. In the anthology *Women of Crisis,* Helen, a working class white woman who works as a maid in the home of a bourgeois white "feminist" expresses her understanding of the contradiction between feminist rhetoric and practice:

> I think the missus is right: everyone should be equal. She keeps on saying that. But then she has me working away in her house, and I'm not equal with her — and she doesn't want to be equal with me; and I don't blame her, because if I was her I'd hold on to my money just like she does. Maybe that's what the men are doing — they're holding on to their money. And it's a big fight, like it always is about money. She should know. She doesn't go throwing big fat pay checks at her "help." She's fair; she keeps on reminding us — but

she's not going to "liberate" us, any more than the men are going to "liberate" their wives or their secretaries or the other women working in their companies.[12]

Women's liberationists not only equated psychological pain with material deprivation to de-emphasize class privilege; they often suggested it was the more severe problem. They managed to overlook the fact that many women suffer both psychologically and materially and for that reason alone changing their social status merited greater attention than careerism. Certainly the bourgeois woman who is suffering psychically is more likely to find help than the woman who is suffering material deprivation as well as emotional pain. One of the basic differences in perspective between the bourgeois woman and the working class or poor woman is that the latter know that being discriminated against or exploited because one is female may be painful and dehumanizing, but it may not necessarily be as painful, dehumanizing, or threatening as being without food or shelter, as starvation, as being deathly ill but unable to obtain medical care. Had poor women set the agenda for feminist movement, they might have decided that class struggle would be a central feminist issue; that poor and privileged women would work to understand class structure and the way it pits women against one another.

Outspoken socialist feminists, most of whom are white women, have emphasized class but they have not been effective in changing attitudes towards class in feminist movement. Despite their support of socialism, their values, behaviors, and lifestyles continue to be shaped by privilege. They have not developed collective strategies to convince bourgeois women who have no radical political perspective that eliminating class oppression is crucial to efforts to end sexist oppression. They have not worked hard to organize with poor and working class women who may not identify as socialists but do identify with the need for redistribution of wealth in the United States. They have not worked to raise the consciousness of women collectively. Much of their energy has been spent addressing the white male left, discussing the connections between marxism and feminism, or explaining to other feminist activists that socialist feminism is the best strategy for revolution. Emphasis on class struggle is often incorrectly deemed the sole domain of socialist feminists. Although I call attention to directions and strategies they have not employed, I wish to emphasize that these issues should be addressed by all activists in feminist movement. When women face the reality of classism and make political commitments to eliminating it, we will no longer experience the class conflicts that have been so apparent in feminist movement. Until we focus on class divisions between women, we will be unable to build political solidarity.

Sexism, racism, and classism divide women from one another. Within feminist movement, divisions and disagreements about strategy and emphasis led to the formation of a number of groups with varied political positions. Splintering into different political factions and special interest groups has erected unnecessary barriers to Sisterhood that could easily be eliminated. Special interest groups lead women to believe that only socialist feminists should be concerned about class; that only lesbian feminists should be concerned about the oppression of lesbians and gay men; that only black women or other women of color should be concerned about racism. Every woman can stand in political opposition to sexist, racist, heterosexist, and classist oppression. While she may choose to focus her work on a given political issue or a particular cause, if she is firmly opposed to all forms of group oppression, this broad perspective will be manifest in all her work irrespective of its particularity. When feminist activists are anti-racist and against class exploitation, it will not matter if women of color are present or poor women, etc. These issues will be deemed important and will be addressed, although the women most personally affected by particular exploitations will necessarily continue in the forefront of those struggles. Women must learn to accept responsibility for fighting oppressions that may not directly affect us as individuals. Feminist movement, like other radical movements in our society, suffers when individual concerns and priorities are the only reason for participation. When we show our concern for the collective, we strengthen our solidarity.

Solidarity was a word seldom used in contemporary feminist movement. Much greater emphasis was placed on the idea of "support." Support can mean upholding or defending a position one believes is right. It can also mean serving as a prop or a foundation for a weak structure. This latter meaning had greater significance in feminist circles. Its value emerged from the emphasis on shared victimization. Identifying as "victims," women were acknowledging a helplessness and powerlessness as well as a need for support, in this case the support of fellow feminist activists, "sisters." It was closely related to the shallow notion of Sisterhood. Commenting on its usage among feminist activists in her essay "With All Due Respect," Jane Rule explains:

Support is a much used word in the women's movement. For too many people it means giving and receiving unqualified approval. Some women are awfully good at withdrawing it at crucial moments. Too many are convinced they can't function without it. It's a false concept which has produced barriers to understanding and done real emotional damage. Suspension of critical judgement is not necessary for offering real support, which has to do instead with self-respect and respect for other people even at moments of serious disagreement.*

Women's legacy of woman-hating which includes fierce, brutal, verbal tearing apart of one another has to be eliminated if women are to make critiques and engage in disagreements and arguments that are constructive and caring, with the intention of enriching rather than diminishing. Woman-to-woman negative, aggressive behavior is not unlearned when all critical judgment is suspended. It is unlearned when women accept that we are different, that we will necessarily disagree, but that we can disagree and argue with one another without acting as if we are fighting for our lives, without feeling that we stand to lose all self-esteem by verbally trashing someone else. Verbal disagreements are often the setting where women can demonstrate their engagement with the win-or-lose competitiveness that is most often associated with male interactions, especially in the arena of sports. Women, like men, must learn how to dialogue with one another without competition. Jane Rule suggests that women can disagree without trashing if they realize they do not stand to lose value or self-worth if they are criticized: "No one can discredit my life if it is in my own hands, and therefore I do not have to make anyone carry the false burden of my frightened hostility."

Women need to come together in situations where there will be ideological disagreement and work to change that interaction so communication occurs. This means that when women come together, rather than pretend union, we would acknowledge that we are divided and must develop strategies to overcome fears, prejudices, resentments, competitiveness, etc. The fierce negative disagreements that have taken place in feminist circles have led many feminist activists to shun group or individual interaction where there is likely to be disagreement which

---

*The essay appears in *Outlander,* by Jane Rule (Tallahassee, Fla.: Naiad Press, 1981). *Ed.*

leads to confrontation. Safety and support have been redefined to mean hanging out in groups where the participants are alike and share similar values. While no woman wants to enter a situation in which she will be psychically annihilated, women can face one another in hostile confrontation and struggle and move beyond the hostility to understanding. Expression of hostility as an end in itself is a useless activity, but when it is the catalyst pushing us on to greater clarity and understanding, it serves a meaningful function.

Women need to have the experience of working through hostility to arrive at understanding and solidarity if only to free ourselves from the sexist socialization that tells us to avoid confrontation because we will be victimized or destroyed. Time and time again, I have had the experience of making statements at talks that anger a listener and lead to assertive and sometimes hostile verbal confrontation. The situation feels uncomfortable, negative, and unproductive because there are angry voices, tears, etc., and yet I may find later that the experience has led to greater clarity and growth on my part and on the part of the listener. On one occasion, I was invited by a black woman sociologist, a very soft-spoken individual, to speak in a class she was teaching. A young Chicana woman who could pass for white was a student in the class. We had a heated exchange when I made the point that the ability to pass for white gave her a perspective on race totally different from that of someone who is dark-skinned and can never pass. I pointed out that any person meeting her with no knowledge of her ethnic background probably assumes that she is white and relates to her accordingly. At the time the suggestion angered her. She became quite angry and finally stormed out of the class in tears. The teacher and fellow students definitely saw me as the "bad guy" who had failed to support a fellow sister and instead reduced her to tears. They were annoyed that our get-together had not been totally pleasurable, unemotional, dispassionate. I certainly felt miserable in the situation. The student, however, contacted me weeks later to share her feelings that she had gained new insights and awareness as a result of our encounter which aided her personal growth. Incidents like this one, which initially appear to be solely negative because of tension or hostility, can lead to positive growth. If women always seek to avoid confrontation, to always be "safe," we may never experience any revolutionary change, any transformation, individually or collectively.

When women actively struggle in a truly supportive way to understand our differences, to change misguided, distorted perspectives, we lay the foundation for the experience of political solidarity. Solidarity is not the same as support. To experience solidarity, we must have a community of interests, shared beliefs, and goals around which to unite, to build Sisterhood. Support can be occasional. It can be given and just as easily withdrawn. Solidarity requires sustained, ongoing commitment. In feminist movement, there is need for diversity, disagreement, and difference if we are to grow. As Grace Lee Boggs and James Boggs emphasize in *Revolution and Evolution in the Twentieth Century:**

> The same appreciation of the reality of contradiction underlies the concept of criticism and self-criticism. Criticism and self-criticism is the way in which individuals united by common goals can consciously utilize their differences and limitations, i.e., the negative, in order to accelerate their positive advance. The popular formulation for this process is "changing a bad thing into a good thing."

Women do not need to eradicate difference to feel solidarity. We do not need to share common oppression to fight equally to end oppression. We do not need anti-male sentiments to bond us together, so great is the wealth of experience, culture, and ideas we have to share with one another. We can be sisters united by shared interests and beliefs, united in our appreciation for diversity, united in our struggle to end sexist oppression, united in political solidarity.

Notes

1. Florynce Kennedy, "Institutional Oppression vs. The Female," in *Sisterhood Is Powerful,* ed. Robin Morgan (New York: Vintage Books, 1970), 438–46.

2. In early contemporary feminist writing (e.g., Redstockings Manifesto) the image of woman as victim is evoked. Joan Cassell's study of sisterhood and symbolism in the feminist movement, *A Group Called Women* (Prospect Heights, Ill.: Waveland Press, n.d.), examines the ideology of bonding among feminist activists. Contemporary writers like Leah Fritz evoke an image of woman as victim to encourage woman bonding. Barbara Smith discusses this tendency in her introduction to *Home Girls,* ed. Smith (New York: Kitchen Table/Women of Color Press, 1983).

---

*(New York: Monthly Review Press, 1974), 133. *Ed.*

3. At the onset of contemporary feminist movement I (and many other black women) often heard white women in Women's Studies classes, consciousness-raising groups, meetings, etc., respond to questions about the lack of black female participation by stressing that this was not related to problems with the structure of feminist movement but an indication that black women were already liberated. The image of the "strong" black woman is evoked in the writings of a number of white activists (e.g., Sara Evans, *Personal Politics* [New York: Random House, 1980]; Bettina Aptheker, *Woman's Legacy* [Amherst: University of Massachusetts Press, 1982]).

4. Jo Freeman, *The Politics of Women's Liberation* (New York: David McKay, 1975), 118.

5. Toni Morrison, "Cinderella's Stepsisters," *Ms.,* September 1979, 41.

6. Toni Morrison, "What the Black Woman Thinks about Women's Lib," *New York Times Magazine,* August 22, 1971, 15.

7. Gloria Joseph, "The Incompatible Menage à Trois: Marxism, Feminism, and Racism," in *Women and Revolution,* ed. Lydia Sargent (Boston: South End Press, 1981), 105.

8. Elizabeth Spelman, "Theories of Race and Gender: The Erasure of Black Women," *Quest* 5(4): 36–62.

9. My experience teaching "Third World Women in the United States" at San Francisco State has deeply enriched my understanding of women from diverse backgrounds. I am grateful to all the students I taught there, especially Betty and Susan.

10. Caroline Bird, *The Two-Paycheck Marriage* (New York: Pocket Books, 1979), 9.

11. Leah Fritz, *Dreamers and Dealers* (Boston: South End Press, 1979), 225.

12. Robert Coles and Jane H. Coles, *Women of Crisis* (New York: Dell, 1978), 266.

19

Women and the Holocaust
A Reconsideration of Research

Joan Ringelheim

I

Thinking is like the veil of Penelope: it undoes every morning what it had
finished the night before.
— *Hannah Arendt, "Thinking and Moral Considerations"*

Even a cursory look at studies about the Holocaust would indicate that
the experiences and perceptions of Jewish women have been obscured or
absorbed into descriptions of men's lives. The similarity among Jewish
victims of the Nazi policy of destruction has been considered more
important than any differentiation, including or especially that of gender. It is not surprising, then, that until quite recently there has been no
feminist perspective in Holocaust scholarship.[1]

Although the research on women and the Holocaust is only just beginning, it already has taken a problematic and troubling direction.
Since my own work has been instrumental in setting this course, I
am going to make it my case study for analysis and criticism. Using
fragments of stories Jewish women survivors have told me in interviews,
I will first recapitulate the assumptions, hypotheses, and categories I
have used in my interpretation and then explore what is problematic in
this approach. I want to look particularly at the influence of cultural

Reprinted from *Signs* 10 (Summer 1985): 741–61, by permission of the author
and the publisher. © 1985 by The University of Chicago. All rights reserved.

feminism on my own work and to pose myself and others some new questions.

When I began research I assumed that gender must have counted for something and that focusing on women's experience would yield new questions and new data: if you were Jewish, in what ways did it matter whether you were a man or a woman? Did gender cause any difference in policies, actions, or reactions of either the Nazis or those opposed to them? In what ways did sexism function in the racist ideology against Jews and other so-called non-Aryans? Is there, for instance, anything to be seen in statistics about the number of men killed as compared to women, differences among those selected to die, or distinctions in types of work assigned? Did the Nazis prolong and intensify an already existing sexism against Jewish women as they prolonged, intensified, and even elaborated anti-Semitism against the Jews as a whole?[2] In what ways was sexism maintained and intensified under Nazism by the Jews themselves?

Were women's experiences during the Holocaust different from men's in some respects? Were there differences in work, relationships, roles, and in maintenance possibilities or capabilities — that is, in what a person did or tried to do simply to keep going, to make it from day to day?[3] Do women and men possess different maintenance skills? Because of traditional gender roles are women better able to bear conditions of deprivation?

At the initial stages of research, I suggested that traditional attitudes and responses toward women, as well as gender-defined conditions, made women especially vulnerable to abuse of their sexuality and of their maternal responsibility — to rape, murder of themselves and their children, the necessity of killing their own or other women's babies, forced abortion, and other forms of sexual exploitation — in the ghettos, in resistance groups, in hiding and passing, and in the camps. I believed it important, moreover, to explore the claim of some survivors and scholars that women's capacities for enduring the trauma of dislocation, starvation, loss of traditional support structures, and physical and mental abuse were different from and sometimes greater than men's.[4]

These assumptions and ideas shaped the form of an interview schedule with a twofold aim: (1) to recapture the Holocaust experience as a whole, and (2) to establish women's sense of their particular experience within it: what was done to them (their vulnerabilities) and what they did (their resources). I began each of the twenty interviews I conducted with some general questions about life prior to the Holocaust: family background, relationships, education, class, and so on. I wanted the women to start their stories in a way that seemed comfortable, even familiar. I expected to be able to hear their understanding of themselves both as Jews and as women from the narrative structures they devised. I asked further questions when they were needed to clarify or expand an idea, or to raise a topic not yet mentioned. In particular, I asked about those things that seemed related to their lives as women: sexuality, sexual abuse, family, children, relationships, food, resistance, and passivity. I asked questions about choices, decisions, and problems. What did they tell me?[5]

In their descriptions of the tragedy of Jews during the Holocaust, the women interviewed discussed women's particular victimization. They spoke of their sexual vulnerability: sexual humiliation, rape, sexual exchange, pregnancy, abortion, and vulnerability through their children — concerns that men either described in different ways or, more often, did not describe at all.[6] Almost every woman referred to the humiliating feelings and experiences surrounding her entrance to the camp (for my interviewees, this was Auschwitz): being nude; being shaved all over — for some being shaved in a sexual stance, straddling two stools; being observed by men, both fellow prisoners and SS guards. Their stories demonstrate shared fears about and experiences of sexual vulnerability as women, not only about mortal danger as Jews.

Some women remember the ways in which sex was used as a commodity in the ghettos; sexual exchanges for food or other goods involved Jewish men at least as often as, perhaps more often than, they did Nazi authorities. S. spoke of her experiences in Theresienstadt — the so-called model ghetto in Czechoslovakia. She was about twenty: "Women survived partly by brains. I worked in the office, in supply, in the education office. I wasn't doing badly. . . . [Up] to [a certain] point you were autonomous . . . you could lead your own life . . . people could get married. You also survived by your male connections. It was the males who had the main offices, who ran the kitchens. . . . [The] *Judenrat* [was] running [the ghetto and the Jewish men] *used* it. And did they *use* it. *Did* they use it. That was how you survived as a woman — through the male. I was done in by one. I suppose I didn't sleep high enough, to put it bluntly. Because in that society, that was the only way you could survive."

Her experiences with sexual abuse did not end when she was sent to Auschwitz. Once when she was working in *Kanada,* an SS officer approached her as she began to take a nap.[7] He tried to wake her by kicking the bunk on which she was resting. She knew what he wanted (she had noticed him staring at her) and feigned sleep, pushing him away or moaning as if he were part of a dream. S. claimed that he would not have forced her to have sex — he would only have had relations if she agreed because a prisoner could report the SS. In such cases the prisoner had some "power," she said, because it was a crime for an SS to have sexual relations with a Jew. This SS man went away. Another time, S. was not so lucky: she was raped by a prisoner.

At the time of the Warsaw Ghetto, G. was about fifteen years old. She remembered seeing a young SS officer spot beautiful Jewish women, go to their houses, and rape them. Afterward, he would shoot them. He always came prepared with a horse-drawn hearse. Since G. was quite pretty, her mother and cousin made paste from flour and water and put it on her face with the hope that she would be less vulnerable if less attractive. She was afraid but never really "knew if it was better to look prettier or terrible."

About three years later, G. was in a camp near Lublin and Maidanek, and the commandant decided to open up the gates of the men's camp and allow them to go over to the women's. "The men came. I was pretty young then. Strangest thing — so many of these men tried right away to screw. . . . [They were] like a horde of animals. . . . I had this vision for a long, long time — this horde of sick men jumping." She was only watching, and this is all she remembers. It was one of her worst memories from the Holocaust.

Although there are many stories about sexual abuse, they are not easy to come by. Some think it inappropriate to talk about these matters; discussions about sexuality desecrate the memories of the dead, or the living, or the Holocaust itself. For others, it is simply too difficult and painful. Still others think it may be a trivial issue. One survivor told me that she had been sexually abused by a number of Gentile men while she was in hiding, when she was about eleven years old. Her comment about this was that it "was not important . . . except to me." She meant that it had no significance within the larger picture of the Holocaust. But why should ideas about the Holocaust as a whole exclude these women's experiences — exclude what is important to women — and thus make the judgment that women's experiences as women are trivial? These aspects of women's daily lives—vulnerability to rape, humiliation, sexual exchange, not to speak of pregnancy, abortion, and fear for one's children—cannot simply be universalized as true for all survivors.

It would be wrong to suggest that abuse characterized the whole of women's sexual experiences during the Holocaust. Some women speak about heterosexual love relationships, great passions, or small romances in the ghettos, resistance groups, and even in the camps. They also speak of liaisons created out of loneliness, friendship, the need for help, or even through the desire to experience sex before one's death.

In sex-segregated camps, as most were, deep friendships occurred among the women that sometimes developed into sexual relationships. Thus far no woman has talked to me about such experiences as her own. S. did say that she knew of lesbian relationships and that "it wasn't an issue; wherever you could get warmth, care, and affection, that was good. That was all that mattered."[8] Her view is not the common one that I have encountered. More often than not those interviewed showed hostility at the question, some associating it with visions of SS women in drag with whips. Attitudes toward lesbian relationships in the camps seem at best ambiguous or ambivalent and require careful study if we are to understand fully relationships and interactions in the camps and elsewhere.

Coping with pregnancy, childbirth, and infant care made Jewish women particularly vulnerable in other ways to physical abuse and mental anguish—whether through abortion by choice, forced abortion, bearing a child, being killed with a child as its actual or supposed mother, bearing a child and not being able to feed it, killing a baby because its cries jeopardized other people or because if the baby were found (at least in Auschwitz) both Jewish mother and baby would be killed.[9] I heard one child survivor say that all adults were enemies to children,[10] but women with children may have been more vulnerable than anyone except children by themselves.

What I am trying to make graphic is the complexity of these Jewish women's lives because of the connections between biology and sexism. There are particular vulnerabilities, such as pregnancy and abortion, resulting from women's biology; others, created by sexism, perpetuate violence against women in the form of humiliation, molestation, rape, and sexual exchange. These vulnerabilities, as well as the sheer terror, degradation, and genocide perpetrated by the Nazis against the Jews, existed for Jewish women in the Holocaust.

Besides their special vulnerability, the other topic that I discussed with the women I interviewed was their special resources. Survivors testify to gender difference in this regard. A number of observers had the impression that women survived better than men, the women "tended to outlive" men, at least in comparable situations.[11] Such perceptions need to be examined.

Study of the Holocaust requires more specific research on the comparative survival rates of women and men than is represented in the sporadic opinions and unrepresentative surveys now available.[12] Without such statistics (and they may never be available) we have only impressions and speculations, a series of questions rather than answers. Were more women killed than men? What was the relation between work and survival? If some sorts of work could save lives, did women and men have similar chances to do it? What was the pattern of food distribution between women and men, among women, and among men — that is, were women eating the same amount as men or sharing their portions more than men did? Are there biological differences to account for the dissimilarities mentioned by survivors and scholars about the effects of starvation?

Some of the differences perceived do appear as transformations related to gender: starving transformed into communal sharing of recipe stories; sex into food, rather than the reverse; rags into clothes; isolation into relationships or surrogate "families." Women were able to transform their habits of raising children or their experience of nurturing into the care of nonbiological family. Men, when they lost their role in the protection of their own families, seemed less able to transform this habit into the protection of others. Men did not remain or become fathers as readily as women became mothers or nurturers. Do women apply and modify previous gender roles more easily than do men?[13]

The so-called trivial, everyday activities of which the women speak constitute the necessary but not sufficient conditions for their survival. "Women's work" — activities centering around food, children, clothing, shelter, social relations, warmth, cleanliness — may be regarded as the only meaningful labor in a time of such dire necessity. It is only with such trivial — and often trivialized — concerns that life among the oppressed becomes possible. And it is important to look at what this means both to women and to men whose relationship to necessity has traditionally been quite different in European as well as other cultures.

Because of the different material conditions and social relations that characterize their lives, women are able to create or recreate "families" and so provide networks for maintenance that may be related to survival rates. Awareness of such responses (and of such variables as class, age, and nationality) is crucial to understanding the lives of the women.[14] Excerpts from the following three interviews give you some preliminary sense of the ways in which a few women have spoken about the importance of relationships to their survival.[15]

Rose

Rose, from a poor family, was born in Hungary in 1919. She was trained as a hairdresser and was deported to Auschwitz in March 1942. After a year on an outside demolition crew, she began work in the sauna, cutting the hair of the incoming prisoners. "There were mountains of dead bodies outside of the barracks which were picked up by trucks every morning. If you had to go to the bathroom [diarrhea was rampant and getting to the latrine difficult], then you went to the bathroom on top of them. Didn't think twice about it. You had no feelings. [Yet] I knew a young girl from Holland, Eva, who was brought to Block 25 [a kind of holding pen for women going to be gassed]. Eva was fifteen or sixteen and got diarrhea which was enough for them to take you away. Took her to Block 25 and I knew where she was going to go. . . . I sneaked there and took her something to eat. . . . My heart was aching for her. You know, here I was walking over dead bodies and it didn't bother me, but it bothered me to see a young girl like this go and nothing I could do for her. There was still feelings. . . . I couldn't cry too much. . . . I felt so bad for her and when you got close to these barracks in Block 25, you can't imagine what you saw in there. Just can't imagine — half-crazy, laid on top of one another, lost their minds . . . horrible."

At about the time Rose got her job in the sauna [1943], Rollie came to Auschwitz from Greece with two sisters. The youngest, Teresa (Rollie's favorite), got sick and died. Rollie was beside herself and wanted to commit suicide. Rose met her. "If it wasn't for me, she wouldn't be alive. We helped each other. We had to cling . . . you had to have somebody. We helped each other. She considers me her best friend, her mother, her father, everything. . . . I considered her as my daughter [Rose was then twenty-four; Rollie was eighteen]. This I felt for her. I was sheltering her. . . . When I had typhus, all I wanted was an apple. Who can get an apple there? [Rollie] sold her bread to exchange for an apple that I should get it."

A small incident. In the chronicle of concentration camp horrors, it may even appear to be minuscule. For Rose, it is only small because it takes a short time to tell. It is an emblem of life for her: "That time you don't think what kind of relation; you just think, I got somebody here I can talk to, somebody close by. That's all what you think about. . . . I fought going off my mind. I thought of taking my life [going to the electrified wires that surrounded the camp and forgetting] the whole thing. But . . . I gotta live. This woman told me, I'm gonna be free, I'm gonna go to America to see my father. . . . [That] gave me a lot. . . . Got Rollie here and she's still a baby—this was how I was thinking about her. Can't do that [commit suicide or lose her mind]. You know, there was always something that was stopping me. Now here was little Eva, she goes in Block 25 and I just want to see her once more—was always something that I say 'No, I'm not gonna do that.' Didn't let myself go."

Rose gave her own reasons for the way in which women kept themselves and others going, and explained what it meant that they did so: Women were "picking each other like monkeys [for lice]. . . . Never remember seeing the men do it. The minute they had lice they just left it alone; the women have a different instinct. Housewives. We want to clean. . . . Somehow the men, . . . the [lice] ate them alive. . . . [During roll call] the women holding each other and keeping each other warm. . . . Someone puts their arm around you and you remember. . . . Can you imagine how much it meant to us over there! Men were crouching into themselves—maybe five feet apart [Rose demonstrated how the men she saw put their arms around their own bodies, rather than around the next person for warmth]. . . . I think more women survived. . . . As much as I saw in Auschwitz, the men were falling like flies. The woman was somehow stronger. . . . Woman friendship is different than man friendship you see. . . . We have these motherly instincts, friend instincts more. If two or three women are friends they can be closer than two or three men. [Men] can be nice to each other, talk to each other, have a beer with each other. . . . But that's as far as it goes, you know? But that's what was holding the women together because everybody had to have somebody to lean on, to depend on. The men, no . . . the men didn't do that. Men were friends there too. They talked to each other but they didn't, wouldn't, sell their bread for an apple for the other guy. They wouldn't sacrifice nothing. See, that was the difference."

Susan

Susan was born in Vienna in 1922 and moved to Czechoslovakia in 1938 with her mother and father. She was deported to Theresienstadt in

1942 and to Auschwitz in January 1943. In the first month there she worked as a typist in the political department. She was sent back to the regular prison population because one of the women in her group was caught passing food and the entire group was punished for it. Susan got typhus soon after returning to the regular camp population.

She had become part of a group of Jewish women from Berlin, and "without them, I wouldn't have gotten through this illness. They helped me through a good eight days of 103–4 degree temperature. . . . I remember like today, every morning standing in roll call, standing close, braced — walked out with their arms under me. These women supported me physically . . . emotionally and spiritually. I was supposed to go to the hospital block [this usually meant death] and my blockleader (*Block-älteste*) Ilka, with whom I had established a relationship, let me stay in the barracks for a day while she covered for me. This was my day of crisis. Without this protection, I would have died. . . . Always part of some group of women for whom you went through fire. . . . Maybe it was egotistical. You knew your group cared for you. . . . It was the reciprocity that kept you alive and going."

I asked if one needed affection: "Oh yes. Yes, you did, oh yes, you did. Women amongst each other . . . for warmth, for feeling of someone caring. That you needed. Most basic point, it kept you warm if you were cuddled. Yes, we were affectionate. Even later in *Kanada*[16] when we were quite comfortable . . . you slept four in a bunk next to each other; sure you cuddle up every so often — that was quite natural. That was not out of the ordinary. When people let themselves go, they also lost touch with other people."

Groups were formed in *Kanada:* "It was a different sort of friendship than in outside *kommandos*. There, it was a matter of survival. Don't know what men did. From what I read, it was not [the same]. The only way you had it with men [was] if they were communists or part of religious groups. . . . There was less of a need for support in *Kanada* because we could get necessities."

So in *Kanada,* the women formed different groups made up of people sharing the same interests or with people who thought alike. In Susan's opinion, these friendships among like-minded people, instead of groups united for maintenance, were possible because death was not imminent in this situation. Friendships here seemed more relaxed and were formed not out of sheer necessity but instead out of mutual sympathy for each other.

Judy

Judy is the youngest of these women. Born in 1929 in Hungary, she came to Auschwitz when she was fifteen, in May 1944. Unlike Rose and Susan, she arrived with her family. They were separated on arrival. Judy was the only one who survived.

She was in Auschwitz for about nine months. She did speak of friendships with the girls in her bunks — she was in a barrack with about one thousand fifteen-year-old girls. She "mothered" those in her bunk whose education and experience were different from hers. She told them stories from such books as *Gone with the Wind* and *My Son, My Son,* and from Deanna Durbin and Shirley Temple movies.

In November, she was sent on a transport to a labor camp, Guben, near Berlin. She was "brought to work in a factory soldering electrical equipment. The conditions were better here. Only fifty people to a room. Each bunk had two or three people. Each person received a blanket. They slept on a wooden board, with no mattress or pillow."

That first evening, she had just fallen asleep when someone came into the room and turned on the lights: " 'Is there anyone here from Uzhorod [her hometown]?' It was Emu, the sister of a childhood friend, [who was looking for her sister]. Even though I was not her sister, there was excitement and from that moment I had somebody and that meant everything to me . . . meant life to me."

Emu was there with her sister-in-law, Rosie. They were between ten and twelve years older than Judy. Emu worked in the kitchen and Rosie in the clothing warehouse. "I became attached to both of them. . . . I got a coat right away from Rosie. . . . [Emu] always had an extra potato or two for me. She would see to it that I got the thicker part of the soup, not the liquid. Every so often, she would have an extra piece of bread which I joyously took back to my room and then shared with the few who were around me who didn't have that fortune as I did. I felt extremely lucky because of the friendship of these two women. They were very devoted, very caring, very kind and . . . good to me."

Her hope and strength were building. She thought the war would be over soon. However, they were evacuated to Bergen-Belsen on a death march. It was cold and snowing; they had no water or food. Judy wanted them to leave her: "I was weak and my feet were blistered and bleeding. But they wouldn't let me go, they dragged me when I couldn't walk, and stood close by when the guards were near so they wouldn't see me."

Somehow they managed. "I ate snow off of the person's shoulder in front of me or pulled frozen roots from the ground."

Judy is simply taken into the lives of Emu and Rosie; there are no discussions, no negotiations. They seem to trust each other in what they do with and for each other. It is part of their practice. Is it partly because they were not total strangers? They do not *ask* Judy to go on; they simply do not let her fall. The acts push and sustain. It is not the will to live that gets Judy through; it is a practice, a set of behaviors between one and the others.

They finally arrived at Bergen-Belsen. Rosie had taken some jewelry with her from Guben for possible bartering. They stuffed the pieces in their mouths as they went through the showers. Judy said that conditions were awful. They slept on the floor. They hardly had any food and "no sanitation . . . people dying by the minute. We were given one meal a day. Often there was no bread. . . . Eventually [there were] lice everywhere. [We were] continually and totally infested by lice [which] carried the typhus germ."

They each got typhus. Rosie was first. "We would drag her to where we could manage to get a little water . . . keep her supported between us, walking, so she's not lying down all the time. Tried to wash her face and slap her face gently. [Tried] to breathe life into her. Somehow these two ladies found a source . . . [and traded] their jewelry for aspirin, some food, sugar cubes, extra pieces of bread. . . . Every time they acquired an extra bite of food they would share it with me as if I was a one-third partner. That was the most amazing thing. I just couldn't believe that. . . . It wasn't mine at all. [Yet] they never even considered not sharing.

"After Rosie got better, Emu got very sick. . . . She developed huge welts—spotted typhus. She was very bosomy and had welts underneath her bosom that were festering. . . . I remember Rosie lifting her breast and me blowing on it to air it, to try to help this . . . to just lift it away from the wound so that the wound would reach some air. . . . We would force feed her and she would say, 'I can't swallow it. Let me die. I can't live anymore. I can't get up.' 'No! You can. You've come this long, and you're not going to go now. You can and you have to and you will.' Just the way they did on the death march for me. . . . We were encouraging this way in Bergen-Belsen."

Judy also got sick. Emu and Rosie did what they could to keep her alive. They still had a piece of jewelry. "They traded it for some cheese and bread. [We] shared it in honor of my sixteenth birthday. It was some sixteenth birthday under those kinds of conditions." Judy was sick for a few days: "I was shivering and my teeth were shaking. I was sure I was not going to live. Someone burst into the room and said, 'All our guards are gone. English soldiers are all over the place.' . . . I couldn't walk. My friends dragged me outside into a sunny, spring day. Liberation, April 15, 1945, about 1:00 P.M. I took this day as my new birthday."

Obviously Rose, Susan, and Judy survived because the Nazis did not kill them, and they were liberated. Ultimately, survival was luck. But that tells us very little if we want to find out about their maintenance strategies and how these strategies relate to their survival. "Luck" does not tell us how they committed life in a world meant for death. In other words, they survived because the Nazis did not kill them; but they lived (trying to be human) because of what they did. Surviving is different from living.[17]

While other things may have been needed in order to keep going — inside work, extra food, cleanliness, willingness to risk, physical and psychological strength — friendships and relationships are central to the stories of Judy, Susan, and Rose.[18] An important clue to these women's understanding of how they carried on, such acts of friendship also suggest questions that need to be asked of others about their experiences. These women recognized that isolation and separation were created by the Nazi system in the camps. They also knew that, if strength mattered, if it was even possible, it could only exist with others. In their "families" they created the possibilities for material and psychological strength. Their relationships — their conversations, singing, storytelling, recipe sharing, praying, joke telling, gossiping — helped them to transform a world of death and inhumanity into one more act of human life.

II

What I propose . . . is very simple: it is nothing more than to think what we are doing.
— *Hannah Arendt*, The Human Condition

The language and perspective in Part I recapitulate some of the research I had written up before May 1984, when I came to see serious problems in my work arising at least in part from my unconscious use of cultural feminism as a frame through which to view Jewish women survivors.[19] Cultural feminism informed the assumptions posited, hypotheses created, and the conclusions reached, and I have come to believe that the perspective it gave must be changed.

Politically cultural feminism can be associated with the breakup of the New Left and the deradicalizing of feminism in the early 1970s; since then, it has been reflected in the work of many involved in women's studies and feminist theory. While I cannot give a complete historical analysis of cultural feminism in these few pages, I can attempt to show what cultural feminism is about, how it has affected my work, how it may reflect liberalism, and why it poses a significant problem for us as feminists.

Cultural feminism was a reaction against at least two views: (1) radical feminism's position that women are an oppressed class, and (2) the position of both New Left politics and radical feminism that personal liberation is impossible without widespread social change. The reaction shifted the territory of liberation from an insistence on the need for changing material conditions to a belief in changing the inner life, consciousness, culture, and so on.

Brooke, an early 1970s feminist critic of cultural feminism, called it "the belief that women will be freed via an alternate women's culture. It leads to a concentration on lifestyle and 'personal liberation,' . . . [and it] is an attempt to transform feminism from a political movement to a lifestyle movement." Cultural feminism thus disavowed the radical feminist position that "the locus of oppression . . . is not culture but power, men's class power."[20] To posit liberation as personal turns the politics of revolution away from the belief that genuine liberation must deal with power first and foremost and not with culture — with changing material conditions, not simply changing hearts and minds.

While those who originally espoused cultural feminism may have thought and even intended that women would rise up and revolt once their consciousness was changed, the result was something else again. The putative politics of revolution turned into a politics of accommodation for individual and personal solutions. Sheila Rowbotham points out that the tendency is "towards preoccupation with living a liberated life rather than becoming a movement for the liberation of women."[21] This political shift to cultural feminism both supported and was supported by an inward turn of women's studies toward a focus on consciousness, women's culture, gender differences, and so on.

Cultural feminism developed not simply as a tactic for battling the antiwoman line in a sexist world,[22] but as a way to detour around it without violent revolution; without confronting the state, family, marriage, or organized religion; and without eliminating institutions intent on keeping women in their place. This detour became a new strategy and ideology. While some may consider cultural feminism to be synonymous with feminism, the two terms cannot serve as substitutes for one another. Rather, cultural feminism substitutes a political activism that was risky and offensive for another that, accidentally or not, conveniently disallows risk. Certainly, feminism is safer if it is cultural rather than political.[23]

The "liberation" that cultural feminism invokes is from women's past. From that recollection comes the discovery or development of a separate women's culture and community based in turn on the belief that women and men are in some sense radically different. Such recollection, goes the claim, can create (and this is true) a positive class consciousness as well as (and this is questionable) a genuinely different society. Proponents offer biological or cultural explanations, alternately, for gender differences, but embedded in both is the judgment that the feminine or the female is superior to the masculine or the male. Thus, cultural feminism overthrows a theory of masculine superiority for its opposite rather than standing such an idea on its head or throwing it out the window.

On these terms, cultural feminism celebrates woman — her values, art, music, sexuality, mothering. In her article "Female Nationalism," Ti-Grace Atkinson succinctly characterizes cultural feminism as "the search for a *mythical history,* the *cult of femaleness,* the *glorification of motherhood, naturalism,* and *separatism,* [so that] female consciousness [became] the source and arbiter of world reality."[24]

While women's consciousness, "herstory," culture, and so on, became the standard by which to understand and judge the world, there was confusion about whether the quintessential woman — the most typical or representative woman — was to be a woman of the past or a new woman of the future. The confusion resolved itself in a psychoanalytic mode: the past is the future. Then struggles arose about which woman of the past would serve as the model. The result was that we did not emerge with a consciousness, let alone a politics, that produced genuine solidarity with all women, though we did advance different claims to superiority. Lesbian separatism may be the most important example politically and motherhood the most egregious expression of the kinds of chauvinism (even nationalism) that developed.[25] The struggles within the women's movement have been "resolved" by cultural feminists who superficially claim the universality of women's culture, "christianized" into the love of women.

Cultural feminists share with liberals a belief in individual solutions as well as in values of individuality, autonomy, and self-determination. Liberals maintain that we are all human beings and, if we but acknowledge this and act out our humanity, the world will change. What counts are our human similarities; thus differences and the structures that established the possibilities for some of those differences are not crucial. If we change ourselves, the world should change. First things first. Liberals say that their discourse includes everyone, and they mean that they are concerned about white Anglo-Saxon Protestants; cultural feminists say that they consider all women, but they refer only to lesbians, and/or mothers, and/or straight women, and/or S/M lesbians, and/or university women, and/or middle-class women, and/or women against pornography, and/or any number of others. While cultural feminists speak about a kind of universal woman, in fact they privilege some women over others. This imitation of, or connection to, liberalism is hazardous. And so, the face of the enemy has become each other; the focus is no longer on men and their institutions — least of all, on the male state. Indeed, with cultural feminism these institutions have become irrelevant or redeemable. Meanwhile the very "femininity" that seemed oppressive earlier in the women's movement has now been made sacred.

Can we so blithely reclaim and make right what has caused so much oppression without some careful scrutiny of our motives and politics? Can Jews reclaim the language of "kike"; or lesbians, "dyke"; or blacks, "nigger" without retaining some of the negativity that infests and infects the oppressors' use of those words, let alone the institutions of which such language is only a part? Even more, can values, ways of life, and skills be reclaimed as if they have not arisen within an oppressive situation? And do they become free of oppression or of its effects simply because we would like them to be so? Such uncritical valorization allows us to retain old patterns without having to believe they are negative.

Thus, cultural feminism entrenches us in a reactionary politics of personal or life-style change, in liberation of the self. What about solidarity with other women? With other feminists? Ann Oakley is right when she says that while not all solidarity with women demonstrates feminist consciousness, "there can be no feminist consciousness without female solidarity."[26] And if female solidarity is to have political import, there must be an active, progressive movement.

The valorization of oppression damages not only our politics but our research. We want to justify our valorization of such beliefs and practices so much that our critical faculties become quiescent when we discuss these questions. The claim of female superiority is not at issue so much as the nature of gender differences and the kind of woman who best exemplifies them. What does all this mean for our research strategies? We must resolve not to use research either to valorize oppression or to blunt or negate its effects. To excavate women's past, to begin to know and understand what has been "hidden from history," does not mean that we use that "herstory" as a model for women's liberation. Our task must be to contribute to a strategy for changing, not simply reinterpreting and obfuscating, women's lives.

The archaeological perspective that we have had on women's culture must be reexamined. Why do we take this point of view? How do we want to use it? Against what are we fighting? What new world are we making? Does our work sustain or even reinforce oppression? Are we articulating ways to understand and combat oppression? How does our work further the liberation of women? And if it does not, in what sense is it feminist?

Political and philosophical or conceptual errors are not far apart from each other. Analysis of my own work on women and the Holocaust has to turn on a critique of both my political and my philosophical perspective on the material and on the world. My use of cultural feminism as a frame (albeit unconsciously) changed respect for the stories of the Jewish women into some sort of glorification and led to the conclusion that these women transformed "a world of death and inhumanity into one more act of human life." It was important, perhaps even crucial for me to see choices, power, agency, and strength in women's friendships, bonding, sharing, storytelling, and conversations in the camps and ghettos, in hiding and passing. And indeed, there are inspiring stories and people, moving tales of help, devotion, and love. However, they describe incidents and are not at the center of the Holocaust. They need to be put into perspective.

The Holocaust is a story of loss, not gain. After all, most Jews were killed in Europe. In addition, one-fourth to one-half of the Gypsy population was killed. Perhaps ten to fifteen thousand homosexual men were killed. The list goes on. Even if we can find differences — even if women did maintain themselves better than men — how is this a real gain? We need to look critically, moreover, at the many ways in which women maintained themselves; their strategies were not always positive, and so a most difficult question has to be asked: "what have the victims wrought?"[27]

It is interesting to look at differences between women and men. It is even interesting to see, if we can, whether women maintained themselves either better than or — perhaps more accurately — differently from men. However, the discovery of difference is often pernicious because it helps us to forget the context of these supposed strengths — oppression — and to ignore the possibility that they may be only apparent. To suggest that among those Jews who lived through the Holocaust, women rather than men survived better is to move toward acceptance or valorization of oppression, even if one uses a cultural and not a biological argument. Oppression does not make people better; oppression makes people oppressed. There is no sense in fighting or even understanding oppression if we maintain that the values and practices of the oppressed are not only better than those of the oppressor but, in some objective sense, "a model [for] humanity and the new society."[28] This is not to say that there are no differences between men and women in the ways that they relate to institutions or in their values. It *is* to question our interpretations of the conceptual and political import of such differences.

My attempt, then, to emphasize friendships among women in the camps gives a false or misleading impression that oppression is only external and not internal as well. Why the silence about the internalized oppression of the Jewish women survivors? To avoid another dimension of the horror of the Holocaust or of oppression in general? In the work represented in Part I, I seemed to be saying that in spite of rape, abuse, and murder of babies; in spite of starvation, separations, losses, terror, and violence; in spite of everything ugly and disgusting, women bonded, loved each other. Rose said: "That's what was holding the woman together." Must we not ask, How many women? At what cost? For how long? Under what conditions?

"Can you imagine what it meant," Rose said to me, "to have affection in spite of the dirt, disease, stench?" I do not doubt that it meant a great deal. It is not that the statement is necessarily false but that the focus on friendship, affection, and so on distorted our understanding of a larger situation in which that experience may have played only a small role. The bonding was limited and exclusive. It was not a bonding against the enemy in solidarity with women. Did the terror of isolation and death *not* affect the women because they bonded? Perhaps these friendship stories cover a deeper and more troubled story of intrigue, bitterness, hurt, pain, and brutality. What else happened in the groups? Between the groups? The talk about friendship allowed those of us who heard the stories to admire these women, even to receive some peace and comfort. It helped to lessen the terrible surrounding sounds of the Holocaust. This "woman-centered" perspective and the questions it addressed were misguided.

Yet if the perspective and questions were wrong, the work is not useless. It needs rather a different political and philosophical context. Different questions must be asked of the survivors — different interpretations made of their replies. To reconstruct the research on women and the Holocaust, we must begin with new questions:

1. What does oppression do to us? What is its process and effect? What is the price of survival? Of oppression? Can anything good come out of oppression?

2. Is women's culture liberating? How can it be if it was nourished in oppression? Can we ever forget the price we pay as oppressed women? Should we? How does a belief that we can *survive* oppression affect our determination to *fight* oppression? If we glorify "the feminine" from a presumably feminist perspective, how do we avoid valorizing oppression in order to criticize or organize against it? Are we unwilling to confront the damage of oppression — how it has killed us? How we kill each other? If sexism makes women better able to survive, why get rid of it? Does suffering make us better people? If these questions make sense, then are there real dangers in the work of Mary Daly, Carol Gilligan, Nancy Chodorow, Adrienne Rich, Dorothy Dinnerstein, and others who begin from a position of difference and end with the judgment (or at least do not deny the judgment) that women — in values, skills, and, some suggest, even in biological makeup — are superior to men? In sum, does cultural feminism, in spite of itself, glorify the oppression of women? To what extent does cultural feminism, with its emphasis on women's values, skills, and so on, contribute to this kind of perspective and itself become part of the problem we have to solve as feminists? What are the "forces of interested ignorance" in the women's movement, in feminist theory, in women's studies?[29] Does "gender pride" or the apparent need for "gender pride" get in the way of the truth?[30] How break this dangerous alliance between trying to understand oppression and needing to mythologize our strengths in oppression or in spite of it? How envision a liberated future without an appeal to an oppressive past?

3. Do we lie in order to survive, no matter what the level of oppression?[31] Do the women survivors of the Holocaust lie? Engage in self deception? Bad faith? Just not tell the truth? Mythologize in order to keep surviving? Does the women's understanding of themselves during the Holocaust differ from what happened? How do the survivors deal with life having been such a ghastly disappointment because of the Holocaust? How live with themselves unless they transform the story? Is the story they tell less about the Holocaust than about present suffering over the past and the attempt to survive its memory? Is the only possibility for survival of any kind the creation of some "cover story" for an individual or a people? How often do survivors say things because they have a sense of obligation to their group, as women or as Jews? Are there patterns to these transformations? Do we have the right as researchers to uncover this story? An obligation? How do we as researchers transform the stories we hear? How should we?

4. Is it a methodological and theoretical mistake to look at women and the Holocaust from the vantage point of their difference from men rather than from that of oppression? Why do many women survivors believe they survived better than men? Does it have to do with the reality of the Holocaust or with women's return to traditional roles and expectations afterward? Is it the only thing to hold onto in a world that pays so little attention to them either as women or as survivors? Why do men believe that women survived better?

5. Were women's friendships in the camps really as crucial, in a positive sense, as those interviewed say? Is there more to the story than the women are likely to report no matter what questions are posed? Are these groups more like a form of tribalism than a form of friendship—exclusive, competitive, damaging to self and others? How much depends on context, position, class, language? How much exploitation is there in these groups? How does sharing really occur in camps? In ghettos? In resistance groups? What does it mean that the women use the term "family" to describe their groups? If biological family loyalties were often a hindrance to the survival of individuals during the Holocaust outside the camps, to what extent did families—surrogate or biological—hamper women in the camps? Why is it important for us to believe that these friendships or relationships were so central to their stories? What is at stake for us?

6. What is resistance? Is anything an oppressed woman does an act of resistance? Is survival resistance? What if a person kills herself? Does

suicide then become resistance? If suicide is sometimes an act of re-sistance, is it always so? Is dying resistance? Is courage resistance? Is singing on the way to the gas chamber resistance? Is maintaining the Jewish religion resistance? Is stealing resistance? Is hiding resistance? Escape? Is helping resistance? Is sabotage? Is killing the enemy resis-tance? See how the term becomes neutralized—worse, destroyed. Such slippage in language suggests that all Jews became heroes or martyrs and all women heroines. Can that possibly make sense of what happened? Do descriptions of the lack of active or armed resistance against the enemy (either by the Jews or women or others) have to lead us not only to defend what they did but also to glorify it, to make of it what it was not? And so we reach what has become a common feminist position: Survival is resistance. Certain values, described as feminine virtues, may get some women through but do not seem to offer most women the resources for fighting the enemy—for genuine resistance. They do not, that is, push one to "cripple or damage" or stop the enemy—or at least to try.[32] Manipulation of the system is not resistance, even though it can mean survival. Do women know more about the manipulation of sys-tems than about resistance to systems? What is the relationship between manipulation and survival? If we believe that survival is resistance, we may end up with the notion that armed or active resistance is not a prior-ity or that it stands on equal footing with living through the Holocaust in any way possible.[33] Is survival a good no matter what the cost? What do we say about cooperation or even collaboration for survival? What about sexual exchanges for food or protection? Is the term "resistance" supposed to describe a kind of heroism about almost anything and anybody? The phrase "resistance is survival" is a mystification in re-sponse to which at least one final question can be posed: What do we say about the dead?

7. What does the transformation of female gender roles really mean in the face of the oppression and genocidal murder perpetrated during the Holocaust? Is our ability to transform ourselves a liability—or are only certain kinds of transformations liabilities? Did any genuine transforma-tions actually take place? Do women become "liberated" in the process of these transformations in sex-segregated circumstances? or merely more deeply embedded in these roles? How did these transformations affect their lives after the Holocaust?

8. Did anyone really survive the Holocaust?

9. How be true to the material given me by those I have interviewed?

How be true to the women? What does that mean? What are my obligations as a woman? As a Jew? As a historian? As a philosopher? As a feminist?

10. What are the political effects or consequences of studying women and the Holocaust? What is the philosophical yield?

These questions and the critique out of which they come not only have enabled me to see where I have been but also show me in what direction I need to move.

Comprehension . . . means the unpremeditated, attentive facing up to, and resisting of reality — whatever it may be.
— *Hannah Arendt,* The Origins of Totalitarianism

Notes

Acknowledgments: The research for this article was partially supported by a Kent Fellowship, Wesleyan University, and an American Council of Learned Societies Fellowship. Parts of this article were written for the conference "Communities of Women" sponsored by *Signs* and the Center for Research on Women at Stanford University, February 1983, and the Sixth Berkshire Conference on the History of Women, June 1984. I want to thank the following people for reading versions of this article, for listening, criticizing, and supporting the work: Pamela Armstrong, Marylin Arthur, Mary Felstiner, Joy Johannessen, Sally Hanley, Esther Katz, Eva Fleischner, Susan Cernyak-Spatz, Irene Eber, Nancy McKenzie. I especially want to thank Ti-Grace Atkinson, whose honesty, insight, and friendship helped me to see, to cut through a wall I was up against, *and* to continue.

1. The first conference on women and the Holocaust took place in March 1983 at Stern College. It was funded by the New York Council for the Humanities and sponsored by the Institute for Research in History. See *Proceedings of the Conference, Women Surviving: The Holocaust,* ed. Esther Katz and Joan Miriam Ringelheim (New York: Institute for Research in History, 1983) (hereafter *Proceedings of the Conference*). See Joan Miriam Ringelheim, "The Unethical and the Unspeakable: Women and the Holocaust," *Simon Wiesenthal Annual* 1 (1984): 69–87, "Communities in Distress: Women and the Holocaust" (Institute for Research in History, 1982, typescript), and "Resources and Vulnerabilities" (Institute for Research in History, 1983, typescript). See also Sybil Milton, "Women and the Holocaust: The Case of German and German-Jewish Women," in *When Biology Became Destiny: Women in Weimar and Nazi Germany,* ed. Renate Bridenthal, Atina Grossman, and Marion Kaplan (New York: Monthly Review Press, 1984), pp. 297–333, and "Is-

sues and Resources," in *Proceedings of the Conference,* pp. 10–21; Vera Laska, ed., *Women in the Resistance and in the Holocaust* (Westport, Conn.: Greenwood Press, 1983); and Marlene Heinemann, "Women Prose Writers of the Nazi Holocaust" (Ph.D. diss., Indiana University, 1981).

2. See Gisela Bock, "Racism and Sexism in Nazi Germany: Motherhood, Compulsory Sterilization, and the State," *Signs: Journal of Women in Culture and Society* 8, no. 3 (Spring 1983): 400–421.

3. I decided to use the term "maintenance" rather than the more customary "survival" because whether one survived or was murdered was determined by the Nazis or by one's fate (that is, luck), whereas "maintenance" was determined by the victims, to some degree.

4. Originally formulated in 1981. See Ringelheim, "The Unethical and the Unspeakable," p. 84.

5. Unless otherwise indicated, the subsequent quotations are from my interviews with Jewish women survivors. I have done twenty-eight interviews with twenty women. Most of the interviews were three hours long; a few lasted between six and ten hours. They were all in English. For the purposes of this article, I have culled some fragments to illuminate issues and concerns. For clarity, I have sometimes added words or explanations in brackets.

6. Twelve out of twenty of the survivors interviewed mentioned fear of rape, feelings of sexual humiliation, or instances of sexual exchange. Two of the twenty said they were raped. Another said she was almost raped.

7. *Kanada* was a section of the *Effektenkammer,* storehouse for the valuables — clothes, jewelry, and so on — of the prisoners who entered Auschwitz. Those who worked there were considered an elite *Kommando* (work crew).

8. See also *Proceedings of the Conference,* pp. 73–74, 141–42; Milton, "Women and the Holocaust," pp. 315–16.

9. See Ringelheim, "The Unethical and the Unspeakable," pp. 74–75, 78, and "Resources and Vulnerabilities," p. 20; and *Proceedings of the Conference,* pp. 40–41.

10. Yaffa Eliach, "The Holocaust and the Family" (paper presented at Lehigh University, March 1984).

11. Elmer Luchterhand, "Social Behavior of Concentration Camp Prisoners: Continuities and Discontinuities with Pre- and Postcamp Life," in *Survivors, Victims, and Perpetrators,* ed. Joel Dimsdale (New York: Hemisphere Publishing, 1980), p. 273.

12. See Alexander Donat, "Jewish Resistance," in *Out of the Whirlwind,* ed. Albert H. Friedlander (New York: Schocken Books, 1968), p. 62; Leonard Tushnet, *The Uses of Adversity: Studies of Starvation in the Warsaw Ghetto* (New York and London: Thomas Yoseloff, 1966), p. 27; Milton, "Women and the Holocaust" (n.1 above), pp. 307–8, and "Issues and Resources" (n.1 above),

pp. 15–19; Raul Hilberg, ed., *Documents of Destruction* (Chicago: Quadrangle Books, 1971), pp. 40–41; Germaine Tillion, *Ravensbruck* (New York: Anchor, 1975), pp. 39, 230; and Lucjan Dobroszycki, ed., *The Chronicle of the Lodz Ghetto* (New Haven, Conn.: Yale University Press, 1984), p. lvii and passim.

13. See Ringelheim, "Communities in Distress" (n.1 above), pp. 35; 43n.27; *Proceedings of the Conference* (n.1 above), p. 176.

14. See Ringelheim, "The Unethical and the Unspeakable" (n.1 above), p. 80.

15. The interviews with Rose and Judy took place in May 1982. Susan was interviewed in August 1979. I have had subsequent conversations with Judy and Susan. Again, the quotations are from these interviews unless otherwise stated. Ten among the seventeen other women survivors interviewed (1981–84) also spoke of relationships with other women as being significant.

16. See n.7.

17. See Ringelheim, "Communities in Distress," pp. 33–34.

18. These categories were worked out in a conversation with Susan Cernyak-Spatz and Pamela Armstrong in August 1982. See also Milton, "Issues and Resources," pp. 17–19, and "Women and the Holocaust," pp. 311–15.

19. I first was made aware of these problems when I read the English (unpublished) version of Ti-Grace Atkinson's "Female Nationalism" ("Le Nationalisme feminin," *Nouvelles questions feministes* 6–7 [Spring 1984]: 35–54). Subsequent discussions with Atkinson about cultural feminism, feminist theory and politics, philosophy, and women and the Holocaust demonstrated that the impasse I had reached had much to do with my unknowing adherence to cultural feminism.

20. Brooke, "Retreat to Cultural Feminism," in *Feminist Revolution: Redstockings of the Women's Liberation Movement* (New York: Random House, 1975), pp. 79, 83.

21. Quoted in Ann Oakley, *Subject Women* (New York: Pantheon Books, 1981), p. 310.

22. Cultural feminism may have had its roots in the pro-woman line. See Carol Hanisch, "The Personal Is the Political," in *Feminist Revolution* (n.20 above), pp. 204–5.

23. Since the cultural feminist position has few, if any, points of conflict with the establishment, the government can more easily adopt or adapt it as a cheap substitute for real change. Cultural feminism is endorsed and supported because it poses no threat.

24. Atkinson, "Le Nationalisme feminin," pp. 35, 53.

25. See ibid.

26. Oakley, *Subject Women*, p. 278.

27. Hope Weissman in a letter to the author, June 1984.

28. See Barbara Burris, "The Fourth World Manifesto," in *Radical Femi-*

nism, ed. Anne Koedt, Ellen Levine, and Anita Rapone (New York: Quadrangle Books, 1973), p. 356.

29. Sandra Harding, "Philosophy and History of Science as Patriarchal Oral History" (University of Delaware, Department of Philosophy, 1982, typescript). She used the phrase about science, not about feminists.

30. Suggested to the author in a letter from Mary Felstiner, July 1984.

31. See Adrienne Rich, *On Lies, Secrets, and Silence: Selected Prose, 1966–1978* (New York: W. W. Norton, 1979), p. 189: "In the struggle for survival we tell lies."

32. Suggested by Raul Hilberg in "Bibliography and the Holocaust" (paper presented at the Scholar's Conference, New York City, April 1981).

33. Compare Ringelheim, "The Unethical and the Unspeakable," pp. 75–81.

20

Feminism and Democratic Community

Jane Mansbridge

Advocates of individualism tend to assume a zero-sum game, in which any advance in community entails a retreat in protecting individuality. Advocates of greater community tend to assume no tradeoff between these goods, ignoring the ways community ties undermine individual freedom. This essay proposes advancing selectively on both fronts. Democracies need community to help develop their citizens' faculties, solve collective action problems, and legitimate democratic decisions. But community is in tension with individualism. The challenge for most polities is to find ways of strengthening community ties while developing institutions to protect individuals from community oppression. Women's experiences, traditionally neglected in political philosophy, help in both prongs of the challenge, by revealing undervalued components of community and underestimated threats to individual autonomy.

I. First Prologue: Democratic Community

Social critics who write about community usually believe that American society in particular and Western societies in general need to redress the balance between individualism and community in favor of community. Redress, they contend, would be good both for the psychological health

Reprinted from *Nomos XXXV: Democratic Community*, ed. John W. Chapman and Ian Shapiro (New York: New York University Press, 1993), 339–51, 369–75, by permission of the publisher.

of the individuals in the society and for the society as a whole.[1] I argue that communal bonds can improve the competitive status of the group as a whole by providing an efficient way of solving problems of collective action.

In a "collective action problem," or social dilemma, each individual's self-interested action interacts with the self-interested actions of others to produce a lower overall product for the group, and, consequently, for the individuals involved. Faced with these dilemmas, communities often use the sanctions as well as the ties of love and duty at their disposal to induce their members to replace some aspects of their self-interested behavior with cooperation. These sanctions and ties can make the community more materially productive, enhancing its competitive status vis-à-vis other communities.[2]

I define a "community" as a group in which the individual members can trust other members more than they can trust strangers not to "free ride" or "defect" in social dilemmas, not to exploit the members of the group in other ways, and, on occasion, to further the perceived needs of other members of the group rather than their own needs. The trust that so defines community derives from ties of love and duty creating mutual obligation, from mutual vulnerability (including vulnerability to the others' sanctions), from mutual understanding and sympathy. The stronger the community, the stronger are the ties of mutual obligation, vulnerability, understanding, and sympathy.[3]

I define a "democratic" community as one that makes decisions in ways that respect the fundamental equality of each citizen, both as a participant in deliberation and as the bearer of potentially equal power in decisions. The appropriate forms of democracy differ depending on the degree of common interest in the polity. The stronger the community, the less useful are aggregative democratic forms like majority rule, developed to handle fundamentally conflicting interests, and the more useful are deliberative democratic forms developed to promote mutual accommodation and agreement. A democracy that is only minimally a "community," with few ties of mutual obligation, vulnerability, understanding, and sympathy, will experience as common interest little more than the coincidence of material interests. As ties of love and duty lead citizens to make the good of others and the whole their own, the incidence of common interest will increase.[4]

All societies depend for their success partly on the ties of community; democracies do so in their own way. Unlike polities based primarily on traditional or charismatic authority, for example, modern democracies claim part of their legitimacy from an egalitarian, individualistic rationality that assumes underlying conflict. The individualistic formula, "each counts for one and none for more than one," comes into play when the interests of some in the community conflict with the interests of others. Yet accepting this individualistic formula in practice requires motivations fostered by community. The socializing agents of a community must help develop citizen commitment to principles of justice such as the principle that each should count for one.

No democracy, however, can meet the absolute requirements of procedural fairness. No polity can guarantee that every individual will count equally in all decisions. Individual preferences are often ordered such that no one outcome is obviously just.[5] And procedures that are just in one context produce injustice in another. (Societies with many cross-cutting cleavages can support systems of majority rule, because each individual can expect, while losing on one, to win on other issues. But in segmented societies, in which one section of the population will be in a minority on most important issues, democratic justice requires proportional outcomes.) In response to these inevitable imperfections, members of a community develop habits and understandings, ideally subject to critical scrutiny, by which they come to accept certain institutions as sufficiently close approximations to the democratic ideal. Without such understandings, democracy cannot work.[6]

The stronger the community in a democracy, the more likely it is that losers will accept a decision by majority rule not only because it is fair (for it can never be perfectly fair), not only because it is a decision (and they benefit from any decision, compared to civil war), and not only because they believe (in polities with cross-cutting cleavages) that they will find themselves in the majority on other issues, but also because, as in traditional non-democratic communities, mutual ties give community members some interest in the fate of others. Even otherwise zero-sum losses may be perceived as not completely losses if the losers see the winners as part of their community.

Most importantly, many democratic decisions are made not by majority rule or even proportional outcomes but by a process of deliberation that generates mutual accommodation and agreement. This process usually requires a strong leaven of commitment to the common good. The classic writers in the liberal democratic tradition, such as John Locke, James Madison, and J. S. Mill, all assumed that democracy as they understood it could not function without such a commitment, at least on the part of the public's representatives. Communal ties of mutual obligation, vulnerability, understanding, and sympathy help create such commitments, making possible a vast range of democratic decisions based in part on common interest.

II. Second Prologue: Gratuitous Gendering

a) "Women's Experiences"

I use the phrase "women's experiences" to mean not just experiences that only women have had or that all women have had, but also experiences that women are more likely than men to have had and experiences that have been "gender-coded" in our society as primarily female rather than male.

Much gender coding is gratuitous, unrelated either to functional necessity or, in some cases, even to observable differences in men's and women's actual behavior. But what I call "gratuitous gendering" is a fact of intellectual life, past and present. Recognizing the subtle yet pervasive influence of gratuitous gendering helps explain why ways of thinking that Western society codes as female have had less influence on its intellectual evolution than ways the society codes as male. The pervasive past influence of gendering also helps explain why feminists want "female" experiences and ways of knowing to play a larger and more respected role in political and philosophical discourse.

To say that women's experiences can add to our understanding of democratic community does not imply that women's experiences are essentially different from those of men, only that the frequency of certain experiences differs by gender. A fairly small average difference in experience or behavior can create a large difference in self-image and an even larger difference in social image. When the social meaning of belonging to a group is strong, cultures magnify the group's distinctive features. Members of each group tend to cleave to the images that their common culture prescribes for them. If one group is dominant, it will tend to avoid the language and images the culture attributes to less powerful groups. Subordinate groups will be torn between pride in their own language and images and a desire to emulate the language and images of the dominant group.

b) The Magnification of Small Differences

Gender is more salient in some societies than in others. Yet in every society gender is one of the three or four most salient traits that distinguish people from one another. When children are born, their gender is one of the few traits reported about them. Among adults, the possibility of sexual contact makes almost everyone notice the gender of others. Sex is sexy. Finally, gender is heavily implicated in reproduction, without which societies cannot continue. It is thus not surprising that some societies consider gender truly cosmic — an organizing principle that explains the fundamental relations in the universe.[7]

Human beings use the categories society gives them to make sense of the world. We learn new information through classification schemes that sort the information as we take it in. When information does not easily fit into familiar categories, we usually forget it. And when a category describes our identities as individuals, we pay even more attention than when it describes something unconnected with ourselves.

Children learn that they are boys or girls before they know much else about themselves, often even their last names. Once they know they are boys or girls, they try to learn what "boy" or "girl" means in order to be it better. Because healthy people want to be who they are, children usually value being a boy or a girl long before they understand the full social connotations of this identity. As a result, socialization to gender is not merely a passive response to punishment and reward, but an active, engaged building of positive self-image.[8]

Human beings also remember the vivid.[9] In two normal distributions, or bell-shaped curves, in which the means of the two groups differ only slightly, an observer would probably not notice differences between the groups for most of the people in that distribution. In a field like math, in which boys excel by a small amount, if the bell-shaped curve of boys is positioned only slightly farther along the skill dimension than the bell-shaped curve of girls and if the curves have generally the same shape, almost half the girls will do *better* than half the boys. For most of the students in a given school, gender differences will not be noticeable. But at the extremes, the differences will become more vivid. Boys will predominate noticeably in the upper "tail" of the distribution. This big difference at the tail provides an interpretative framework for differences elsewhere in the distribution. A girl who is doing better than half the boys at math but better than sixty percent in reading will think of herself as "not good at math."

When differences between groups are tied to relations of domination and subordination, the dominant group will also have an interest in magnifying the salience of these differences.

Because gender is so salient, and its salience has been for these reasons and others greatly reinforced, it has in many societies become an organizing feature for the whole universe. In such societies, every identifiable feature of the universe can be assimilated into either Yin or Yang, the female or the male principle. Every noun in the language can be given a gender, making a table feminine and a wall masculine.

The cultures of this world have produced a great deal of gratuitous gendering ascribing gender definitions and taboos to many features of social and physical life. Anthropologists report that among the Aleut of North America, for example, only women are allowed to butcher animals. But among the Ingalik of North America, only men are allowed to butcher animals. Among the Suku of Africa, only the women can plant crops and only the men can make baskets. But among the Kaffa of the Circum-Mediterranean, only the men can plant crops and only the women can make baskets. Among the Hansa of the Circum-Mediterranean, only the men can prepare skins and only the women can milk. But among the Rwala of the Circum-Mediterranean, only the women can prepare skins and only the men milk.[10] In the culture of the United States, I would venture, we have created similar, though less mutually exclusive, patterns. We code empathy, for example, as women's work, so that the more both men and women are aware that empathy is the object of attention, the more they slide into their cultural roles.

If gender-coding followed a pattern of "separate but equal" and if all the actions of every individual perfectly fit the appropriate gender code, the pervasiveness of gender coding might be only a charming idiosyncrasy of the human race. But men's unequal power has made male practices and traits the norm for "mankind." In the United States, to give only a few examples from Catharine MacKinnon's impressive list, "men's physiology defines most sports, their needs define auto and health insurance coverage, their socially-designed biographies define workplace expectations and successful career patterns."[11] In practice, the labor, traits, and even philosophical terms that are coded as male are usually more highly valued.

c) Gendered Meanings in the Concept of Community

In the United States today, the term "community" is not gender-free. Its two components, local geographical rootedness and emotional ties, have female connotations. Local communities are the province of women far more than are state or national affairs. Women organize, run, and staff many activities of local communities, which as a cause and consequence feel close to home, almost domestic. Even in the formal political realm, from which women have been excluded in almost every traditional society, local communities in the United States have allowed women the most access. Considerably before women won the vote nationally, several states and localities allowed women to vote in local school elections; today, the percentage of women in city and town councils and the percentage of women mayors far exceeds the percentage of women in state and national legislatures or executive positions. In the recent past, the gendered division of labor insured that when men earned the family wage, and particularly when they worked away from the community, women became the caretakers of local community life.

An even more salient component of "community" involves the quality of human relations.[12] In the United States today, women have particular responsibility for intimate human relations. Talcott Parsons and Robert Bales codified the reigning gender schema in 1955 when they wrote that in households men generally took the more "instrumental" roles and women the more "expressive" roles, maintaining "integrative" relations among the household members.[13] Mothers and wives still tend disproportionately to take on the family's "emotion work" and "kinwork," fostering the relations of connection.[14] One recent review of psychological research noted that the two orientations it studied "have been labeled *masculine* and *feminine, instrumental* and *expressive,* and *assertive* and *communal.*"[15] In this analysis, "communal" is almost synonymous with "feminine."

As the triad "liberty, equality, fraternity" has evolved into "liberty, equality, community," the third element has experienced a gender evolution from male to female.[16] In this evolution, the term has lost legitimacy in a way that affects the balance between individual and community. As a consequence, those who today urge renewed emphasis in liberal individualism on ties of connection in the social world and on the possibility of common interests in politics have to fight not only the well-founded fears of those who see in any move toward commonality the potential for domination, but also, more insidiously, the subtle association of connection and commonality with womanliness. Pamela Conover suggests, for example, that among political scientists eager to be seen as tough-minded, altruism has come to seem sissified.[17] It seems likely that several components of community — the legitimation of intimate connection, emotional ties, particularity, and common interests — suffer the same disability.

In making the case for ties of love and duty, for mutual vulnerability, and for the possibility of common interest in democratic politics, proponents of democratic community are hampered by the female connotations of love, certain kinds of duty, vulnerability, and even common interest. Some feminist theorists have therefore attempted a radical revaluation, recognizing the gender connotations of these elements of community and insisting on their worth. As the next section demonstrates, these theorists draw heavily from women's experiences of intimate human "connection." A later section explores the ways women's experiences of unequal power reveal the potential oppression, blatant and subtle, inherent in communal ties.

III. Connection

Empathy, the quality of being able to put oneself emotionally in another's place, exemplifies the process through which gender differences take on magnified social significance. In the United States, both men and women see women as intuitive, good at understanding others, and sensitive to personal or emotional appeals. Empirical research on empathy shows, however, that gender differences in empathy vary dramatically according to the measure used. The more the person being measured knows that empathy is being measured, the more a gender difference appears. When psychologists try to take physiological measurements of empathy — such as galvanic skin responses on seeing others receive an electric shock; skin conductance, blood pressure, heart rate, or pulse on seeing or hearing newborn infants cry; or sweating while seeing another take a test — they usually find no significant difference between women and men or between girls and boys. When psychologists tell stories to children of other children experiencing happiness, sadness, fear, and anger, and ask after each story, "How do you *feel?*" "Tell me how you *feel?*" or "How did that story make you *feel?*" — a procedure that might lead the child to think that responsive feelings were being measured — either girls score higher than boys on empathy when the experimenter is female and boys score higher than girls when the experimenter is male, or else the differences are not significant. Yet when either children or adults are asked to fill out a questionnaire asking individuals to describe themselves with statements like "I tend to get emotionally involved with a friend's problems" and "Seeing people cry upsets me," the difference between males and females is consistently significant and in the expected direction. On these measures, females always appear more empathetic. The differences are larger among adults than children, and larger still among those who rate themselves high on other measures of stereotypical "femininity" and "masculinity."[18] The more the person knows what is being measured, the older the person is, and the more attached to gender stereotypes, the stronger the relations between gender and empathy.

Gender differences on other themes involving intimate connection may well follow the same pattern as gender differences in empathy. If research on nurturance, care, and other correlates of intimate connection parallels that on empathy, the largest differences will be obtained from female experimenters, fully socialized adults, stimuli likely to elicit empathetic-nurturance responses from women, and clear cues in the stimuli that empathy, nurturance, and care are the subject of investigation. This pattern would not make the differences less "real." When women define themselves and are defined as more attuned to empathy or intimate connection, specific practices draw from and reinforce that connection. Women allow themselves, for example, to demonstrate their empathy openly. Girls and women look more for emotion and expression in their friendships, centering their conversations with friends more on discussions of relations, whereas men develop more instrumental or goal-oriented friendships, based more on shared activities.[19] These gender-coded practices then have effects on the way both genders view the political and social world.

The gender-coding of intimate connection has had a long history in American feminist political argument. The first wave of feminism evolved the idea that women were likely to act more nurturantly not only in the home but also in political life. Six years before women won the vote, Charlotte Perkins Gilman's classic novel *Herland* envisioned a utopia composed only of women, whose communal form of maternal nurturance produced a politics of loving cooperation.[20] Particularly toward the end of the struggle for women's suffrage, arguments for the vote stressed the virtues women would bring to the polity from their experiences as wives and mothers.[21]

The second wave of the feminist movement almost from the beginning incorporated interest in the ways that "women's culture" could be more caring and less rapacious than men's. A 1970 movement article on women's culture quoted Marlene Dixon's derivation of the special skills of "intuition" and "empathy" from women's relative powerlessness, and three years later Jane Alpert attributed to the experience of motherhood the empathy, intuitiveness, and protective feelings toward others of the developing feminist culture.[22]

Related ideas entered the academy a decade or so later. In 1976, the psychologist Dorothy Dinnerstein argued that it is harder for women than men to separate themselves from their mothers.[23] Her work, and in 1978 Nancy Chodorow's greatly more influential *The Reproduction of Mothering,* set the stage through psychoanalytic speculation for academic feminists to recognize and celebrate women's "connection." Chodorow ascribed what she called "women's relatedness and men's denial of relation" to the male child's need to differentiate himself from his mother and create a separate, oppositional, entity. Although for both boys and girls mothers represent lack of autonomy, for boys dependence on the mother and identification with her also represent the not-masculine; a boy must "reject dependence and deny attachment and identification."[24] "The basic feminine sense of self," Chodorow concluded, "is connected to the world, the basic masculine sense of self is separate."[25]

The theme moved into philosophy when in 1980 Sara Ruddick drew attention to the strengths of "maternal thinking,"[26] and in 1981 Sheila Ruth concluded that male philosophers tended to shun or show contempt for female connection: "Flight from woman is flight from feeling, from experiencing, from the affective; it is flight into distance."[27]

In 1982, Carol Gilligan's *In a Different Voice* adopted much of Chodorow's analysis, arguing that "since masculinity is defined through separation while femininity is defined through attachment, male gender is threatened by intimacy while female gender identity is threatened by separation. Thus males tend to have difficulty with relationships, while females tend to have problems with individuation."[28] Gilligan's investigations of women's reactions to moral dilemmas led her to conclude that women define themselves "in a context of human relationship" and judge themselves according to their ability to care.[29] Chodorow and Gilligan inspired an outpouring of theoretical writing, including Nel Noddings's 1984 argument that the approach to ethics through law and principle "is the approach of the detached one, the father," whereas the caring approach, the "approach of the mother," is "rooted in receptivity, relatedness, and responsiveness."[30]

I suggest that feminist analyses of maternal and other forms of intimate connection can generate new insights into democratic community. Yet the relation of these insights to actual differences in experience between American men and women is not clear. Chodorow's psychoanalytic theory, although intellectually suggestive, remains to be tested empirically. Gilligan's finding—that in the United States today women are more likely than men to adopt a morality based on preserving relations rather than one based on individual rights—appears primarily among the highly educated, because it is primarily in this class that men distinctively adopt a "rights" or "justice" orientation to which Gilligan's "care" or "relationships" orientation can be compared.[31] Even within this group, we do not yet know how large are the differences between men and women, and whether they might not, like differences in empathy, appear only or most dramatically when the persons being interviewed have some idea of what is being measured. In the population as a whole, the differences are unlikely to be large, since several studies cannot find any difference.[32]

Research since Gilligan's *In a Different Voice* has made it clear that even when no differences appear between men and women on the dimensions of relationships and rights, when researchers describe two orientations to moral conflict, one based on relationships and one on rights,[33] those men and women distinguish between the two orientations in a way that fits traditional gender stereotypes. Both men and women tend to rate Gilligan's care orientation as more feminine and the rights orientation as more masculine.[34] If the American public in the late twentieth century codes connection as female and separation as male, it would not be surprising if the women and feminist theorists of that society tended to make the value of connection their "own."

I find it most useful to treat this literature not as demonstrating any large difference between the actual behavior or even the normative orientations of most men and women in American society, but as drawing attention to the deeply gender-coded nature in this society of the dichotomy of separation versus connection. It is not simply that some groups of modern American women seem in fact to be somewhat more deeply embedded in intimate relationships than some groups of men. It is also, more importantly, that the cultural reification and exaggeration of these gender differences in behavior has influenced popular and philosophical thinking about the various possibilities in human relations.

Anglo-American democratic theory, for example, often portrays the polity as constructed by free and unencumbered individuals who associate to promote self-interest. Such a theory cannot easily draw inspiration from or use metaphors derived from the typically "female" experiences of empathetic interdependence, compassion, and personal vulnerability.

Drawing from experiences of intimate connection, on the other hand, makes it easier to envision preserving individuality and furthering community at the same time. These experiences help generate a vision of democratic community in which autonomy derives from social nurturance, some obligations are given, communal ties derive from emotional connection as well as from principle, the local and particular has legitimately a special moral weight, and a leaven of common interest makes possible a politics based on persuasion as well as power. . . .

IV. Women's Perspectives on Community

. . . In drawing political insight from various realms of private life, this essay embodies a tension, but not a logical contradiction, between "minimalist" and "maximalist" approaches to gender differences. Pointing out the extent of gratuitous gendering in every society suggests a "minimalist" approach to gender differences. This approach, to which I subscribe, holds that although men and women undoubtedly differ in biological characteristics like the ability to give birth and upper body strength, technological advances in contraception, childrearing, and material production have significantly reduced the social importance of these differences in the last several centuries. Much of the remaining social stress on gender differences is "gratuitous," resting on differences or magnitudes of difference that are neither innate nor socially efficient.[35]

In this essay, however, I also emphasize gender differences throughout, in a way that may seem to align implicitly with the "maximalist" school of feminist analysis, which emphasizes the differences between men and women.[36] Members of this school sometimes suggest that these differences are large and perhaps impossible to change, although few, if any, conclude that they are innate.[37] Nor is innateness the issue. The great variation in women's experience by class and across individuals even in one culture suggests that whether or not the roots of some differences are innate, the differences are susceptible to social change. Moreover, the psychological differences implicated in intimate connection do not seem large compared to many cultural differences.[38]

To make the points about cultural dominance that I have been making, it is not necessary to argue that women are "essentially connected" to other human beings through their biology in a way that differs from men, or even that they have a more connected relation than men to their mothers. There may be some truth to both points. But if there were no truth to either, simply typing women as connected and men as separate would do the trick. If many women grew up thinking of themselves as relatively connected with others and men grew up thinking of themselves as relatively separate, and if men produced the dominant literature, that literature would tend to emphasize the virtues of separation. Connection, or at least "going on" about connection, would have about it just a touch of the effeminate.

In this situation one obvious intellectual strategy would be simply to point out and try to eliminate the gratuitous gendered implications that accrue to various philosophical positions, make the case on its own grounds for the "feminine" position, and move on from the subject of gender. This is a good strategy, with much to recommend it, including prefiguring its goal in its form of argument. It has, however, several weak points.

Most importantly, it is a better strategy for what I perceive as a distant goal than for the present. In the different cultures of the world, the association of gender with various social ideals will presumably begin to wither away as women and men have more of one another's "typical" experiences and recognize the diversity within their own and the other group. However, because it is unlikely that the salience of gender will ever be eliminated, and because the full androgynization of childrearing and workplace roles is in any existing society almost unimaginably distant, it will be hard in the imaginable future to reach a stage at which, when arguments for one or another ideal imply constellations of linked behaviors, those implications could be teased apart and examined without inferences derived from gender. Moreover, if in the future some gendered division of labor should prove socially efficient and normatively acceptable, some ideals would probably remain gendered. A more proximate goal than the abolition of all gender implications, a goal aimed at a world in which some association of gender with particular social ideals persists, prescribes first, that gendering should be reduced to a realistic minimum, and second, that ideals for which there are equally good independent normative arguments should enjoy an equal normative status.

These two prongs of the proximate goal are in tension. Reducing gendering to a minimum, that is, eliminating "gratuitous" gendering, requires downplaying gender implications when they arise in social and philosophical discourse. But arguing for the equal normative status of "female" ideals requires bringing those ideals to center stage and trumpeting their virtues. Moreover, because "male" virtues will be better in some ways and contexts and worse in others, and "female" virtues will be better in some ways and contexts and worse in others, trying to achieve equality in an already hierarchical world will require stressing the ways in which "female" virtues are better.

This essay tries to accomplish both goals. It is logically possible, and I believe an accurate description of much of today's social reality, to say, first, that much of the human race's carrying on about gender could be eliminated without much loss and with a good deal of gain, and second, that so long as gender is still extremely salient and society is still hierarchically organized in regard to gender, some of the ideals more frequently associated with women should be valued more highly than they are now — indeed, that in some ways and contexts those ideals serve human needs better than some ideals more frequently associated with men. Simply pointing out the gendered component of ideals and passing on is not enough.

Another problem with the idea that an argument should stand "on its own," regardless of the gender-coding of its content or the gender of those who espouse it, is that this proposition, while generally an excellent guide to productive thought, tends to obscure the many ways that arguments themselves are gendered. Normative arguments do not consist solely, or even primarily, of deduction from agreed or self-evident principles. These arguments involve telling stories, making analogies, and asking readers to imagine themselves in situations they have never experienced. They can be persuasive only to the degree that they build on something in a reader's experience that the reader values either positively or negatively. To the degree that experience is heavily gendered, and readers do not share in an experience from which an author draws, it becomes possible for readers of a gender different from that of an author simply not to understand the point the author is making. If gendered differences in experience are unequally valued socially, it becomes even harder for readers with the more valued experience to understand points drawn from the less valued experience. (To succeed in the dominant world, however, those with less valued experiences must be able to understand at least in part the dominant experiences.) An argument "standing on its own" may be surreptitiously an argument that draws heavily on male experience. To make this possibility conscious, women must draw consciously on specifically women's experiences. Before we set out to "translate" our insights to men, as to some extent I try to do here, women must also sometimes write as women to women, working out those insights in a context of greater common experience, particularly in those areas neglected by traditional male discourse.

Finally, the strategy of simply pointing out the gender connotations of existing values and moving on fails to take full account of the role in intellectual life of emotional identification with ideas. People often come to think differently about their ideas and values because others exert effort to persuade them to change. Those who exert effort often do so because they identify themselves emotionally with the ideals they are promoting. "Schools of thought" often advance intellectually through emotional as well as cognitive reinforcement, each member reassuring the others that the ideas on which they are working deserve their efforts. Academics who think of the methodological structuralism they espouse as "French" or the methodological individualism they espouse as "Anglo-American" draw some of their intellectual energy from identification with their nation. Women theorists as a group will put more effort into unfolding certain arguments when they identify as women with those ideas.

Even insight itself sometimes requires commitment. Women are more likely than men to have insights on connection and unequal power not only because women are more likely to have had experiences that generate these insights, but also because they are more likely to feel strongly about their insights. Anger, pride, and other of the more disreputable emotions also fuel the intellectual machine. As a woman, I feel angry, and deserve to feel angry, that "our" values have been denigrated. I also feel proud, and deserve to feel proud, of those values, adopting some version of them after scrutiny even more consciously as my own. When the anger women feel on these issues touches off an opposing anger in men, and our pride an opposing pride, these are often acceptable costs of a process that brings the ideas to the surface for critical examination.

Because anger and pride by and large tend to obscure rather than illuminate, this stage in the intellectual process works best if it is only one stage in an ongoing dialectic. It may well be a recurring stage until greater social equality is achieved, because ultimately, in spite of the best efforts of feminist theorists, "female" values are unlikely to be accorded equal worth until women are perceived as the social, political, and intellectual equals of men. But harnessing now for the process of revaluation the anger and resentment generated by the existing system of gendered ideals is likely to make a useful difference in how future generations, at least of philosophers, think of autonomy, obligation, emotion, particularity, persuasion, power, privacy, and other components of a dual stance of welcome and vigilance toward democratic community.

V. Deepening Community: Enhancing Individuality

"Ties" tie you down. Increasing the number and strength of communal ties usually decreases personal freedom. But recognizing the frequent tradeoff between ties and choices does not entail accepting the present mix between the two. Just as a child who has mastered the bicycle must learn street safety before venturing forth, so progress from a previous equilibrium often requires a move and a countermove to regain a satisfactory equilibrium farther along. Although American society has established an equilibrium of sorts between the competing claims of individualism and community, thought and experimentation should allow us to create a better equilibrium strengthening the community ties that most advance the ends we desire while at the same time creating and strengthening institutions that guard against community domination.[39]

Individualists and communitarians would both gain from recognizing that any step that strengthens people's ties to a democratic community usually requires heightened, institutionalized vigilance against the illusion that all members of the community have common interests. If we look to long-standing groups for cues to which equilibria work in practice, we see that in the realm of democratic procedure, groups that pursue the quest for democratic community to an extreme, by refusing to make any decisions not perceived by all as in the common good, also institutionalize safeguards against the creation of false consensus. Quaker communities make decisions only by consensus, but also fight the social pressure not to disrupt a consensus by making it a religious duty to hold out against a decision one genuinely thinks is immoral or wrong. The Bruderhof, an even more communal association, institutes similar mechanisms.[40] Other smoothly functioning groups that make many decisions by consensus find ways of investigating verbal or nonverbal signs of dissatisfaction to give the possibly silenced members a hearing, to meet their needs in ways not included in the formal decision, or to reopen the question. In all these cases, a move toward community works in tandem with moves to recognize and protect individual difference.

Individualists and communitarians need to recognize the possibility that a polity can strengthen community ties and respect for the individual at the same time. Contemporary feminist theory helps us think about how to perform these seemingly contradictory tasks simultaneously. If, as I argue, liberal individualism and an adversary system of democracy over-emphasize atomistic conflict, the greater self-consciousness of women regarding intimate connection makes available metaphors and experiences in which individuals are not so starkly pitted against one another. If, as I argue, all moves toward assuming commonality need monitoring, feminist insights into pervasive and unequal power provide for all individuals conceptual defenses against the pronouncements of the community on who we are or what our good should be.

The main task of feminist theory must be to clarify and help redress gender inequality. In doing so, however, it contributes to a more general understanding of democratic community in ways not available to a liberalism restricted to individuals sprung into adulthood fully grown and a politics that excludes the private.

Notes

Acknowledgments: I would like to thank Pauline Bart, Nancy Fraser, Virginia Held, Christopher Jencks, Jennifer Nedelsky, Robert Merton, Susan Okin, Robert Post, my two NOMOS commentators, Carol Gould and David Richards, and Kenneth Winston, who read the manuscript carefully twice, for useful and insightful comments. In particular, I urge that Carol Gould's commentary be read in conjunction with this essay. Some of the ideas in the essay were developed earlier in my "Feminism and Democracy," *The American Prospect* 1, no. 1 (1990). I would also like to thank the Center for Urban Affairs and Policy Research at Northwestern University and the Russell Sage Foundation for support.

1. E.g., Robert H. Bellah, Richard Madsen, William M. Sullivan, Ann Swidler, and Steven M. Tipton, *Habits of the Heart: Individualism and Commitment in American Life* (Berkeley: University of California Press, 1985); Alan Wolfe, *Whose Keeper: Social Science and Moral Obligation* (Berkeley: University of California Press, 1989); Elizabeth Fox-Genovese, *Feminism without Illusions: A Critique of Individualism* (Chapel Hill: University of North Carolina Press, 1991).

2. On communal bonds as a way of solving collective action problems, see Jane J. Mansbridge, "On the Relation between Altruism and Self-Interest," in Mansbridge, ed., *Beyond Self-Interest* (Chicago: University of Chicago Press, 1990). Communal bonds can also deter material success, as when the community expectation that members will share accumulated wealth produces disincentives for individuals to exert effort in earning.

3. Roberto Mangabeira Unger characterizes communities as "those areas of social existence where people stand in a relationship of heightened mutual vulnerability and responsibility toward each other" (*The Critical Legal Studies Movement* [1982] [Cambridge: Harvard University Press, 1986], p. 36), and considers sympathy "the sentiment that animates community" (*Knowledge and Politics* [New York: Free Press, 1975], p. 220). Thomas Bender (*Community and Social Change in America* [New Brunswick: Rutgers University Press, 1978], p. 7) describes communities as "held together by shared understandings and a sense of obligation." Although conflict also creates and maintains mutual ties, it undermines "community" when it lowers the trust between members below that which they would feel with strangers.

4. In *Beyond Adversary Democracy* [1980] (Chicago: University of Chicago Press, 1983) I elaborate on these distinctions, including the forms of equality democracy requires in contexts of common and conflicting interests, and the use of friendship, based on equality of respect, as a model for democratic community. I assume there and elsewhere that both forms of democracy require the protection of minority rights.

5. Kenneth Arrow, *Social Choice and Individual Values* [1951] (New York: Wiley, 1963). William H. Riker, *Liberalism against Populism: A Confrontation between the Theory of Democracy and the Theory of Social Choice* [1982] (Prospect Heights, Ill.: Waveland Press, 1988).

6. Community understandings of what constitutes "good enough" (sufficing rather than maximizing) democracy parallel similar understandings of "good enough" (or "mediated") morality (see Mansbridge, "On the Relation between Altruism and Self-Interest," 1990). Such broad understandings facilitate democracy, while not constituting an "agreement on fundamentals," which Carl Friedrich (*The New Belief in the Common Man* [Boston: Little, Brown, 1942], p. 153ff) argued democracies do not require.

7. Whereas "gender" has social connotations and "sex" connotations of biology and sexual intercourse, I do not make a sharp distinction between the two. On interchangeable usage, see, from different perspectives, Francine Watman Frank and Paula A. Treichler, *Language, Gender, and Professional Writing* (New York: Modern Language Association, 1989), pp. 10–14; and Catharine A. MacKinnon, *Toward a Feminist Theory of the State* (Cambridge: Harvard University Press, 1989), pp. xiii, 113.

8. Lawrence Kohlberg, "A Cognitive-Developmental Analysis of Children's Sex-Role Concepts and Attitudes," in Eleanor E. Maccoby, ed., *The Developmental Sex Differences* (Stanford: Stanford University Press, 1966).

9. See Amos Tversky, Daniel Kahneman, and Paul Slovic, eds., *Judgment under Uncertainty: Heuristics and Biases* (Cambridge: Cambridge University Press, 1982), on the availability heuristic.

10. Analysis derived from data in George P. Murdoch and Caterina Provost,

"Factors in the Division of Labor by Sex: A Cross-Cultural Analysis," *Ethnology* 12 (1973): 203–25, table 8. "Circum-Mediterranean" is Murdoch's own neologism. Data of this kind derive from the reports of anthropologists who often did not check their conclusions with the people they described. Had they done so, they might have found that these practices were contested, changing, or more ambiguous than reported (personal communication from David Cohen, Professor of History and Director of African Studies, Northwestern University).

11. Catharine MacKinnon, "Difference and Dominance," in *Feminism Unmodified* (Cambridge: Harvard University Press, 1967), pp. 32–45, p. 36. See also Mary Austin, *Earth Horizon* (Boston: Houghton Mifflin, 1932), cited by Nancy Cott, "Feminist Theory and Feminist Movements," in Juliet Mitchell and Ann Oakley, eds., *What Is Feminism?* (New York: Pantheon, 1986); and Martha Minow, "Justice Engendered," a feminist "Foreword to the Supreme Court 1986 Term," *Harvard Law Review* 101 (1987): 10–95, p. 32ff.

12. Although in 1955 George A. Hillary, Jr., concluded after inspecting ninety-four different definitions of community that "social interaction within a geographic area" was part of a "minimum" definition ("Definitions of Community: Areas of Agreement," *Rural Sociology* 20 [1955]: 111–23), subsequent thinkers have downplayed the importance of locality. Raymond Plant reported in 1987 that compared to the dispute over whether locality is a necessary component of the meaning of community, "all are agreed that it is something about the quality of the relationships that makes a social grouping into a community" ("Community," in *The Blackwell Encyclopedia of Political Thought* [Oxford: Basil Blackwell, 1987], p. 90). Reviewing "the meanings of community" in 1978, Thomas Bender concluded that it "is best defined as a network of social relations marked by mutuality and emotional bonds," or, in a formal definition, "a community involves a limited number of people in a somewhat restricted social space or network held together by shared understandings and a sense of obligation" (*Community and Social Change in America* [New Brunswick: Rutgers University Press, 1978], p. 7).

13. Talcott Parsons and Robert F. Bales, *Family, Socialization, and Interaction Process* (New York: Free Press, 1955), p. 47.

14. For "emotion work," see Arlie Russell Hochschild, "The Sociology of Feeling and Emotion: Selected Possibilities," in Marcia Millman and Rosabeth Moss Kanter, eds., *Another Voice: Feminist Perspectives on Social Life and Social Science* (New York: Doubleday/Anchor, 1975), pp. 280–307; for "kinwork," see Micaela di Leonardo, "The Female World of Cards and Holidays: Women, Families and the Work of Kinship," *Signs* 12 (1987): 440–53.

15. Alice H. Eagly and Blair T. Johnson, "Gender and Leadership Style: A Meta-Analysis," *Psychological Bulletin* 108 (1990): 233–56, p. 236, emphasis in original.

16. For the strong male content of "fraternity," see Wilson Carey Mc-

Williams, *The Idea of Fraternity in America* (Berkeley: University of California Press, 1973), chap. 1; and Carole Pateman, "The Fraternal Social Contract," in *The Disorder of Women* (Stanford: Stanford University Press, 1989), and *The Sexual Contract* (Stanford: Stanford University Press, 1988).

17. Pamela Johnston Conover, "Who Cares? Sympathy and Politics: A Feminist Perspective," paper presented at the annual meeting of the Midwest Political Science Association, 1988.

18. Nancy Eisenberg and Randy Lennon, "Sex Differences in Empathy and Related Capacities," *Psychological Bulletin* 94 (1983): 100–131.

19. Ruth Sharabany, Ruth Gershoni, and John E. Hofman, "Girl Friend, Boy Friend: Age and Sex Differences in Development of Intimate Friendships," *Developmental Psychology* 17 (1981): 800–808; Margery Fox, Margaret Gibbs, and Doris Auerbach, "Age and Gender Dimensions of Friendship," *Psychology of Women Quarterly* 9 (1985): 489–502; E. Douvan and J. Adelson, *The Adolescent Experience* (New York: Wiley, 1966); Matya A. Caldwell and Letitia A. Peplau, "Sex Differences in Same-Sex Friendships," *Sex Roles* 8 (1982): 721–32; Lynne R. Davidson and Lucile Duberman, "Friendship: Communication and Interactional Patterns in Same-Sex Dyads," *Sex Roles* 8 (1982): 809–22. For a recent review of the literature, see Hazel Markus and Daphna Oyserman, "Gender and Thought: The Role of Self-Concept," in Mary Crawford and Margaret Gentry, eds., *Gender and Thought: Psychological Perspectives* (New York: Springer-Verlag, 1989). There is no meta-analysis of psychological studies involving connection. Much of the work cited in support of greater connection among women is, in the original research, more ambiguous than the citations suggest.

20. Charlotte Perkins Gilman, *Herland* [1915] (New York: Pantheon, 1979).

21. Aileen Kraditor, *The Ideas of the Woman Suffrage Movement* (Garden City: Doubleday, 1971). Although Kraditor stresses the predominance of arguments from women's special virtues toward the end of the suffrage movement, more recent historians (cited in Cott [1986], pp. 50–51) demonstrate that both kinds of arguments flourished throughout the period from 1792 (Mary Wollstonecraft's *Vindication of the Rights of Women*) to 1921. Cott (1986) provides an excellent short account of "sameness" versus "difference" strands in the first wave of feminism in the United States.

22. Marlene Dixon in *It Ain't Me Babe*, April 7, 1970, p. 8; Jane Alpert, "Mother Right: A New Feminist Theory," *off our backs* 3 (8 May 1973): 6; *Ms.* 2 (1973): 52–55, 88–94. Alice Echols, *Daring to Be Bad: Radical Feminism in America, 1967–1975* (Minneapolis: University of Minnesota Press, 1989), p. 7, dates the term "cultural feminism" to 1972, but indicates correctly that the ideas predated the term. Echols, who wants to associate the "rise of cultural feminism" with a turn "away from opposing male supremacy" (p. 5), attributes

to "conceptual confusion" (pp. 6, 7, 10) the interlacing of concern with women's culture through much of the early radical women's movement.

"Women's culture" undoubtedly has its roots in women's powerlessness as well as other sources. But as Dixon suggests, roots in a harmful situation do not automatically invalidate a cognitive or emotional insight. A brush with death can make one more appreciative of life in a way one may want to maintain after reducing the threat of death. Per contra, see MacKinnon, *Toward a Feminist Theory of the State,* pp. 51–58, 153.

23. Dorothy Dinnerstein, *The Mermaid and the Minotaur: Sexual Arrangements and Human Malaise* [1976] (New York: Harper Colophon, 1977), p. 193. Dinnerstein also concludes that the need to invest major energy in perpetuating the species tended to make women specialists in the exercise of capacities "crucial for empathic care of the very young and for maintenance of the social-emotional arrangements that sustain everyday primary-group life" (p. 20). See also p. 68 on the more permeable boundaries of self among women. Dinnerstein drew from Norman O. Brown's conclusion that male domination is the product of the boy's "revolt against biological dependence on the mother" (p. 182, citing Norman O. Brown, *Life against Death* [Middletown: Wesleyan University Press, 1959], n.p.).

24. Nancy Chodorow, *The Reproduction of Mothering: Psychoanalysis and the Sociology of Gender* (Berkeley: University of California Press, 1978), p. 181. Chodorow linked connection with empathy: "Girls emerge from this [oedipal] period with a basis for 'empathy' built into their primary definition of self in a way that boys do not. Girls emerge with a stronger basis for experiencing another's needs or feelings as one's own (or of thinking that one is so experiencing another's needs or feelings)" (p. 167).

25. Chodorow, *The Reproduction of Mothering,* p. 169.

26. Sara Ruddick, "Maternal Thinking," *Feminist Studies* 6 (Summer 1980): 353; see also Jean Bethke Elshtain, *Public Man, Private Woman: Women in Social and Political Thought* (Princeton: Princeton University Press, 1981), p. 336, and "Feminist Discourse and Its Discontents: Language, Power and Meaning," *Signs* 7 (1983): 603–21, p. 621.

27. "Methodocracy, Misogyny and Bad Faith: The Response of Philosophy," in D. Spender, ed., *Men's Studies Modified: The Impact of Feminism on the Academic Disciplines* (New York: Oxford University Press, 1981), p. 47, cited in Jean Grimshaw, *Philosophy and Feminist Thinking* (Minneapolis: University of Minnesota Press, 1986), p. 54. See also Jane Flax, "Political Philosophy and the Patriarchal Unconscious: A Psychoanalytic Perspective on Epistemology and Metaphysics," in S. Harding and M. Hintikka, eds., *Discovering Reality: Feminist Perspectives on Epistemology, Metaphysics, Methodology, and the Philosophy of Science* (London: D. Reidel, 1983), for a critique, based on Chodorow, of the denial of primary relatedness in philosophy.

28. Carol Gilligan, *In a Different Voice* (Cambridge: Harvard University Press 1982), p. 8. Several years later, however, in "Moral Orientation and Moral Development," in Kittay and Meyers, eds. *Women and Moral Theory* (Totowa, N.J.: Rowman and Littlefield, 1987), Gilligan criticized Chodorow for tying self-development to the experience of separation, thus sustaining "a series of oppositions that have been central in Western thought and moral theory, including the opposition between thought and feelings, self and relationship, reason and compassion, justice and love" (p. 29). Although I concentrate here on the empirical question of gender differences in "connection," Gilligan was reacting to a line of research that, for reasons probably linked in part to implicit gender coding, considered a rights, or Kantian, orientation higher than other moral orientations. See below on the moral emotions for the feminist critique of this form of Kantian orientation. See also Joan C. Tronto, "Women and Caring: What Can Feminists Learn about Morality from Caring?" in Alison M. Jaggar and Susan R. Bordo, eds., *Gender/Body/Knowledge* (New Brunswick: Rutgers University Press, 1989); and Owen Flanagan and Kathryn Jackson, "Justice, Care and Gender: The Kohlberg-Gilligan Debate Revisited," *Ethics* 97 (1987): 622–37 for a review and critique of the literature.

29. Gilligan, *In a Different Voice*, p. 17. Like Chodorow, Gilligan explicitly linked care with empathy, concluding that women's moral judgments "are tied to feelings of empathy and compassion" (p. 69), and that girls' smaller and more intimate playgroups foster the development of "empathy and sensitivity" (p. 11).

30. Nel Noddings, *Caring: A Feminine Approach to Ethics and Moral Education* (Berkeley: University of California Press, 1984), p. 2.

31. Diana Baumrind, "Sex Differences in Moral Reasoning: Response to Walker's (1984) Conclusion that There Are None," *Child Development* 57 (1986): 511–21.

32. Nona Plessner Lyons reports the largest differences of any of Carol Gilligan's students. In her sample of thirty upper-middle-class people, identified through personal contact and recommendation, 63 percent of the sixteen women were coded as "predominantly connected" compared to none of the fourteen men, and 79 percent of the men as "predominantly separate" compared to 13 percent of the women (Nona Plessner Lyons, "Two Perspectives: On Self, Relationships, and Morality," in Carol Gilligan, J. Victoria Ward, and Jill McLean Taylor, eds., *Mapping the Moral Domain: A Contribution of Women's Thinking to Psychological Theory and Education* [Cambridge: Harvard University Press, 1988]).

Other studies do not find significant gender differences, even in college-educated populations. See Maureen R. Ford and Carol R. Lowery, "Gender Differences in Moral Reasoning: A Comparison of the Use of Justice and Care Orientations," *Journal of Personality and Social Psychology* 50 (1986): 777–83 (college students); William J. Friedman, Amy B. Robinson, and Britt L. Friedman, "Sex Differences in Moral Judgments? A Test of Gilligan's Theory," *Psychology of Women Quarterly* 11 (1987): 37–46 (college students); Robbin Derry, "Moral Reasoning in Work-Related Conflicts," *Research in Corporate Performance and Policy* 9 (1987): 25–49 ("first-level managers"). On Kohlberg's measures, see Laurence J. Walker, "Sex Differences in the Development of Moral Reasoning: A Critical Review," *Child Development* 55 (1984): 677–91.

Such differences may be highly context specific. When no other cues are given, the classic Bem Sex-Role Inventory finds American college students linking the words "understanding," "sensitive to the needs of others," and "compassionate" to the "feminine" role (Sandra L. Bem, "The Measurement of Psychological Androgyny," *Journal of Consulting and Clinical Psychology* 42 [1974]: 155–62; and Hazel Markus, Marie Crane, Stan Bernstein, and Michael Siladi, "Self-Schemas and Gender," *Journal of Personality and Social Psychology* 42 [1982]: 38–50). When no cues are given, students also associate the "communal goals" of "selflessness, concern with others and a desire to be at one with others" with women more than men (women 3.81, men 3.03 on a 5-point scale). Yet the same students also see male *homemakers* as more likely to have communal traits than female *employees* (4.11 vs. 3.31), suggesting that the stereotypes derive at least in part from the work in which the two sexes are thought typically to engage. Alice H. Eagly and Valerie J. Steffen, "Gender Stereotypes Stem from the Distribution of Women and Men into Social Roles," *Journal of Personality and Social Psychology* 46 (1984): 735–54.

The anthropologist Ronald Cohen concludes that "empathy" is "not a proper way to behave" in some African tribal societies, and suggests that the Anglo-European focus on empathy may be the historical result of many generations of small, inwardly focused nuclear families with a relatively low instance of infant death. "Altruism: Human, Cultural, or What?" *Journal of Social Issues* 28 (1972): 39–57. On the other hand, Sandra Harding, "The Curious Coincidence of Feminine and African Moralities," in Kittay and Meyers, eds., *Women and Moral Theory*, and Patricia Hill Collins, *Black Feminist Thought* (London: Allen and Unwin, 1990), p. 206ff., suggest that an ethics of "connection" and "caring" may typify the behavior and norms not only of women in the United States, but also of both men and women in Africa. Empirical research on these issues is in its infancy.

33. That a researcher can construct two distinct operationalizations of these two orientations does not mean that analytically the two are entirely separate. On the overlap, see Susan Moller Okin, "Thinking Like a Woman," in Deborah L. Rhode, ed., *Theoretical Perspectives on Sexual Difference* (New Haven: Yale University Press, 1990); George Sher, "Other Voices, Other Rooms? Women's Psychology and Moral Theory," in Kittay and Meyers, eds.,

Women and Moral Theory; and Flanagan and Jackson, "Justice, Care, and Gender." Nondiscretionary rights can be based on relations, as when the primary caretaker has the right to custody after divorce (Mary Becker, University of Chicago Law School, personal communication). Moreover, although about two-thirds of D. Kay Johnston's ("Adolescents' Solutions to Dilemmas in Fables" in Gilligan et al., *Mapping the Moral Domain*) eighty middle-class students focused on one orientation rather than another in interpreting a moral fable, all were eventually able to adopt the other orientation (about half spontaneously, after being asked, "Is there another way to think about this problem?" and the rest after prompting).

34. Ford and Lowery, "Gender Differences in Moral Reasoning."

35. In some philosophic readings, neither innateness nor efficiency is automatically good. Nor does innateness or efficiency automatically trump other goods. Societies work hard and often successfully to reduce or eliminate the effects of many innate impulses, such as the impulse to defecate spontaneously. Societies may also decide against implementing certain efficient ways of functioning, such as plantation slavery, on the grounds that these forms of efficiency are incompatible with other social ideals.

36. The terms "minimalist" and "maximalist" derive from the work of Catharine R. Stimpson, e.g., "Knowing Women," the Marjorie Smart Memorial Lecture, St. Hilda's College, University of Melbourne, August 1990. For divisions in the women's movement on this issue, see Ann Snitow, "Gender Diary," in Marianne Hirsch and Evelyn Fox Keller, eds., *Conflicts in Feminism* (New York: Routledge, 1990).

37. Robin West, "Jurisprudence and Gender," *University of Chicago Law Review* 55 (1988): 1–72, comes close to making a claim for innateness when she says that "women, uniquely, are physically and materially 'connected' to those human beings when the human beings are fetuses and then infants. Women are more empathic to the lives of others because women are physically tied to the lives of others in a way that men are not" (p. 21). West states the "connection thesis" as follows: "Women are actually or potentially materially connected to other human life. Men aren't. This material fact has existential consequences" (p. 14). West also somewhat exaggerates the evidence of gender difference by writing, "According to the vast literature on difference now being developed by cultural feminists, women's cognitive development, literary sensibility, aesthetic taste and psychological development, no less than our anatomy, are all fundamentally different from men's, and are different in the same way: unlike men, we view ourselves as connected to, not separate from, the other" (p. 17). Or, "Intimacy is not something which women fight to become capable of. We just do it. It is ridiculously easy. It is also, I suspect, qualitatively beyond the pale of male effort" (p. 40). In her conclusion West modifies her emphasis on biology by saying that "material biology does not *mandate* existential value: men *can* connect

to other human life. . . . *Biology is destiny only to the extent of our ignorance*" (p. 71, emphases in original), but her stress throughout on "material" and "physical" connection, and her use of phrases like "fundamentally" and "qualitatively beyond the pale of . . . effort" make the differences sound insurmountable.

38. My own experience suggests that the differences between college-educated men and women in the United States today are no greater than the differences between college-educated residents of France and the United States. I have found no systematic comparison, across different norms or behaviors, of the size of gender differences to the size of class or other cultural differences. Janet Shibley Hyde's recent study, demonstrating that gender differences in cognitive abilities are generally not large and differences in social behavior depend greatly on context, implies that comparisons of the size of gender differences with the size of class or other cultural differences are rare or nonexistent. Janet Shibley Hyde, "Meta-Analysis and the Psychology of Gender Differences," *Signs* 16 (1990): 5–73, esp. 63–64, 72.

39. Community may be valued both as an end in itself and as a means to other ends. When community is at least in part a means, clarity about ends allows us to look for ways of achieving those ends with lower costs. Communities cohering through interdependence, for example, allow more individuality than communities cohering through sameness (Emile Durkheim, *The Division of Labor in Society* [1893], trans. George Simpson [New York: Free Press, 1964]); chosen communities with easy exit allow greater individuality than "given" communities with non-voluntary obligations (Friedman [1989]; Chap. 13, this volume). Evaluating these alternatives requires asking what aspects of community different kinds of people most value, and why.

40. Benjamin Zablocki, *The Joyful Community* (Baltimore: Penguin, 1971).

21

Feminist Communities and Moral Revolution

Ann Ferguson

Introduction: Three Mainstream Approaches

Traditional Western approaches to ethical theory have attempted to provide some general methodological principle or set of criteria for determining in individual cases what is right and wrong. They have usually been ahistorically grounded in a priori thought experiments, that is, thinking what "we" (the philosopher and *his* presumed audience) would say about hypothetical situations "we" can imagine. For example, is this type of action what we would agree to be good, right, obligatory, or permitted, or wrong or forbidden? Except for Marx and Nietzsche, classical ethical thinkers did not ask themselves what the purpose of formulating ethical theory was. Thus, they hardly noticed that the "we" they were consulting were wealthy, leisure-class, and usually white European men, some of them slaveholders and nearly all having legal and economic control over women and children. Marx and Nietzsche, on the other hand, assumed that hegemonic ethical codes served the ideological and manipulative function of keeping some social groups in power over others by forcing the second to internalize and act on norms that perpetuated the power of the first.[1]

Feminist ethics has this in common with Marx and Nietzsche: it does not want to accept any conventional value systems that operate as ideologies to perpetuate the power of a particular group of dominants (specifically, men) over a particular group of subordinants (i.e., women). Alison Jaggar and Sarah Hoagland (Jaggar, 1991a; Hoagland, 1988) point out that one of the main purposes of doing feminist ethics is to unmask conventional value systems or ethical theories that perpetuate male domination.[2] After that, feminist ethicists part company as to exactly how we should transform ethics. The divisions between us stem in part from the mainstream theories, from which we begin, so it is worth summarizing these different paradigms.

There are three mainstream theories of the foundations of rights and duties, goods and evils. There are, first: universalism, including rights theory; second, communicative or discourse ethics; and third, communitarianism. Just as there are three mainstream views as to how to ground ethical claims, there are three competing feminist approaches that use these traditional starting points but come to different conclusions.

Universalism is the view that there are one or more principles of goodness or obligation that will tell us what to do in any situation. Theories of justice often start from the a priori, or assumed-without-proof, intuition that there are certain universal human rights or principles of justice that apply to all human societies. John Rawls (1971) has developed one such famous theory of justice; Susan Moller Okin (1989) is a feminist who accepts Rawls's starting point but insists that his principles ought to be extended to give women and children rights against men in the family, thus breaking down the public-private split that Rawls and others see as marking off a sphere of personal freedom.

A second starting point is communicative ethics or discourse theory, as put forward by Jurgen Habermas (1987). His view is that ethical statements ought to be justified by a dialogical process in which those affected could communicate their needs and perspectives, agree on formal equality and reciprocity in the dialogical process, and attempt to get agreement based on the uncoerced force of the best argument presented for resolving the problem. Seyla Benhabib is the feminist ethicist whose position is the closest to that of Habermas. She also makes an ambitious attempt to put together some of Carol Gilligan's insights about the ethics of care while retaining an ethics of justice and universal principles (Benhabib, 1992). Alison Jaggar critiques Habermas's idea of a dialogical ethics because it ignores the structural inequalities of some participants (e.g., women to men, people of color to whites, lesbians and gays to heterosexuals, uneducated to educated). She maintains that a feminist practical reason was developed in feminist self-help movements in the 1960s and 1970s that used an egalitarian process to incorporate the voices of those structurally oppressed, including an emphasis on consensual process and emotional support (Jaggar, 1991b).

Iris Young's feminist theory of justice (1991) starts with a Habermasian emphasis on the importance of a commitment to dialogue. She expands Habermas's views with the idea that justice is a process value that requires self-determination or participatory democracy. However, these are excluded by structures of oppression and domination in welfare-state capitalist and socialist societies, which deny such self-determination to anyone except white, wealthy or elite men. Caucus vetoes, affirmative action, and block voting, in addition to effective constitutional protections for women and minorities, would have to be put into place before justice could become a reality.

The third starting point for mainstream theory and for some feminist approaches is the communitarian position of people like Michael Sandel (1982) and Alasdair MacIntyre (1981, 1983). For these thinkers, morality is neither an abstract individual reasoning process, as it is for the universalists, nor a process to be hammered out by abstract "talking heads," as in the communicative ethics model. Rather, individuals understand values as intimately connected with their identification with a particular community and the social practices and roles assumed in that community. Thus, rather than define morality as a universalist code that becomes clear through a process of internal reasoning or ideal dialogue, MacIntyre argues that what we ought to do depends on our moral tradition, that is, on the particular historically specific narratives and communities in which we are embedded, for example, the narratives of Christianity or Judaism or Native American religions.[3]

Interestingly enough, we can place in this communitarian tradition those feminist ethicists like Nel Noddings (1984), Carol Gilligan (1982), and Sara Ruddick (1989), who attempt to develop an ethic of feminine care as an alternative to masculinist universalist theories of rights and justice. They appeal to a distinctive woman's ethical voice that prioritizes concern and ability to care for concrete others, and they connect this voice to the specific virtue of mothering. Since this is women's primary social role in traditional societies, it would seem they are also communitarians in their insistence on valuing an already given aspect of most existing communities. They critique male ethicists who have ignored this feminine moral point of view and demand the substitution or extension of mainstream ethical thinking to include the feminine voice as a necessary prelude to the elimination of male domination.

As rhetorical strategies, feminists in all three camps, by insisting on extending rights talk, communicative ethics, and communitarian virtues to include women's issues, moral skills, and priorities, are partially transforming our moral values — first, in extending the sphere of rights to the personal sphere; second, in demanding that female recipients of state welfare be considered deserving of participation in public-policy decision making; and third, in demanding that men coparent in order to learn to prioritize caring in context rather than universalistic principles of justice. In this way all feminist ethical approaches have been partially successful in creating a transformation or "transvaluation of values," that is, in starting the process of moral revolution.

However, I maintain that we need to complement and correct the work of these other tendencies in feminist ethics with a fourth starting point, which we could call the existential communitarian position. Those of us who want to challenge the presuppositions and privileges involved in social roles that perpetuate social inequality are faced with a Nietzschean existential choice to rebuild ourselves and our virtues, although clearly we will not choose the aristocratic, Dionysian values he favored (Nietzsche, 1966, 1967). This starting point acknowledges that human identities are importantly defined by our relation to the social order. Thus feminists, uppity women, and profeminist men cannot change ourselves individually by "pulling ourselves up by our own individual bootstraps." Instead, we will require alternative supporting communal frameworks to deconstruct our internalized sexism, racism, heterosexism, and class attitudes. To reconstitute ourselves as antiracist, antisexist, and so forth requires work, struggle, new habits, new virtues, and new social practices as well as reconstructed social identities.

In her book *Lesbian Ethics* (1988) Sarah Hoagland gives her vision of how such a process could work for women who identify with a lesbian-feminist community. Hoagland argues that commitment to a lesbian-feminist community allows lesbians to challenge not only "heterosexualism," the ideology that women should be dependent on men, but also the value choices offered us under patriarchal social roles, those of being either independent, hence abstracted from relationships and commitments to others, or dependent on relationships, hence submissive and lacking a sense of separate self and self-worth. She argues that we can transform autonomy and community, which are values usually thought to oppose each other, into a synthesis of autonomy-in-community, or what she calls "autokoeneny." In other words, in the right context, women can support each other to develop their individual powers of independent choice, something patriarchal communities have restricted.[4]

Transvaluation of Values and Oppositional Communities

I agree with Sarah Hoagland that in a sexist society there exists a gender dualism that posits distinctive masculine and feminine virtues that exclude each other. For example, in the symbolic gender value system of the United States at the present time, character traits held to involve particularly "feminine" virtues, like nurturance, caring, and altruism, will be contrasted with "masculine" virtues like principled behavior and rational self-interest, or enlightened egoism. A person will be expected to embody only one or the other of these sets of virtues, depending on their gender. Such qualities as self-sacrifice will be associated with the feminine virtues and aggressive individualism with the masculine virtues (Ferguson, 1991).

Not only do those of us who want to challenge these gender models need to change the context of such virtues so that such meaning implications change but we need to strengthen a new and different sense of self by developing different social relationships with others. For example, we need to create new practices of caring and nurturing that do not require the caregiver regularly to accept suffering or the sacrifice of his or her own needs in order to promote the interests of those cared for. We need new meanings and practices of assertiveness that do not imply lack of receptivity to others' needs and thoughts; new practices of criticism and self-criticism that do not involve paralyzing guilt or self-abasement; and new meanings and practices of love as a basis for ethical priorities that do not imply that one privileges one's private life over broader issues of social equality and justice.

Transvaluing or redefining and reconstructing our values, by, for example, eliminating the gender dualism in them, is not a project that can simply be done by an individual feminist who progresses in so-called moral maturity to the stage of postconventional care plus responsibility à la Gilligan. Rather, our character traits and the values connected to them are products of our social relations with each other in particular primary communities that give us our sense of self and self-worth. Thus, in order for women to redefine the value of caring or nurturance so as to be compatible with a rebellious defense of our own rights to self-development outside of the home we need the support of others. To be ambitious, to value our own projects as much as our commitment to the projects of the men and children to whom we have affective connections, we have to create for ourselves new communities of others who, like ourselves, resist accepting the dominant meanings and values associated with the role of nurturer in patriarchal societies. This means we need to form intentional or chosen communities of resistance, or what I call "oppositional communities." Such communities are attempts to partially realize some of our ideals in the present as we struggle to change the world in the future. They are spaces in which we can both empower and strengthen ourselves to struggle against those who wish to maintain the status quo outside of this space. Thus, they are both present-looking and forward-looking, and in their best cases concerned both with self and others in ways that the standard distinction between egoism and altruism just doesn't allow.[5]

But what exactly is an "oppositional community"? I have in mind not just people who live together or in the same neighborhood, such as in a communal household or progressive barrio or neighborhood, but a network of actual and imagined others to whom one voluntarily commits oneself in order to empower oneself and those bonded with others by challenging a social order perceived to be unjust, usually by working on a shared project for social change. Connecting to an oppositional community is at some level an act of rebellion or resistance. The choice to do so involves a resolve to reconstitute one's personal identity and, in so doing, to reasess the values to which one is committed and the responsibilities one has for others. All social movement involved in "identity politics" try to construct such oppositional communities, communities in which members attempt to redefine their gender, racial, ethnic, or sexual identities so as to eliminate the negative implications hitherto associated with them—for example, to adopt an identity as Black and proud, gay and proud, or as a woman-identified woman. But oppositional communities are more successful in the long run when they are not just formulated around identity politics but involve also affinities and political affiliations with those in other identity positions who share critiques of the dominant order, for example, anarchists critical of production for profit, environmental activists critical of consumerist lifestyles, vegetarians defending animal rights, or pacifists opposed to military spending.

Given that most of us lead complicated lives in which economic and social constraints force us to live within certain structures (e.g., the capitalist market and workplace, biological kin networks, geographical communities of place ranging from neighborhoods to nations), hardly any women can be empowered by participation in only one oppositional community, such as Hoagland's model lesbian-feminist community. Rather, our fragmented subjectivities require support by a number of oppositional communities that provide alternative meanings and material support. As I will argue shortly, a postmodern notion of self suggests a model of empowerment through a number of relational networks rather than one unique "pool of energy" one receives through abstract sisterhood.

Networks that constitute oppositional communities can occur in many ways in social life. They can be groups who validate a stigmatized lifestyle, such as lesbian and gay communities. They include alternative nonprofit businesses, such as cooperatives running a food store or bookstore, like New Words, the feminist bookstore in Cambridge, Massachusetts, or a parent-run childcare group or school organized around nonracist, nonsexist education. They can involve networks of professionals who set up organizations committed to changing their theories and practices in ways that require reconstituting their members' sense of self and their ethical responsibilities, such as the Society for Women in Philosophy. They can involve trade unions or social service providers' coalitions that are interested not merely in pay raises or job security for their members, but in broader issues of social justice, such as challenging racism or sexism or the lack of democratic input by workers or clients in determining management or state policy. And, finally, they can involve progressive organizations for social change, such as antiracist coalitions or caucuses of people of color, solidarity groups supporting liberation struggles in the Third World, and antimilitarist, peace, and tax resisters' networks.

I hope it has become clear by my examples that there are many types of overlapping oppositional communities and that many of these networks have members who would not identify themselves as feminists, perhaps because they have not really thought about the value of combating sexism or because their priority is opposing some other pressing social injustice, such as racism, anti-Semitism, militarism, or class inequalities. But for women to empower ourselves to develop new values, most of us require more than one oppositional community to empower the many aspects of self we are because of our racial, ethnic, class, and sexual identities, which are implicated in social structures of domination.

With respect to transforming sexist values, women need feminist communities or communities of "uppity women" — that is, networks of women who are consciously critical of the gender roles, or the implicit meanings of the gender roles, we have been taught. Such communities intend to redefine themselves and their values by associating themselves with others of like mind while at the same time challenging the institutional sexism of the larger society.[6]

Women of color like Audre Lorde, Trinh Minh Ha, bell hooks, Gloria Anzaldúa, and Patricia Hill Collins have pointed out the implicit racism of white feminists who assume that fighting sexism should take priority to fighting racism or that we all have the same experiences of sexism. As Audre Lorde says, "By and large within the women's movement today, white women focus upon their oppression as women and ignore difference of race, sexual preference, class and age. There is a pretense to a homogeneity of experience covered by the word 'sisterhood' that does not in fact exist" (Lorde, 1984:116). Patricia Hill Collins points out that the racist-sexist images of the Black mammy and matriarch are unique to African American women (Collins, 1990). On the other hand, once white women are forced by women of color to acknowledge differences, Trinh Minh Ha argues that since white women's sense of self is predicated on women of color as the Other, there is the sense of an unbridgeable gulf, as women of color are perceived as outsiders whose experience and tradition is too alien to comprehend (Minh Ha, 1989).

For these and other reasons the oppositional communities that women of color may create for themselves will not automatically be connected to those of white women. Making coalitions across the color line to deal with sexism will therefore be a struggle and not an automatic identification. For example, many African American women would rather define themselves as "womanist" than "feminist," feeling that the latter term has been identified with white women who wish to prioritize sexism over racism and other issues of social justice, such as poverty and class privilege.[7]

Because of class, racial, and sexual privileges that serve to divide women from each other, I would argue that self-defined feminists who want to form oppositional communities to empower women need to commit themselves to challenging at least the four "isms" of sexism, classism, racism, and heterosexism — though of course there may be political disagreement within our communities as to the best strategies for accomplishing these goals.

How do the goals of autonomy and empowerment for women connect to the formation of oppositional communities? In order to know

whether these goals are even feasible, particularly the idea of the empowerment of women as a social group that cuts across race, class,
sexual, and national differences, we need to understand what the goals
involve. Feminist writers have stressed the idea that the kind of empowerment that a group of women receives, both collectively and individually, from participating in a good consciousness-raising group is not
power based on control over others or a simple increase in the individual
capacities of each woman. Rather than being "power over" or "power
to," empowerment is "power with" — that is, an interrelationship in
which the whole group creates more energy to change the world in its
joint support of each individual than any one individual would have on
her own.

But solidarity with other women across barriers of race, class, ethnicity, sexual orientation, and nationality is problematic. If we try to
ignore these differences simply in order to empower ourselves *as women,*
we ignore the "power over" dynamics that continue to exist between
us due to institutionalized and internalized racism, ethnicism, homophobia, and classism. Indeed, only white Euro-American heterosexual
middle- and upper-class women will be empowered by ignoring the other
"isms" that oppress other women. Bell hooks suggests that what she calls
"the ideology of common oppression" has been used by bourgeois feminists to usurp the feminist movement (hooks, 1984). How then can a
feminist ethical approach that stresses the need for building oppositional
communities of women avoid this consequence?

It seems to me that the solution to the dilemma of whether feminists
can unite across race, class, and ethnic lines depends on understanding
that empowerment for women can never come from merely *one* oppositional community through which to reconstitute a positive and powerful
sense of self. As María Lugones points out, Sarah Hoagland's vision of a
separatist lesbian-feminist community will not empower lesbian women
of color or working-class or immigrant women who need a way to bond
with their racial, class, and national communities of origin in order
to reconstruct their identities and overcome internalized oppression
(Lugones, 1990). Since one's gender identity, or sense of being a woman,
is never entirely separable from one's other identities, such as racial,
ethnic, and class background, we cannot assume that the networks of
self-defined feminists and uppity women will automatically form the
same one community or network. Indeed, it seems more likely that, in
the United States at least, feminist/"womanist" networks will divide

by race and some major ethnic groups, such as white/Anglo, African-American, Asian, Latino, and Jewish. It is therefore more accurate to speak of oppositional feminist *communities* rather than just one feminist *community*.

Thinking of multiple feminist communities also is helpful for autonomous feminists in dealing with "the man question," if they reject either separatism or integration in mixed-sex groups as the answer to fighting sexism. Many feminists find ourselves with both womanly and manly identifications and bonds because of our personal histories and thus we cannot be personally empowered simply by one or the other, that is, either a woman-only or a mixed oppositional community. For example, I am a lesbian mother who has been co-parenting but not living with my ex-husband. I have an adopted Black daughter and have several grown white stepsons whom I continue to relate to maternally. I work in a male-defined field, philosophy, and have male allies who support my feminist courses and Women's Studies in my university against other male colleagues and some female colleagues who would love to eliminate them. I have found myself equally empowered by utopian visions of Amazon women able to live independently of men and by androgynous visions of genderless egalitarian societies, since one of my self-aspects is a "female man" (Russ, 1975). Since I suspect there are many of us with such multiple gender identifications, to empower ourselves we require a complicated set of single-sex and mixed-sex alliances around issues of social justice that combine partial visions in a process of struggle without one static end point or vision. But this does not imply that we can give up utopian thinking, for to do that is to give up hope, which creates cynicism and passivity (Ferguson, 1992).

The above considerations suggest some implications for developing the feminist virtue of "sisterhood." Feminists, womanists, and uppity women have to understand that this is not a goal that can be achieved without struggle or work to change ourselves. And changing ourselves is an ongoing process that we cannot do alone. Instead we must develop what I call "sex-affective" practices of bonding, friendship, and emotional-psychological processing (Luepnitz, 1992) that, on the one hand, break down our internalized racism, ethnicism, and classism and, on the other, involve activist coalitions for social justice that challenge the institutionalized aspects of these social domination relations. Thus "sisterhood" becomes an *achievement* rather than a biologically given kinship relation (hooks, 1984). It will involve understanding the impor-

tance of women expressing their anger toward other women with privilege, learning constructive ways to deal with political disagreements,
guilt, and shame, ways to empower a feminist/womanist leadership,
and ways to distinguish constructive from destructive competition
(Brown, 1992). All of this will also involve the development of revolutionary love in feminists, the kind of love that can motivate us to
weather such difficult processes and yet find it all worth the effort. I will
talk more about what "revolutionary love" involves shortly.

A Postmodernist Aspect Theory of Self

Let's approach the problem of the kinds of oppositional communities a
feminist ethics requires by exploring some metaphysical presuppositions
of the concept of self-empowerment. Feminist object-relations theorists
such as Nancy Chodorow (1978) and moral-development theorists such
as Carol Gilligan (1982) have critiqued the classical liberal individualist
view of the self as an atomistic entity, defined as autonomous and
independent of others. They claim this is a masculinist model stemming
from the sort of masculine gender identity fostered by maternal responsibility for infant care. They have argued that this model ignores feminine gender development, which defines the self as dependent on and in
relation to others. Feminine gender identity, they argue, tends to develop
a more contextual ethics based on mediating the needs of concrete
others, rather than the abstract principled ethics of justice and rights that
men tend to develop.

But positing such a division between socially constructed masculine
and feminine gendered personalities does not help to determine to what
extent these self-understandings are themselves ideology and to what
extent reality.[8] Further, even if it can be shown that women generally do
approach ethical questions differently from men, it is a simplistic naturalism to infer that therefore women (and men) *ought* to so value things.[9]
Furthermore such a position needs to address the underlying metaphysical question of the *nature* of the self's relation to others. Some feminists,
notably those coming from either a Marxist or a liberal feminist tradition, have assumed that at base all individuals are atomistic, rational,
self-interested agents but that patriarchal conditioning has deluded
many women into misconceiving their interests to be relational in the
self-sacrificing sense of the term. For these theorists, such as Friedan
(1963), Delphy (1984), Benston (1969), Folbre (1982), and Hartmann

(1981), the feminist solution would be that *women should act more like men* and organize instrumentally with other women to defend our rational self-interests. Caroline Whitbeck is a feminist who has argued the opposite, that at base all individuals are selves defined in relation to each other, and that it is men whom patriarchal conditioning deludes into holding a modernist, atomistic, and individualist view of themselves (Whitbeck, 1983). Thus *men should become more like women* and stop denying the unconscious relational connections with others on which their sense of selfhood rests.

The problem with these two conceptions of the self is that they are too modernist in their assumption that most individuals in today's world should be conceived of as having *one* coherent self, whether this is defined as an autonomous rational agent separate from others or as a self defined in relation to particular others. Each of these extreme poles is suspect. Both ignore the ways in which both masculine and feminine selves in advanced capitalist societies are engaged in a multiplicity of relationships, some of which encourage an instrumental, self-interested response and some of which involve an incorporative response in which the self's interests are identified with others' interests. In addition, each pole eliminates by metaphysical fiat an ethical possibility that feminists need to take seriously. The rational, self-interested theory of selfhood assumes that altruism is impossible since selves always maximize their own perceived self-interests to the best of their knowledge and ability. The self-as-relational theory, as derived from object-relations theory, assumes that egoism is impossible since selves always define their interests by incorporating them with those of others, which seems to rule out oppositional relationships in which one rejects any identification with the interests of others.

I propose that both altruism and egoism are possible, depending on what social relations one is involved in. Patriarchal capitalist societies tend to foster egoism as a form of self-defense among those who are entrepreneurs and those who define themselves primarily as wage laborers because of the competitive relations of the capitalist market. However, altruistic connections with specific others, particularly kin, are encouraged in those who define themselves primarily as homemakers. But we cannot conclude that therefore masculine selves are egoists and feminine selves are altruists. This ignores the contradictory overlap that many women and some men face, as we engage in wage labor and competitive careers *as well as* childcare and homemaking.

We must develop a postmodernist metaphysic of self in order to critique a patriarchal capitalist ethics based on a conception of community as egoistic and instrumental and to imagine its successful overturn. María Lugones (1987) has argued that we must reject the modernist theory of one core self in favor of a theory of multiple selves, each defined in terms of an actual or possible "world" of meaning and value relations with others. I agree with María's key insight about different worlds of meaning that define the self in relation, but I prefer to speak of a self that has multiple aspects rather than multiple selves.[10]

On my view, each aspect of self is defined by its relation to a different set of social practices in communities with different built-in norms and expectations and therefore different meaning-relations with others. The self is a multifaceted conscious and unconscious process. Memory is importantly involved, though not all aspects of the self-process are known to itself, since there is often a disparity between self-understanding and others' understanding of self. Nonetheless, since the self is defined in terms of its relations with others in concrete social practices, any aspect of self is in principle able to be remembered, called to consciousness, and understood through dialogue with others. The self-process involves multiple aspects, each defined differently through its relation to different practices. Some of these aspects involve conscious agency and intentional action, and others involve unconscious intentions that can be brought to light by therapy or by angry confrontation of dominators by the oppressed, as María Lugones discusses in her paper on the importance of anger (Lugones, 1991).

All self-defining social practices involve what I call "sex/affective" connections with others, that is, emotional identification or bonding with those considered *like* oneself. Such practices often also involve *disidentification* with those defined as different or in oppositional roles.[11]

Aspects of self may lie in ambivalent and uneasy relation to each other, since they may involve contradictory values and meanings. For example, a woman in wage labor may find herself in competitive relations with other workers with respect to whether she keeps her job, is promoted, or receives pay raises. But if there is a strong trade union at her workplace, she may also have an incorporative relation to sister workers and an instrumental and oppositional relation to her boss or supervisor. On the other hand, at home she may define herself through her ability to empathize with and advance the interests of her children and her mate as if they were her own. Thus in one set of social practices, the woman may develop a self-aspect whose values are egoistic while in others she may have one whose values are altruistic.

One way to reconcile the insights of the theory of the rational, self-interested agent with the theory of the self as relational is to understand the self-process as involving conscious *projects* for the future as well as remembered (and misremembered) past aspects. These projects are relational as well, but they may operate at cross-purposes with each other. Projects relate to the self on one or more levels. They all involve practical reasoning to achieve goals, but conflicting conceptions of interests are involved. Thus, on one level, the material-survival level, the self-process defines an interest in continuing to exist, to enjoy physical pleasures and comforts, and to avoid physically unpleasant experience. We can call this *the level of material self-interest*. On a second level, the self-process defines an interest in social acceptability that allows for easy bonding with others in one's cultural milieu. We can call this the *level of status-quo social interest*. Finally, there is a level in which the self-process defines goals for what he or she would like to become. We can call this *the level of reconstitutive interests* (cf. McCrate, 1991).[12] It is this latter level that must be engaged by feminist transformative values if the person's moral reasoning is to escape from conventional ethical values connected to status-quo social interests. Thus, for example, a woman who wants to act on her desires for other women must find a way to reconstitute herself in order to counter her status-quo interests in continuing to identify herself as a "normal" (i.e., heterosexual) woman. And a man who desires to be a pacifist has a reconstitutive, but not a status-quo, interest in redefining his masculinity to avoid thinking of himself as a failed man. One way, of course, to do this is to develop a counter-identity as a gender outlaw in which he rejects status-quo gender categories altogether.

Masses of people can come to reject their status-quo interests in favor of feminist constitutive interests only by bonding sex/affectively with others in actual and imagined oppositional communities that challenge sexism as part of their vision. If we are concerned with global feminism and desire to create international feminist connections that go beyond national identities, we must do more than state with Virginia Woolf (in *Three Guineas*) that "As I woman I have no country. As a woman I want no country. As a woman my country is the whole world." We will have to create imagined communities with unseen others that are not merely abstract fantasies but connect to a revolutionary love that allows us to reconstitute ourselves as promoters of care and justice for these others as an ethical responsibility.

There are two important conditions necessary to create such extensive feminist oppositional communities. First, we need to create actual friendships across race and class difference and natural boundaries. Secondly, we need to develop a culture that accommodates political disagreement between us without destroying the trust and respect necessary for our common purposes, and for this we need to agree on an ethics of disagreement.

An Ethics of Disagreement

Although oppositional communities can empower women, we can also become very disempowered by political disagreements and power struggles for leadership. Most of us who have been feminists for a while have experienced such disagreements — for example, with the sectarian left in the 1960s and 1970s, the lesbian-straight split in the 1970s, class, ethnic, and racial divisions from the 1970s to the present, and the conflict over pornography and consensual S/M between radical and pluralist feminists in the 1980s. It is essential to formulate and defend an ethics of disagreement that will prevent the kind of destructive trashing and fragmentation that keeps us all weak. Though obviously face-to-face discussion and mediation are one solution, this strategy is not available to those who are not in the same locale.

A second strategy is to find ways, whether or not they are face-to-face meetings, to explore common ground. For example, women organizing against pornography and women opposed to censorship, though they disagree about how to assess the harms of pornography to women, may agree that women's voices should be heard in response to degrading media images of women. Though we cannot assume that those who disagree have enough in common to make coalitions about their commonalities and agree to disagree on the rest, we need to make the effort to find such commonalities.

A "no-trashing" rule — that is, not to argue *ad feminam* or to attack an individual's character, but instead to discuss the issue itself — seems to be a very important maxim. It is hard to believe that women who critique each other as "sexual puritans" and "fascists" or as "in league with male pornographers to use women," as the pluralists and radical feminists do to each other in the sex debate, can possibly see each other as allies in the struggle against institutional sexism. For example, Andrea Dworkin has been attacked as a sexual puritan and fascist lesbian separatist by feminists calling themselves "pro-sex" feminists. While I don't agree with all of Dworkin's views, I do agree with her that this kind of political trashing is destructive to feminism and completely inappropriate (cf. Dworkin, 1992).

It is harder to maintain such a no-trashing rule when it comes to challenging a person's social privilege, especially since such privilege causes anger in those oppressed by it, which if not expressed, can be internalized, creating a sense of lack of self-worth. On the other hand, when one person accuses another of racism or classism or homophobia, it is easy for the woman so attacked to respond with paralyzing feelings of guilt, which can allow her to distance the attacker as alien Other, and thus the process can perpetuate racism, classism, and heterosexism. Women who want to network together for empowerment must find ways to express their anger and resolve their guilt feelings. One way to do this is for all involved to engage together in a constructive project to challenge together the institutionalized aspects of the particular privilege at issue, so that both or all the involved individuals feel a sense of common commitment. For example, a women's studies program accused of structural racism can overcome mistrust and guilt by working to construct a nonracist curriculum.

Revolutionary Love

The best possibility for developing a viable process ethic to deal with the unavoidable anger and guilt that come out of working across gender, race, and class privilege arises when individuals involved in political disagreement act out of revolutionary love rather than ego needs, guilt, or obligation to principles of justice held only as abstract beliefs. Revolutionary love involves a commitment to a set of ideals connected to social justice, such as the rights of all humans to material and social equality, to be heard, and to democratic participatory decisionmaking and autonomous self-development. It also involves emotional bonding with, and care and concern for, others who are denied these rights, a feeling of social kinship and imagined community with them, and a desire to renounce one's own social and material privileges in order to challenge such existing inequalities.

When speaking of love, philosophers have distinguished *eros* and *agape,* that is, the sensualized love of particular others and the general, principled and unselfish love that people can have to causes and to unknown others. For example, those who love the poor in a way that causes them to give massively to charity, or those who so love the unconverted to their religion that they are led to become missionaries, are said to love in the sense of agape. As Katie Cannon points out in *Black Womanist Ethics* (1988), Martin Luther King, Jr., felt that agape is an essential virtue of radicals fighting for civil rights because it prioritizes the goals of a "beloved community" over one's own self-interests and responds altruistically to the need of other human beings for their own sakes. Cornel West has recently argued that the African American community needs to find a way to deal with Black rage against the dehumanization and invisibility of racism, and this requires accessing the love within the Black community now directed at kin and expanding it to empower the Black community as a whole in a search for radical democracy (West, 1993).

I hesitate to define revolutionary love as agape because of the latter's historical connection to the notion of altruistic or generalized love as opposed to egoistic love. I prefer to think of revolutionary love as the effect of a social relation only possible with a community of friends constituted to fight for social justice. In such a community the distinction between egoism and altruism does not really apply, since each individual gains something important, namely, a reconstitution of his or her sense of self — for example, as a feminist activist or as antiracist or anti-imperialist. For members of a dominant group, revolutionary love develops by developing friendships with particular others in subordinate groups as well as with others in one's social groups of origin who are interested in challenging their role as dominants. When women have such revolutionary love toward each other, they feel themselves to be sister revolutionaries connected to at least one common oppositional community or network. This in turn allows them a common context to work out their angers and guilt with respect to particular privileges. It follows from this analysis that a key value to aim for in the building of oppositional communities and networks is the creation of friendships of uppity feminists and womanists across race, class, and nationality.[13]

Perhaps I should add that most of us will also need to develop mixed-gender oppositional communities or networks with men who are pro-feminist, not only to allow the men we love a context in which to reconstitute themselves but also to reconstitute ourselves in nonsexist relations with men. In proposing this I am not of course implying that our oppositional communities will be sufficient to eliminate sexism. Obviously they are only a beginning while institutional structures of sexism continue to exist in the larger society.

Global Feminism and Imagined Community

Marilyn Friedman (1990) recently remarked about the fragility of feminist concern to create global feminism. Hard as it is to create an inclusive women's movement at home, how can it be possible for women to bond with women across national borders in oppositional communities? In order for global feminism to be possible, people must be motivated to create oppositional communities that prioritize gender, racial, class, ethnic, and sexual identity connections over national identities. This means women must be able to prioritize a commitment to an imagined community of others over one's communities of origin. But what exactly would this commitment involve?

An imagined community is that group of real or imagined humans through which an individual identifies an aspect of her- or himself. In order to act as a locus for constitutive self-identification, an imagined community cannot be merely a fantasy community dreamed up in the person's head. Rather, she or he must believe it to be an actual group of people and relate to it by ongoing social practices that involve emotionally engaging social interactions with, or concerning, these others.

Identifying with a nation-state is an example of identifying with an imagined community. Benedict Anderson (1983) documents the way that territorial conquests and the imposition of national languages, along with the rise of a common territorial time made possible by national newspapers and the fictive community of literary novels, created a context in which the nation-state could rise as a socio-psychological entity in which its citizens felt a common membership. As such an entity, the nation is in a position to command patriotism from its members. Those of us who wish to surpass the nation toward broader, global communities can confirm that such an emotional commitment is possible on the model of the nation-state and patriotism.

Patriotism is based on a feeling of community that must be regularly reinspired. The self-identified American or Canadian engages in nation-bonding rituals and activities — even if they are merely reading the daily newspaper, watching television, or discussing politics or sports — with other self-identified Americans or Canadians.

To counter patriotism with a more global commitment to the value of world peace, the pacifist reads about, speaks about, defends, or otherwise interacts and bonds with other pacifists. Usually the committed pacifist also finds a way to engage emotionally, often on a face-to-face basis, with people in other countries who are or may be labeled the "enemy" by his or her country's foreign policy. Just so, the global feminist, in order to reconstitute herself as such, must engage in actual meaning- and value-making rituals with women not of her national group. Such constitutive global sisterhood is not an automatic result of the desire to be a global feminist. Rather, the necessary cross-cultural meaning making involves interactive work and political commitment through practice. For example, it often requires learning other languages in order to communicate with women from other cultures face to face. It involves studying the histories of other peoples in order to understand their culture and values. And it can involve forming support networks for donating material aid or cooperative productive work or exchanges so as to feel affective bonds with particular people.

How would global feminist oppositional communities in which first-world feminists related to women in poorer countries avoid the "woman-as-do-gooder" syndrome that repeats the stereotype of Eurocentric middle-class feminine values? If women from North America don't want to relate to women in other nations as charity cases, we will have to deal with the power imbalance between us caused by our relative wealth and our countries' imperialist relations with these nations.

The way to do this, I would argue, is to combine a feminist politics of local organizing around women's self-interest with solidarity politics. That is, we must continue to organize our communities at home to deal with local empowerment issues, whether these concern trade unions, rape crisis or battered women's services, reproductive rights, women's health care, lesbian and gay rights, federal spending on the inner cities, or problems of homelessness and housing. Once we have our local organizations in place, we can relate as peers to similar existing organizations or to women interested in forming such organizations in other communities and nations. Relating not just on the individual level, but through grassroots organizations, we can put in place feminist dialogical processes involving affective communications, participatory democracy, and constructive evaluations of communicative processes. This way we are learning from and empowering each other rather than having one side merely giving "handouts." Thus, rather than a politics based on individual guilt over privilege, we will be substituting constructive support for each others' empowerment projects.[14]

A Vision for Feminist Global Imagined Communities

First we must understand that the only plausible global feminism we can create at the moment must involve a pluralist vision. Since feminism is an existential project that has grown and will continue to develop in different cultural contexts, there is no way we can eliminate the likelihood that different value priorities will be elected by different feminists to deal with the contradictions between their various self-aspects or multiple selves. Thus, with Iris Young, we should define feminist community as partly heteronymous, or composed of different subcommunities, as a network of overlapping empowerment communities, of feminisms rather than one Feminism with a capital F.

Second, we must refuse to define feminist issues as those only and narrowly relating to women, such as equal pay, affirmative action, reproductive rights, lesbian rights, and violence against women. Feminism redefined as a global feminist network must instead seek to empower as many dominator-challenging self-aspects of individuals as possible. An example of broadening what counts as a feminist issue is the practice of eco-feminism, which has reconceived environmental concerns as feminist issues by developing a feminist analysis of the destruction of the environment that is linked to an analysis of imperialism (Shiva, 1988). Similarly, we can define imperialism, racism, war and militarism, health care, economic democracy (housing, hunger, participatory democracy, workers' control) as feminist issues, even though combating, solving, or instituting them will also empower many men.

Finally, it is a mistake for feminists to define the constitutive goal of global feminist community as merely pluralism or respect for difference. We also need some basis for sameness, since the identification required for revolutionary love must be based on a minimal set of shared values. Thus, we need to define both end goals and process values for our constitutive community with others. What kind of a normative goal of community do we want to struggle for in the world as a whole? What kind of transitional or process goals should we try to incorporate into our constitutive social practices with others to change our values as we go?

In 1968, in *The Poverty of Liberalism,* Robert Paul Wolff contrasted the normative goal of individualism with the normative goal of community and in so doing identified several components of community as an ideal. His is an intellectual gloss on ideas presented in more imaginative ways by feminists like anarchist Emma Goldman (1969) and novelists Charlotte Perkins Gilman in *Herland* (1979) and Marge Piercy in *Woman at the Edge of Time* (1978). I believe it is time for feminist philosophers to develop further the details of this vision. I try to do this in my two books by developing a feminist anarcho-socialist model (cf. also Ferguson, 1992). But my blueprint was meant as a national vision for an ideal U.S. society. How would it be applicable to a *global* feminist ideal?

In answer I will summarize the components of the ideal of community Wolff discusses, add some more of my own, and suggest how each could apply to a global feminist politics and ethics. The first aspect Wolff discusses is rational community with others, by which he means joint, reasoned democratic decision making, as in the idea of participatory democracy. The second-wave women's movement has attempted through its self-help projects to develop process goals that emphasize participatory democracy. Although there are numbers of problems with this as a model for all decision making (see Phillips, 1991), global feminism should support the creation of spaces for direct participation in decisions that affect one's life, particularly in the family and at worksites outside the family.

Second, Wolff mentions productive community, that is, cooperative work to meet joint needs. Of course, in some sense, all economies involve productive community since they involve cooperation to create products and exchange them. But combining productive community and participatory democracy suggests the ideal of an egalitarian planned economy with both worker and consumer input. The international and intercommunity productive projects in which feminists engage can at most involve market socialism in the face of the ubiquity of the international capitalist market. Nonetheless we can insist that such projects try to democratize control by a structure that shares decision-making power among those providing capital and workers and consumers. A good example of global feminist political practice in this regard have been the women's work brigades from North America and Europe that have gone to Central America to work with women there to build schools and in the process share construction skills. Ultimately, I would argue, we need to develop as our long-range goal worker-controlled and -planned but decentralized economies. This requires feminists to develop a democratic socialist vision in order to achieve the fullest possible empowerment of the world's women through rational and productive community.

Wolff's third criterion for community includes aesthetic bonding, that is, a collective appreciation of a common culture. We can develop this insight for our purposes by pointing out the need to create in ourselves and others an ability to interact with and appreciate the cultural rituals of women outside our cultures of origin. That is, we must build a common, eclectic global feminist culture that appreciatively incorporates different national cultures as well as minority cultures in our own nation. Such cultural elements include language, food, dance, cinema, music, history, literature, and possibly religion. The women's music projects and festivals in the United States go some way toward offering a diversity of musical styles from different cultures and redefining feminist musical taste. But we need more emphasis on reconstituting ourselves as multicultural appreciators than first-world feminists have yet demanded of ourselves. Of course I do not mean to imply that creating such an eclectic global feminist culture and a national antiracist and anti-ethnicist feminist culture would, in the process, eliminate our national and local cultures. Nor do I see ourselves as simply becoming passive culture consumers. Rather, I see these aesthetic links as encouraging bonds that will foster the minimum similarity we need to work in political coalition with each other even when we do not agree on political priorities and strategies.

I would argue for two more components to the feminist ideal of community. Sex, love, and friendship must become part of global feminism, together with a commitment to distributive justice in the world. One cannot become a global feminist in the abstract or even on the level of cultural appreciation. If one has not found particular others outside one's race, class, and culture of origin to relate to as lovers or friends, one will not be able successfully to reconstitute oneself away from one's status-quo interests. And unfortunately, even for those of us who consider ourselves feminist social outlaws, our status-quo interests to prioritize the needs of our kin and friends tend to make us passive moral collaborators in perpetuating racism, class hierarchy, ethnicism, and imperialism.

We also need to have an intellectual and emotional grasp of the massive disparities in the distribution of basic social and material goods in the world—to be actively concerned with the problems of starving children and adults, lack of health care and education and personal freedoms — in order to have an effective feminist moral commitment to a world community that achieves some modicum of distributive justice.

To reconstitute ourselves to prioritize world distributive justice, we must involve ourselves in personal and political practices that place us in imaginative community with those oppressed by economic want. Such practices could include building feminist coalitions with leftist groups to attack national foreign policies that perpetuate such maldistributions, since we know that their impact is worse for women and children than for adult males. Also, middle-class and wealthy feminists could agree to tithe a considerable percentage of their incomes for redistributive projects at home and abroad. Such tithing symbolizes a moral attack on consumerist preoccupations and is part of the process of reconstituting oneself away from status-quo values. Finally, first-world feminists should participate in organizing material-aid projects involving the underprivileged at home and in the underdeveloped world. Such grassroots projects could include both those that immediately improve lives by meeting material needs and those that support national liberation movements for social justice.

To conclude, we need a new ethical motto to correct that of Virginia Woolf. Although I cannot match Woolf's eloquence, I suggest something like: "As a woman, I refuse to let my status and country keep me from demanding justice for the whole world!"

Notes

1. However, both Nietzsche and Marx have their own implicit ethical values, although there is considerable controversy about this claim. Some insist, for example, that Marx is a radical historicist who felt that values and the standards of justice were always changing (West, 1991; Wood, 1971), while others believe that Marx retained freedom as a basic universal value (Young, 1981).

2. Kathy Addelson, in her essay "Nietzsche and Moral Change" (Addelson, 1991), argues that like Nietzsche's critique of slave morality, feminist reformers can be seen as demanding a moral revolution, or in Nietzsche's terms, a "transvaluation of values."

3. MacIntyre maintains that the contemporary context of individualist capitalist nations is morally problematic. According to him, morality was not problematic for premodern societies since goodness, virtue, and duty were what would best achieve the goals embedded in one's social role and social practices. Bureaucratic individualist societies such as modern capitalist societies create a moral problem in that they break the assumed connection between what is good

for the individual, who is now assumed to be an egoist, and the good of the society or community, which is assumed to be connected somehow to production for profit and the highest GNP. The breakdown of commitment to local communities and the moral traditions embedded in them has created some individuals who are "moral solipcists" like Nietzsche's "great man" Zarathustra, who can accept no external authority. Liberals attempt to avoid dealing with this moral problem by insisting that although no agreement can be reached on the good life, we can agree on principles of right or justice. But communitarians like Michael Sandel argue that John Rawls's project (1971) to prioritize justice as abstract moral principles universally agreed to by individualist selves is untenable, since human selves are not so abstractable from their communities of origin as to be able to make any intelligible choice of the sort Rawls presupposes. Instead, Sandel argues for what he calls a "constitutive" sense of community in which people share the end of furthering the well-being of the community in a way that creates a mode of self-understanding partly constitutive of each member's identity. Thus one's values are tied to the values of the community by one's moral sense of self even though one may be critical of certain community opinions or practices. (Sandel, 1982).

4. Hoagland gives another example of a concrete "transvaluation of values" by critiquing the value of altruism as a model for the lesbian-feminist community because of the denial of self this ordinarily implies. The implicit self-sacrifice connected with nurturing others need not be necessary in a social context where patriarchal relations are not present and women can create relations of what she calls Amazon care. As she points out, the problem of seeing motherhood as a base for women's distinctive ethical point of view, as do Carol Gilligan, Nel Noddings, and Sarah Ruddick, is that it ignores what Adrienne Rich (1976) calls the patriarchal institution of motherhood. That is, most women mother in a context in which they are economically and politically dependent on men, which creates a situation of self-sacrifice for mothers and a tendency for them to perpetuate the status quo by devoting themselves to bettering their own children's life chances without critiquing the unjust structures of the dominant order.

5. June Arnold's *The Cook and the Carpenter,* one of the many 1970s feminist utopian novels, is about a commune of feminist women and their children. As the carpenter says, using the author's pronoun "nan" as a substitute for "his" or "her": "Look, I really don't believe that anyone can work for a revolution separate and distinct from nan [her] own personal happiness or love-needs. Such a person wouldn't have any way of knowing the difference between what is true and what is false. If isn't that we're trying to do two things at once — set up a counterlife and work for a revolution: the two are halves of the same whole and the absolutely essential thing is to keep juggling them" (Arnold, 1973:50).

6. Groups and networks may do this to a greater or lesser degree of course.

For example, the Bunting Institute for Women at Radcliffe/Harvard University does not require sister fellows to define themselves as feminists or to choose a topic of research connected to the issue of sexism. Nevertheless, even the women whose research projects have nothing to do with gender issues are by their participation in an all-women's scholarly institute challenging the idea that only men can be scholars. As another example, the women Black blues artists such as Bessie Smith, who constituted themselves as "uppity women" through their style and lyrics, created a culture of resistance to the image of women as dependent and passive in sexuality and love as espoused by the dominant white culture. Women who fought as militants for the FSLN against Nicaraguan dictator Anastasio Somoza were certainly challenging the gender stereotype that soldiers must be men, and changing themselves in the process. Thus their membership in the oppositional networks of the FSLN had feminist effects, even though they may not have defined themselves as feminists in the process. We might call these examples "incipient oppositional communities" and note that they provide the conditions for more self-conscious feminist activity to arise, for example as has happened recently with the development of the autonomous women's movement in Nicaragua.

7. As Alice Walker defines it in *In Search of Our Mother's Gardens* (1983:xi), "womanist" means in part: "1. From *womanish*. (Opp. of "girlish," i.e., frivolous, irresponsible, not serious.) A black feminist or feminist of color. . . . Usually referring to outrageous, audacious, courageous or *willful* behavior. . . . 2. *Also:* A woman who loves other women, sexually and/or nonsexually. Appreciates and prefers women's culture. . . . Sometimes loves individual men, sexually and/or nonsexually. Committed to survival and wholeness of entire people, male *and* female. Not a separatist, except periodically, for health."

8. By the question of whether these self-understandings are ideology or reality I have in mind the question of whether women's ways of valuing in reality are all that distinct from men's, or whether we are misled by the social norm that women *ought* to be more altruistic than men, that is, more nurturant and caring to particular others, into thinking that we in fact are that way. My own view is that women can be just as egoistic and abstractly principled as men *in certain contexts,* but that we tend to define ourselves connectedly and altruistically in others. See my discussion of self-aspects theory below.

9. By "naturalism" I mean any ethical theory that assumes that by describing the way the world is (human nature, the function of ethical codes in society) we can automatically deduce what *ought* to be. Hume characterized this as the "is-ought" deduction and rightly questioned its validity.

10. Perhaps this is because I don't quite understand how multiple selves relate to each other in Lugones's conception, that is, how she can avoid a schizophrenic notion of multiple persons inhabiting the same body. For my view see Ferguson, 1991.

11. For either Lugones or my postmodernist theories of selfhood, it is mistaken to believe that women who are lesbians have lesbianism as an essential aspect of a core self. Rather, being a lesbian relates to only one aspect of self-understanding developed through experiences of desiring other women, erotic practices with them, and a sense of identification with an actual or imagined community of women-desiring-women. But another self-aspect of some women like myself who are lesbians is being mothers. And another self-aspect is race, another class, while still others involve national and ethnic and religious origins. Each of these self-aspects is defined in relation to experiences and practices with others, some of which give one social privilege in relation to others (e.g., race and class privileges) and some of which oppress one in relation to others.

Under the aspect theory of self, we cannot assume that Sarah Hoagland's strategy of "re-moralizing" the lesbian self-aspect of some of us by creating a lesbian-feminist community will empower the multiple-aspect persons that we are. If such a community fails to deal with race or class privileges, or ignores lesbian mothers or handicapped lesbians, or stigmatizes bisexual women, or refuses to acknowledge the empowering bonds that many lesbians derive from their friendships and political work with heterosexual feminists (or even with women who are not feminists or with pro-feminist men), then the multiple-aspected self that each lesbian is will fail to be empowered to change her internalized oppression in existing systems of social domination.

12. McCrate calls such interests "constitutive interests." I have changed the name because of confusion about whether a constitutive interest refers to an essential aspect of self. Since I don't hold an essentialist theory of the self, I am more in sympathy with Judy Butler here, who posits that social identities are always provisional and always involve a project of becoming through performances (Butler, 1991). In a way, one's plans even to continue to be a certain way require one to reconstitute oneself at every moment by social practices that reaffirm one's identity. However, I am using the concept of "reconstitutive interests" to contrast with one's status-quo interests in what one is presently taken to be by others. Thus, I will not count as a reconstitutive interest the project of continuing to be what one is taken and expected to be in the dominant culture.

13. From the point of view of revolutionary love, we can now see why Sarah Hoagland's lesbian ethic is inadequate for moral revolution, for she argues that lesbian communities should not judge each other with respect to class or racial justice issues, since these are bound to be disruptive of cohesion. But if feminist social justice requires empowering all women by challenging all forms of social domination, then our feminist oppositional communities must constantly struggle to challenge class, racial, sexual, and other social privileges that impair reciprocal relations between members of our communities. Revolutionary love requires that each of us adopt as a reconstitutive interest challenging those character traits and habits that perpetuate social inequality in our relations with

each other while at the same time recognizing that social justice requires a common struggle to eliminate institutional structures of injustice.

14. An example of how North American women can relate to women in Third World countries as peers on the organizational level, rather than as individual do-gooders giving handouts, was given to me by Nettie Wiebe, women's president of the Canadian National Farmer's Union. Their union brought material aid to the women in the ATC, the Nicaraguan farmworkers' union. Although the Canadian women brought gifts, they also gained from the act of solidarity, since the two groups learned from each other as they shared experiences of and strategies for organizing as farmers.

References

Addelson, Kathryn Pyne. 1991. *Impure Thoughts: Essays on Philosophy, Feminism, and Ethics*. Philadelphia: Temple University Press.

Albert, Michael, and Robin Hahnel. 1991. *Looking Forward: Participatory Economics in the Twenty-First Century*. Boston: South End Press.

Anderson, Benedict. 1983. *Imagined Communities: Reflections on the Origins and Spread of Nationalism*. London: New Left Books.

Arnold, June. 1973. *The Cook and the Carpenter*. Plainfield, Vt.: Daughters, Inc.

Bartky, Sandra. 1990. *Femininity and Domination*. New York: Routledge.

Benhabib, Seyla. 1992. *Situating the Self: Gender, Community and Postmodernism in Contemporary Ethics*. New York: Routledge.

Benston, Margaret. 1969. "The Political Economy of Women's Liberation." *Monthly Review* 21 (Sept. 1969): 13–25.

Bookchin, Murray. 1990. *Remaking Society: Pathway to a Green Future*. Boston: South End Press.

Brown, Cherie. 1992. "Healing Pain and Building Bridges." *Women of Power* no. 22 (Summer 1992): 16–21.

Butler, Judith. 1991. "Imitation and Gender Insubordination." In *Inside/Out: Lesbian Theories, Gay Theories*, edited by Diana Fuss, 13–31. New York: Routledge.

Cannon, Katie. 1988. *Black Womanist Ethics*. Atlanta: Scholars Press.

Card, Claudia. 1990. "Caring and Evil." *Hypatia* 5, no. 1:101–8.

———, ed. 1991. *Feminist Ethics*. Lawrence: University of Kansas Press.

Chodorow, Nancy. 1978. *The Reproduction of Mothering*. Berkeley: University of California Press.

Collins, Patricia Hill. 1990. *Black Feminist Thought: Knowledge, Consciousness, and the Politics of Empowerment*. London: Harpercollins.

Davion, Virginia. 1990. "Pacifism and Care." *Hypatia* 5, no. 1 (Spring 1990).

Delphy, Christine. 1984. *Close to Home*. Amherst: University of Massachusetts Press.

Dworkin, Andrea. 1992. "An Honorable Ethic: Interview." *Women of Power* no. 22 (Summer 1992): 52–59.

Ferguson, Ann. 1987. "A Feminist Aspect Theory of the Self." In *Science, Morality, and Feminist Theory. Canadian Journal of Philosophy,* supplementary vol. 13, edited by Marsha Hanen and Kai Nielsen, 339–56. Calgary, Alberta: University of Calgary Press.

———. 1989. *Blood at the Root: Motherhood, Sexuality and Male Dominance.* London: Pandora.

———. 1991. *Sexual Democracy: Women, Oppression and Revolution.* Boulder, Colo.: Westview.

———. 1992. "Herland or Ourland: Feminist Utopias as Visions of Social Change." Talk delivered at Theological Opportunities Program, November 12, 1992, Harvard Divinity School. Unpublished ms.

Folbre, Nancy. 1982. "Exploitation Comes Home: A Critique of the Marxian Theory of Family Labour." *Cambridge Journal of Economics* 6, no. 4: 317–29.

Foucault, Michel. 1977. *Power/Knowledge.* Edited and translated by Colin Gordon. New York: Pantheon.

Fraser, Nancy. 1989. *Unruly Practices: Power, Discourses and Gender in Contemporary Society.* Minneapolis: University of Minnesota Press.

Friedan, Betty. 1963. *The Feminine Mystique.* New York: Bantam.

Friedman, Marilyn. 1987. "Beyond Caring: The De-moralization of Gender." In *Science, Feminism, and Morality. Canadian Journal of Philosophy* supplementary vol. 13, edited by Marsha Hanen and Kai Nielsen, 87–110. Calgary, Alberta: University of Calgary Press.

———. 1990. "Feminism and Modern Friendship: Dislocating the Community." In *Feminism and Political Theory,* edited by Cass Sunstein, 143–58. Chicago: University of Chicago Press.

Gilligan, Carol. 1982. *In a Different Voice: Psychological Theory and Women's Development.* Cambridge: Harvard University Press.

———. 1987. "Moral Orientation and Moral Development." In *Women and Moral Theory,* edited by Eva Kittay and Diana Meyers. Totowa, N.J.: Rowman and Littlefield, 1987.

Gilman, Charlotte Perkins. 1979. *Herland.* New York: Pantheon.

Goldman, Emma. 1969. *Anarchism and Other Essays.* New York: Dover.

Habermas, Jürgen. 1987. *Theory of Communicative Action.* Vols. 1 and 2. Translated by Thomas McCarthy. Boston: Beacon Press.

Hanen, Marsha, and Kai Nielsen, eds. 1987. *Science, Morality, and Feminist Theory.* Calgary, Alberta: University of Calgary Press.

Hartmann, Heidi. 1981. "The Unhappy Marriage of Marxism and Feminism." In *Women and Revolution,* edited by Lydia Sargent. Boston: South End Press.

Held, Virginia. 1987. "Feminism and Moral Theory." In *Women and Moral Theory,* edited by Eva Kittay and Diana Meyer. Totowa, N.J.: Rowman and Littlefield, 1987.

———. 1990. "Feminist Transformations of Moral Theory." *Philosophy and Phenomenological Research* 1 (supplement, Fall 1990): 321–44.

Hoagland, Sarah. 1988. *Lesbian Ethics: Toward New Value.* Palo Alto, Calif.: Institute of Lesbian Ethics.

———. 1991. "Some Thoughts about 'Caring.' " In *Feminist Ethics,* edited by Claudia Card, 246–64. Lawrence: University of Kansas Press.

hooks, bell. 1984. *Feminist Theory from Margin to Center.* Boston: South End Press.

Irigaray, Luce. 1985. *This Sex Which Is Not One.* Edited by Catherine Porter and Carolyn Burke. Ithaca, New York: Cornell University Press.

Jaggar, Alison. 1991a. "Feminist Ethics: Projects, Problems, Prospects." In *Feminist Ethics,* edited by Claudia Card, 78–106. Lawrence: University of Kansas Press.

———. 1991b. "Telling Right from Wrong: Toward a Feminist Conception of Practical Reason." Paper read at the North American Society for Social Philosophy's national conference, Colorado Springs, August 10, 1991.

Kittay, Eva Feder, and Diana T. Meyers, eds. 1987. *Women and Moral Theory.* Totowa, N.J.: Rowman and Littlefield.

Lauritzen, Paul. 1989. "A Feminist Ethic and the New Romanticism — Mothering as a Model of Moral Relations." *Hypatia* 4, no. 2 (Summer 1989): 29–44.

Lorde, Audre. 1984. *Sister Outsider.* Trumansburg, N.Y.: Crossing Press.

Luepnitz, Deborah. 1992. "Defining Our Own Desires." *Women of Power* no. 22 (Summer 1992): 60–66.

Lugones, María. 1987. "Playfulness, 'World'-Traveling and Loving Perception." *Hypatia* 2, no. 2 (Summer 1987): 3–19.

———. 1990. "Hispaneando y Lesbiando: On Sarah Hoagland's *Lesbian Ethics.* *Hypatia* 5, no. 3 (Fall 1990): 138–46.

———. 1991. "On the Logic of Pluralist Feminism." In *Feminist Ethics,* edited by Claudia Card, 35–44. Lawrence: University of Kansas Press.

Lugones, María, and Elizabeth V. Spelman. 1986. "Have We Got a Theory for You! Feminist Theory, Cultural Imperialism, and the Demand for 'The Woman's Voice.' " In *Women and Values: Readings in Recent Feminist Philosophy,* edited by Marilyn Pearsall, 19–32. Belmont, Calif.: Wadsworth.

MacIntyre, Alasdair. 1966. *A Short History of Ethics.* New York: Macmillan.

———. 1981. *After Virtue.* Notre Dame, Ind.: University of Notre Dame Press.

MacIntyre, Alasdair, and Stanley Hauerwas. 1983. *Revisions.* Notre Dame, Ind.: University of Notre Dame Press.

Marx, Karl. 1977. *Karl Marx: Selected Writings.* Edited by David McLellan. Oxford: Oxford University Press.

McCrate, Elaine. 1991. "Rationality, Gender and Domination." Unpublished ms., Economics Department, University of Vermont, Burlington.

Minh Ha, Trinh T. 1989. *Woman, Native, Other: Writing Postcoloniality and Feminism.* Bloomington: University of Indiana Press.

Nietzsche, Friedrich. 1966. *Beyond Good and Evil.* Translated and edited by Walter Kaufmann. New York: Random House.

———. 1967. *On the Genealogy of Morals and Ecce Homo.* Translated and edited by Walter Kaufmann. New York: Random House.

Noddings, Nel. 1984. *Caring: A Feminine Approach to Ethics and Moral Education.* Berkeley: University of California Press.

Okin, Susan Moller. 1989. *Justice, Gender and the Family.* New York: Basic.

Parsons, Susan. 1990. "Feminism and the Logic of Morality: A Consideration of Alternatives." In *Socialism, Feminism and Philosophy: A Radical Philosophy Reader,* edited by Sean Mayers and Peter Osborne, 69–99. London: Routledge.

Phillips, Anne. 1991. *Engendering Democracy.* University Park: Pennsylvania State University Press.

Piercy, Marge. 1978. *Woman at the Edge of Time.* New York: Fawcett.

Puka, Bill. 1990. "The Liberation of Caring: A Different Voice for Gilligan's 'Different Voice,'" *Hypatia* 5, no. 1 (Spring 1990): 58–82.

Rawls, John. 1971. *A Theory of Justice.* Cambridge, Mass.: Harvard University Press.

Rich, Adrienne. 1976. *Of Woman Born: Motherhood as Experience and Institution.* New York: Norton.

Ruddick, Sara. 1984. "Preservative Love and Military Destruction: Some Reflections on Mothering and Peace." In *Mothering: Essays in Feminist Theory,* edited by Joyce Trebilcot, 231–62. Totowa, N.J.: Rowman and Allenheld.

———. 1987. "Remarks on the Sexual Politics of Reason." In *Women and Moral Theory,* edited by Eva Kittay and Diana Meyers, 237–60. Totowa, N.J.: Rowman and Littlefield.

———. 1989. *Maternal Thinking: Toward a Politics of Peace.* Boston: Beacon Press.

Russ, Joanna. 1975. *The Female Man.* New York: Bantam.

Sandel, Michael. 1982. *Liberalism and the Limits of Justice.* Cambridge: Cambridge University Press.

Shiva, Vandana. 1988. *Staying Alive.* New Delhi: Kali for Women.

Sunstein, Cass, ed. 1990. *Feminism and Political Theory.* Chicago: University of Chicago Press.

Tronto, Joan C. 1989. "Woman and Caring: What Can Feminists Learn about

Morality from Caring?" In *Gender/Body/Knowledge,* edited by Alison Jaggar and Susan Bordo, 172–87. New Brunswick, N.J.: Rutgers University Press.

Walker, Alice. 1983. *In Search of Our Mothers' Gardens.* New York: Harcourt Brace Jovanovich.

Welch, Sharon D. 1990. *A Feminist Ethic of Risk.* Minneapolis: Augsburg Fortress.

West, Cornel. 1991. *The Ethical Dimensions of Marxist Thought.* New York: Monthly Review Press.

———. 1993. *Race Matters.* Boston: Beacon Press.

Whitbeck, Caroline. 1983. "A Different Reality: Feminist Ontology." In *Perspectives on Women and Philosophy,* edited by Carol C. Gould. Totowa, N.J.: Rowman and Allenheld.

Wolff, Robert Paul. 1968. *The Poverty of Liberalism.* Boston: Beacon Press.

Wood, Allan. 1971. "The Marxian Critique of Justice." *Philosophy and Public Affairs* 1 (1971–72): 244–82.

Young, Gary. 1981. "Doing Marx Justice." In *Marx and Morality,* edited by Kai Nielsen and Steven C. Patten, 251–68. Guelph, Ontario: Canadian Association for Publishing in Philosophy.

Young, Iris. 1991. *Justice and the Politics of Difference.* Princeton: Princeton University Press.

22

If Not with Others, How?

Adrienne Rich

I have been reflecting on what feels so familiar about all this: to identify actively as a woman and ask what that means; to identify actively as a Jew and ask what that means. It is feminist politics — the efforts of women trying to work together as women across sexual, class, racial, ethnic, and other lines — that have pushed me to look at the starved Jew in myself; finally, to seek a path to that Jewishness still unsatisfied, still trying to define its true homeland, still untamed and unsuburbanized, still wandering in the wilderness. Over and over, the work of Jewish feminists has inspired and challenged me to educate myself, culturally and politically and spiritually, from Jewish sources, to cast myself into the ancient and turbulent river of disputation which is Jewish culture.

Jews, like women, exist everywhere, our existence often veiled by history; we have been "the Jewish question" or "the woman question" at the margins of Leftist politics, while Right Wing repressions have always zeroed in on us. We have — women and Jews — been the targets of biological determinism and persistent physical violence. We have been stereotyped both viciously and sentimentally by others and have often taken these stereotypes into ourselves. Of course, the two groups interface: women are Jews, and Jews are women; but what this means for the

Reprinted from *Blood, Bread, and Poetry*, by Adrienne Rich (New York: W. W. Norton, 1986), 202–9, by permission of the author and the publisher. Excerpted from a keynote address for the New Jewish Agenda National Convention, Ann Arbor, Michigan, July 1985, and first published in *Genesis 2: An Independent Voice for Jewish Renewal*, February–March 1986.

Jewish vision, we are only beginning to ask. We exist everywhere under laws we did not make; speaking a multitude of languages; excluded by law and custom from certain spaces, functions, resources associated with power; often accused of wielding too much power, of wielding dark and devious powers. Like Black and other dark-skinned people, Jews and women have haunted white Western thought as Other, as fantasy, as projected obsession.

My hope is that the movement we are building can further the conscious work of turning Otherness into a keen lens of empathy, that we can bring into being a politics based on concrete, heartfelt understanding of what it means to be Other. We are women and men, *Mischlings* (of mixed parentage) and the sons and daughters of rabbis, Holocaust survivors, freedom fighters, teachers, middle- and working-class Jews. We are gay and straight and bisexual, older and younger, differently able and temporarily able-bodied; and we share an unquenched hope for the survival and sanity of the human community. Believing that no single people can survive being only for itself, we want a base from which to act on our hope.

I feel proud to be identified as a Jew among Jews, not simply a progressive among progressives, a feminist among feminists. And I ask myself, What does that mean? What is this pride in tribe, family, culture, heritage? Is it a feeling of being better than those outside the tribe? The medieval philosopher Judah ha-Levi claimed a hierarchy of all species, places on earth, races, families, and even languages. In this hierarchy, the land, language, and people of Israel are naturally superior to all others. As a woman, I reject all such hierarchies.

Then is pride merely a cloak I pull around me in the face of anti-Semitism, in the face of the contempt and suspicion of others? Do I invoke pride as a shield against my enemies, or do I find its sources deeper in my being, where I define myself for myself?

Difficult questions for any people who for centuries have met with derogation of identity. Pride is often born in the place where we refuse to be victims, where we experience our own humanity under pressure, where we understand that we are not the hateful projections of others but intrinsically ourselves. Where does this take us? It helps us fight for survival, first of all, because we know, from somewhere, we deserve to survive. "I am not an inferior life form" becomes "There is sacred life, energy, plenitude in me and in those like me you are trying to destroy." And if, in the example of others like me, I learn not only survival but the plenitude of life, if I feel linked by a texture of values, history, words, passions to people long dead or whom I have never met, if I celebrate these linkages, is this what I mean by pride? Or am I really talking about love?

Pride is a tricky, glorious, double-edged feeling. I don't feel proud of everything Jews have done or thought, nor of everything women have done or thought. The poet Irena Klepfisz has confronted in her long poem "Bashert" the question of sorting out a legacy without spurning any of it, a legacy that includes both courage and ardor, and the shrinking of the soul under oppression, the damages suffered. In any one like me, I have to see mirrored my own shrinkings of soul, my own damages.

Yet I must make my choices, take my positions according to my conscience and vision now. To separate from parts of a legacy in a conscious, loving, and responsible way in order to say "This is frayed and needs repair; that no longer serves us; this is still vital and usable" is not to spurn tradition, but to take it very seriously. Those who refuse to make these distinctions — and making distinctions has been a very Jewish preoccupation — those who suppress criticism of the Jewish legacy suppress further creation.

As an American Jew, I fear the extent to which both Americans and Israelis, in their national consciousness, are captives of denial. Denial, first, of the existence of the peoples who, in the creation of both nations, have been swept aside, their communities destroyed, pushed into reservations and camps, traumatized by superior might calling itself destiny. I fear that this denial, this unaccountability for acts which are still continuing, is a deep infection in the collective life and conscience of both nations.

America wants to forget the past, and the past in the present; and one result of that was Bitburg.* Israeli denial is different. Years ago, I remember seeing, with great emotion, on the old Jerusalem–Tel Aviv road,

---

*In 1985 then-president Ronald Reagan decided to visit the German military cemetery at Bitburg for ceremonies marking the fortieth anniversary of Germany's liberation from the Nazis, despite the fact that the cemetery contained the graves of at least forty-nine SS soldiers. Responding to criticism before the trip, Reagan said, "I don't think we ought to focus on the past. I want to focus on the future. I want to put that history behind me." The only concession he made was adding a visit to the Bergen-Belsen concentration camp site on his trip. For more, see Geoffrey H. Hartman, *Bitburg in Moral and Political Perspective* (Bloomington: Indiana University Press, 1986). *Ed.*

rusted tanks left from the 1948 war, on one of which was painted "If I forget thee, O Jerusalem . . ." But Palestinian memory has been violently obliterated. I fear for the kind of "moral autism" (Amos Oz's phrase) out of which both the United States and Israel, in their respective capacities of power, have made decisions leading to physical carnage and to acute internal disequilibrium and suffering.

I say this here, knowing my words will be understood or at least not heard as anti-Semitism. But many of us have experienced a censorship in American Jewish communities, where dissent from official Israeli policies and actions is rebuked and Jewish critical introspection is silenced. "The armored and concluded mind" (Muriel Rukeyser's phrase)[1] is not what the Jewish mind has been overall. Torah itself is not a closed system; we have been a people unafraid of argument, a people of many opinions. Our forebears were instructed to commit suicide rather than idolatry; yet Israel has become a kind of idol for many American Jews. Israel is not seen and cared about as an unfinished human effort, harrowed and flawed and full of gashes between dreams and realities, but as an untouchable construct: The Place Where Jews Can Be Safe. I think that the taboo on dissent among American Jews damages all Jews who, in the wake of the Holocaust and the birth of a Jewish state, are trying to imagine a Jewish future and a Jewish consciousness that does not stop with Hillel's first question.[2]

The word *safe* has two distinct connotations: one, of a place in which we can draw breath, rest from persecution or harassment, bear witness, lick our wounds, feel compassion and love around us rather than hostility or indifference. The safety of the mother's lap for the bullied child, of the battered-women's shelter, the door opened to us when we need a refuge. Safety in this sense implies a place to gather our forces, a place to move from, not a destination. But there is also the safety of the "armored and concluded mind," the safety of the barricaded door which will not open for the beleaguered Stranger, the psychotic safety of the underground nuclear-bomb shelter, the walled and guarded crime-proof condominium, the safety bought with guns and money at no matter what cost, the safety bought and sold at the cost of shutting up. And this safety becomes a dead end in the mind and in the mapping of a life or a collective vision. I want to say that though the longing for safety has been kept awake in us by centuries of danger, mere safety has not been the central obsession of the Jewish people. It has not been an ultimate destination. How to live in compassion, pursue justice, create a society in which "what is hateful to you, do not do to your neighbor," how to think, praise, celebrate life — these have been fundamental to Jewish vision. Even if strayed from, given lip service, even if in this vision Jewish women have remained Other, even if many Jews have acted on this vision as social reformists and radicals without realizing how Jewish — though not exclusively Jewish — a vision it is. And I don't believe that the Jewish genius has completed itself on this earth: I think it may be on the verge of a new, if often painful and disorienting, renascence.

All of us here live in two dissonant worlds. There is the world of this community and others like it in America: Jewish and gentile, men and women, Black and brown and red and yellow and white, old and young, educated in books and educated in what Tillie Olsen has named "the college of work," in poverty or in privilege — the communities of those who are trying to "turn the century," in Black activist musician Bernice Reagon's words.[3] In this world of vision and struggle, there is still myopia, division, anti-Semitism, racism, sexism, heterosexism. But there is also passion, and persistence, and memory, and the determination to build what we need, and the refusal to buy safety or comfort by shutting up. We affirm the diversity out of which we come, the clashes and pain we experience in trying to work together, the unglamorous ongoing labors of love and necessity.

And there is that other world, that America whose history is Disneyland, whose only legitimized passion is white male violence, whose people are starving for literal food and also for intangible sustenance they cannot always name, whose opiate is denial. As progressives, we live in this America, too, and it affects us. Even as we try to change it, it affects us. This America that has never mourned or desisted in or even acknowledged the original, deliberate, continuing genocide of the indigenous American people now called the Indians. This America that has never acknowledged or mourned or desisted in the ordinary, banal murderousness of its racism — murderous of the individuals and groups targeted by skin color, and murderous of the spiritual integrity of all of us.

As Jews, we have tried to comprehend the losses encompassed by the Holocaust, not just in terms of numbers or communities or families or individuals, but in terms of unknown potentialities — voices, visions, spiritual and ethical — of which we and the world are irreparably deprived. As American Jews, our losses are not from the Holocaust alone. We are citizens of a country deprived of the effective moral, ethical, and aesthetic visions of those whom white racism has tried to quench in both subtle and violent ways; whose capacity, nonetheless, to insist on their humanity, to persevere and resist, to educate their fellow citizens in political reality, to carry their "message for the world," as W. E. B. Du Bois called it, should be supported and celebrated by Jews everywhere.

For progressive American Jews, racism as it exists here in America, around and also within us, in the air we breathe, has both an ethical and a pragmatic urgency. We cannot continue to oppose the racism of Kahane and his like or of South African apartheid and take less oppositional stands on the malignancy of racism here where we live. The depth of the work we do depends on its rootedness — in our knowledge of who we are and also of where we are — a country which has used skin color as the prime motive for persecution and genocide, as Europe historically used religion. As Elly Bulkin indicates in a mind-stretching essay, "Hard Ground": "In terms of anti-Semitism and racism, a central problem is how to acknowledge their differences without contributing to the argument that one is important and the other is not, one is worthy of serious attention and the other is not."[4] It is difficult to move beyond these polarizations, but we are learning to do so and will, I believe, continue to help each other learn.

We must continue to insist that the concepts of Jewish survival and "what is good for the Jews" have an expanding, not a constricting, potential. I long to see the widest range of progressive issues defined as Jewish issues everywhere in this country. I long to see the breaking of encrustations of fear and caution, habits of thought engrained by centuries of endangerment and by the spiritual sterility of white mainstream America. I long to see Jewish energy, resources, passion, our capacity to celebrate life pouring into a gathering of thousands of American Jews toward "turning the century." I believe the potential is there; I long to see it stirred into glowing life. I believe we may be at the watershed for such a movement. And I would like to end by quoting Hillel's three questions, which can never really be separated, and by adding a fourth, which is implicit in what we are doing:

If I am not for myself, who will be for me?
If I am only for myself, what am I?
If not now, when?

If not with others, how?

Notes

1. *The Collected Poems of Muriel Rukeyser* (New York: McGraw-Hill, 1978), 102.

2. "If I am not for myself, who will be for me?" See *Sayings of the Fathers, or Pirke Aboth, the Hebrew Text, with a New English Translation and a Commentary by the Very Rev. Dr. Joseph H. Hertz* (New York: Behrman House, 1945), 25.

3. Bernice Reagon, "Coalition Politics: Turning the Century," in *Home Girls: A Black Feminist Anthology,* ed. Barbara Smith (New York: Kitchen Table/Women of Color Press, 1983), 356–68.

4. Elly Bulkin, "Hard Ground: Jewish Identity, Racism, and Anti-Semitism," in Elly Bulkin, M. B. Pratt, and B. Smith, *Yours in Struggle: Three Feminist Perspectives on Anti-Semitism and Racism* (Brooklyn, N.Y.: Long Haul, 1984; distributed by Firebrand Books, Ithaca, N.Y.).

About the Contributors

Lila Abu-Lughod, associate professor of anthropology at New York University, is the author of two books on the Bedouin of Egypt, *Veiled Sentiments: Honor and Poetry in a Bedouin Society* and *Writing Women's Worlds: Bedouin Stories*. Her article "The Romance of Resistance: Tracing Transformations of Power through Bedouin Women" takes up directly the issues of feminism and resistance in the women's community. She is now doing research on the role of Egyptian television soap operas in contemporary contests over national, class, and gender identities and plans next to tackle the relationship between nationalism and feminism in the serials.

Byllye Y. Avery, founding president of the National Black Women's Health Project since its inception in 1981, has been a women's health care activist for twenty years. A dreamer, "visionary," and grassroots realist, Avery has combined activism and social responsibility in developing a national forum for the exploration of health issues of African American women. Before entering the health care arena, she taught special education to emotionally disturbed students and consulted on learning disabilities in public schools and universities. She has received the MacArthur Foundation Fellowship for Social Contribution, the Essence Awards for community service, and the Academy of Science Institute of Medicine's Gustav O. Lienhard Award for the Advancement of Health Care.

Pauline B. Bart is a professor of sociology in the Department of Psychiatry, University of Illinois at Chicago. Trying to demystify the world *for* women, she has written about depressed middle-aged women, a feminist illegal abortion collective, and women who were attacked and avoided rape. She is the author of *Stopping Rape: Successful Survival Strategies*, co-editor of *Violence against Women: The Bloody Footprints*, and co-author of *The Student Sociologists' Handbook*. Her work is grounded in women's experiences as she attempts to lessen women's subordination for which violence is the linchpin. She tells the truth and pays the consequences. Thus she has been banned from teaching in liberal arts and science. She agrees with the Mongolian proverb "When you are about to tell the truth, you should have one foot in the stirrup."

Rita Mae Brown is the author of *The Hand That Cradles the Rock, Songs to a Handsome Woman, Rubyfruit Jungle, In Her Day, Six of One, Southern Discomfort, Sudden Death, High Hearts, Bingo, Venus Envy,* and *Starting from Scratch: A Different Kind of Writers' Manual.* She is an Emmy-nominated screenwriter and a poet.

Jean Bethke Elshtain, Centennial Professor of Political Science and a professor of philosophy at Vanderbilt University, is a political philosopher whose task has been to show the connections between our political and our ethical convictions. Her books include *Public Man, Private Woman: Women in Social and Political Thought; Meditations on Modern Political Thought; Women and War;* co-editor, *Women, Militarism, and the Arms Race;* co-editor, *Rebuilding the Nest: A New Commitment to the American Family; Power Trips and Other Journeys;* editor, *Just War Theory;* co-author, *But Was It Just? Reflections on the Morality of the Persian Gulf War;* and *Democracy on Trial.* Works in progress include: *Freud and Politics; Political Mothers;* and her biography of Jane Addams.

Ann Ferguson is a lesbian socialist-feminist philosopher who has written two books in feminist theory, *Blood at the Root: Motherhood, Sexuality and Male Dominance* and *Sexual Democracy: Women, Oppression, and Revolution,* plus numerous articles in which she has tried to develop a multi-system theory of male dominance. She is currently working on a book on feminist ethics. Her political work includes working with the Women's Studies program at the University of Massachusetts at Amherst in a period of multicultural curriculum restructuring that requires multiple committee work. She also tries to practice what she preaches by working in a community-based women's group doing solidarity work with women in Central America called Feminist Aid to Central America.

Estelle Freedman is a professor of history at Stanford University, where she also teaches in the Program in Feminist Studies. She is the author of *Their Sisters' Keepers: Women's Prison Reform in America, 1830–1930,* co-author of *Intimate Matters: A History of Sexuality in America,* and co-editor of *Victorian Women: A Documentary Account* and *The Lesbian Issue: Essays from Signs.*

Marilyn Friedman teaches philosophy at Washington University in St. Louis. She has published widely in the areas of feminist theory, social philosophy, and ethics. She is the author of *What Are Friends For? Feminist Perspectives on Personal Relationships and Moral Theory* and co-author (for the affirmative) of *Political Correctness: For and Against.*

Marilyn Frye teaches philosophy and women's studies at Michigan State University. Her essays are in two anthologies: *The Politics of Reality* and *Willful Virgin.* She is a founding member and has served on the board of the Lesbian Alliance in Lansing, Michigan, a city famous among U.S. lesbians for its lesbian community.

Virginia Held is a professor of philosophy and professor of women's studies at the City University of New York, Graduate School and Hunter College. Her most recent books are *Feminist Morality: Transforming Culture, Society, and Politics,* and *Rights and Goods: Justifying Social Action.*

Sarah Lucia Hoagland is a middle-aged, anglo chicago dyke and philosopher. She has been making meaning in lesbian community creating for twenty years. She is the author of *Lesbian Ethics: Toward New Value* and co-editor of *For Lesbians Only: A Separatist Anthology.* In addition, she is a professor of philosophy and women's studies at Northeastern Illinois University in Chicago.

Emily Honig is a professor of women's studies and history at the University of California, Santa Cruz. She is the author of *Sisters and Strangers: Women in the Shanghai Cotton Mills, 1919–1949,* co-author of *Personal Voices: Chinese Women in the 1980's,* and author of *Creating Chinese Ethnicity: Subei People in Shanghai, 1850–1990.*

bell hooks is a writer, feminist theorist, cultural critic, and professor of English and women's studies. Her books include *Ain't I a Woman: Black*

Women and Feminism, Feminist Theory: From Margin to Center, Breaking Bread (with Cornel West), *Yearning: Race, Gender, and Cultural Politics*, and *Talking Back: Thinking Feminist, Thinking Black*.

María C. Lugones is a folk educator and feminist philosopher. She teaches at the Escuela Popular Nortena, a folk school for radical movement among Latinos and Latinas. She directs Latin American Studies at the State University of New York at Binghamton. Her work centers on struggling against oppressions as intermeshed.

Jane Mansbridge is Jane W. Long Professor of the Arts and Sciences in the Department of Political Science at Northwestern University, a faculty fellow of the Center for Urban Affairs and Policy Research, and a member of the American Academy of Arts and Sciences. She is the author of *Beyond Adversary Democracy* and *Why We Lost the ERA*, and editor of *Beyond Self-Interest*. A member of Bread and Roses, a Boston women's movement collective federation in the late 1960s, she is the co-author of the chapter "Sexuality" in the first edition of *Our Bodies, Ourselves* and has been involved in feminist issues since that time.

Del Martin is a leading authority on the problem of battered women and coordinator of the NOW Task Force on Battered Women. She is the author of *Battered Wives* and co-author of *Sappho Was a Right-On Woman*.

Adrienne Rich has published more than thirteen volumes of poetry and four books of prose. Her most recent work is *What Is Found There: Notebooks on Poetry and Politics*. She is an advisory board member of *Bridges: A Journal for Jewish Feminists and Our Friends*. She has been the recipient of the National Book Award, the Ruth Lilly Poetry Prize, the *Los Angeles Times* Book Award in Poetry, the Common Wealth Award in Literature, the Lenore Marshall/*Nation* Poetry Prize, the Lambda Book Award for Lesbian Literature, and Poets' Prize, among other recognitions.

Joan Ringelheim has taught courses on prejudice and oppression, guilt and shame, freedom and responsibility, philosophy of social science, political philosophy, philosophy of history, and feminist theory. Eventually, two subjects became the major foci: the Holocaust and feminist theory. Together they opened up a new area of investigation — women and the Holocaust. She recently moved to Washington, D.C., to be Research Director for the Permanent Exhibition of the United States Holocaust Memorial Museum and is now the director of the Oral History Department of its Research Institute. She recently finished a manuscript, "Double Jeopardy: Women and the Holocaust."

Kate Rushin is an African American poet and teacher, currently Visiting Writer and director of the Center for African American Studies at Wesleyan University. Her first book of poems, *The Black Back-Ups,* was chosen by the New York Public Library for its list "Books for the Teen Age 1994." She has received the Massachusetts Artists' Foundation Fellowship and the 1988 Grolier Poetry Prize. Her poems have appeared in numerous publications, including *The Black Woman's Health Book, Double Stitch, This Bridge Called My Back: Writings by Radical Women of Color,* and *An Ear to the Ground: An Anthology of Contemporary American Poetry.*

Penny A. Weiss teaches political theory at Purdue University and is especially interested in the history of feminist theory. She is the author of *Gendered Community: Rousseau, Sex, and Politics.* Along with her partner and three children, she is a founding member and has served on the board of The New Community School in Lafayette, Indiana, an alternative pre- and elementary school.

Patricia J. Williams, author of *The Alchemy of Race and Rights,* is an associate professor of law at the University of Wisconsin. She lectures and writes on the relation of questions of identity and subjectivity to race and gender.

Iris Marion Young teaches ethics and political theory in the Graduate School of Public and International Affairs at the University of Pittsburgh. She is author of *Justice and the Politics of Difference* and is currently working on a book on democratic theory.